テニスの王子様

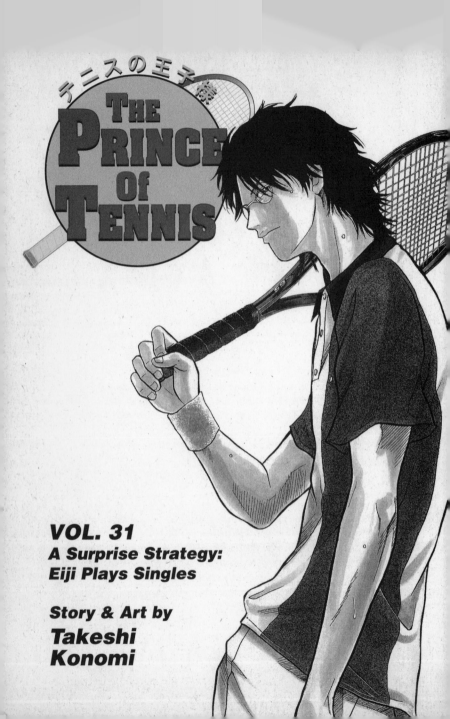

THE PRINCE OF TENNIS

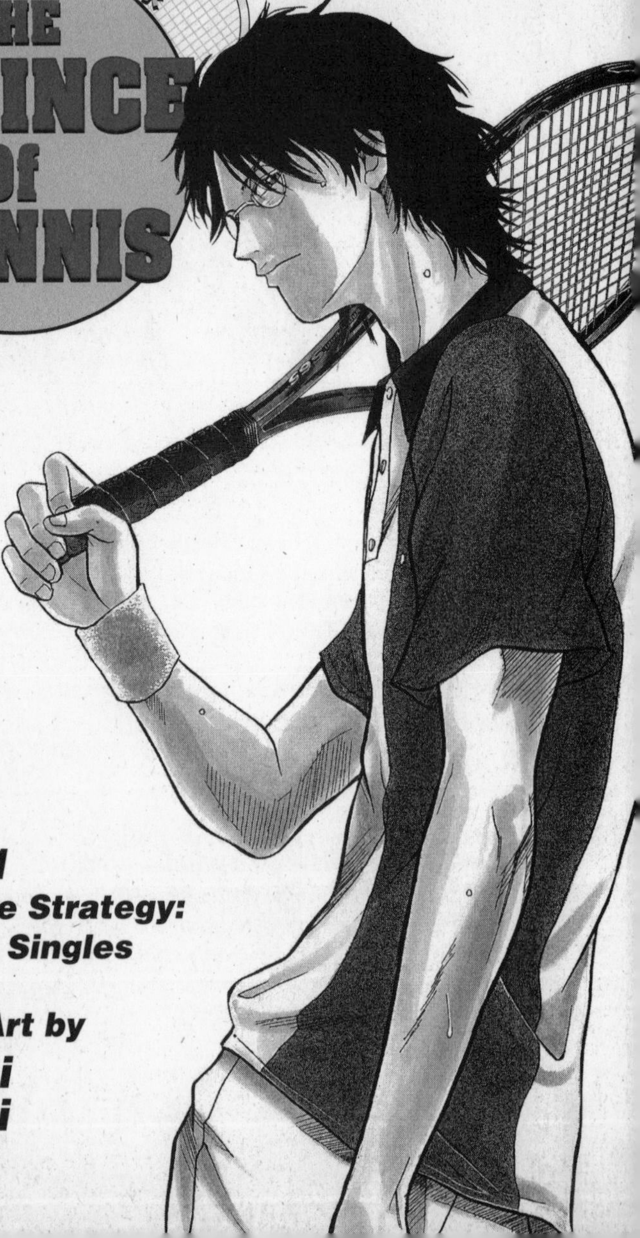

VOL. 31

A Surprise Strategy: Eiji Plays Singles

Story & Art by

Takeshi Konomi

ENNIS CLUB

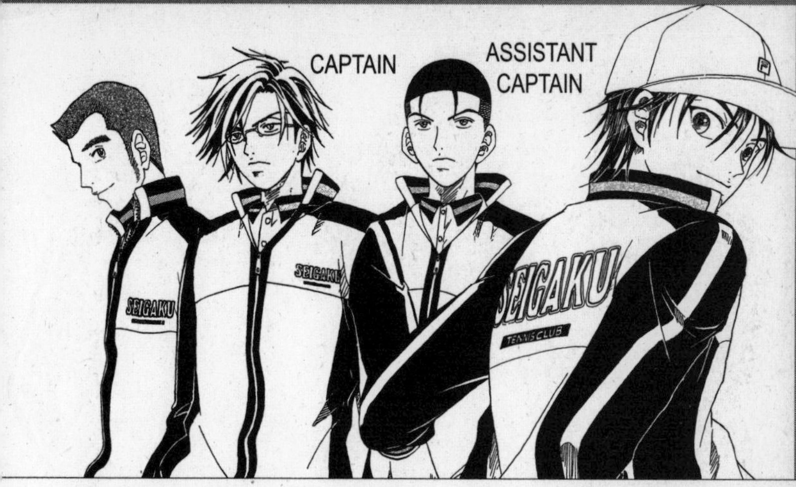
CAPTAIN
ASSISTANT CAPTAIN
SEIGAKU
SEIGAKU
SEIGAKU
SEIGAKU
TENNIS CLUB

• TAKASHI KAWAMURA • KUNIMITSU TEZUKA • SHUICHIRO OISHI • RYOMA ECHIZEN •

STORY & HARACTERS

Seishun Academy student Ryoma Echizen is a tennis prodigy, with wins in four consecutive U.S. Junior Tennis Tournaments under his belt. He became a starter as a 7th grader and led his team to the District Preliminaries! Despite a few mishaps, Seishun won the District Prelims and the City Tournament, and earned a ticket to the Kanto Tournament. The team came away victorious from its first-round matches, but captain Kunimitsu injured his shoulder and went to Kyushu for treatment. Despite losing Kunimitsu and assistant captain Shuichiro to injury, Seishun pulled together as a team, winning the Kanto Tournament and earning a slot at the Nationals!

With Kunimitsu recovered and back on the team, Seishun enters the Nationals with their strongest line-up to face Okinawa's Higa Junior High! Ryoma, playing in No. 3 Singles, overcomes Kei Tanishi's Big Bang serve and wins. Shusuke follows up with an easy victory using his Fourth Counter, the Dragonfly Wrap! With two consecutive victories locked, Seishun now sends Eiji out to play in No. 2 Singles!

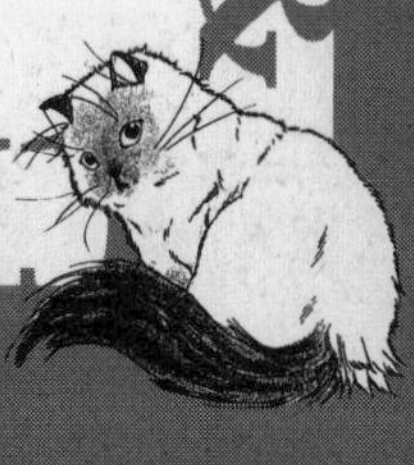

SEIGAKU T

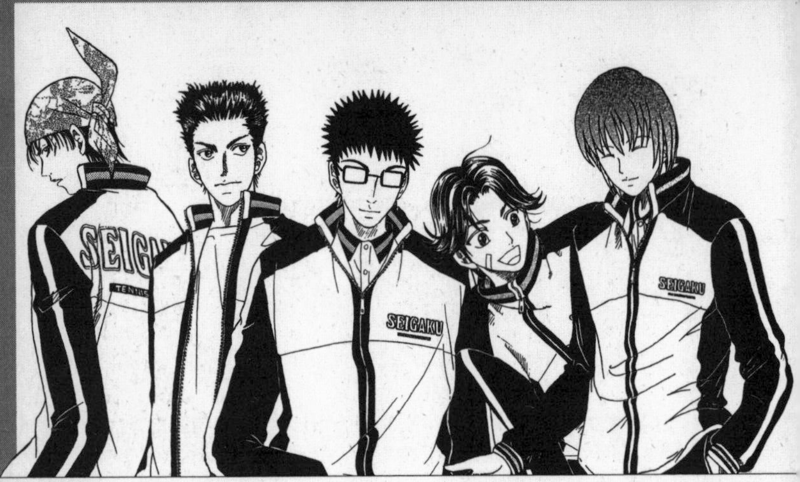

• KAORU KAIDO • TAKESHI MOMOSHIRO • SADAHARU INUI • EIJI KIKUMARU • SHUSUKE FUJI •

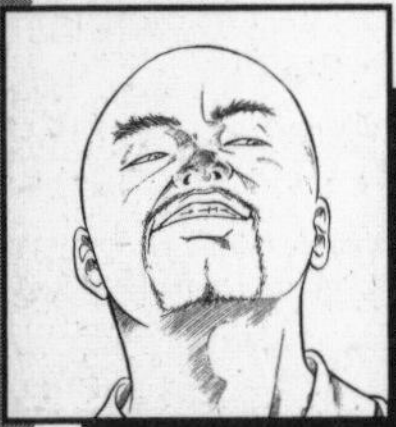

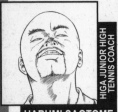

HARUMI SAOTOME
HIGA JUNIOR HIGH TENNIS COACH

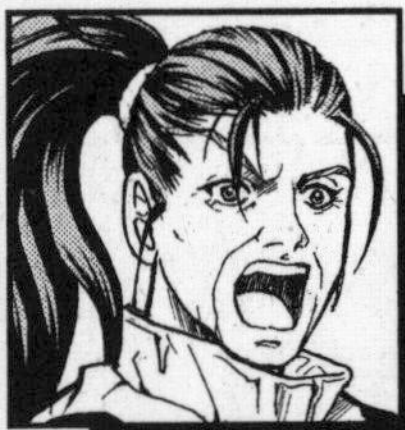

SUMIRE RYUZAKI
SEISHUN ACADEMY TENNIS COACH

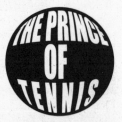

THE PRINCE OF TENNIS

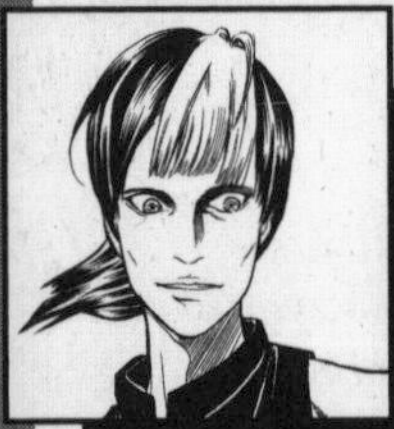

HIROSHI CHINEN
HIGA JUNIOR HIGH

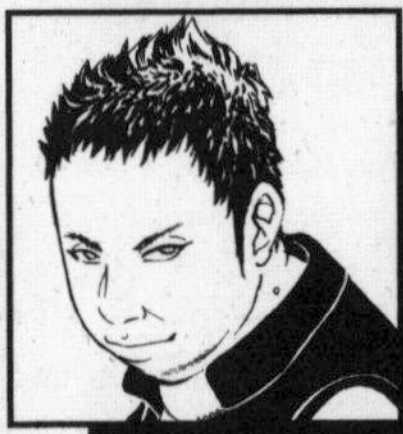

KEI TANISHI
HIGA JUNIOR HIGH

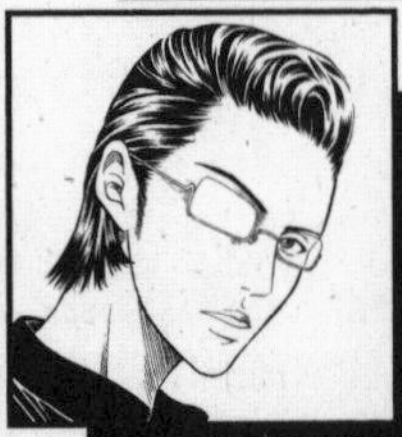

EISHIRO KITE
HIGA JUNIOR HIGH

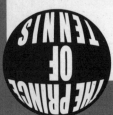

THE PRINCE OF TENNIS

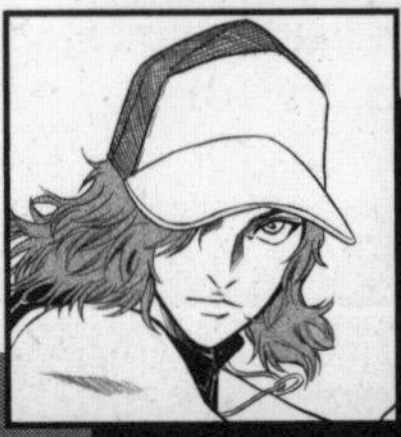

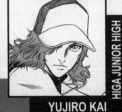

YUJIRO KAI
HIGA JUNIOR HIGH

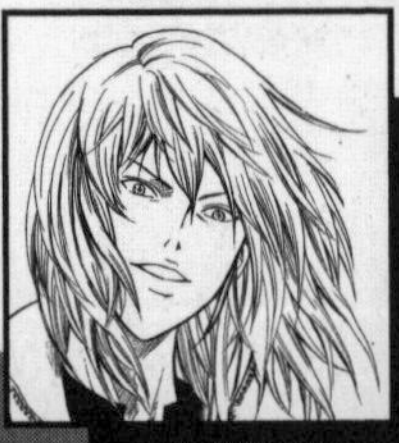

RIN HIRAKOBA
HIGA JUNIOR HIGH

CONTENTS

Vol. 31
A Surprise Strategy:
Eiji Plays Singles

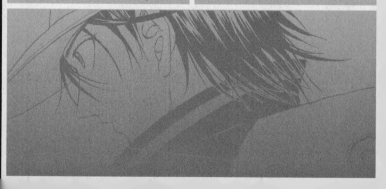

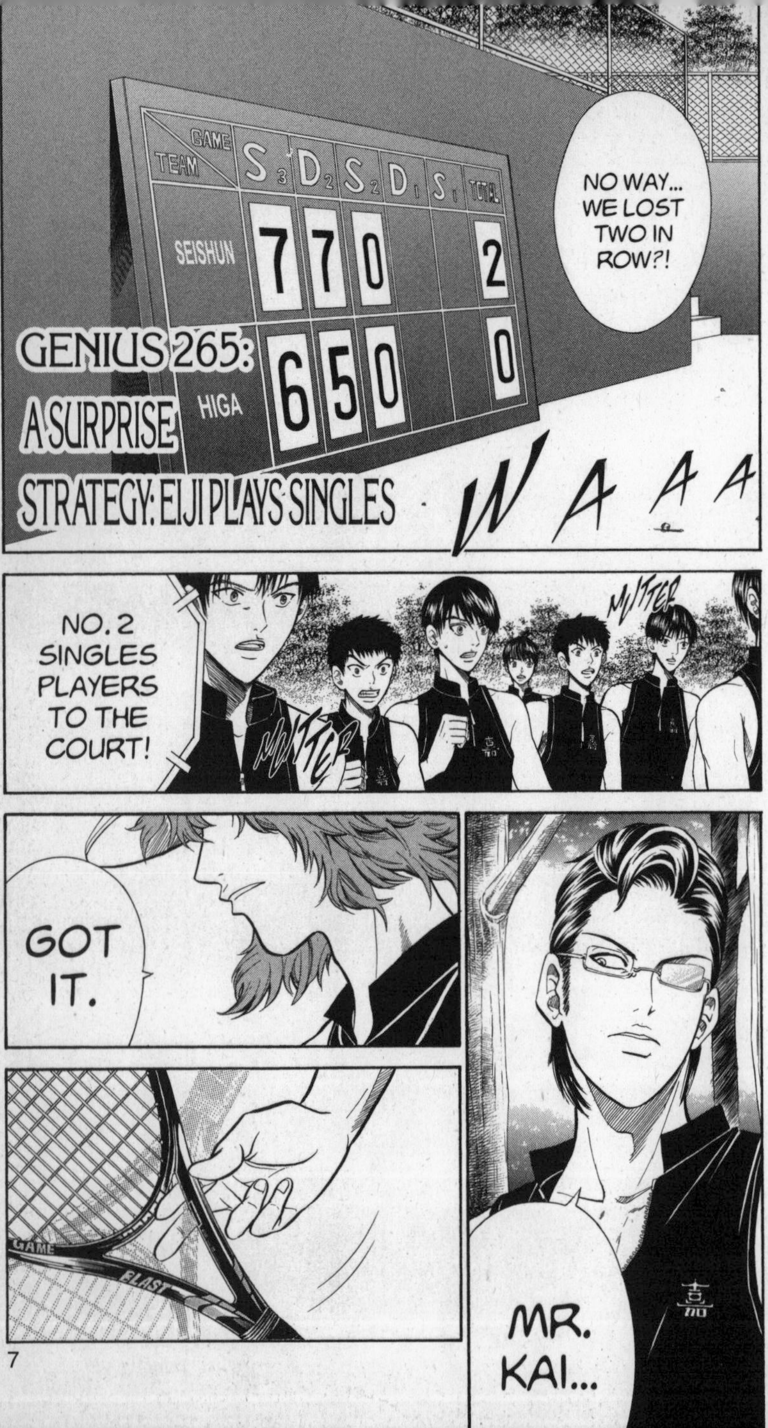
GENIUS 265:
A SURPRISE
STRATEGY: EIJI PLAYS SINGLES
GAME
TEAM
S3 D2 S2 D1 S1 TOTAL
SEISHUN 7 7 0 2
HIGA 6 5 0 0
NO WAY... WE LOST TWO IN ROW?!
WAAA
MUTTER
NO. 2 SINGLES PLAYERS TO THE COURT!
MUTTER
MR. KAI...
GOT IT.
GAME
BLAST

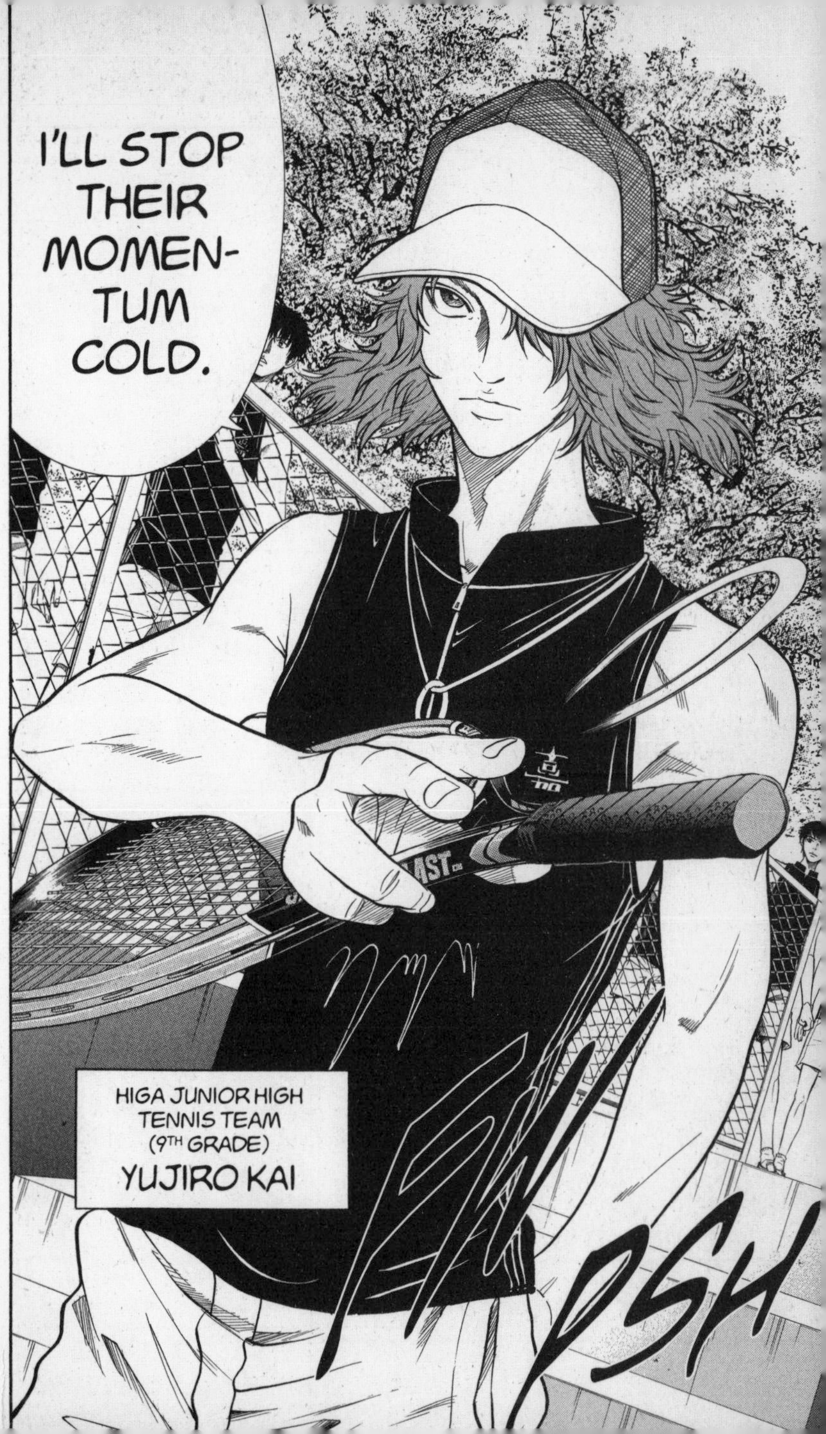
I'LL STOP THEIR MOMEN-TUM COLD.
HIGA JUNIOR HIGH TENNIS TEAM (9TH GRADE) YUJIRO KAI
PSH

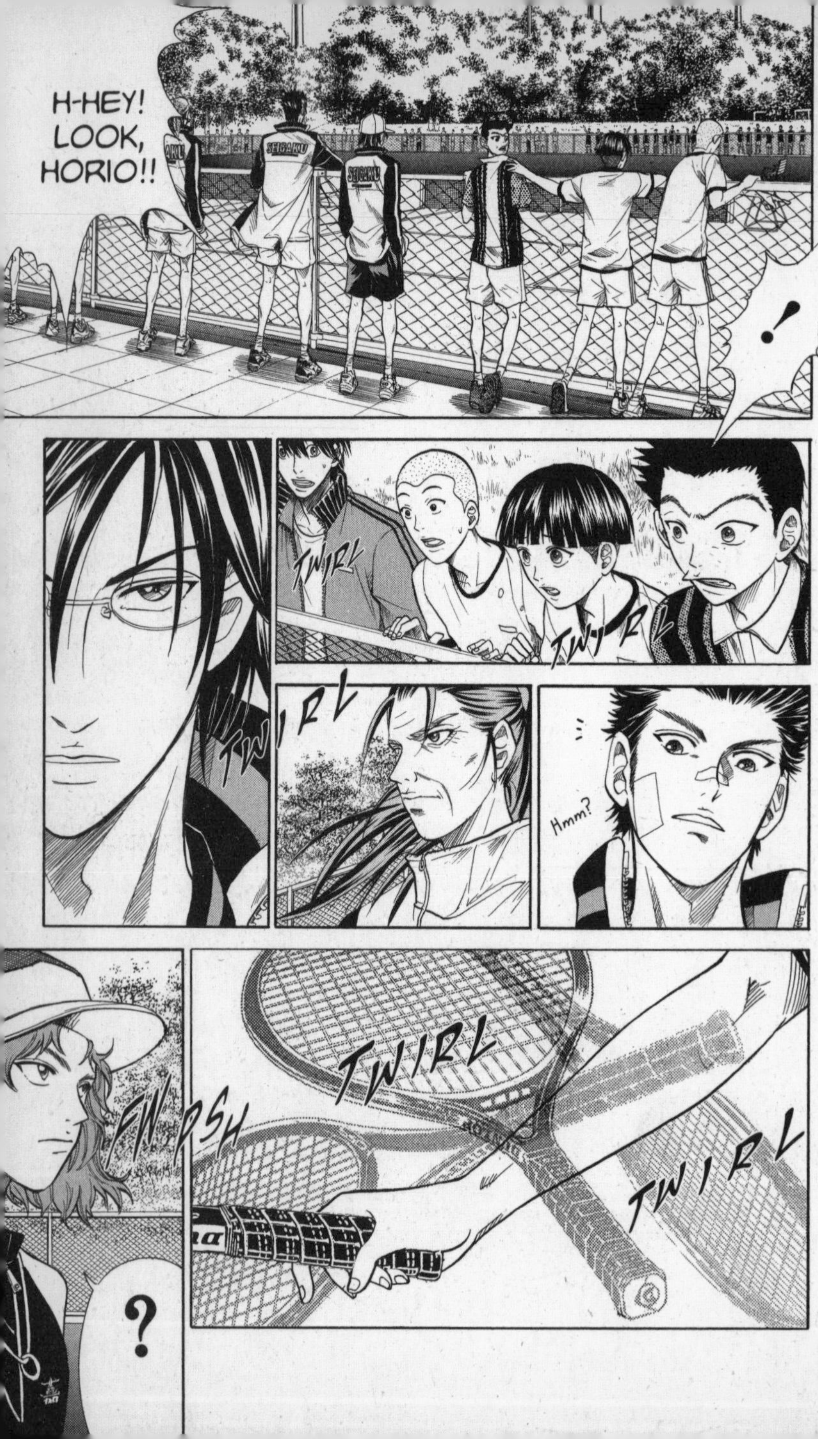
H-HEY! LOOK, HORIO!!
!
TWIRL
TWIRL
Hmm?
TWIRL
TWIRL
TWIRL
TWIRL
FWOSH
?

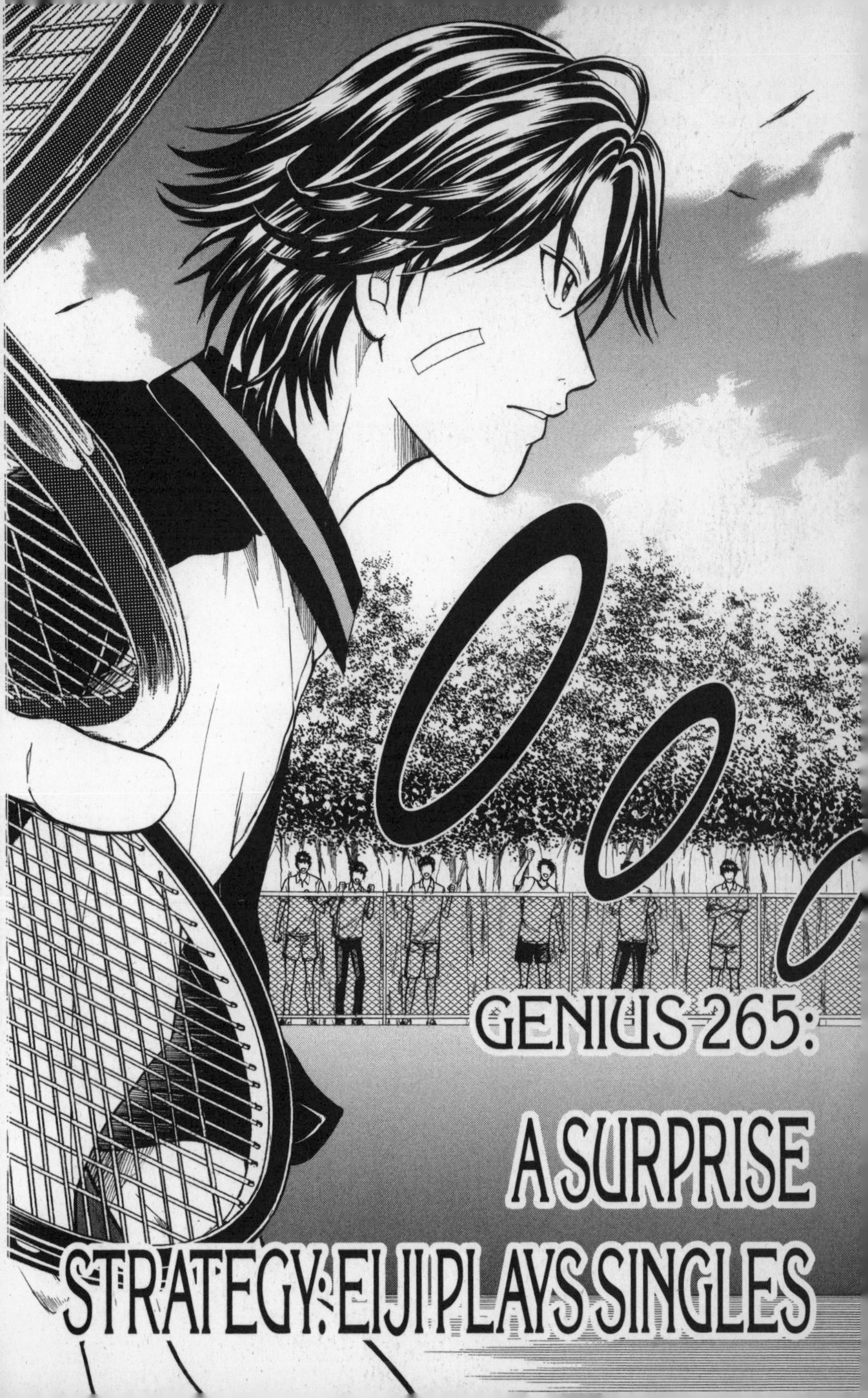
GENIUS 265:
A SURPRISE
STRATEGY: EIJI PLAYS SINGLES

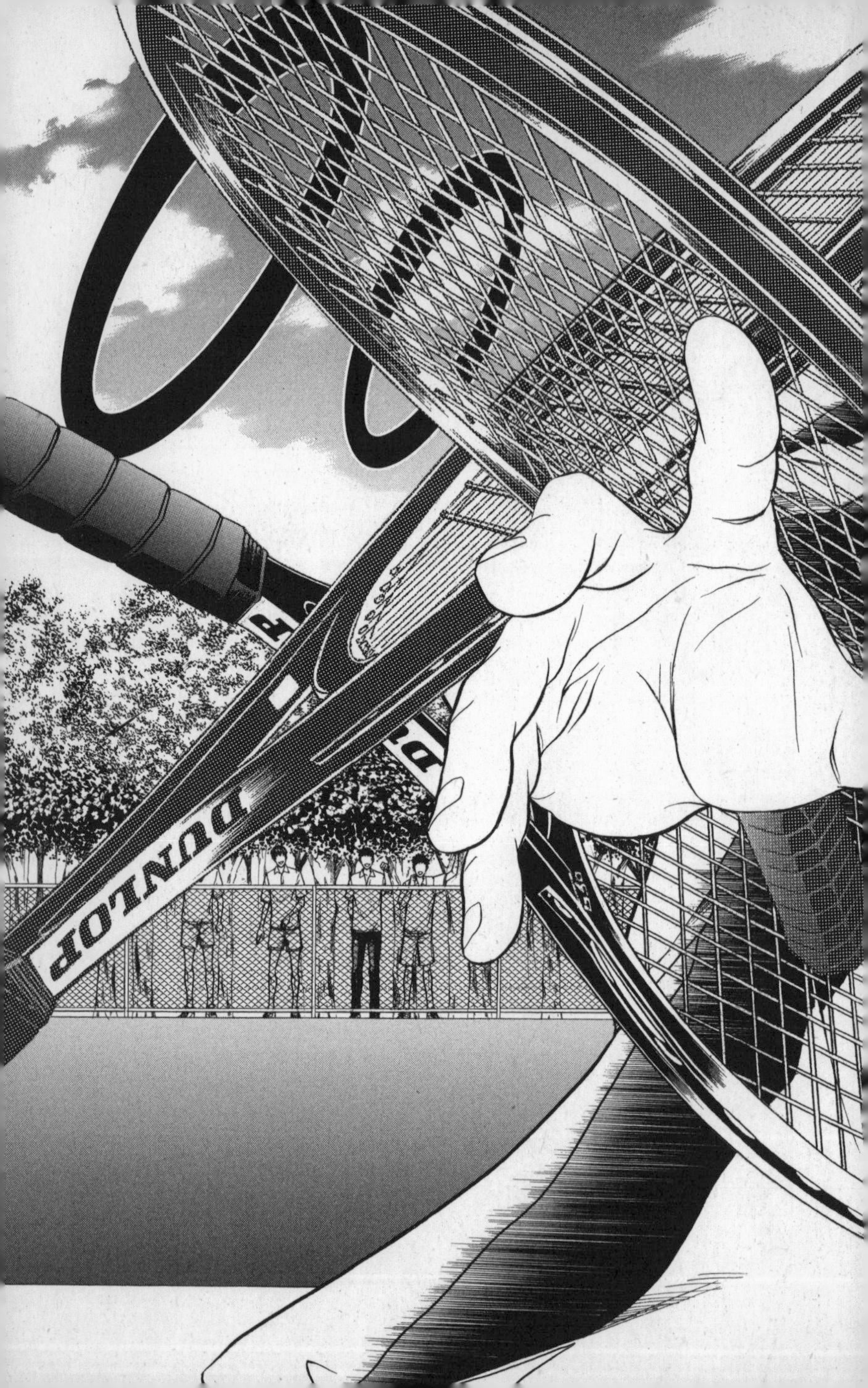
DUNLOP

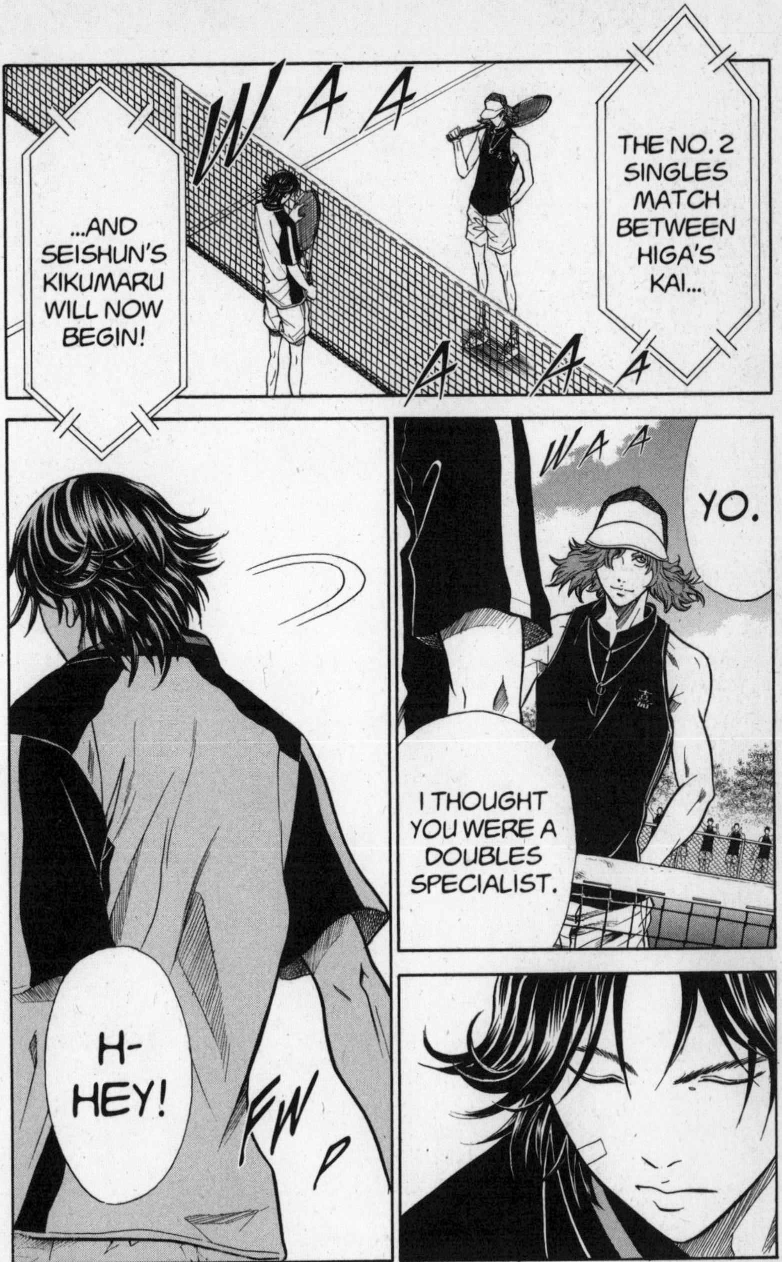

WAAAAAA
THE NO. 2 SINGLES MATCH BETWEEN HIGA'S KAI...
...AND SEISHUN'S KIKUMARU WILL NOW BEGIN!
WAA
YO.
I THOUGHT YOU WERE A DOUBLES SPECIALIST.
H- HEY!
FWP

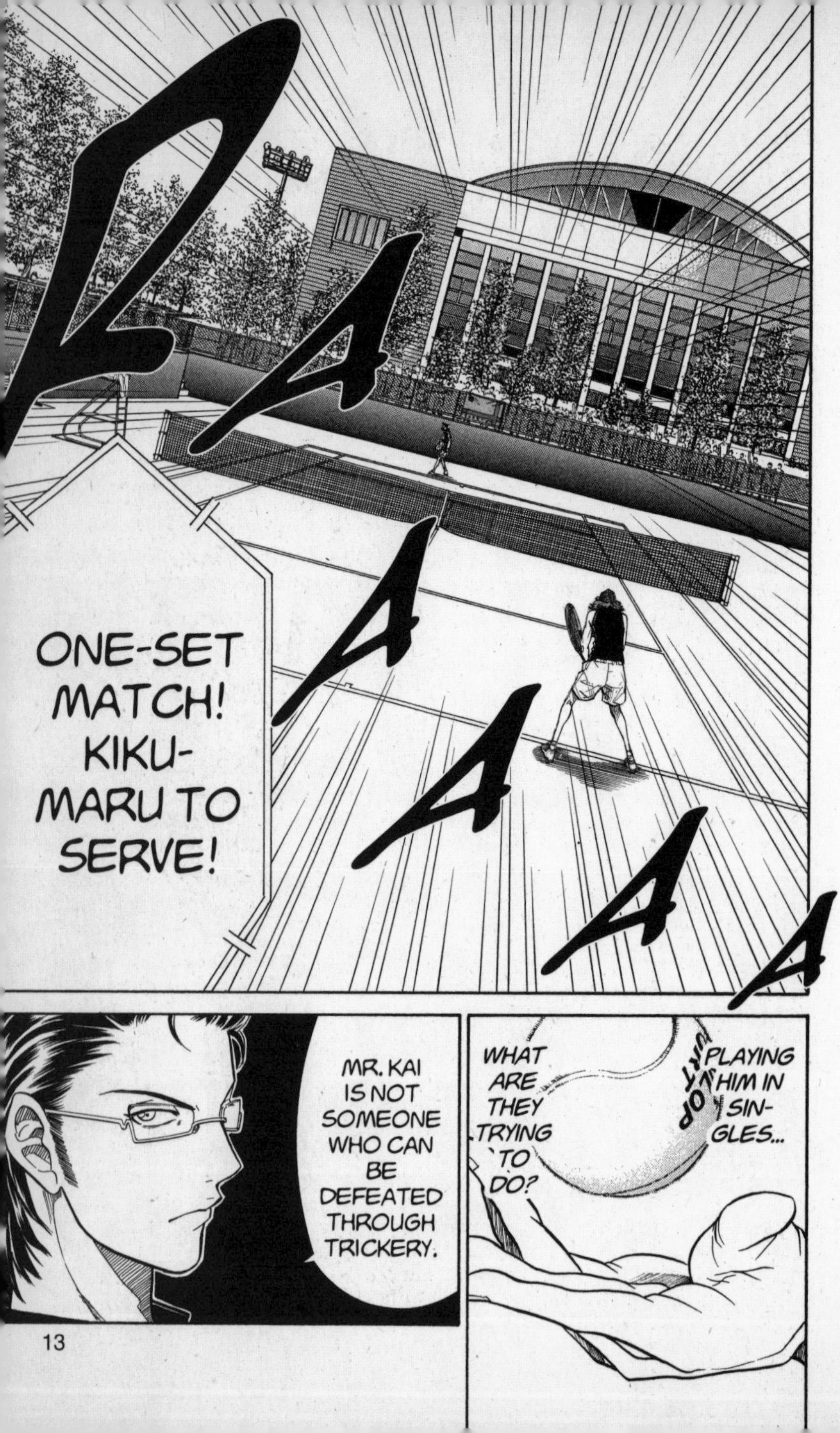
KAAAAA
ONE-SET MATCH! KIKU-MARU TO SERVE!
PLAYING HIM IN SIN-GLES...
WHAT ARE THEY TRYING TO DO?
MR. KAI IS NOT SOMEONE WHO CAN BE DEFEATED THROUGH TRICKERY.

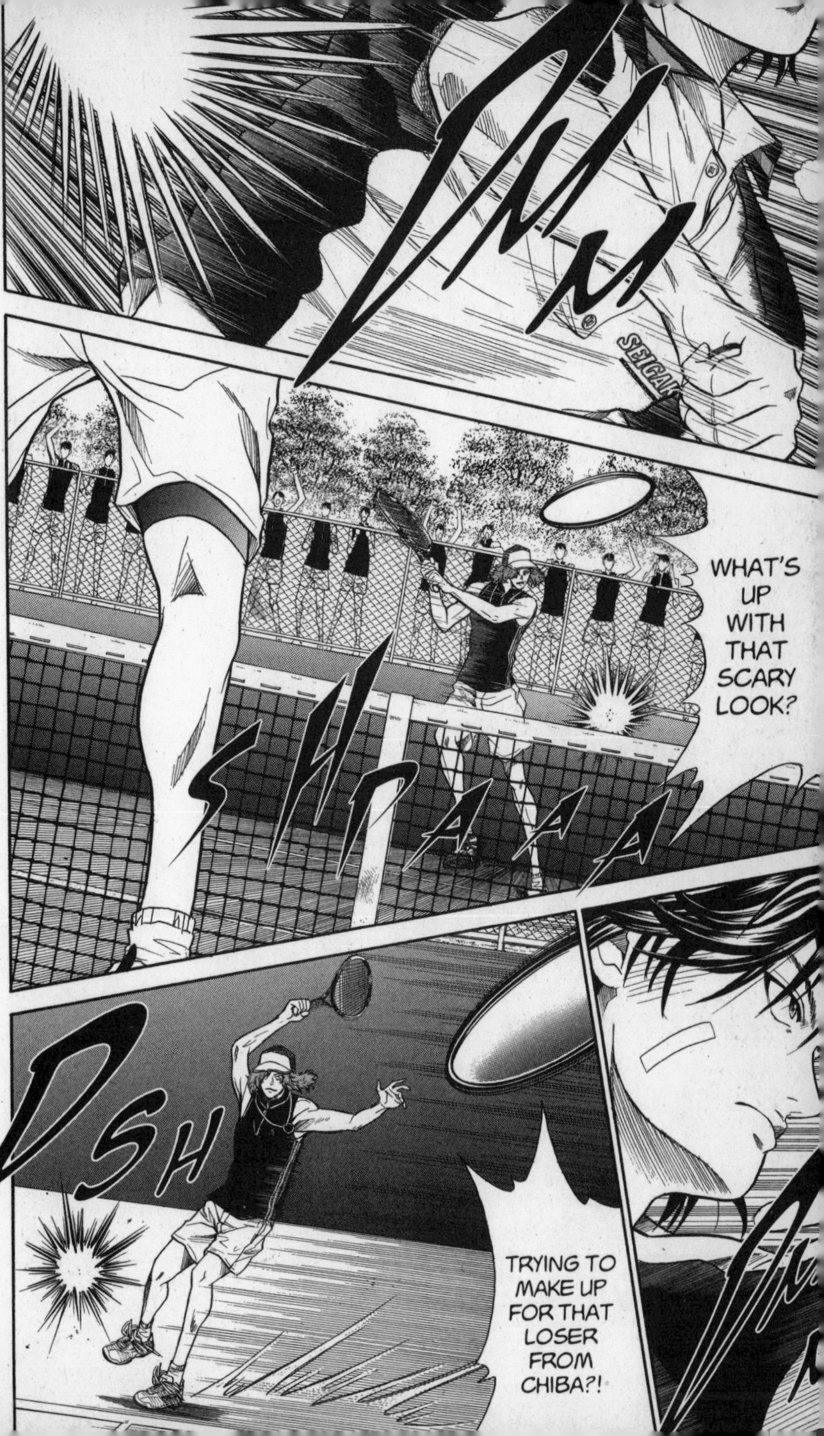
VMM
SEIGAKU
WHAT'S UP WITH THAT SCARY LOOK?
SHRAAAA
TRYING TO MAKE UP FOR THAT LOSER FROM CHIBA?!
DSH

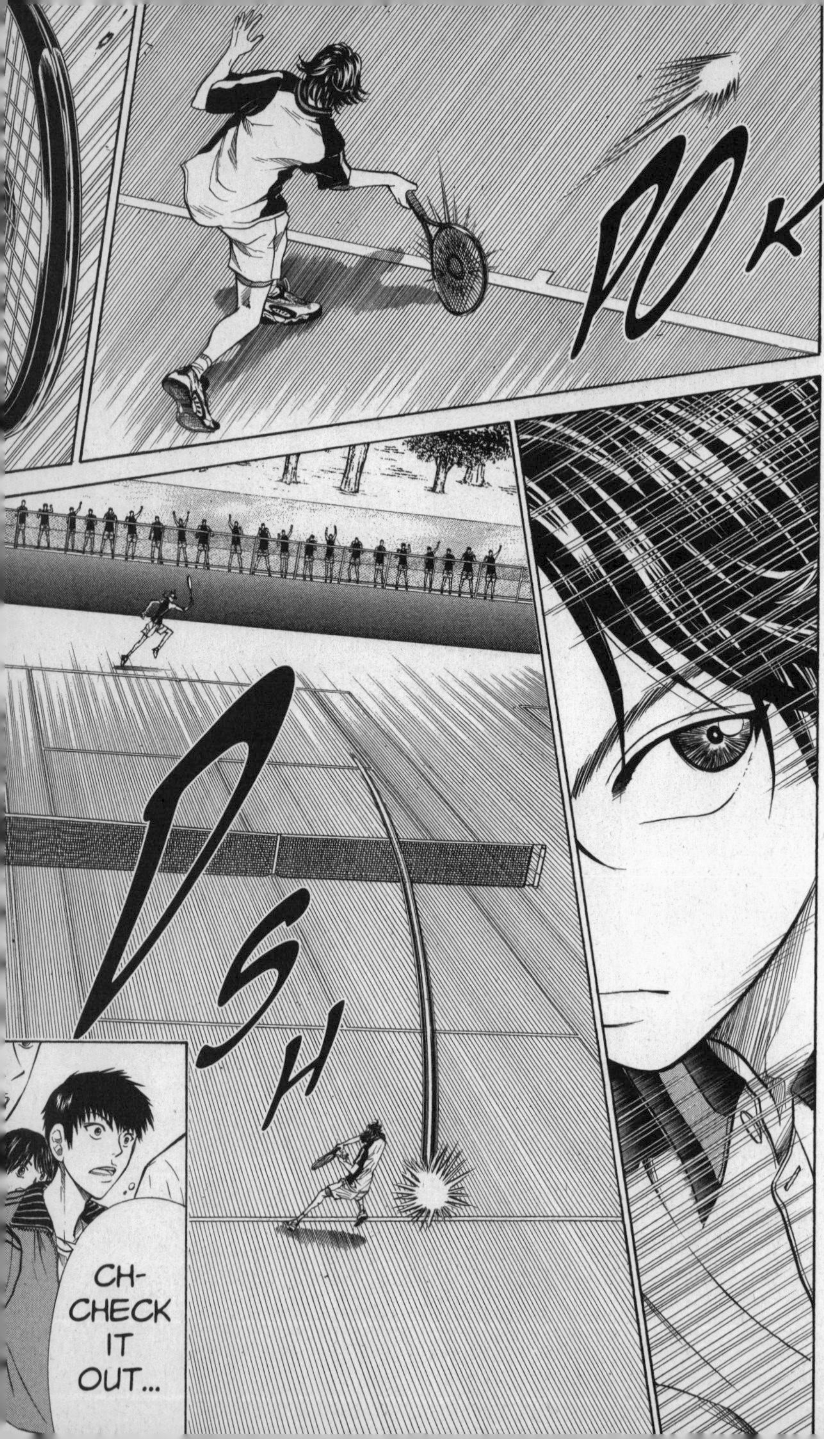
POK
DSH
CH-CHECK IT OUT...

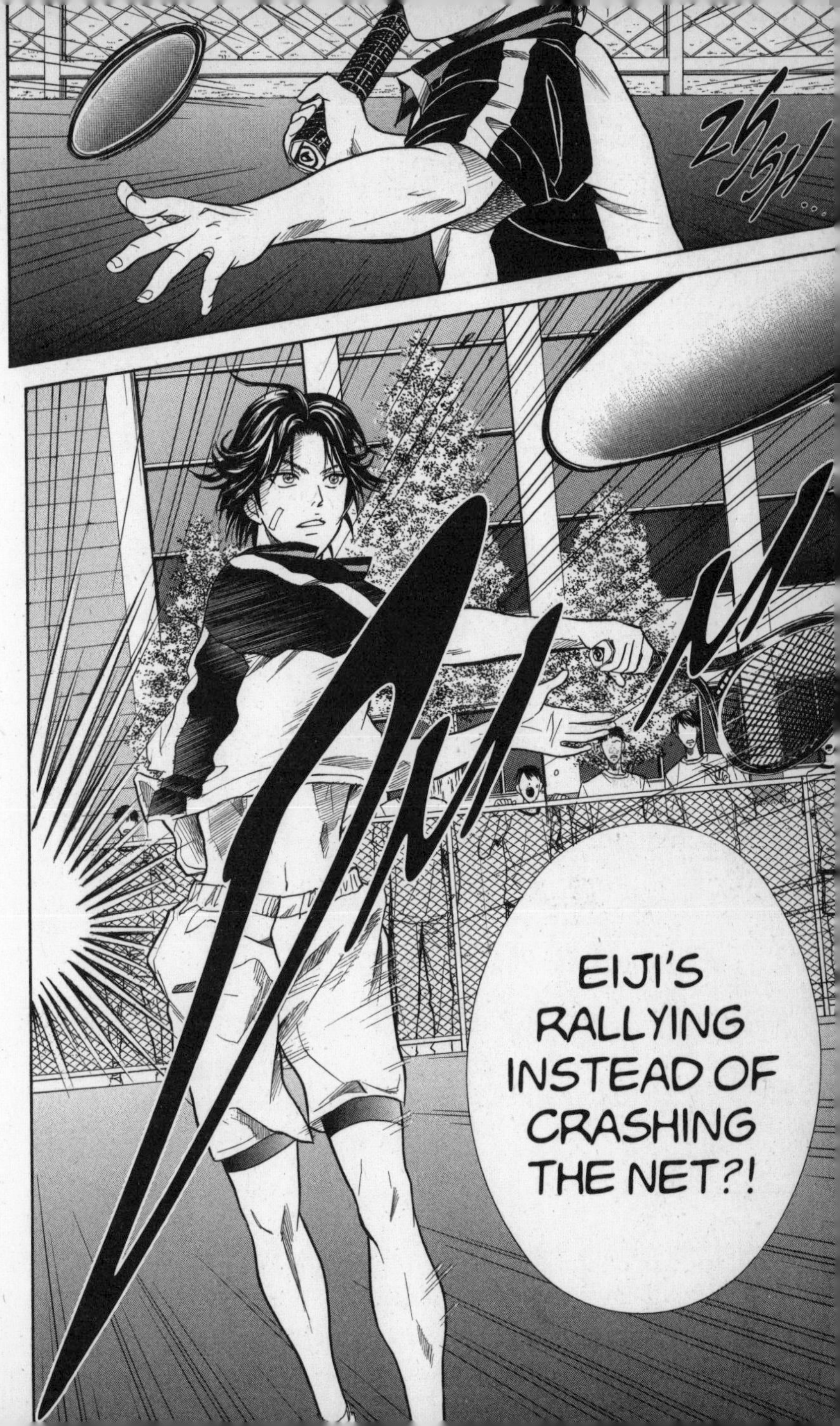
EIJI'S RALLYING INSTEAD OF CRASHING THE NET?!

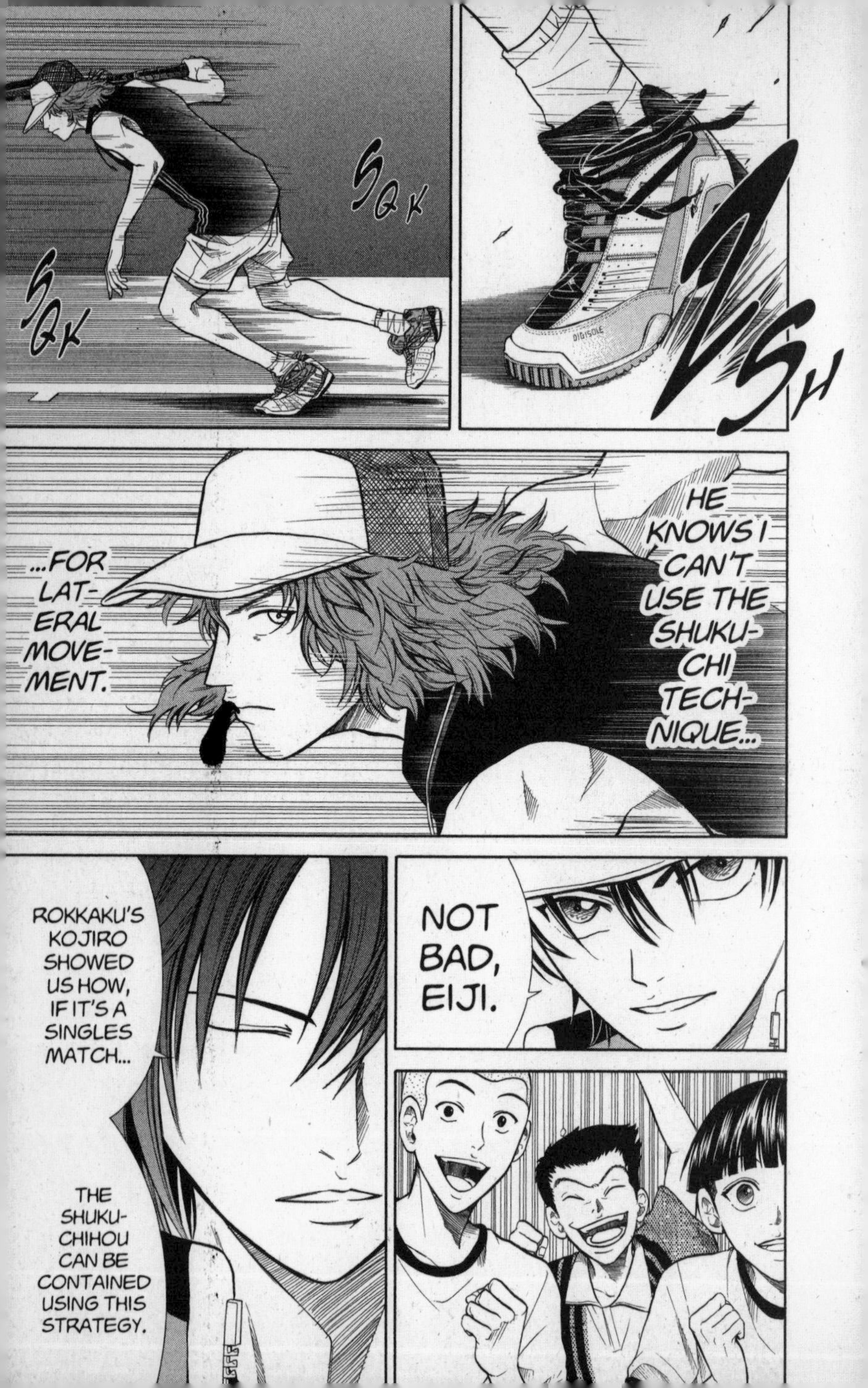
VISH
SQK
SQK
HE KNOWS I CAN'T USE THE SHUKU-CHI TECH-NIQUE...
...FOR LAT-ERAL MOVE-MENT.
NOT BAD, EIJI.
ROKKAKU'S KOJIRO SHOWED US HOW, IF IT'S A SINGLES MATCH...
THE SHUKU-CHIHOU CAN BE CONTAINED USING THIS STRATEGY.

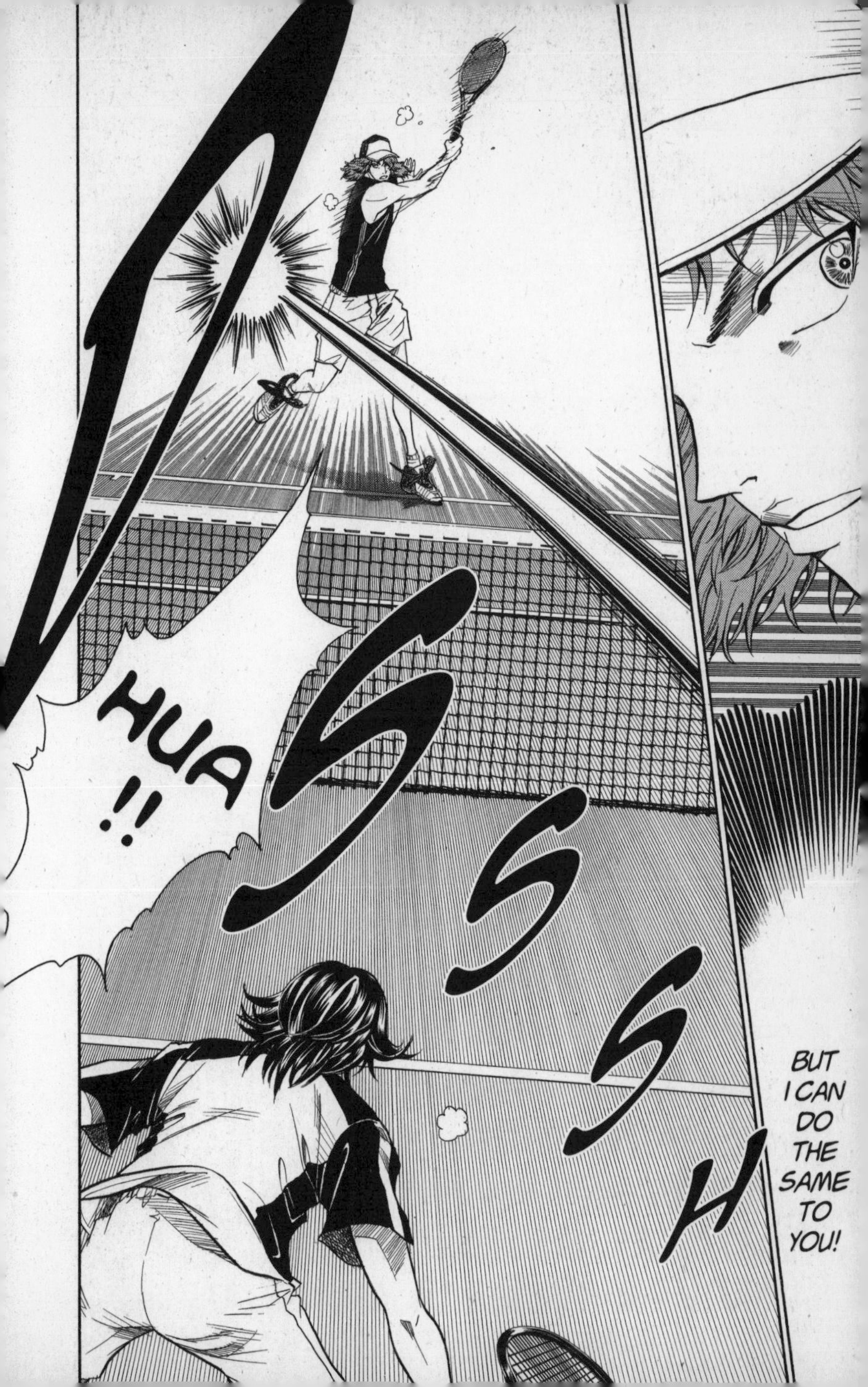
BUT I CAN DO THE SAME TO YOU!
SSSSH
HUA!!

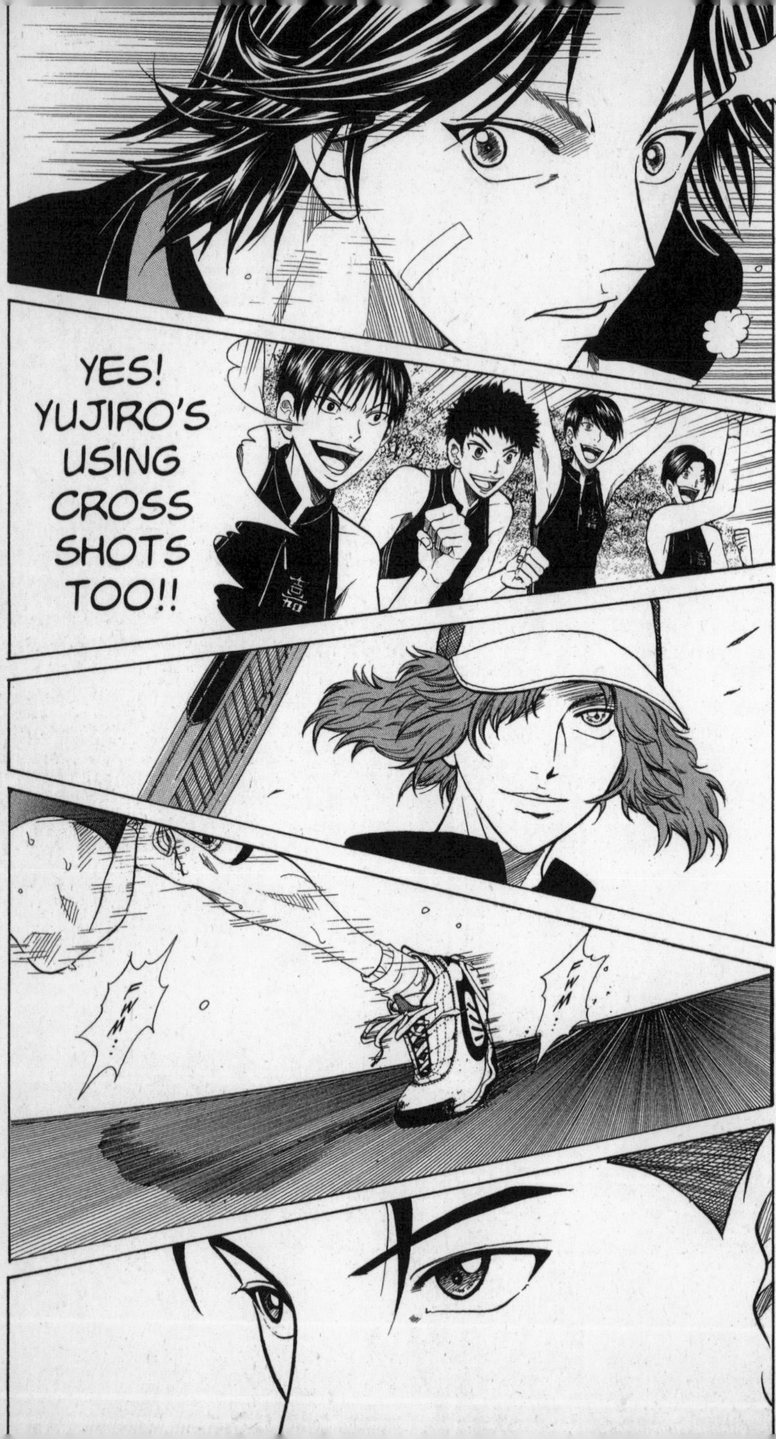
YES! YUJIRO'S USING CROSS SHOTS TOO!!
FWM...
FWM...

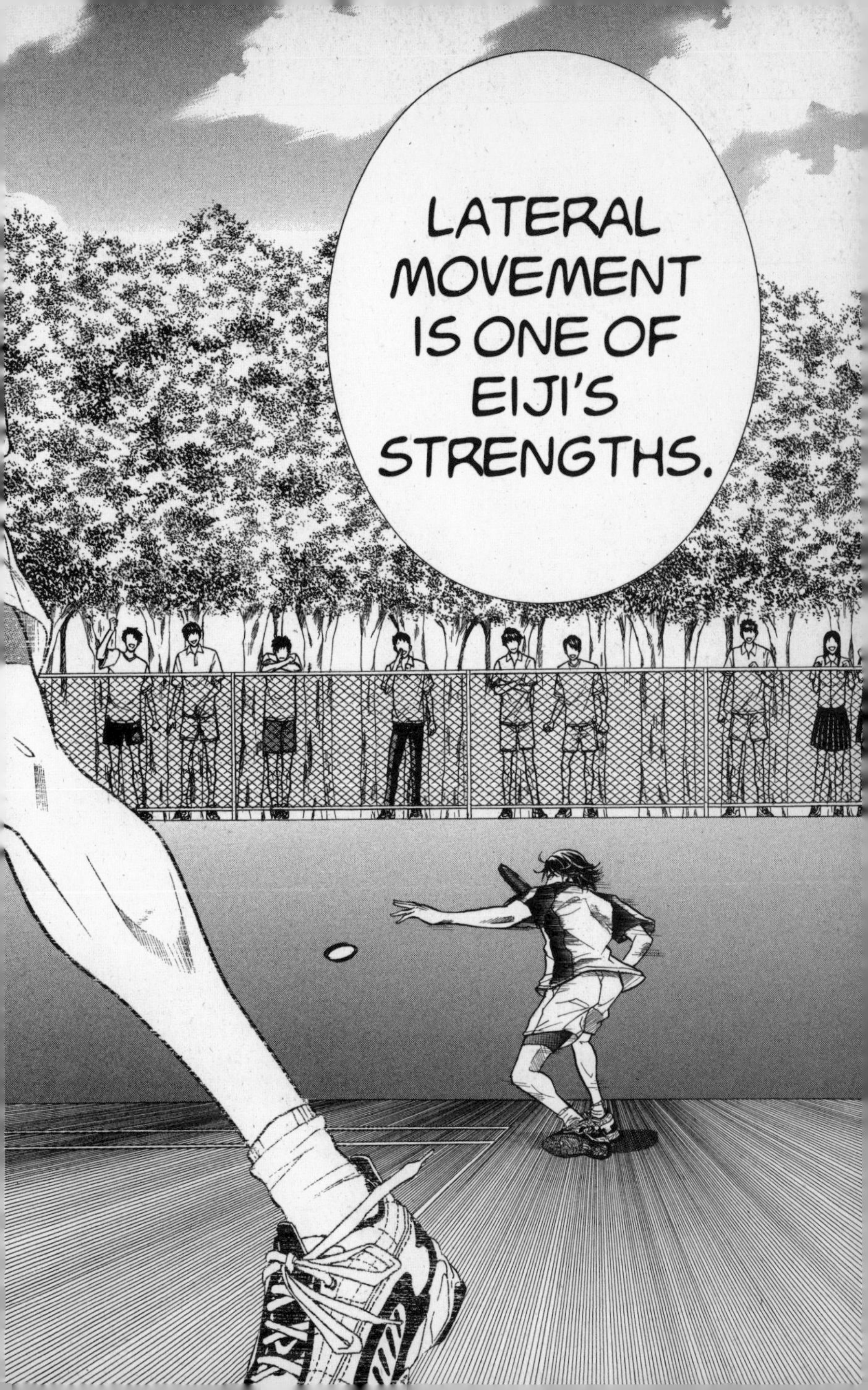
LATERAL MOVEMENT IS ONE OF EIJI'S STRENGTHS.

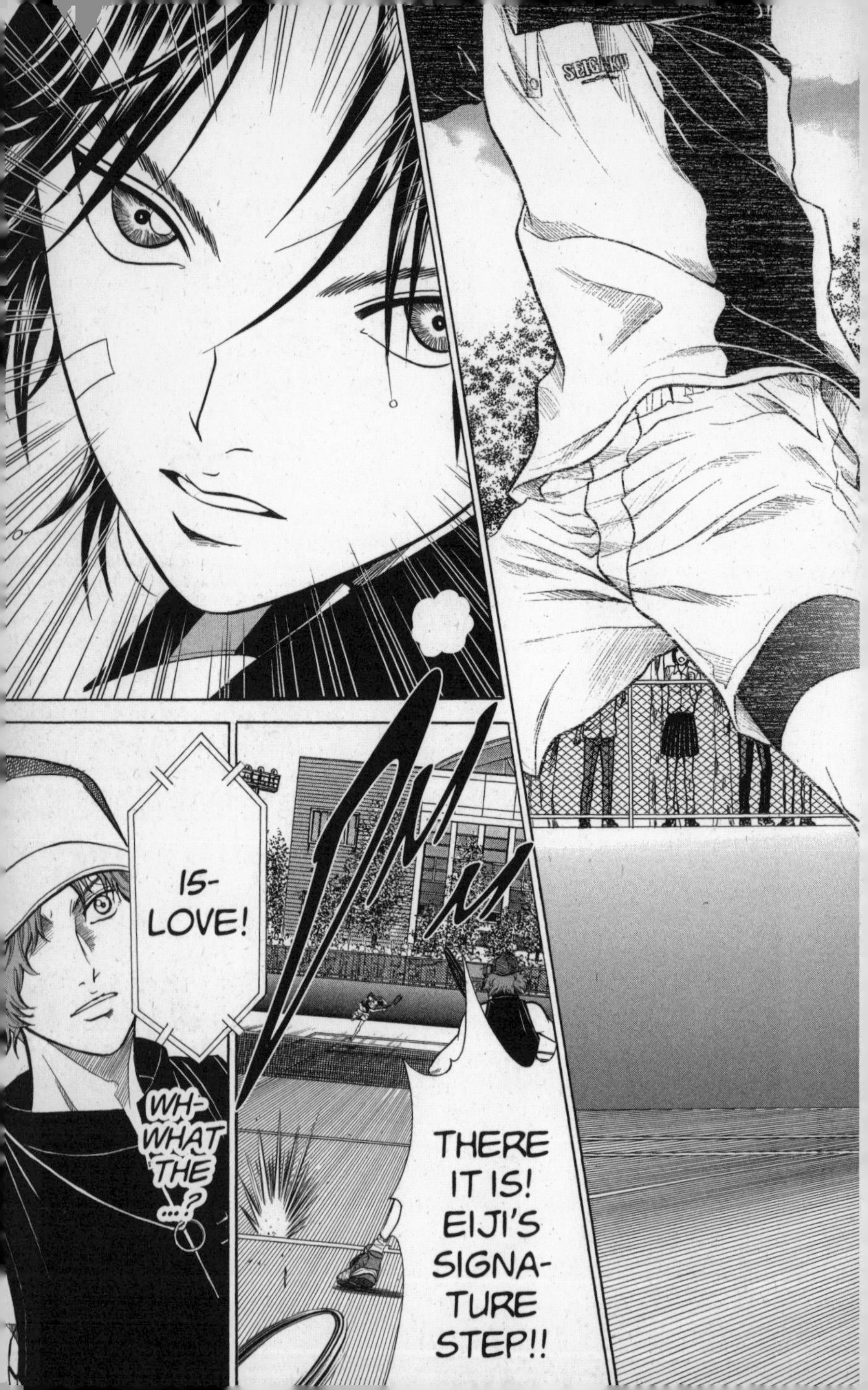
SEIGAKU
THERE IT IS! EIJI'S SIGNATURE STEP!!
IS-LOVE!
WH-WHAT THE...?

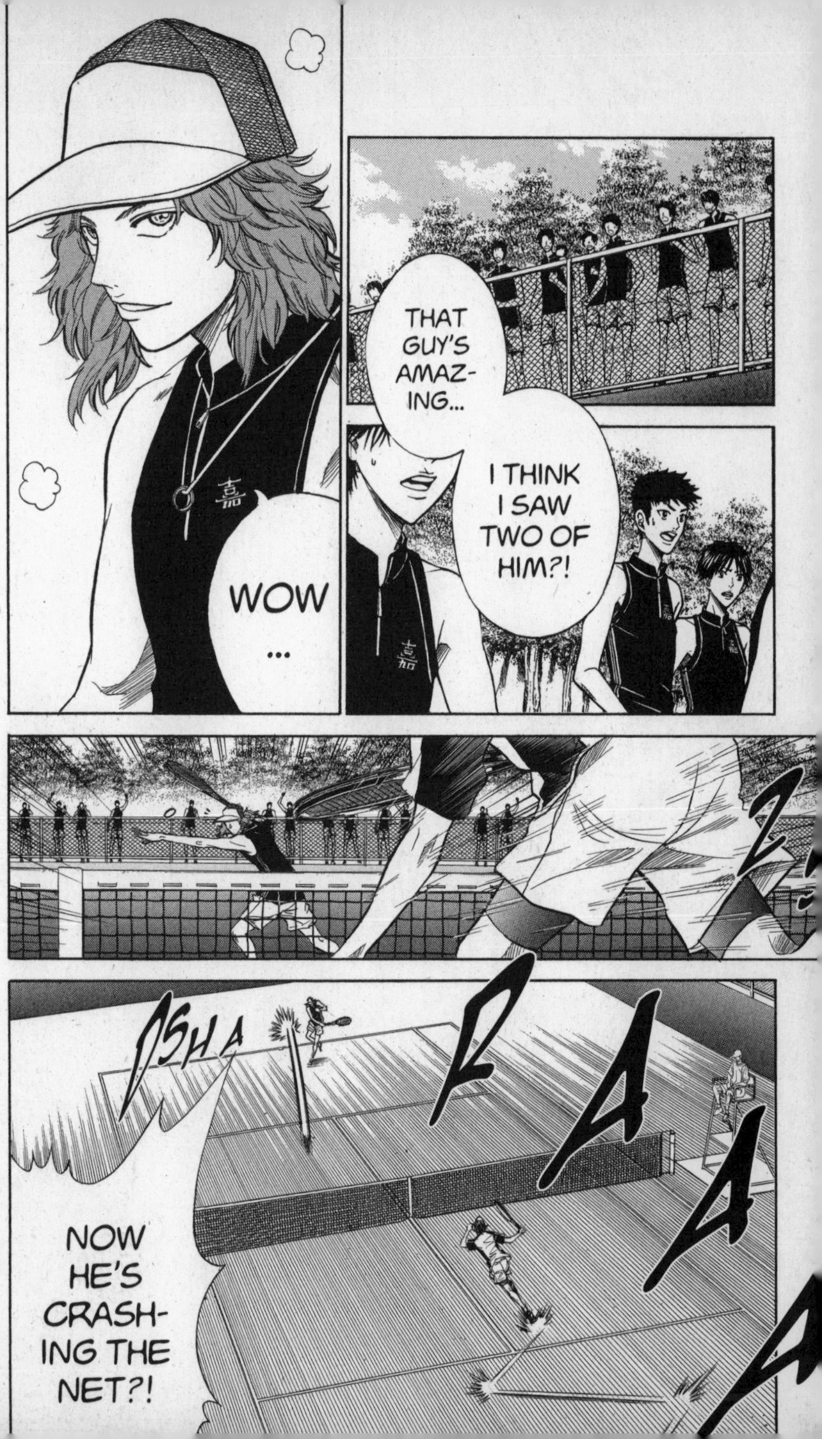

THAT GUY'S AMAZ-ING...
I THINK I SAW TWO OF HIM?!
WOW ...
NOW HE'S CRASH-ING THE NET?!

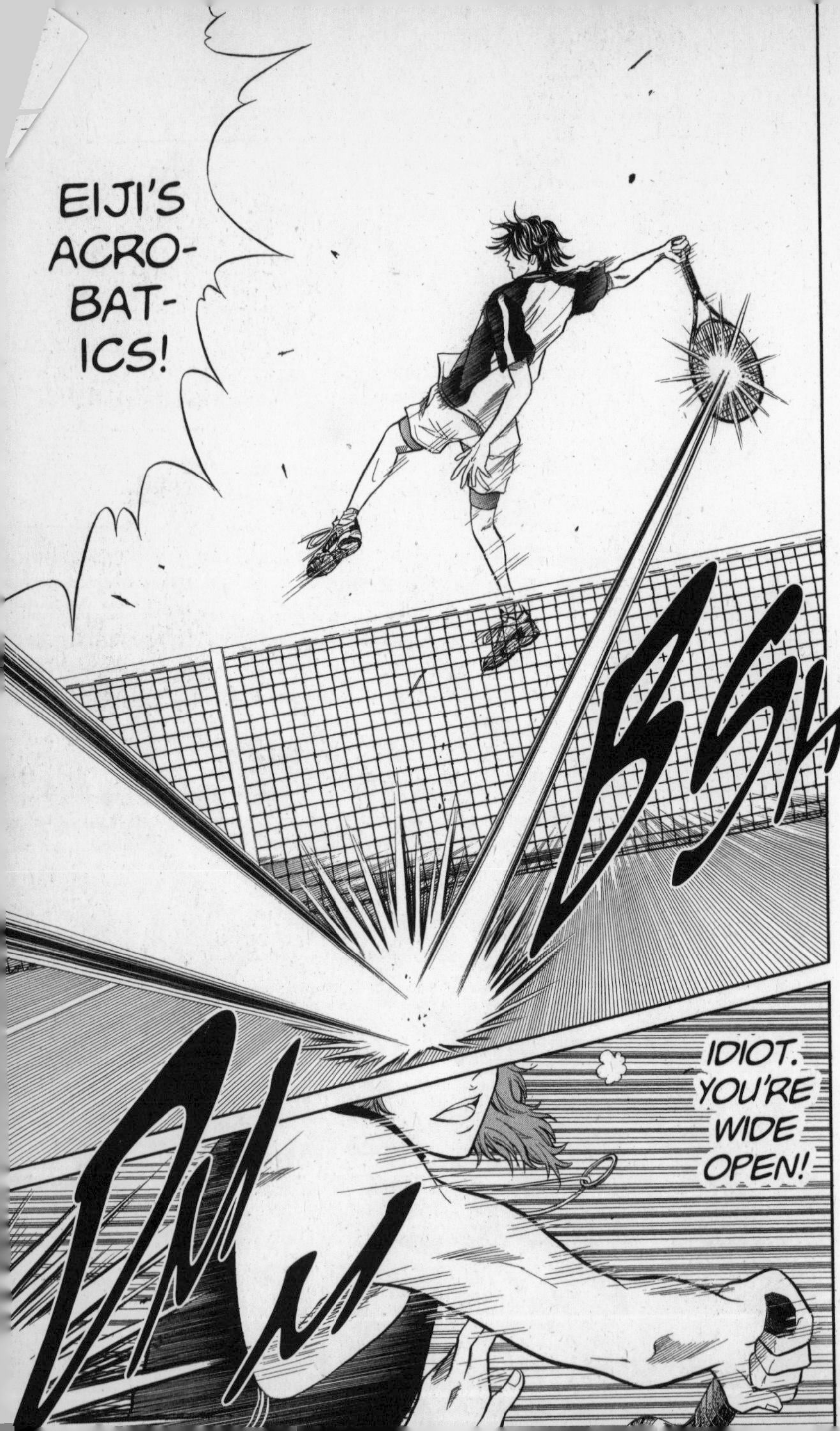
EIJI'S ACRO-BAT-ICS!
BSH
IDIOT. YOU'RE WIDE OPEN!

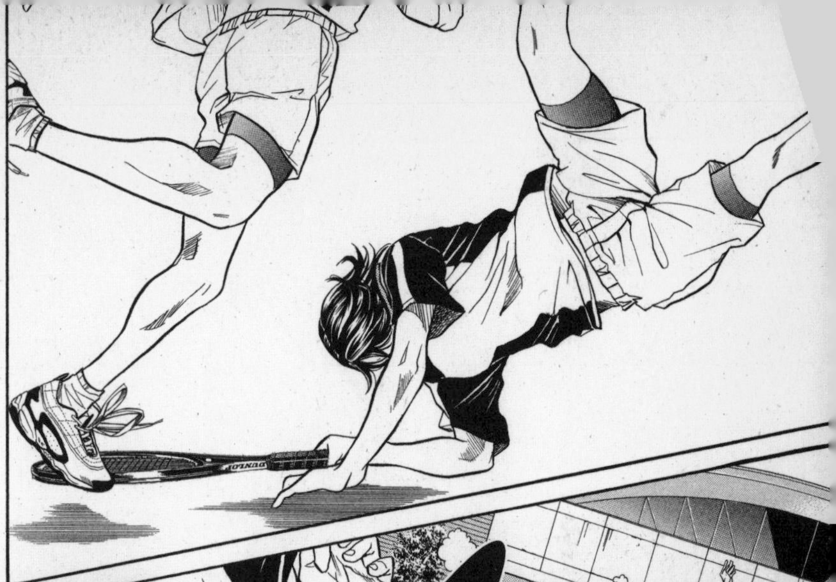
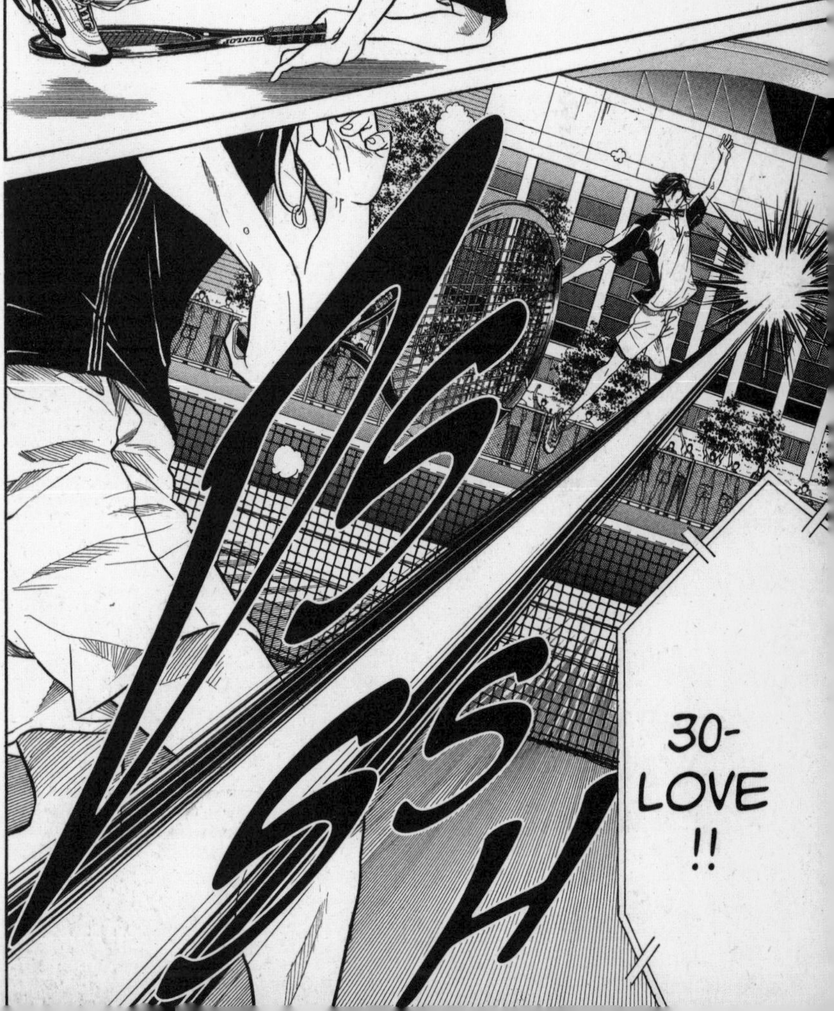
VSSH
30-LOVE!!

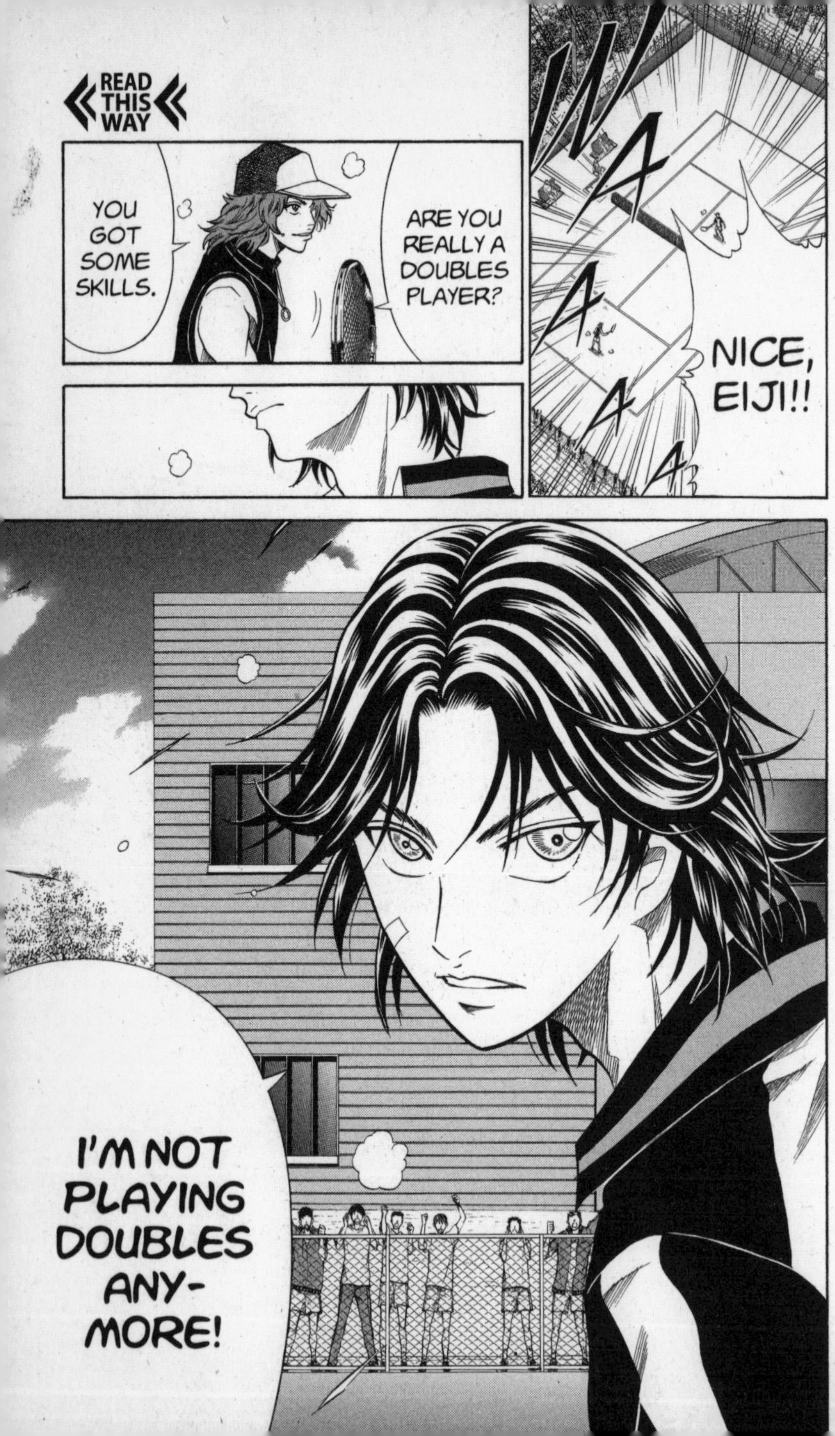
READ THIS WAY
WAAAA
NICE, EIJI!!
ARE YOU REALLY A DOUBLES PLAYER?
YOU GOT SOME SKILLS.
I'M NOT PLAYING DOUBLES ANYMORE!

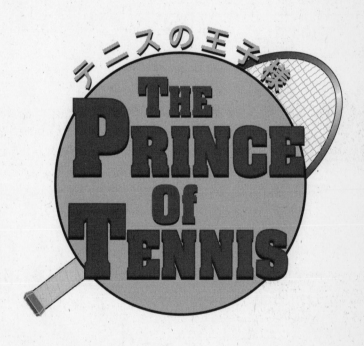

テニスの王子様

THE PRINCE OF TENNIS

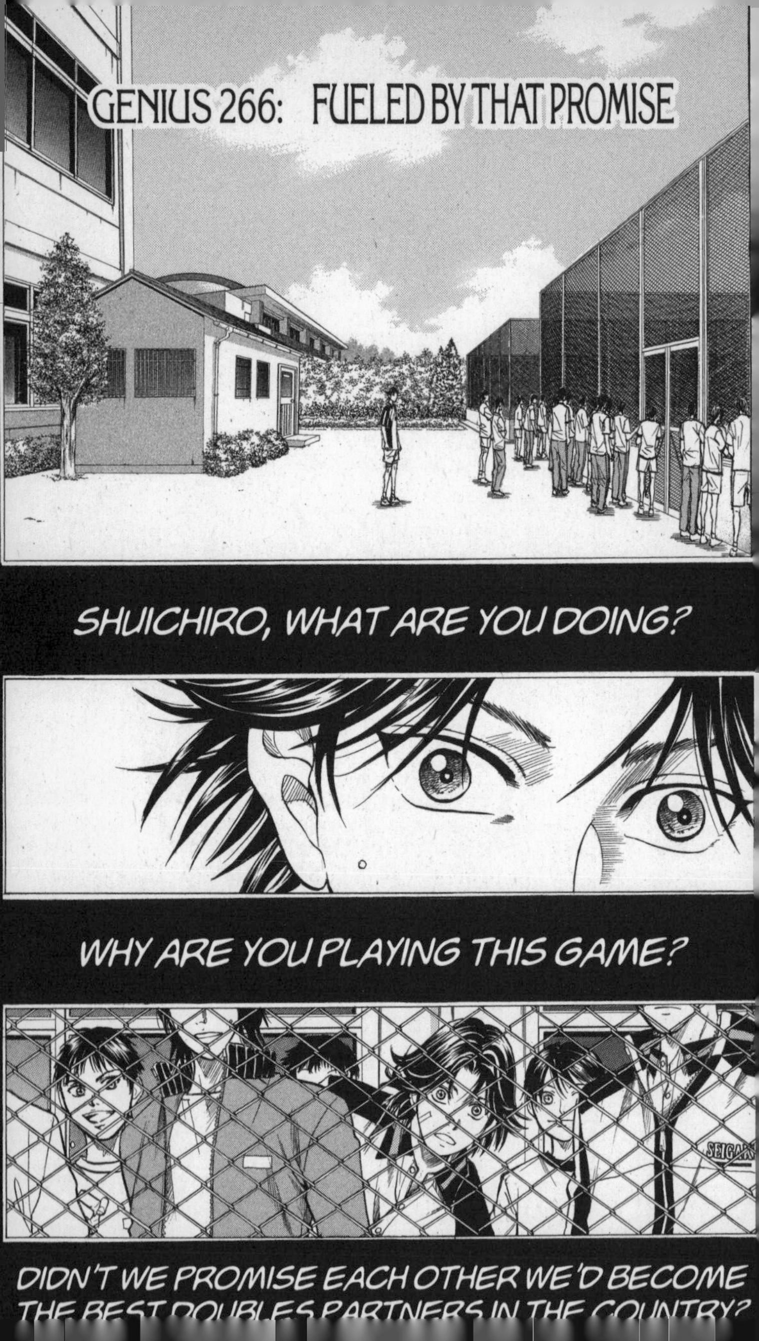
GENIUS 266: FUELED BY THAT PROMISE
SHUICHIRO, WHAT ARE YOU DOING?
WHY ARE YOU PLAYING THIS GAME?
DIDN'T WE PROMISE EACH OTHER WE'D BECOME THE BEST DOUBLES PARTNERS IN THE COUNTRY?

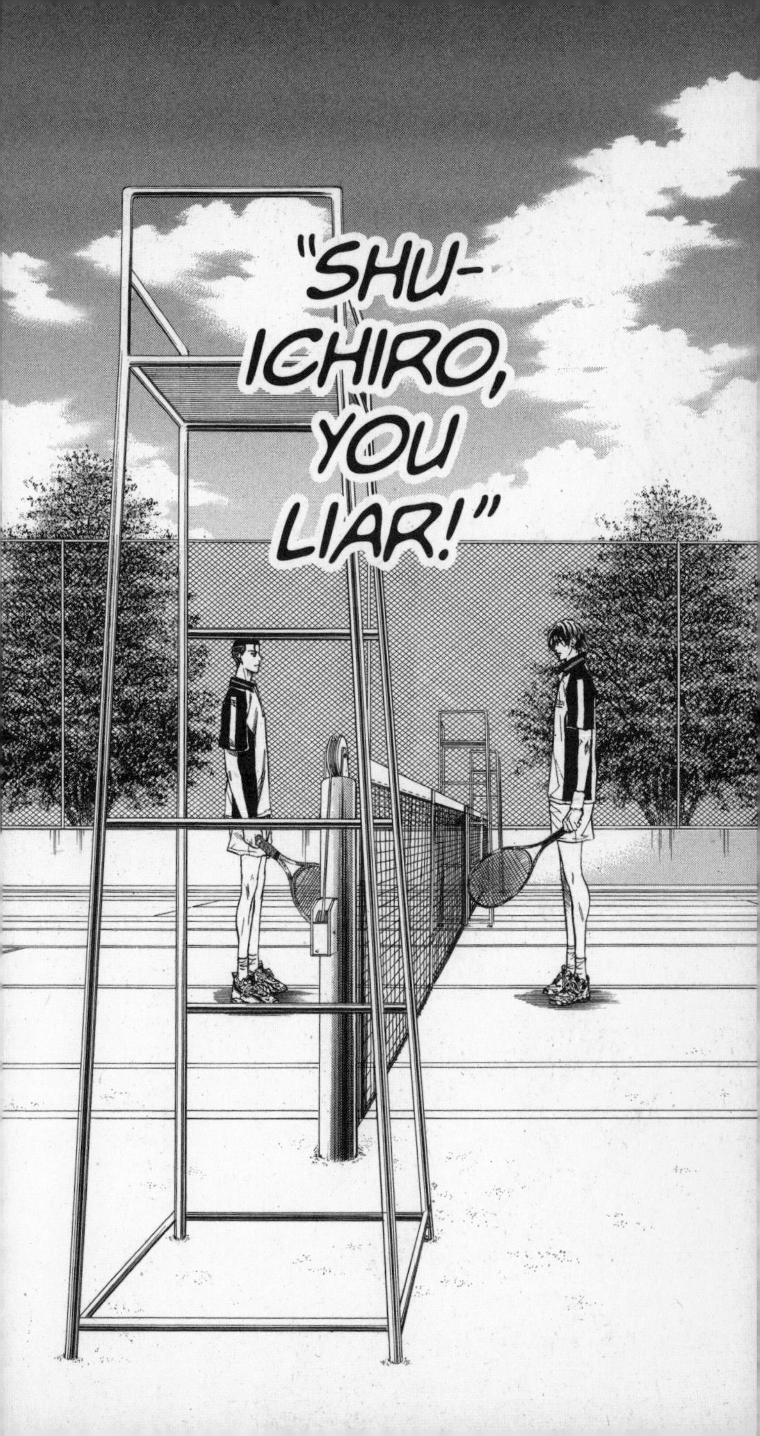
"SHU-ICHIRO, YOU LIAR!"

GENIUS 266: FUELED BY THAT PROMISE

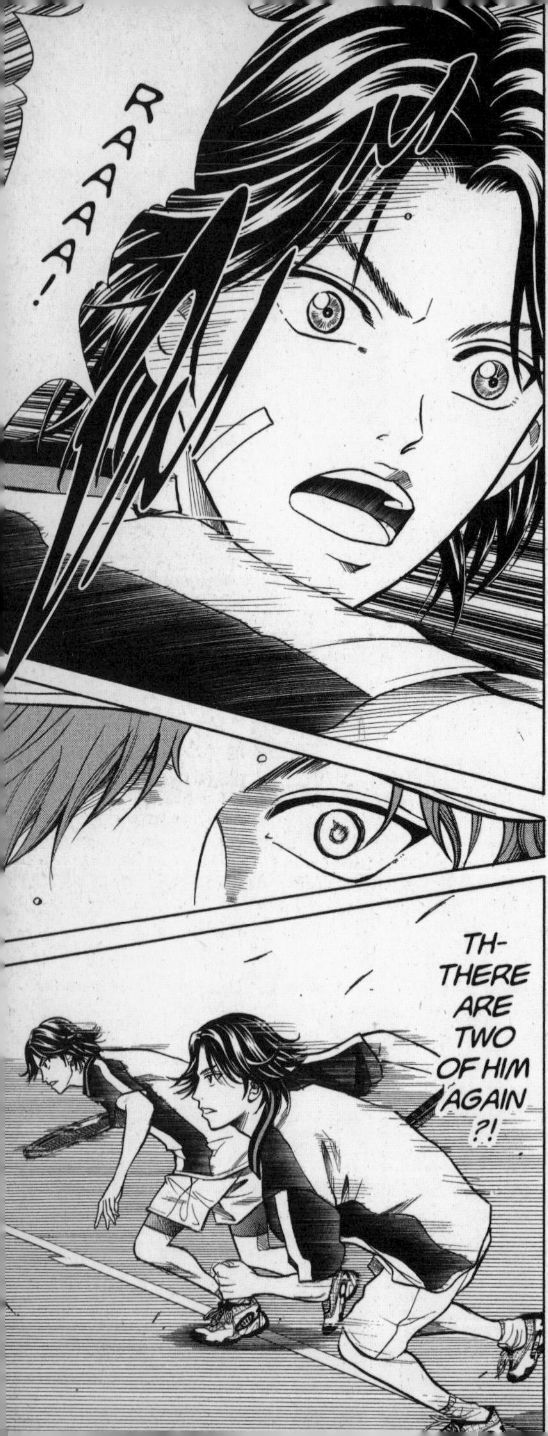
RAAAAA-!
TH- THERE ARE TWO OF HIM AGAIN ?!

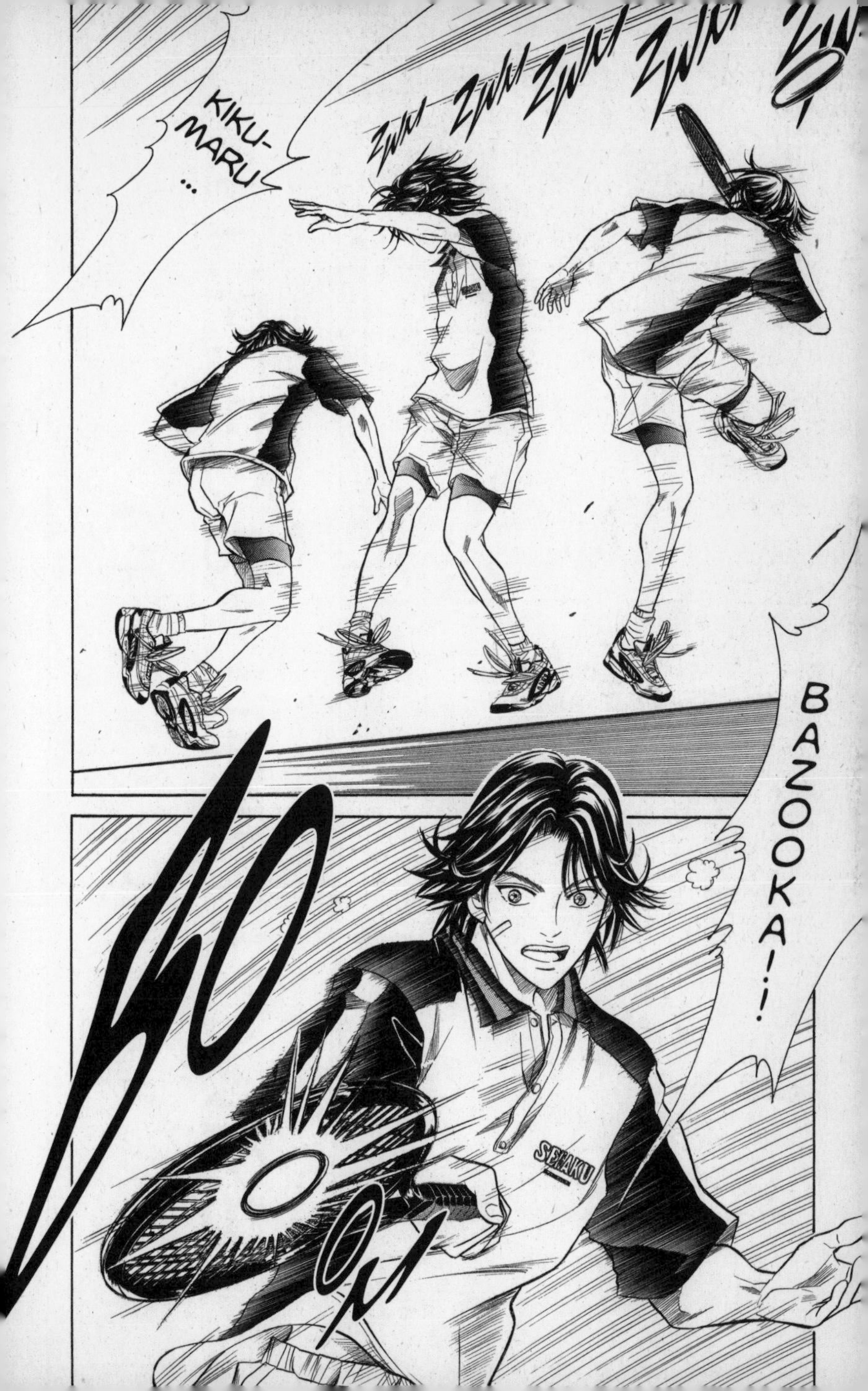
KIKU-MARU...
BAZOOKA!!

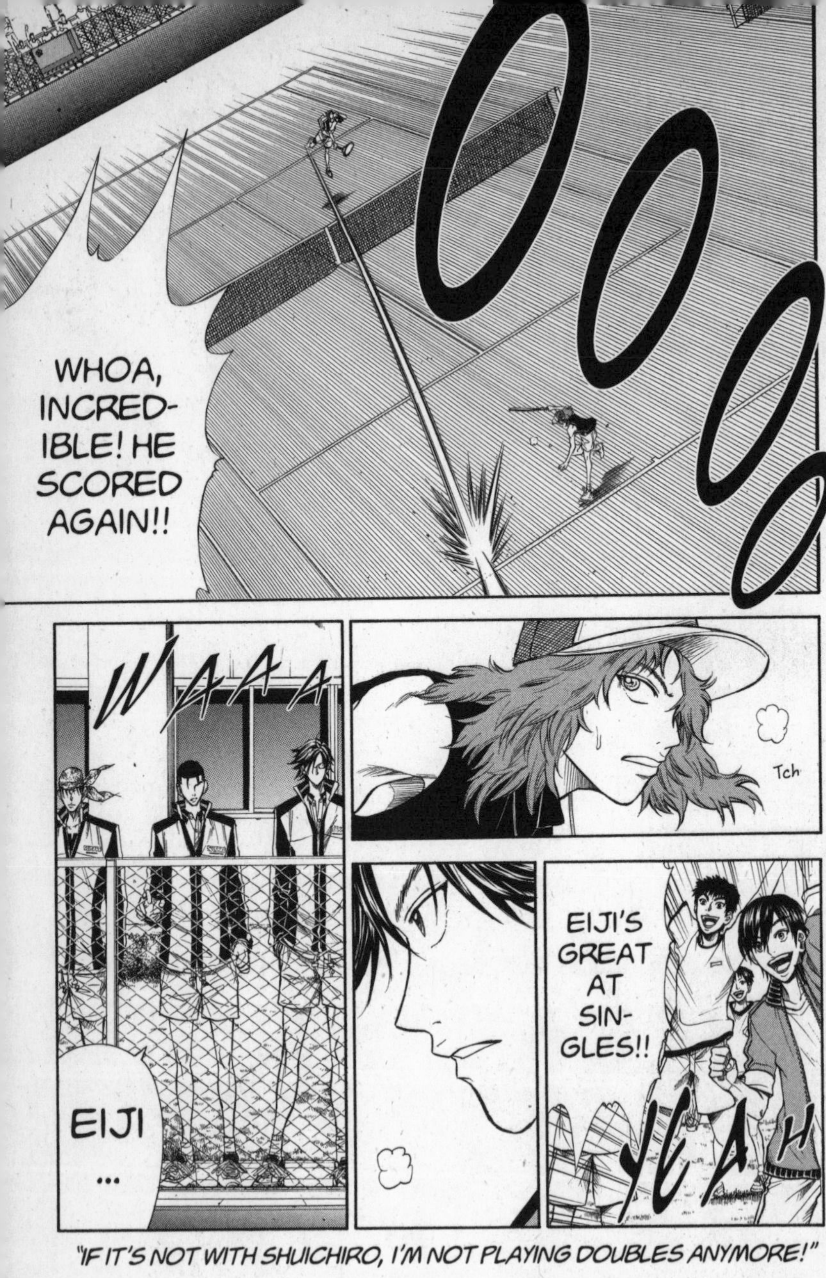
WHOA, INCRED-IBLE! HE SCORED AGAIN!!
Tch
EIJI'S GREAT AT SIN-GLES!!
YEAH
WAAAA
EIJI ...

"IF IT'S NOT WITH SHUICHIRO, I'M NOT PLAYING DOUBLES ANYMORE!"

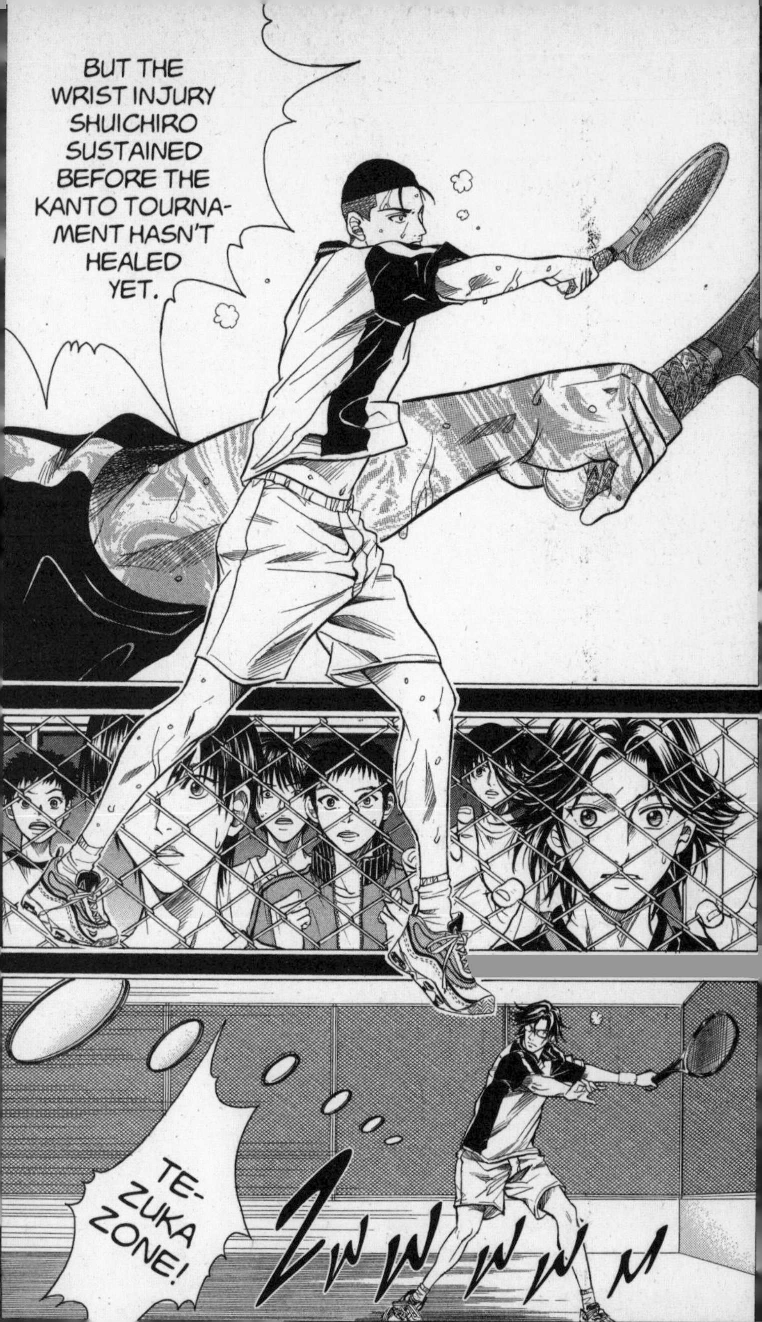
BUT THE WRIST INJURY SHUICHIRO SUSTAINED BEFORE THE KANTO TOURNAMENT HASN'T HEALED YET.
TE-ZUKA ZONE!
ZWWWWWM

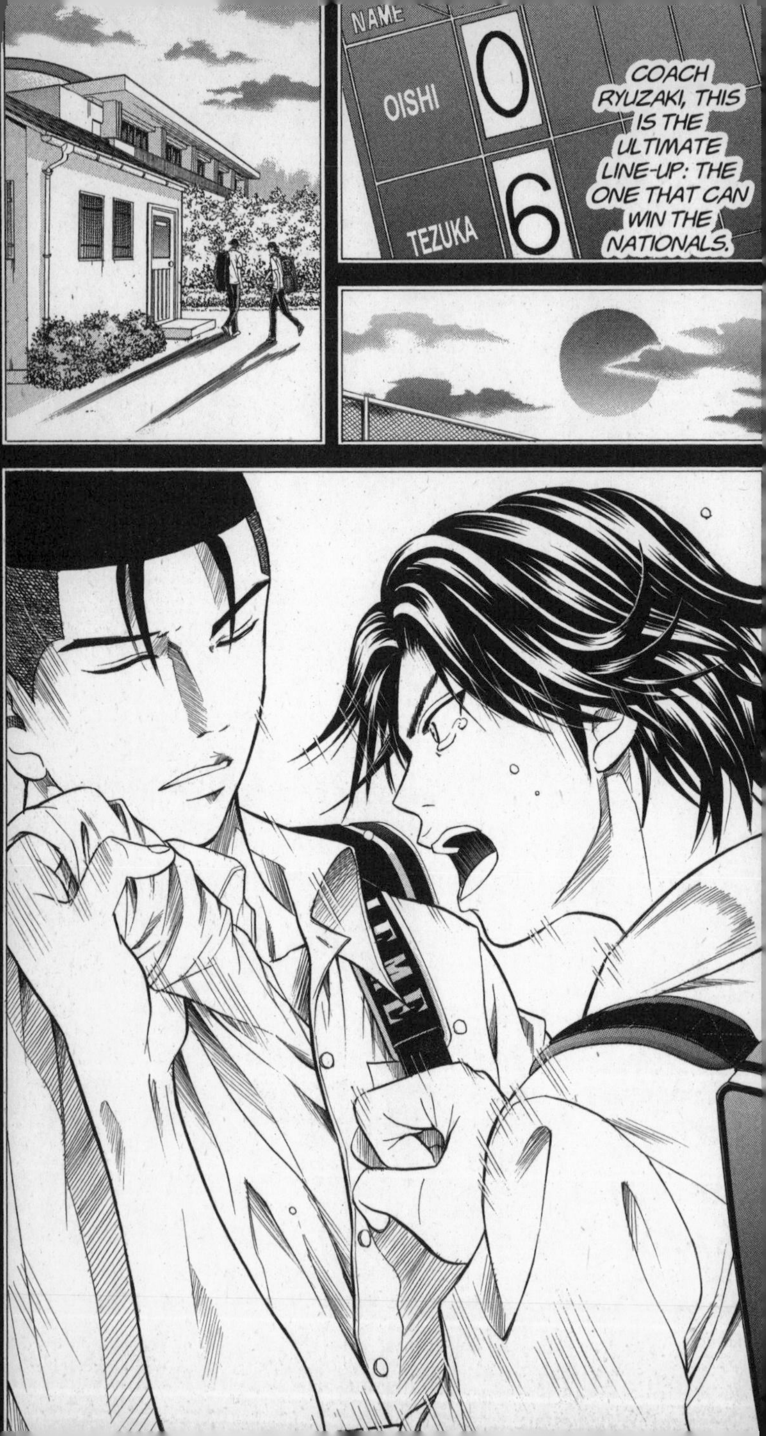
NAME
OISHI
0
TEZUKA
6
COACH RYUZAKI, THIS IS THE ULTIMATE LINE-UP: THE ONE THAT CAN WIN THE NATIONALS.

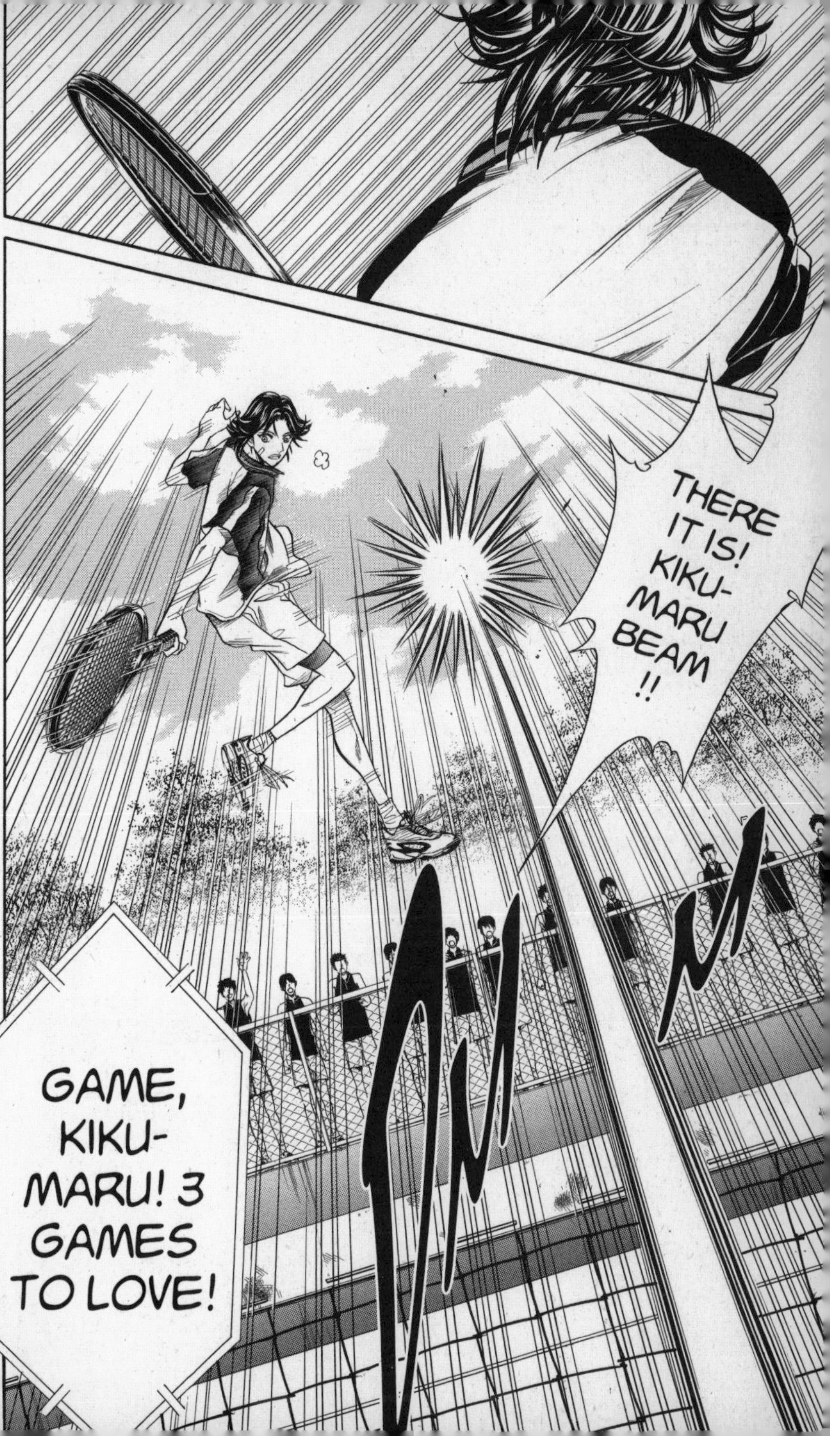
THERE IT IS! KIKU-MARU BEAM !!
GAME, KIKU-MARU! 3 GAMES TO LOVE!

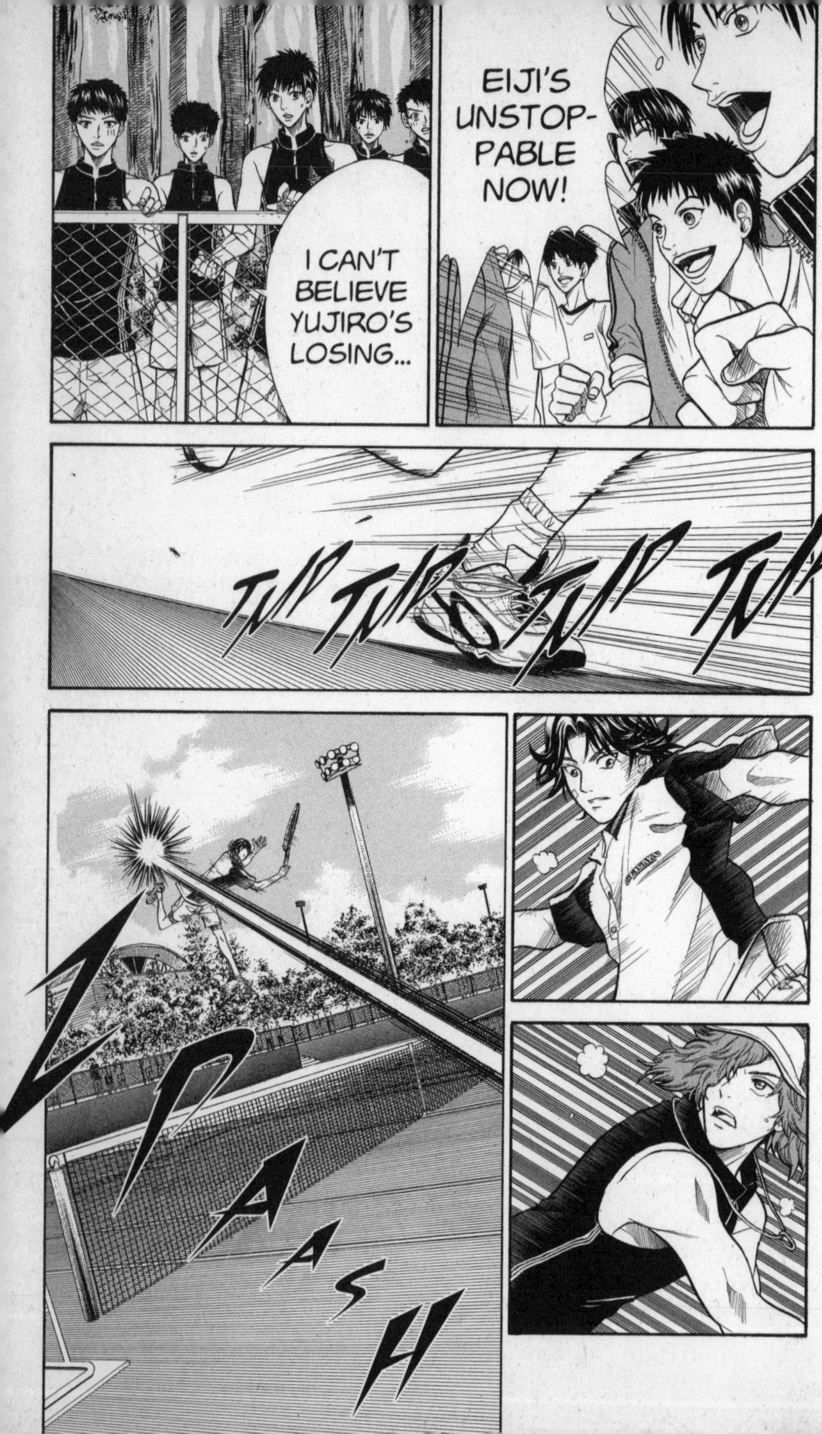
EIJI'S UNSTOPPABLE NOW!
I CAN'T BELIEVE YUJIRO'S LOSING...
TMP TMP TMP TMP
ZPAASH

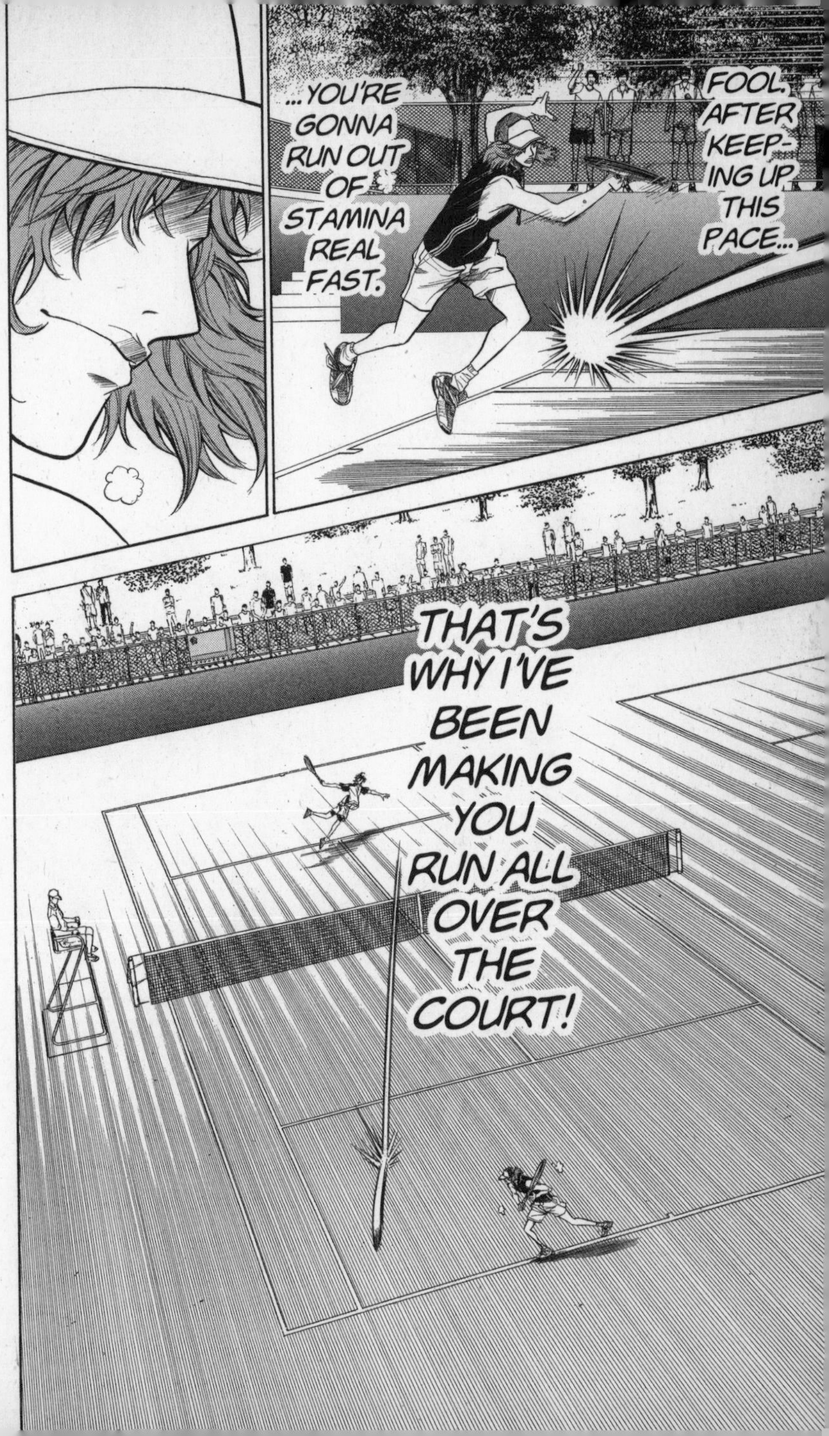
FOOL. AFTER KEEPING UP THIS PACE...
...YOU'RE GONNA RUN OUT OF STAMINA REAL FAST.
THAT'S WHY I'VE BEEN MAKING YOU RUN ALL OVER THE COURT!

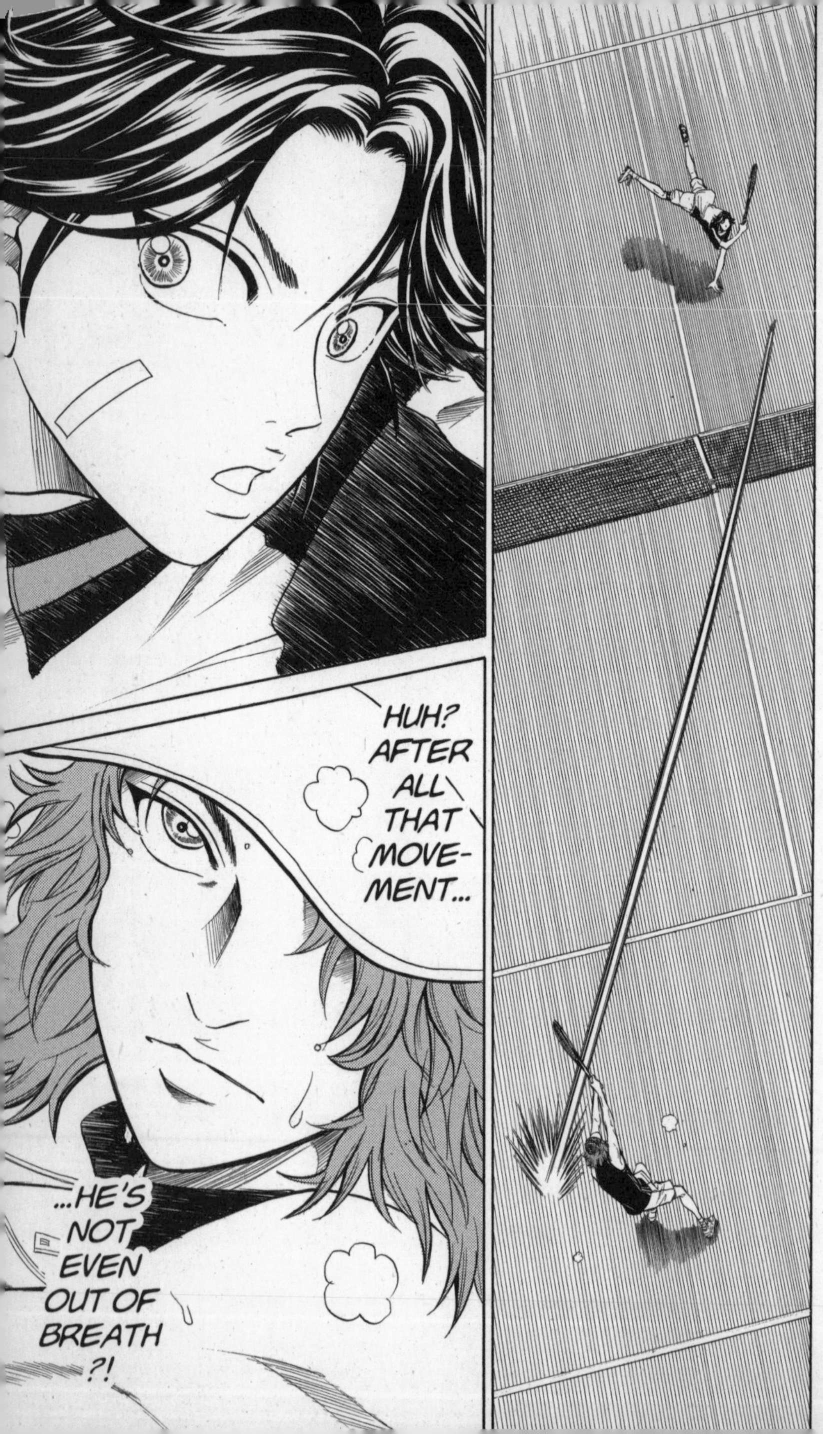
HUH? AFTER ALL THAT MOVEMENT...
...HE'S NOT EVEN OUT OF BREATH ?!

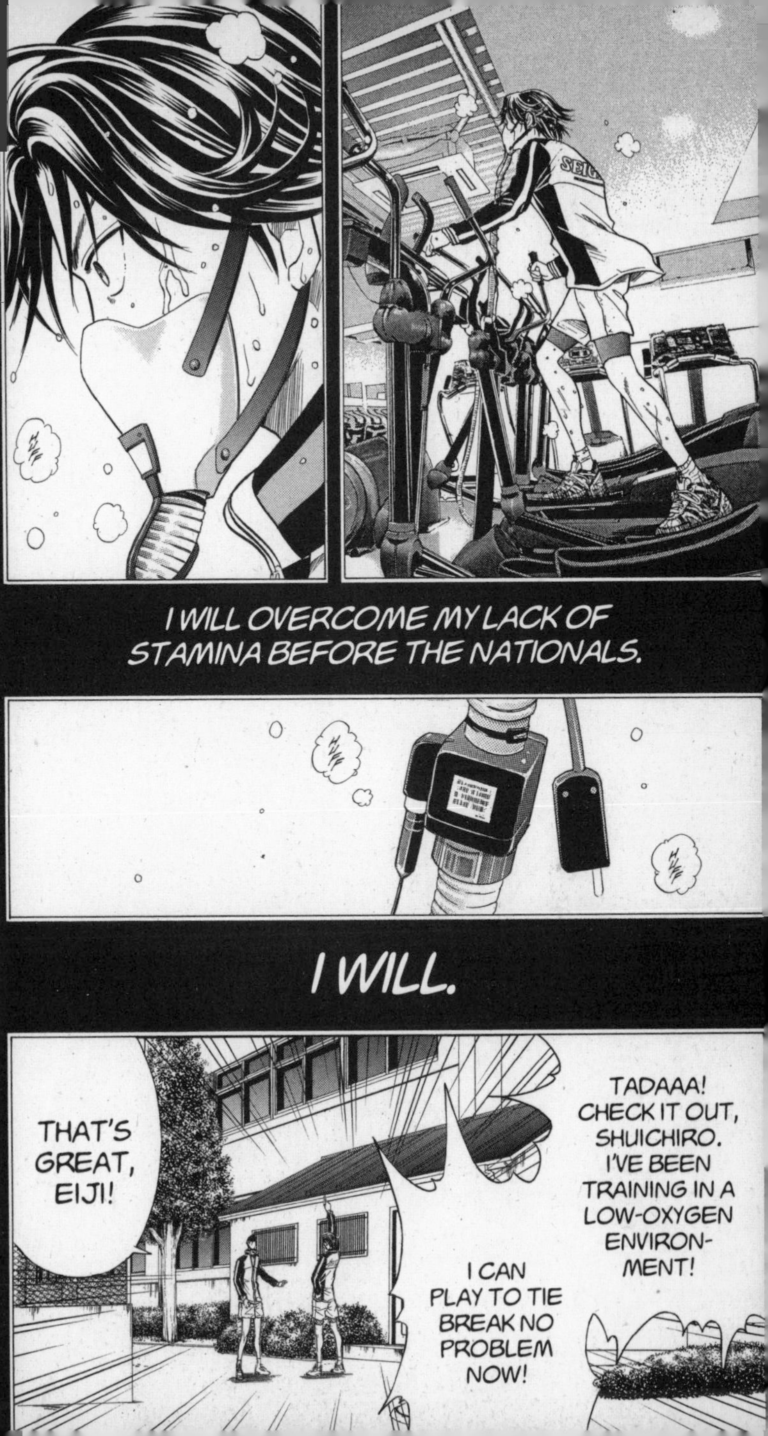
I WILL OVERCOME MY LACK OF STAMINA BEFORE THE NATIONALS.
I WILL.
TADAAA! CHECK IT OUT, SHUICHIRO. I'VE BEEN TRAINING IN A LOW-OXYGEN ENVIRON-MENT!
I CAN PLAY TO TIE BREAK NO PROBLEM NOW!
THAT'S GREAT, EIJI!

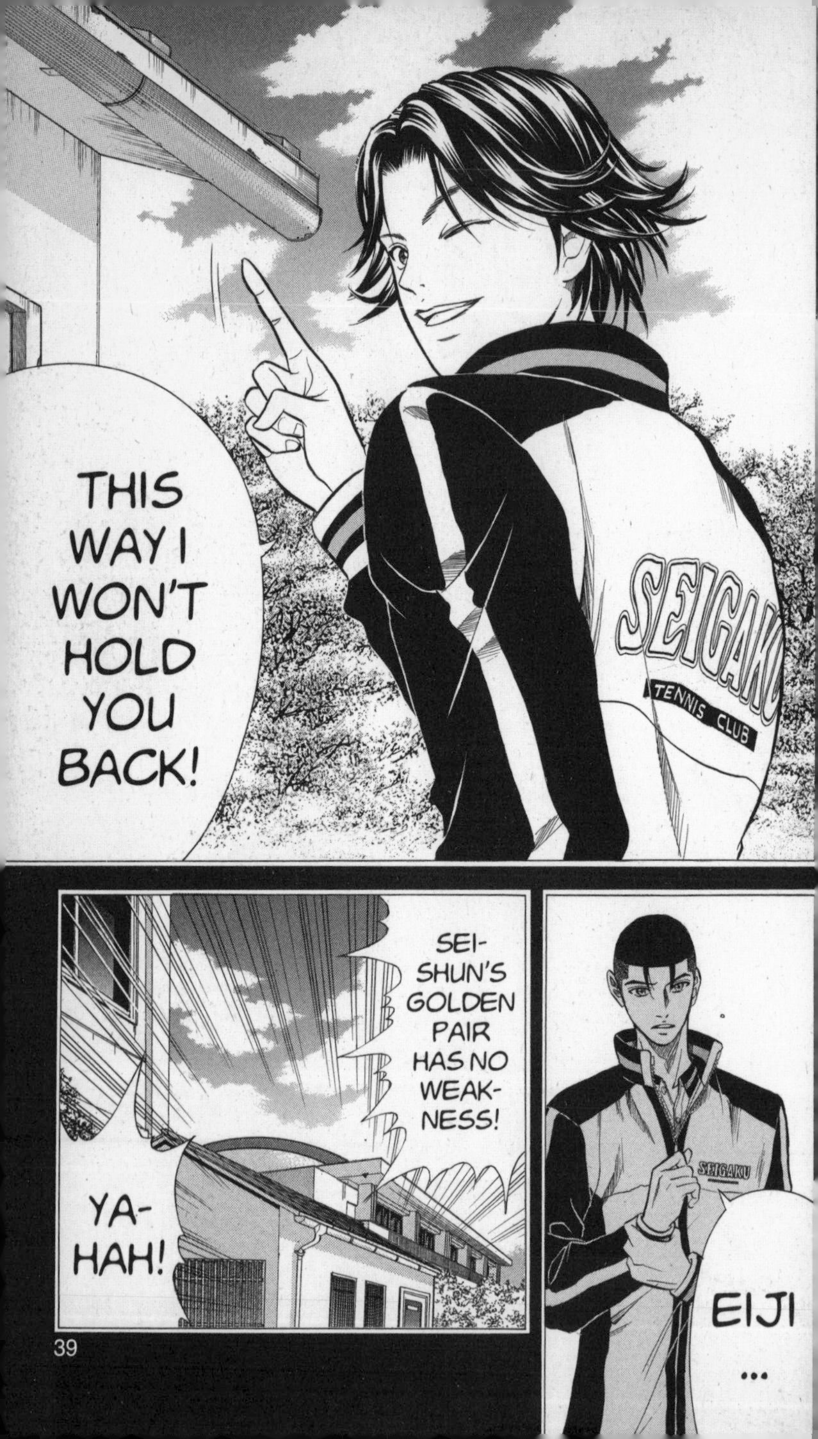
THIS WAY I WON'T HOLD YOU BACK!
SEIGAKU
TENNIS CLUB
SEIGAKU
EIJI ...
SEI-SHUN'S GOLDEN PAIR HAS NO WEAK-NESS!
YA-HAH!

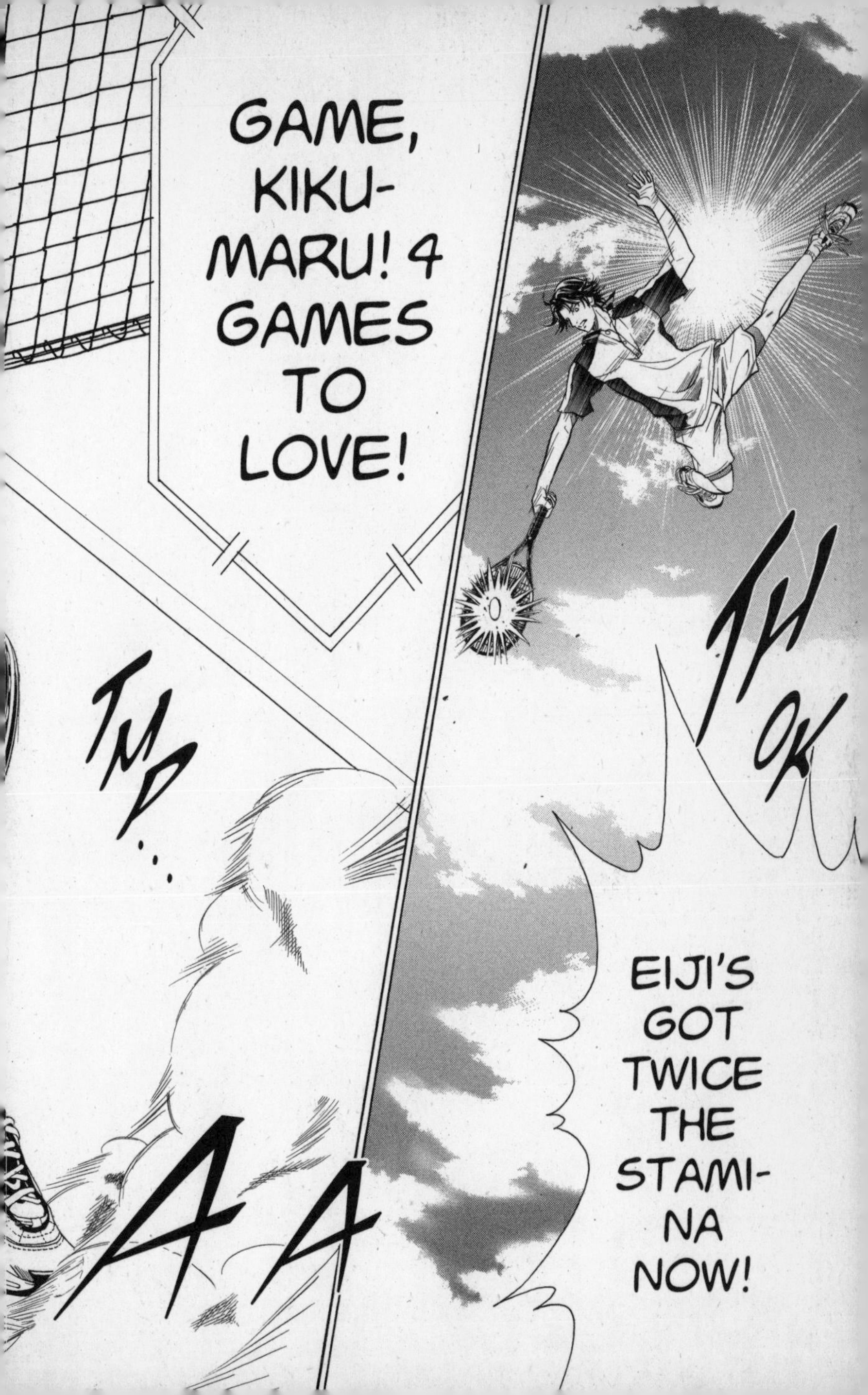
THOK
EIJI'S GOT TWICE THE STAMINA NOW!
GAME, KIKUMARU! 4 GAMES TO LOVE!
TMP...
AA

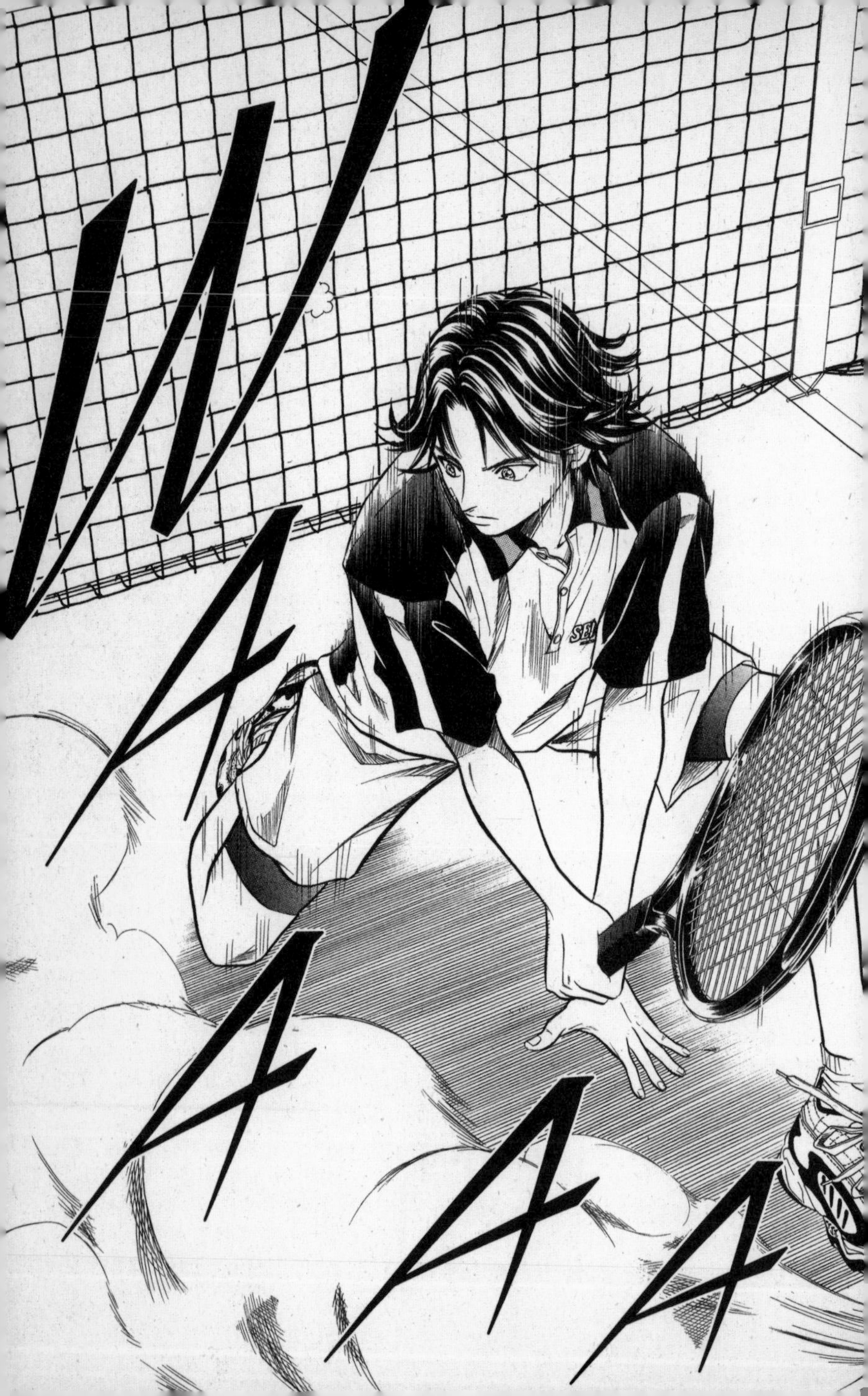
WAAAAA

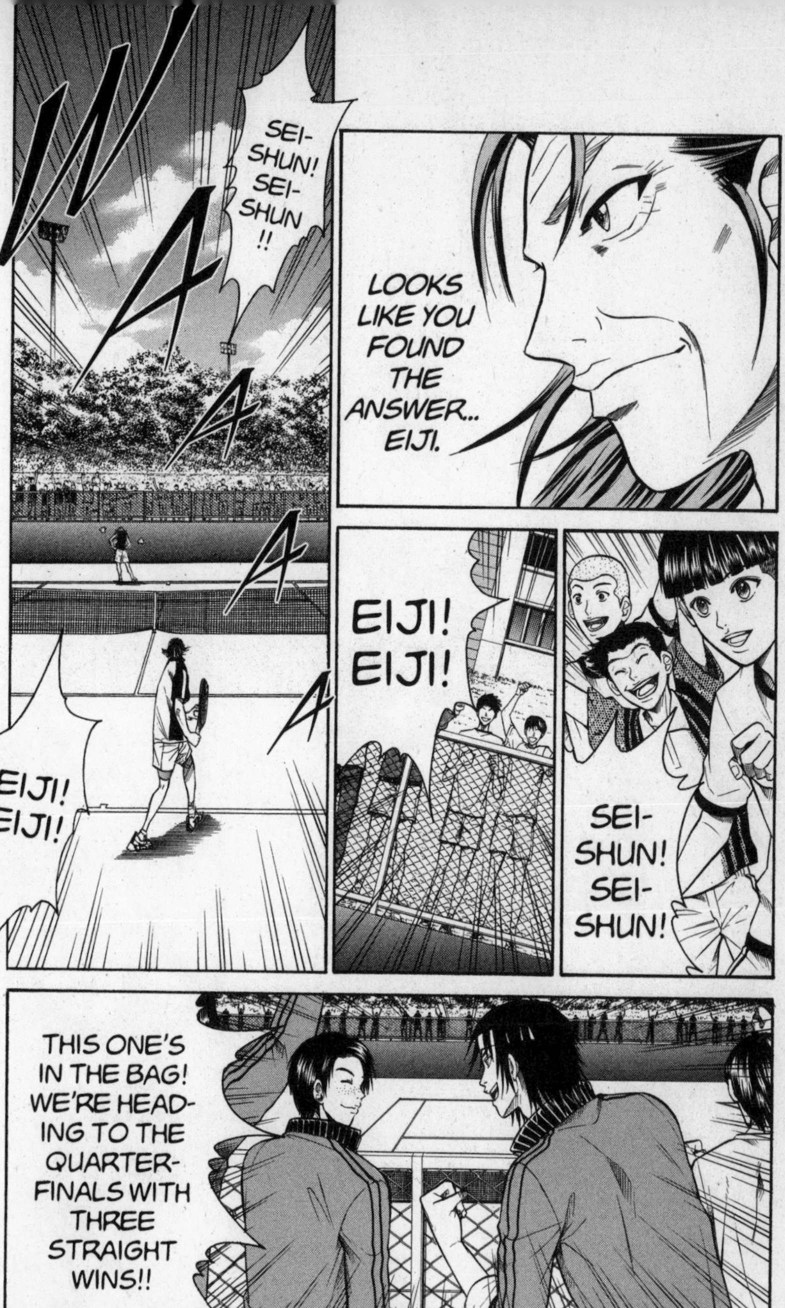
LOOKS LIKE YOU FOUND THE ANSWER... EIJI.
SEI-SHUN! SEI-SHUN!
EIJI! EIJI!
SEI-SHUN! SEI-SHUN!!
WAAAA
EIJI! EIJI!
THIS ONE'S IN THE BAG! WE'RE HEADING TO THE QUARTERFINALS WITH THREE STRAIGHT WINS!!

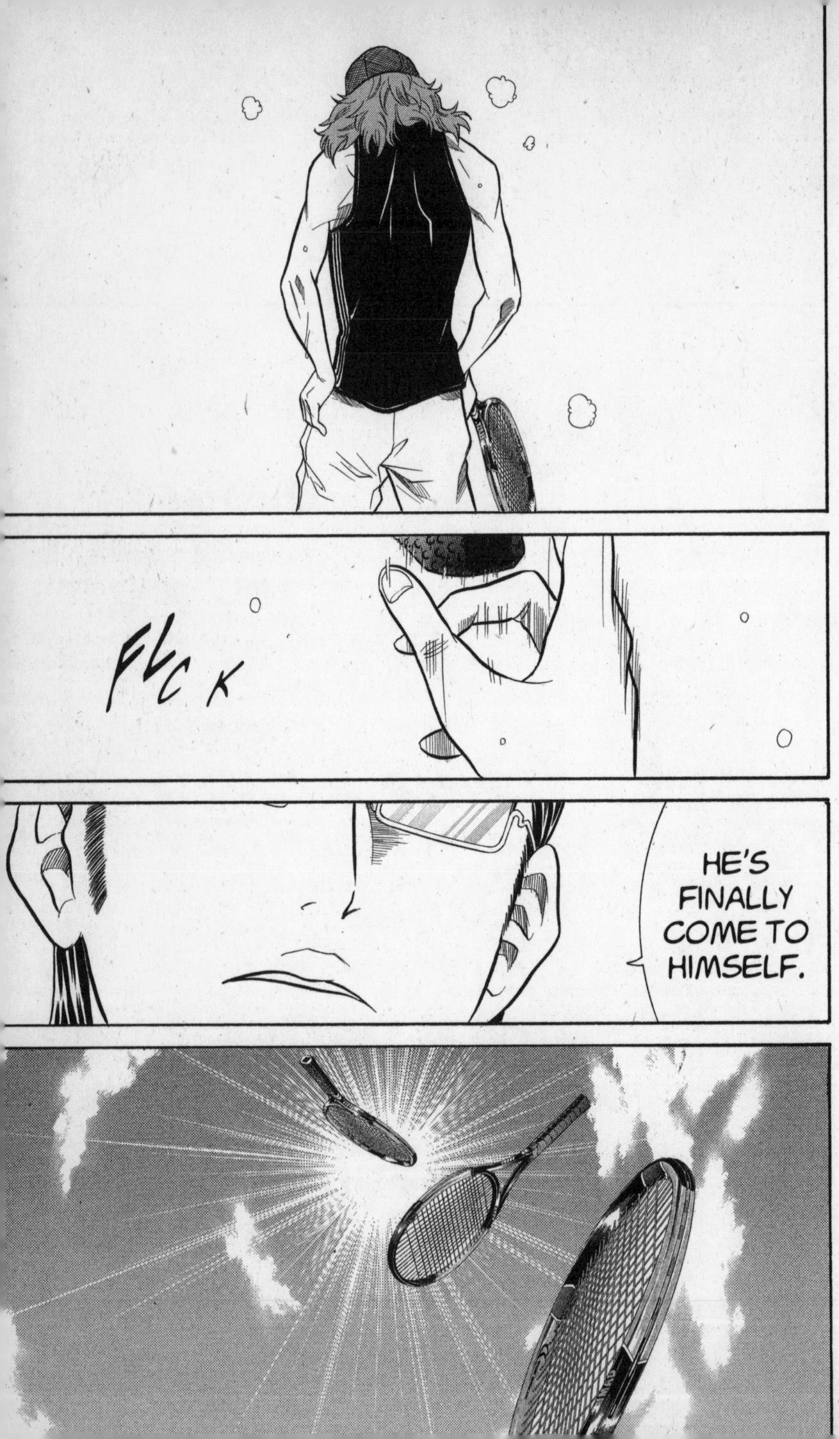
FLICK
HE'S FINALLY COME TO HIMSELF.

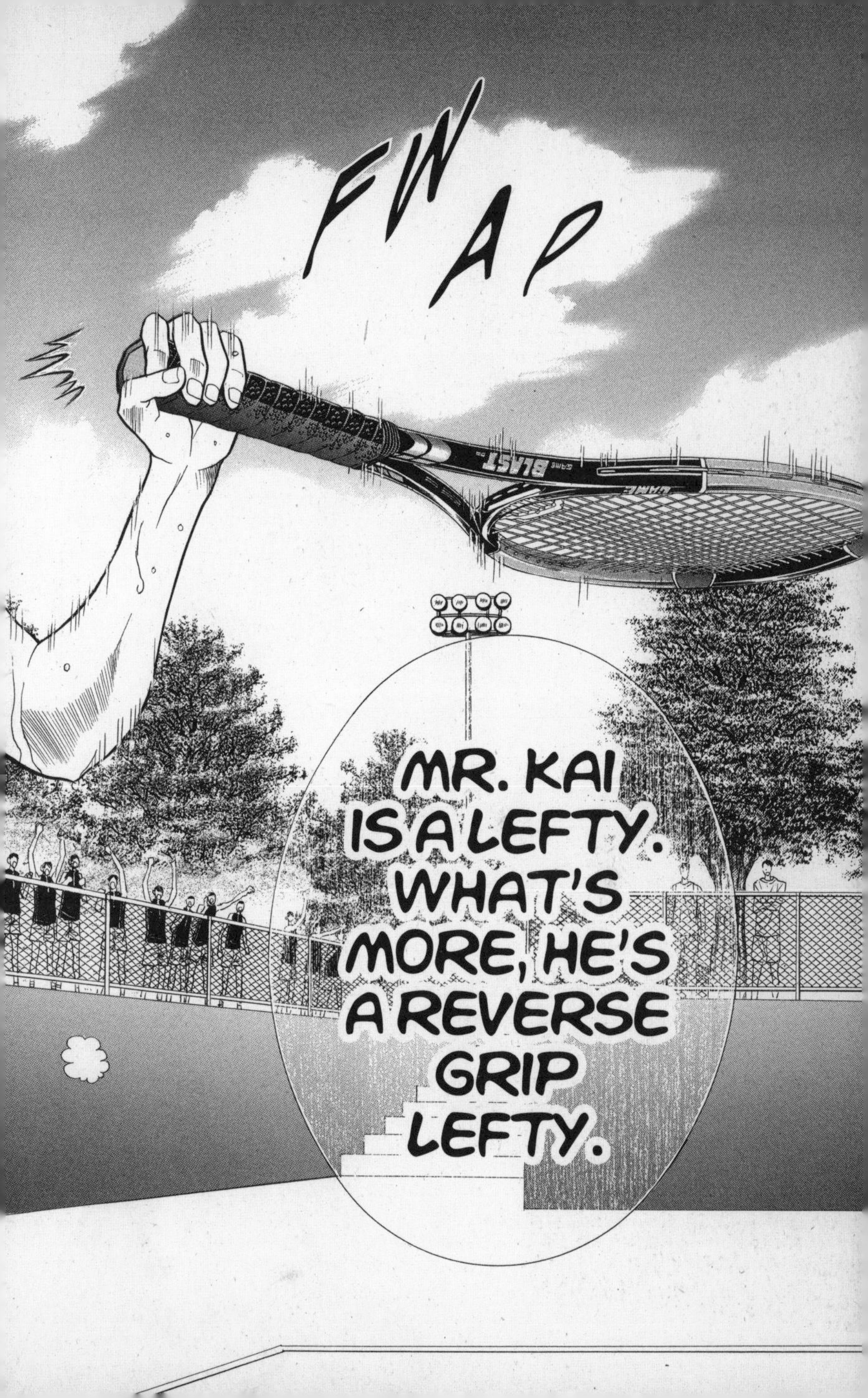
FWAP
MR. KAI IS A LEFTY. WHAT'S MORE, HE'S A REVERSE GRIP LEFTY.

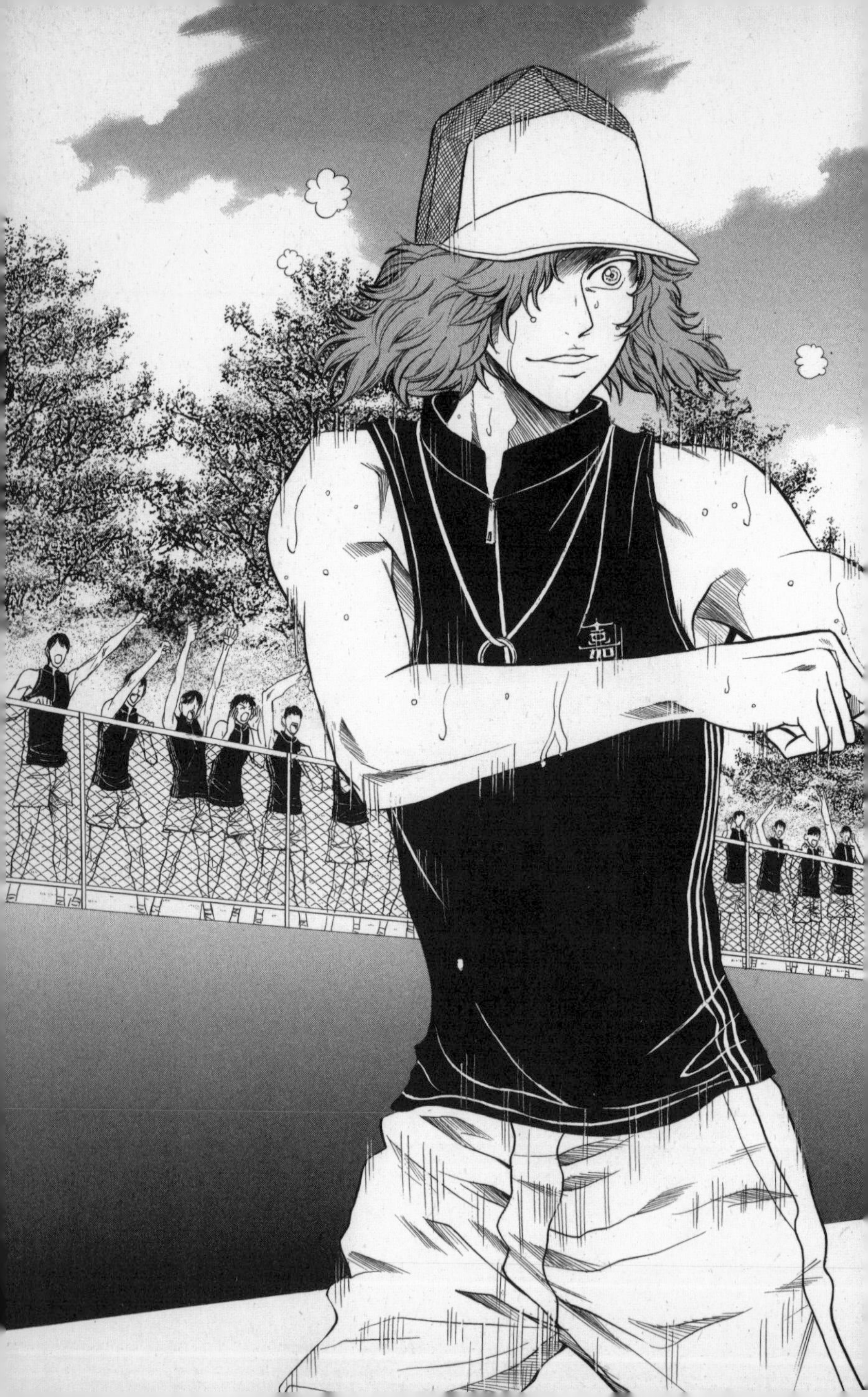

テニスの王子様

THE PRINCE OF TENNIS

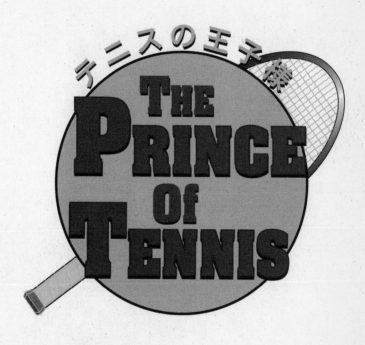

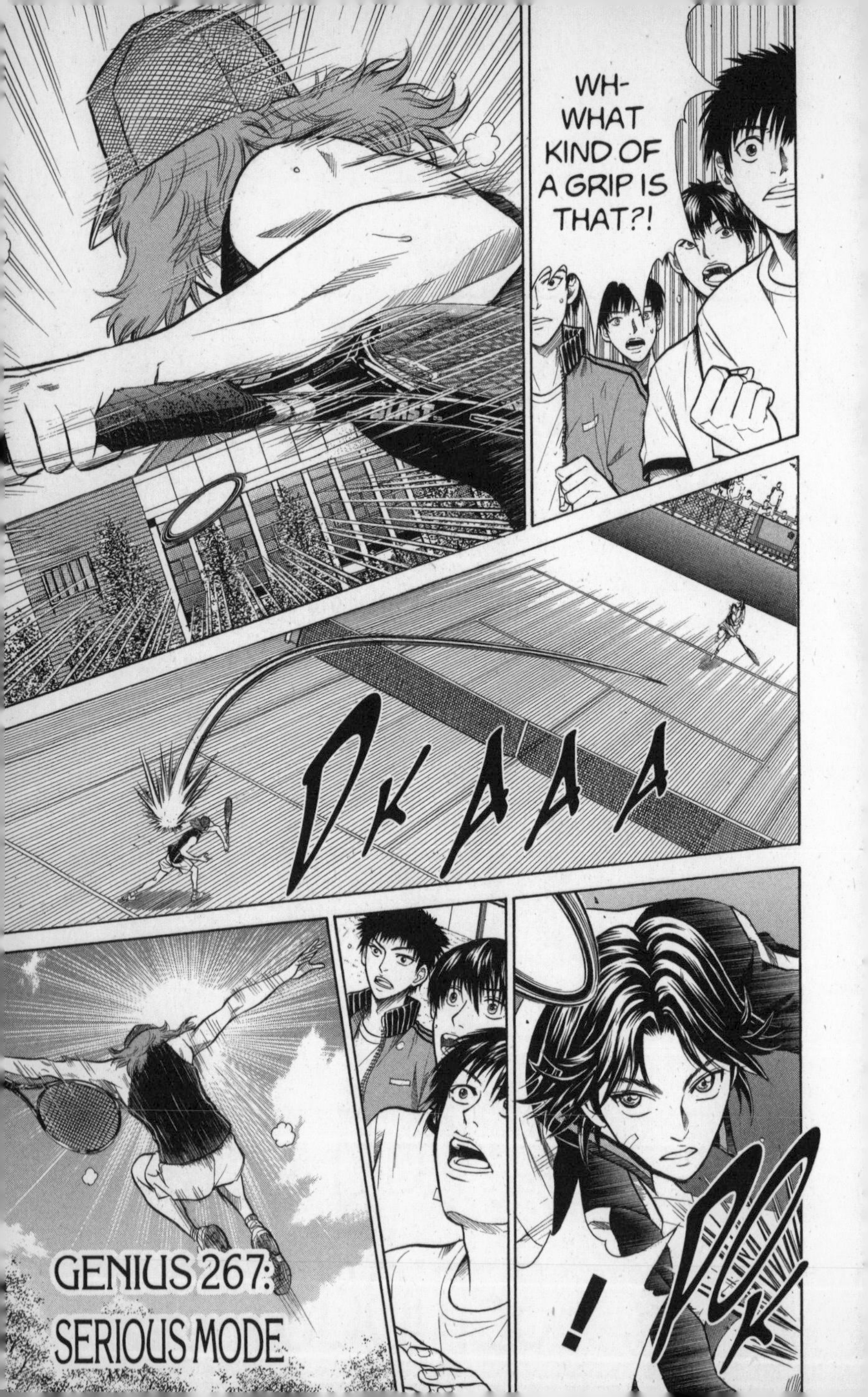
WH-
WHAT
KIND OF
A GRIP IS
THAT?!
DKAAAA
!
GENIUS 267:
SERIOUS MODE

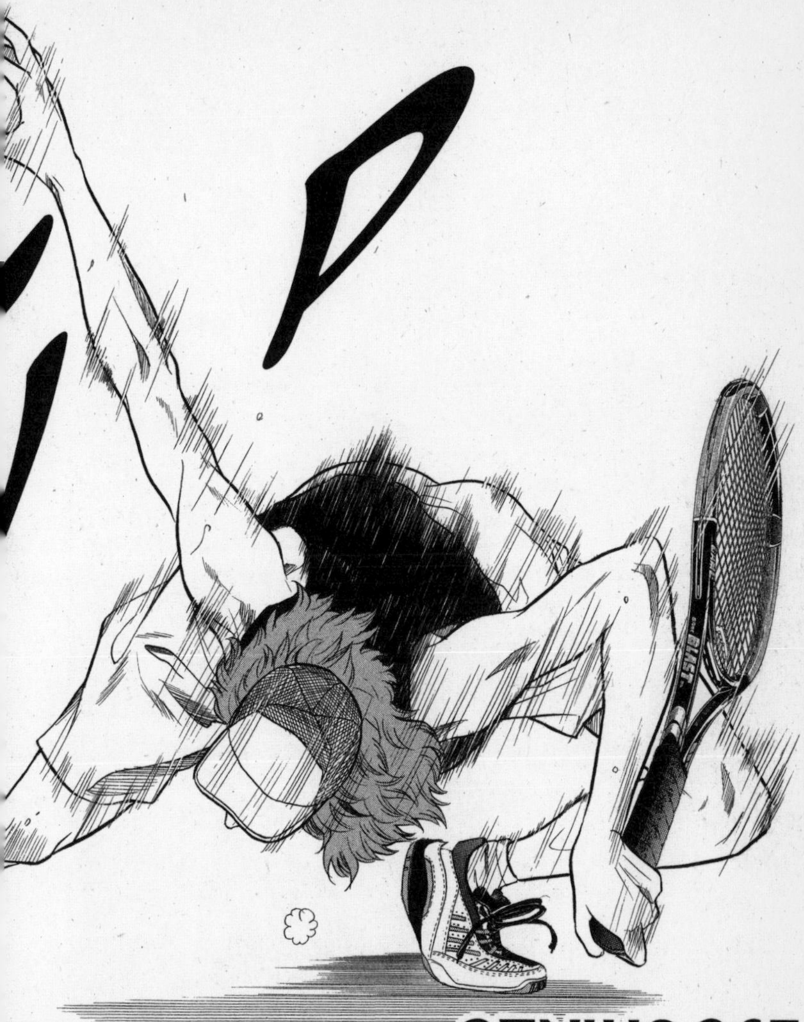

GENIUS 267:

SERIOUS MODE

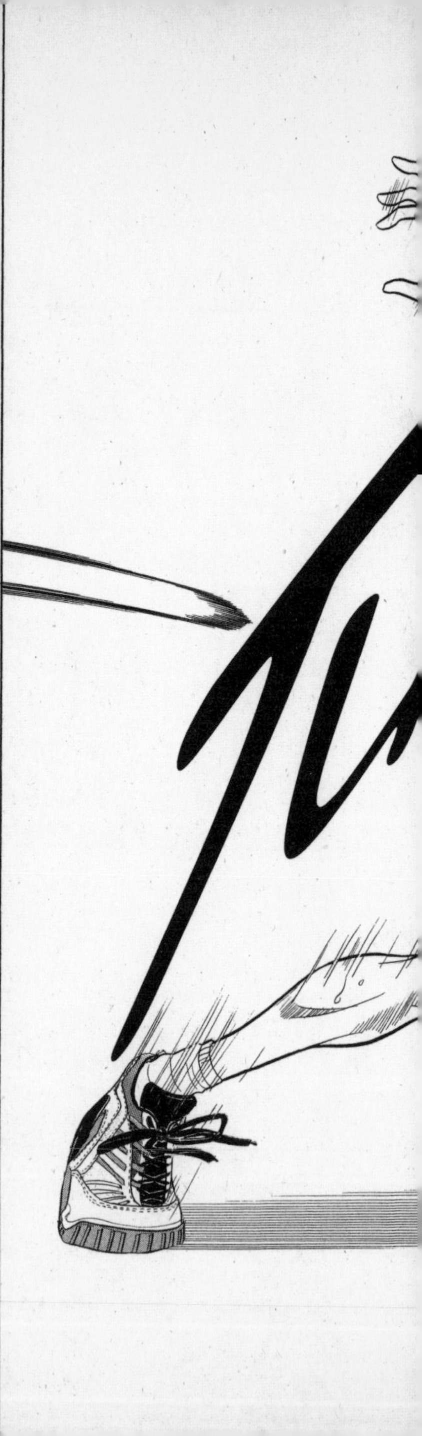
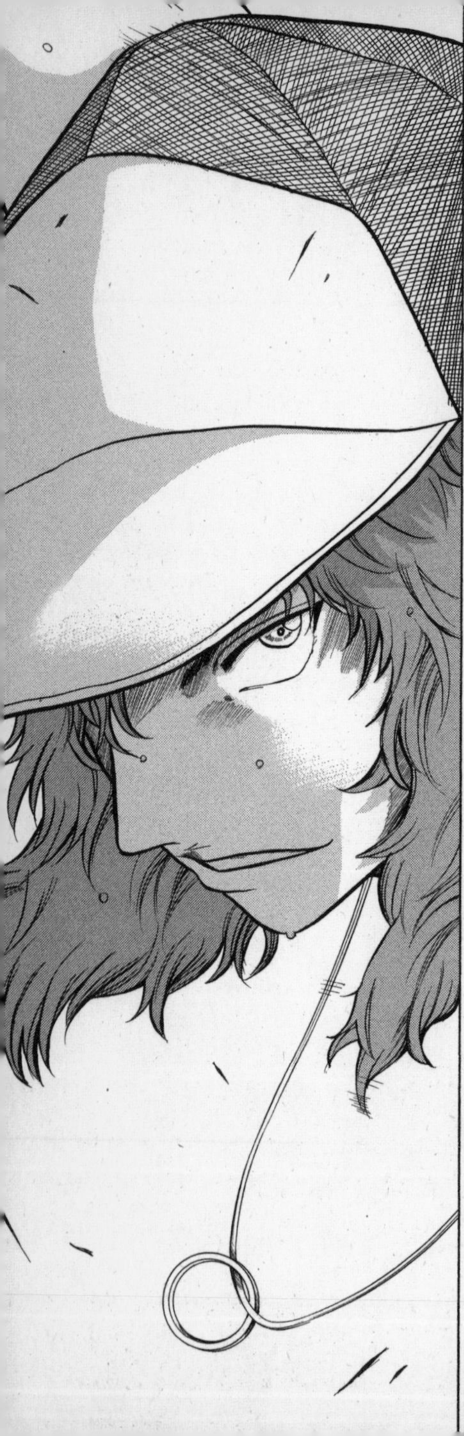

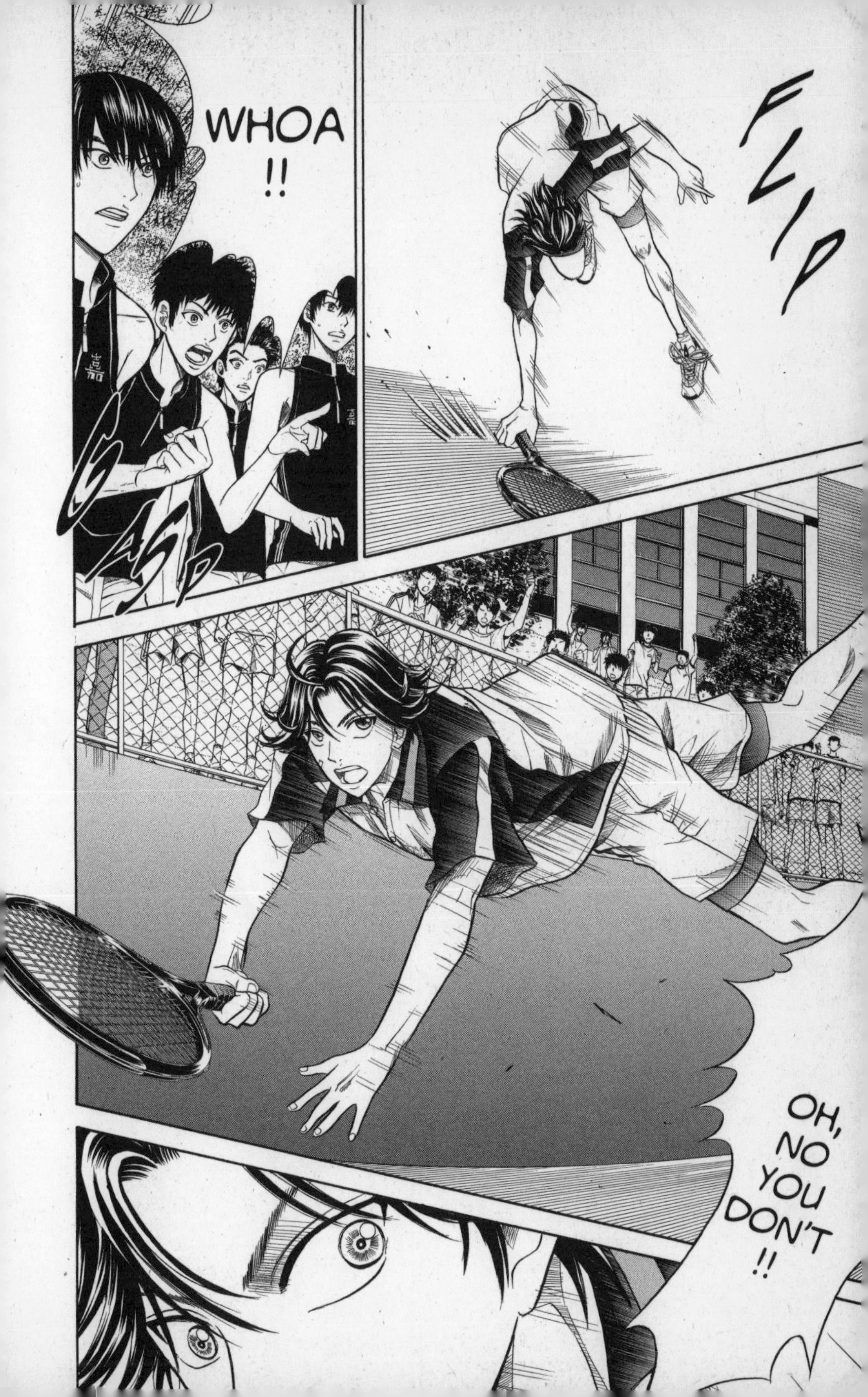
FLIP
WHOA !!
GASP
OH, NO YOU DON'T !!

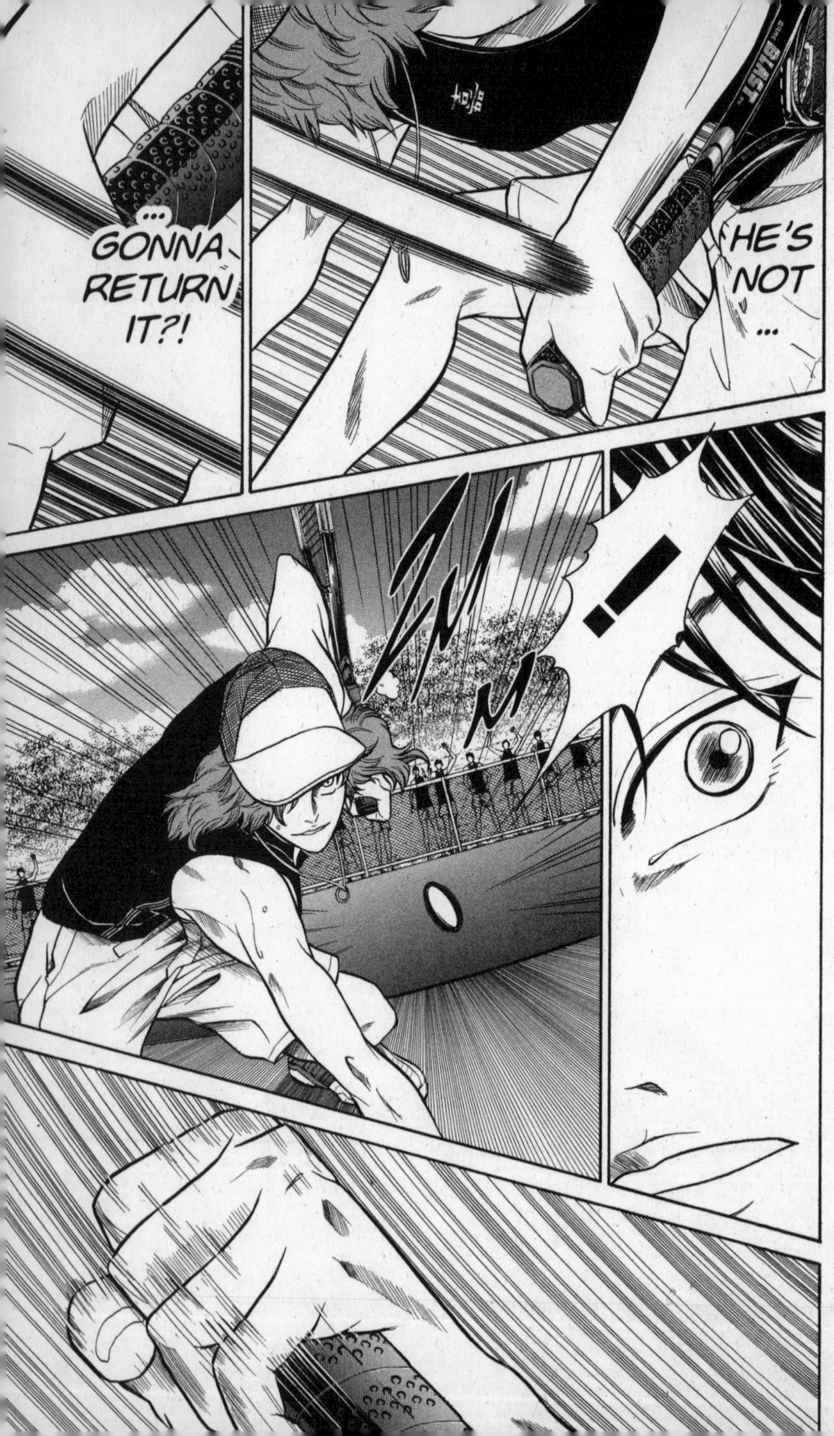
HE'S NOT ...
... GONNA RETURN IT?!
!

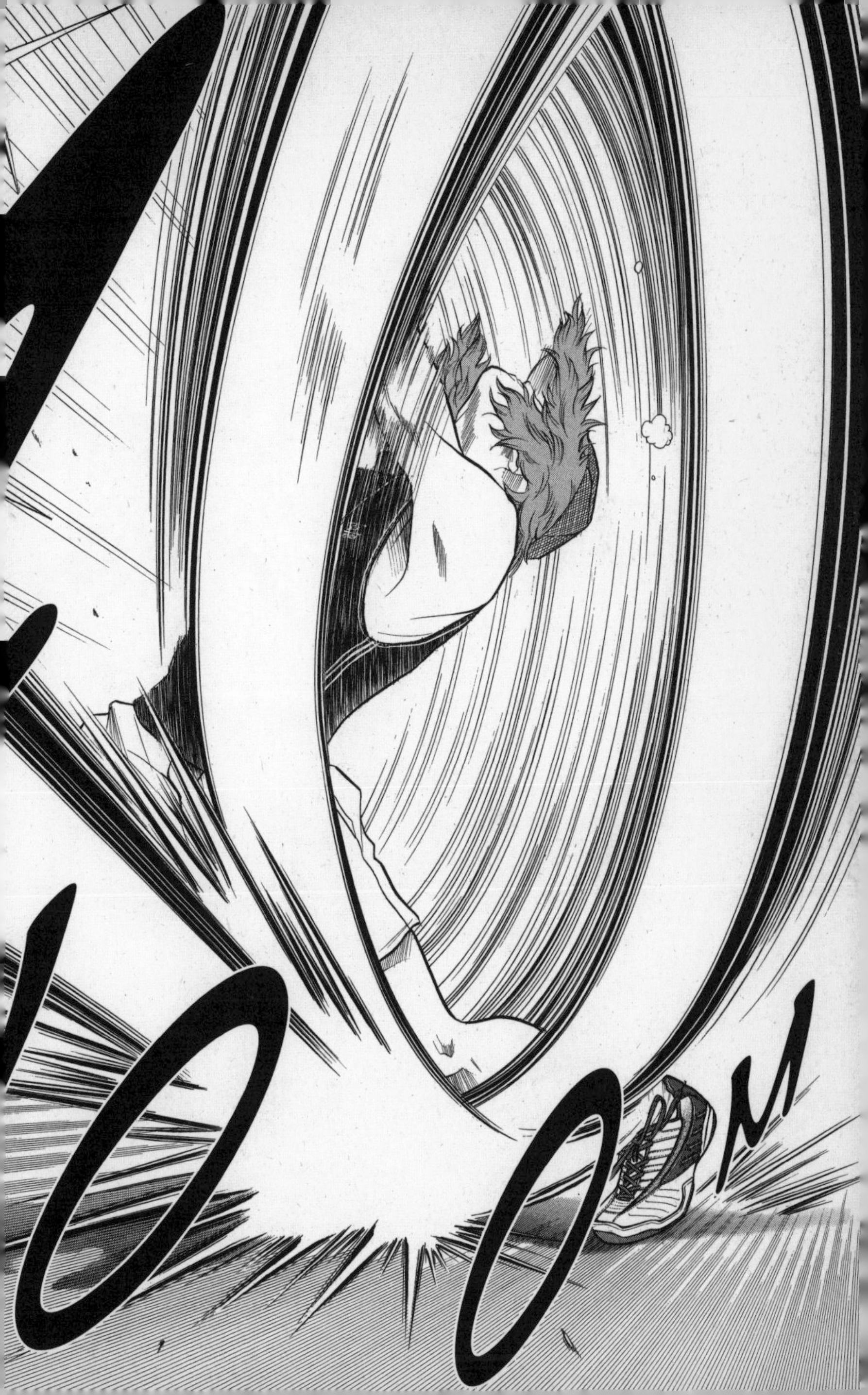
OOM

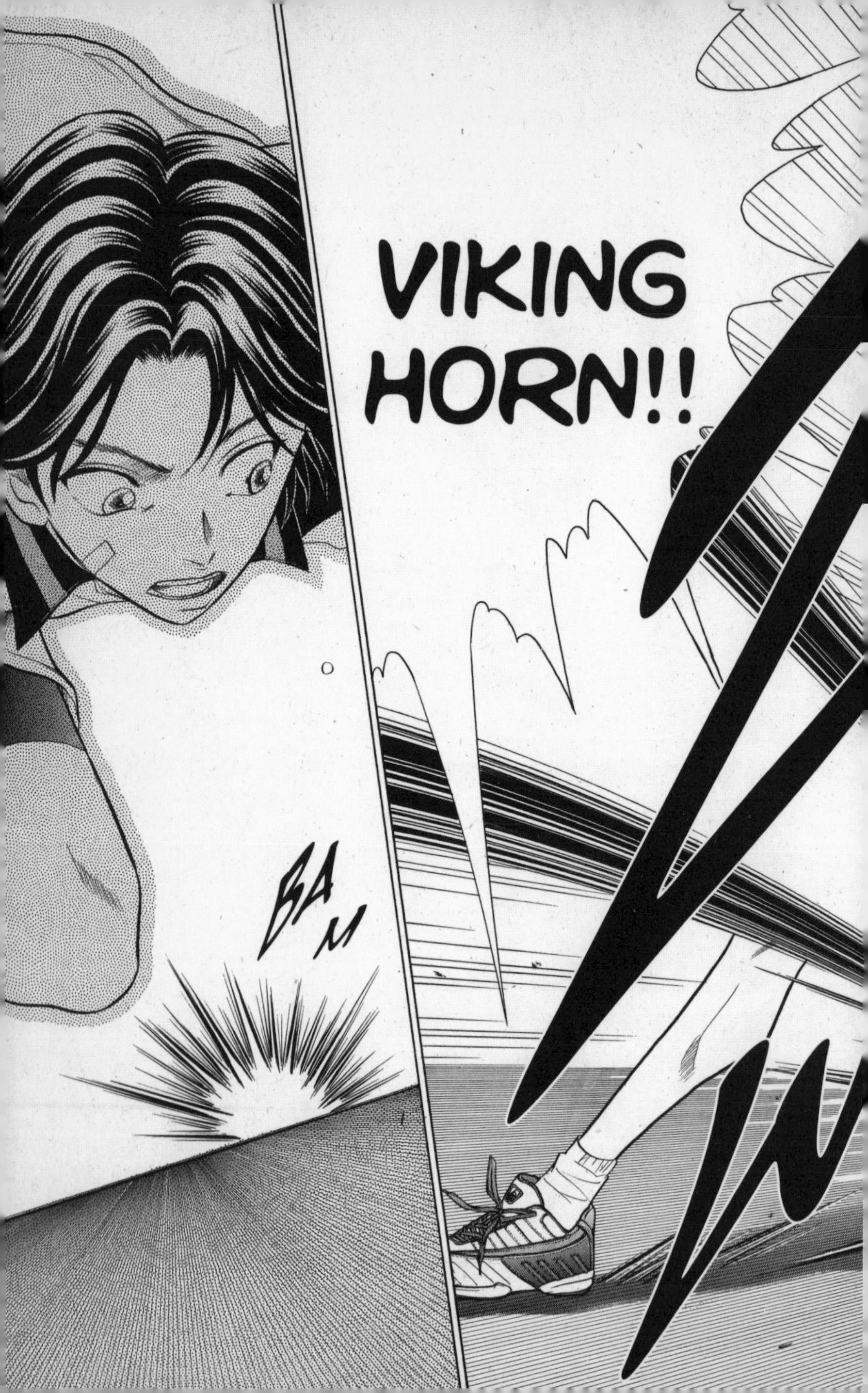
VIKING HORN!!
BAM

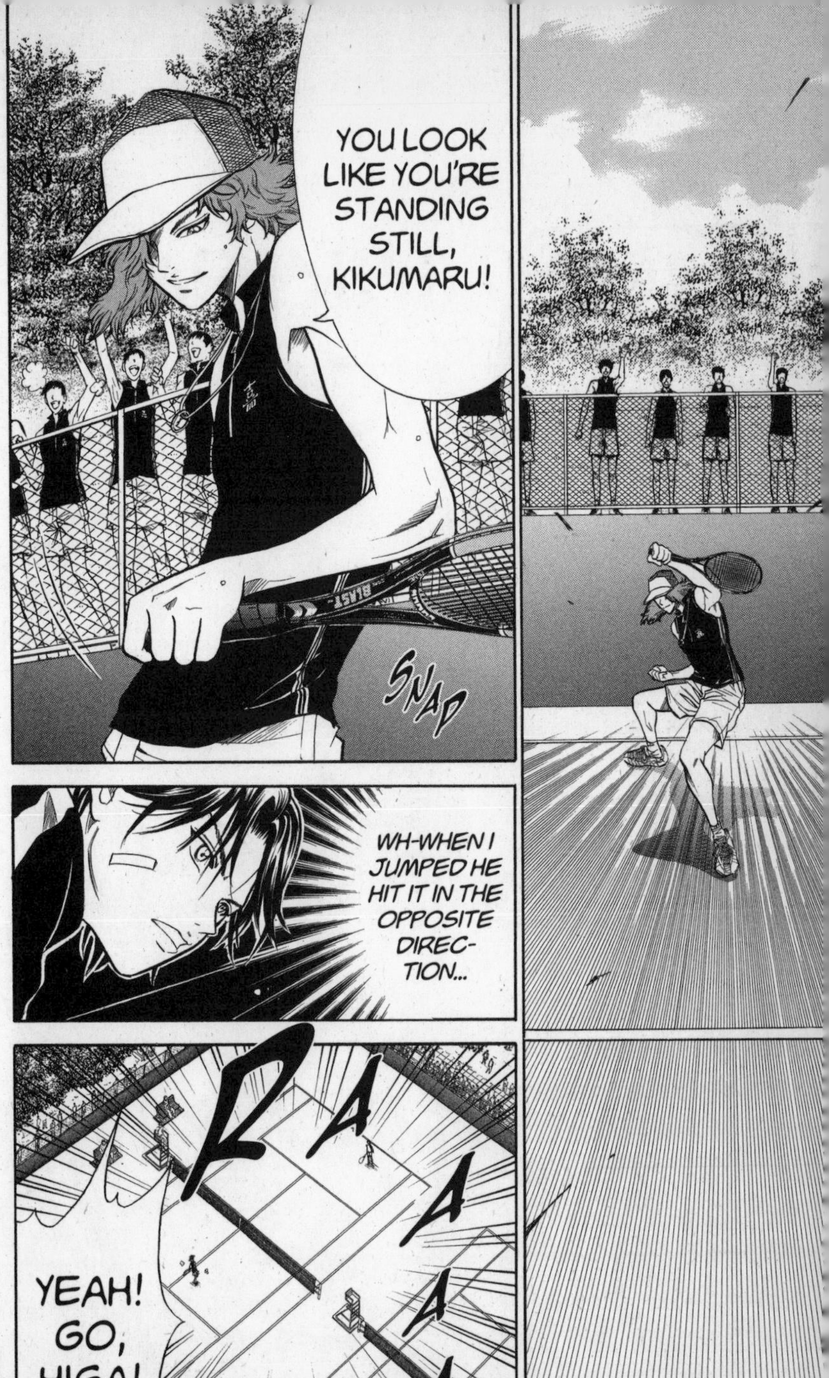
YOU LOOK LIKE YOU'RE STANDING STILL, KIKUMARU!
SNAP
WH-WHEN I JUMPED HE HIT IT IN THE OPPOSITE DIREC-TION...
RAAAAA
YEAH! GO, HIGA!

READ THIS WAY

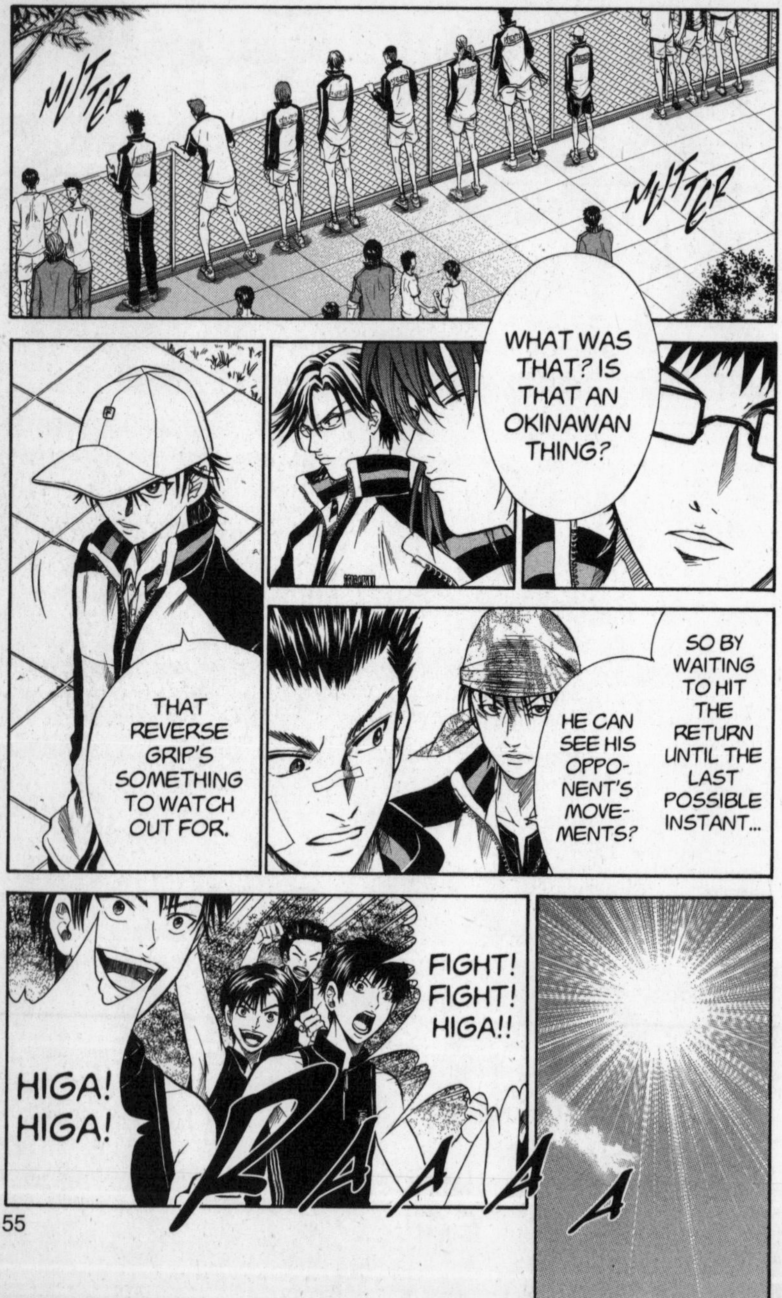
MUTTER
MUTTER
WHAT WAS THAT? IS THAT AN OKINAWAN THING?
SO BY WAITING TO HIT THE RETURN UNTIL THE LAST POSSIBLE INSTANT...
HE CAN SEE HIS OPPONENT'S MOVEMENTS?
THAT REVERSE GRIP'S SOMETHING TO WATCH OUT FOR.
FIGHT! FIGHT! HIGA!!
HIGA! HIGA!

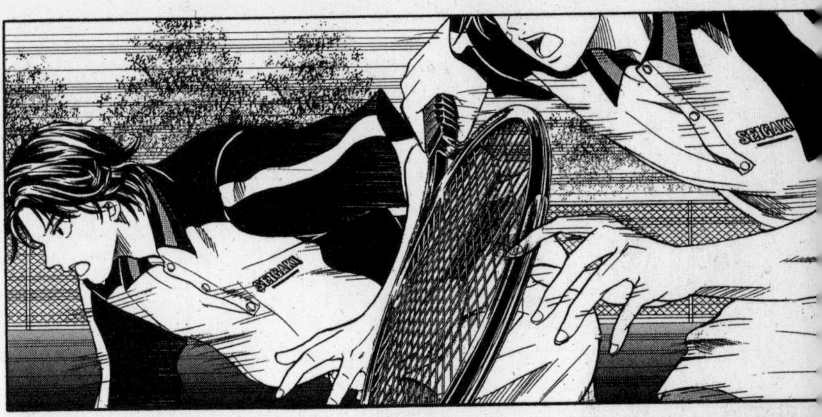
SEIGAKU
SEIGAKU

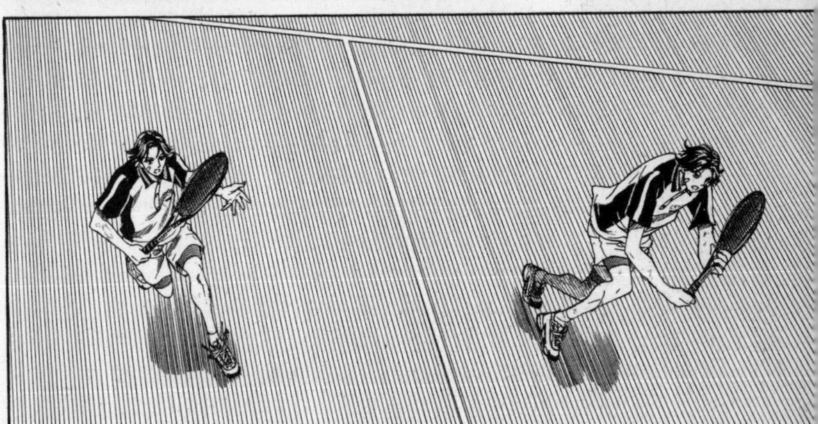

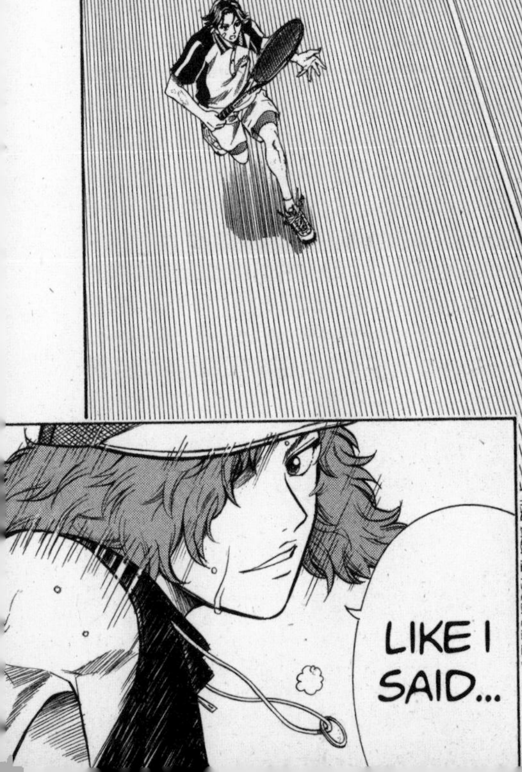
LIKE I SAID...

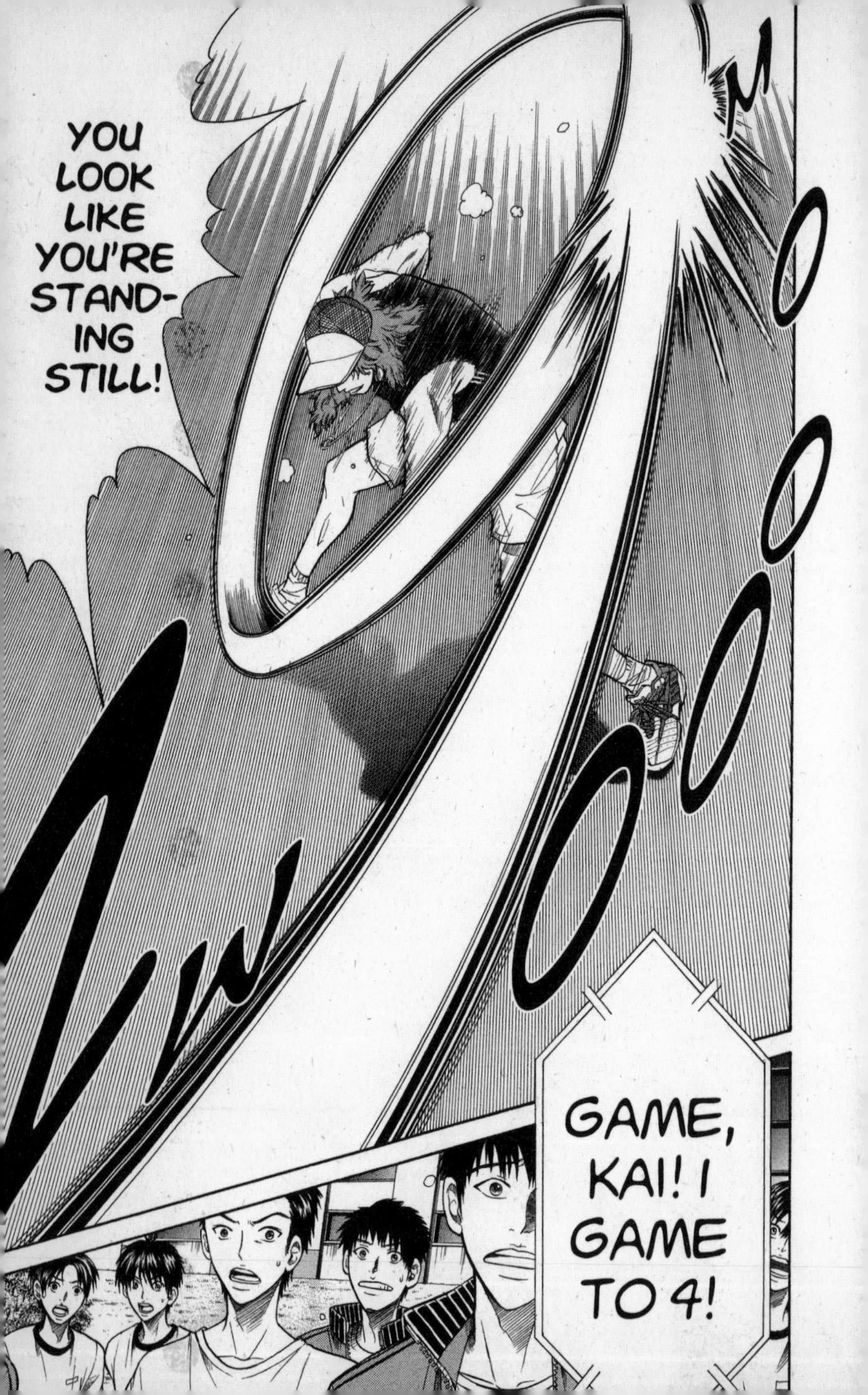
YOU LOOK LIKE YOU'RE STAND-ING STILL!
MOOOOOOOOO
GAME, KAI! 1 GAME TO 4!

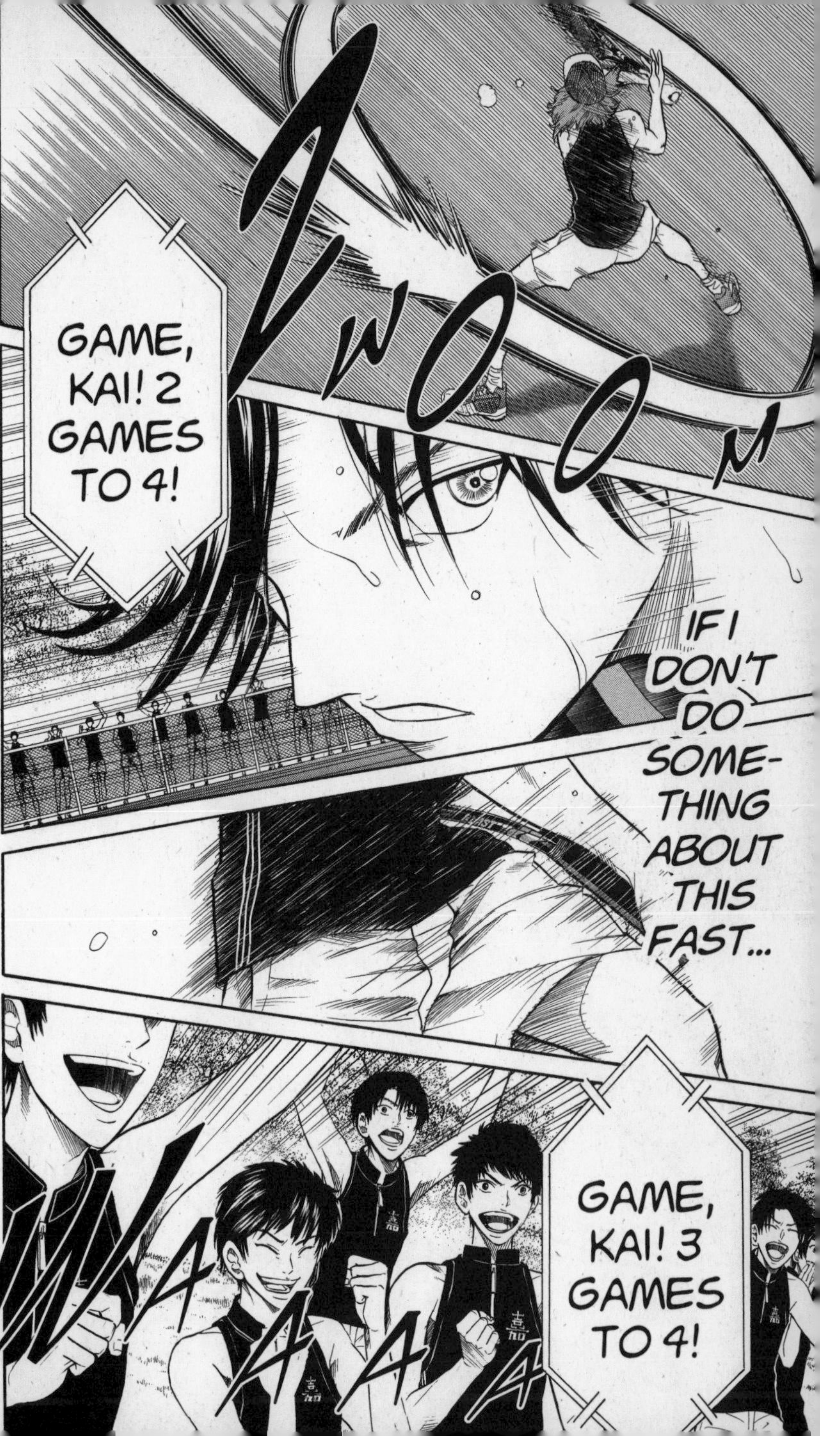
VWOOOM
GAME, KAI! 2 GAMES TO 4!
IF I DON'T DO SOMETHING ABOUT THIS FAST...
GAME, KAI! 3 GAMES TO 4!
WAAAA

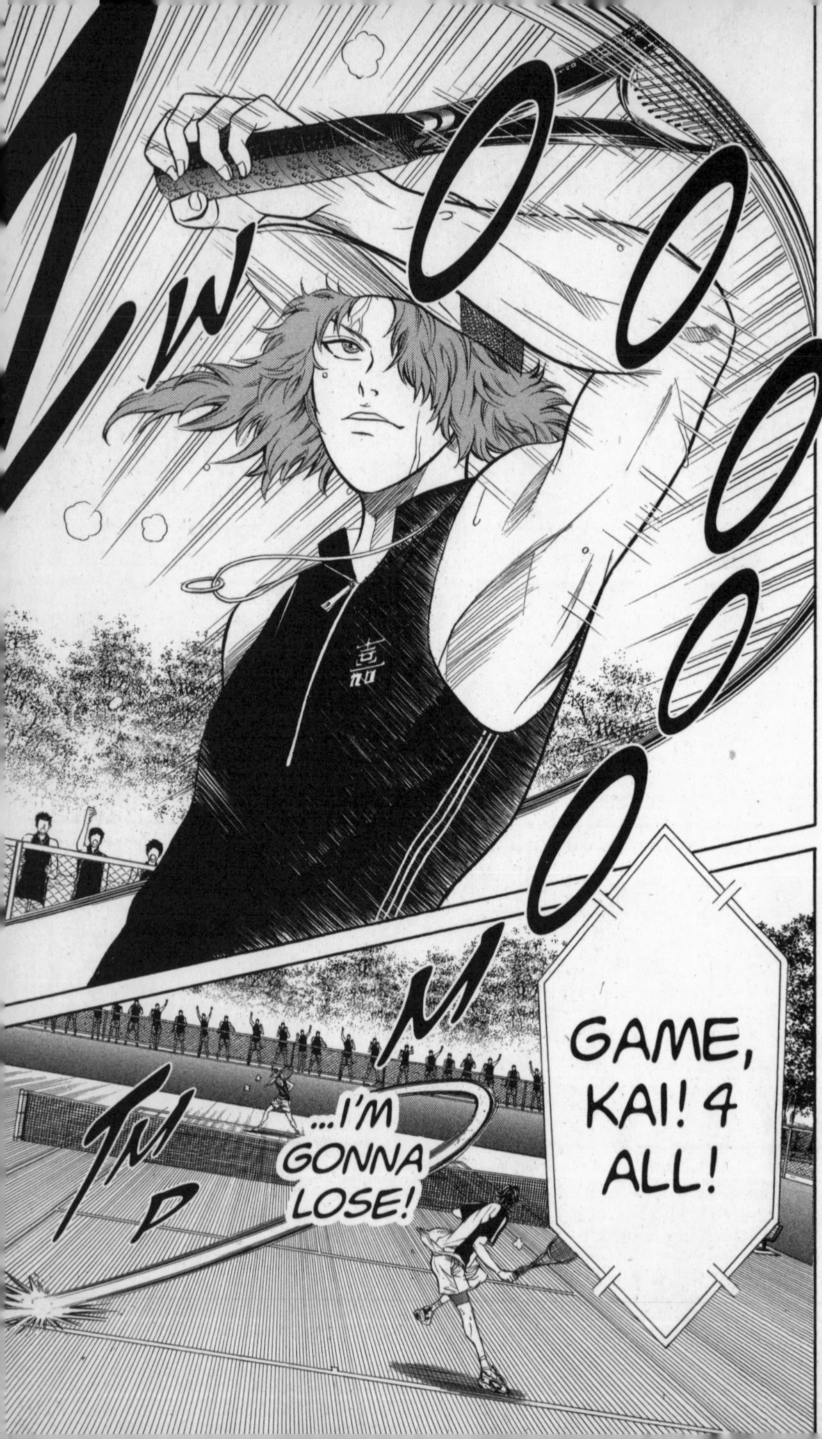
GAME, KAI! 4 ALL!
...I'M GONNA LOSE!

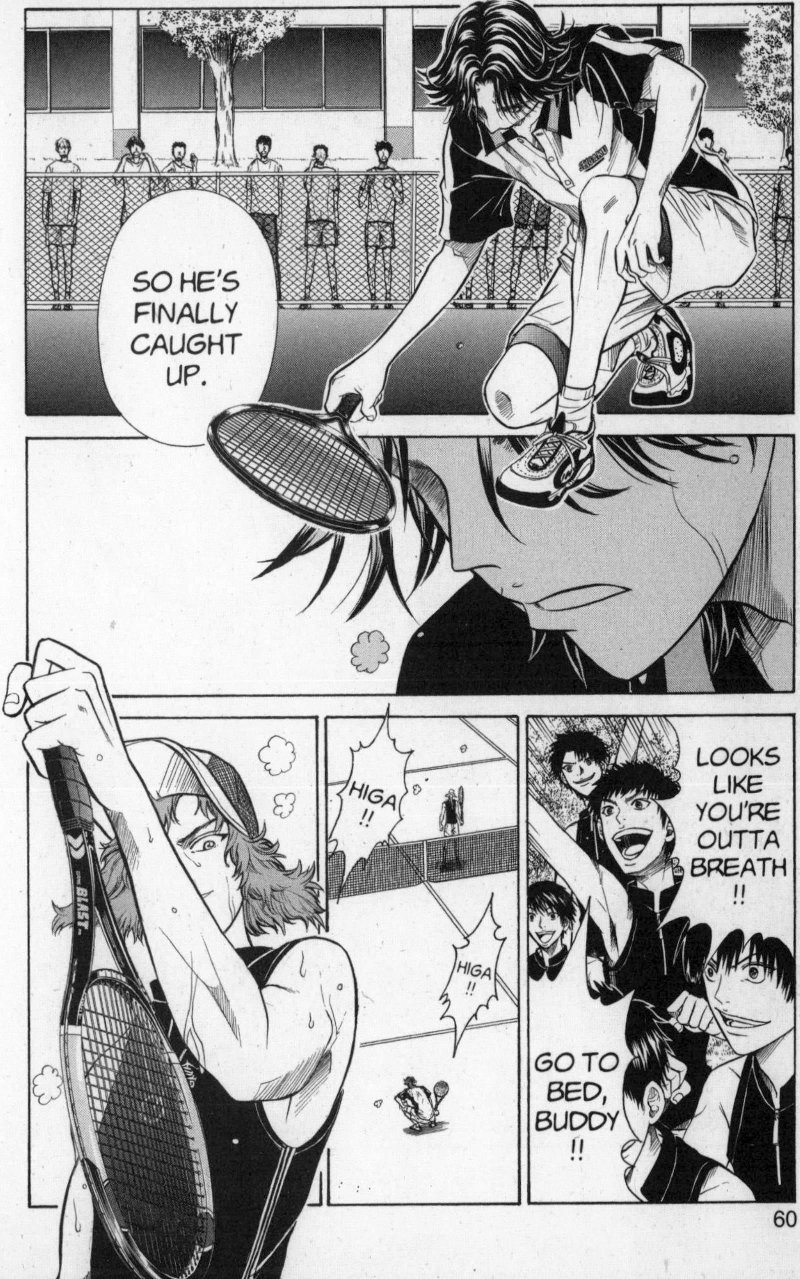
SO HE'S FINALLY CAUGHT UP.
LOOKS LIKE YOU'RE OUTTA BREATH !!
GO TO BED, BUDDY !!
HIGA !!
HIGA !!

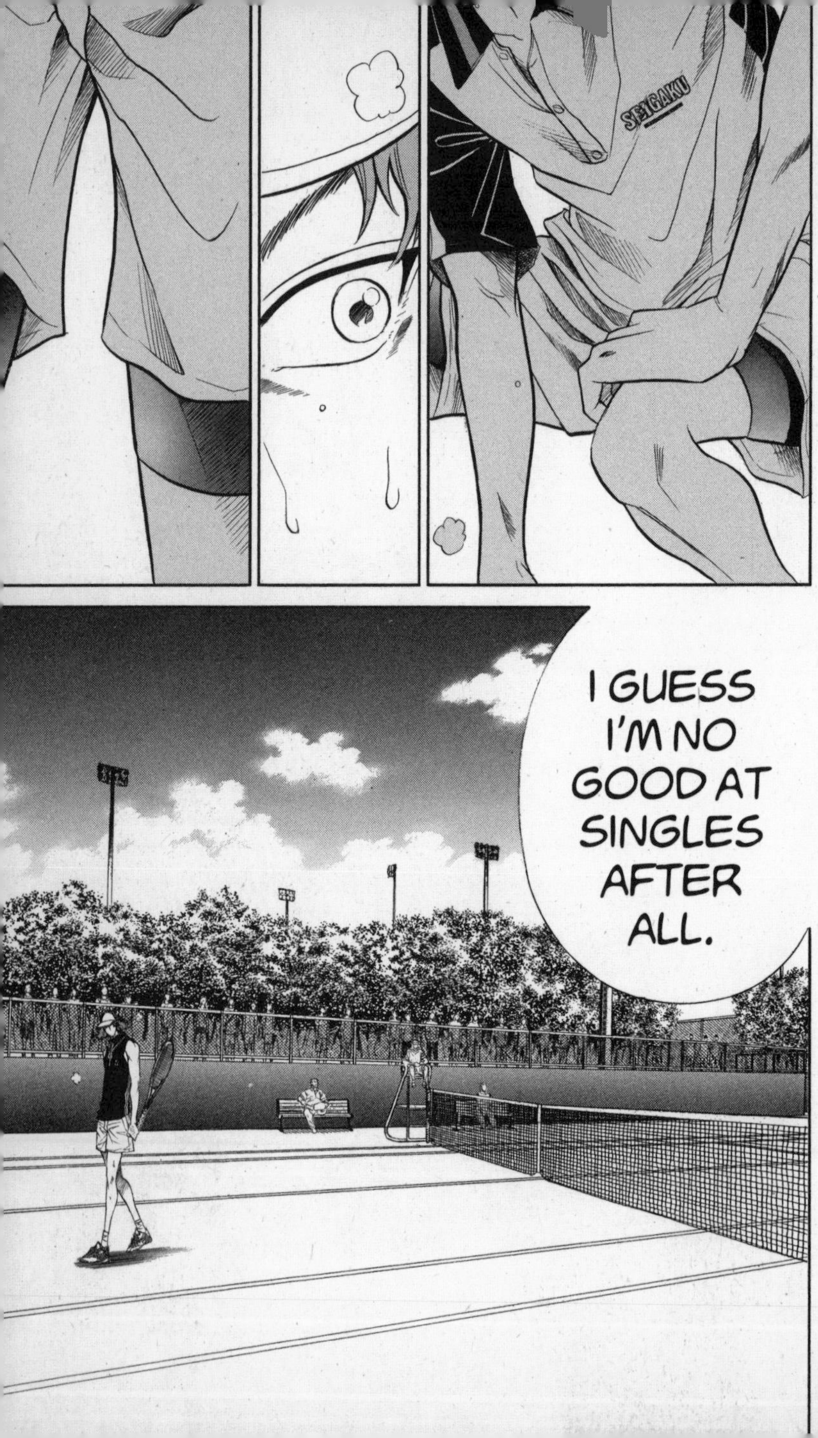
SEIGAKU
I GUESS I'M NO GOOD AT SINGLES AFTER ALL.

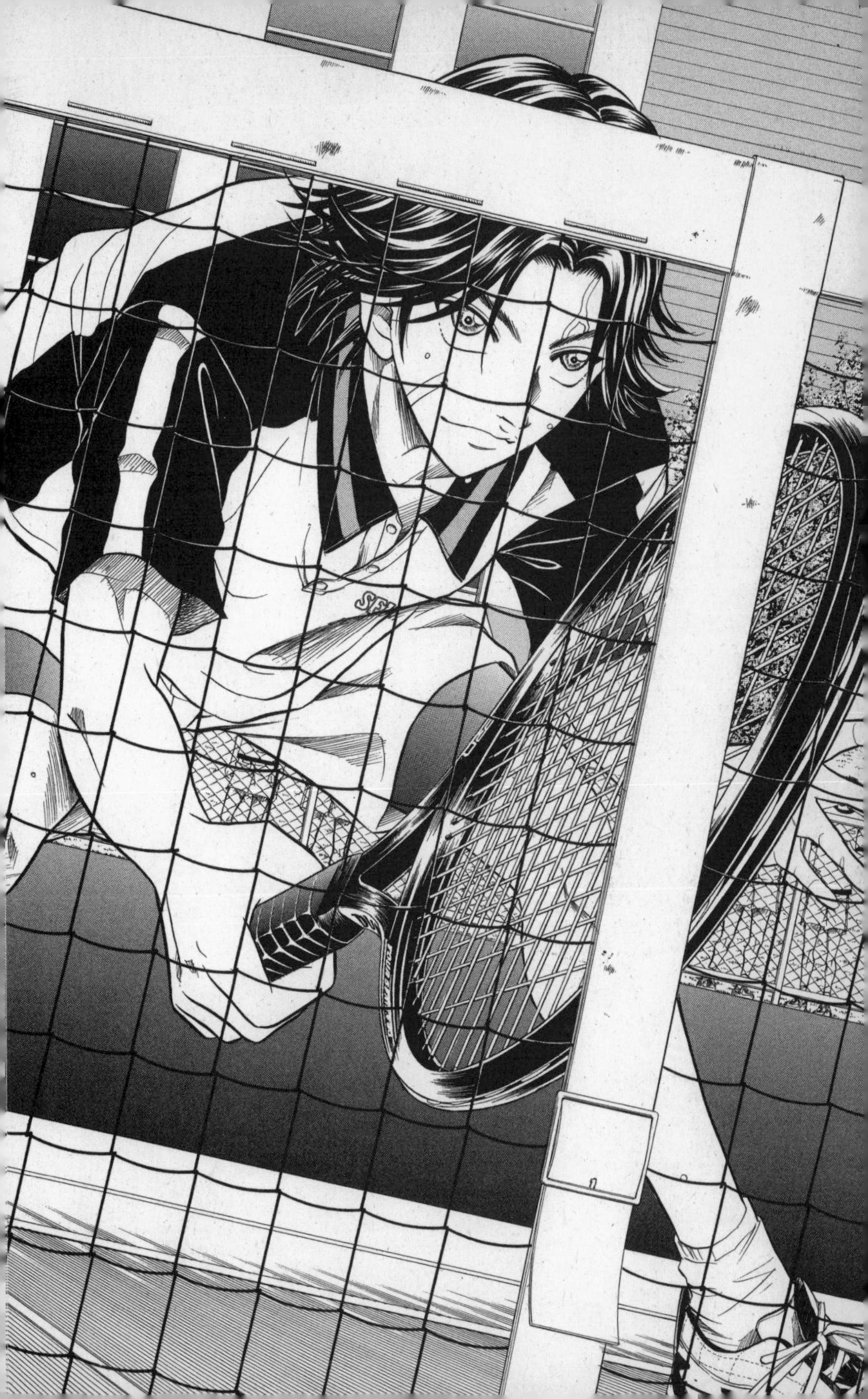

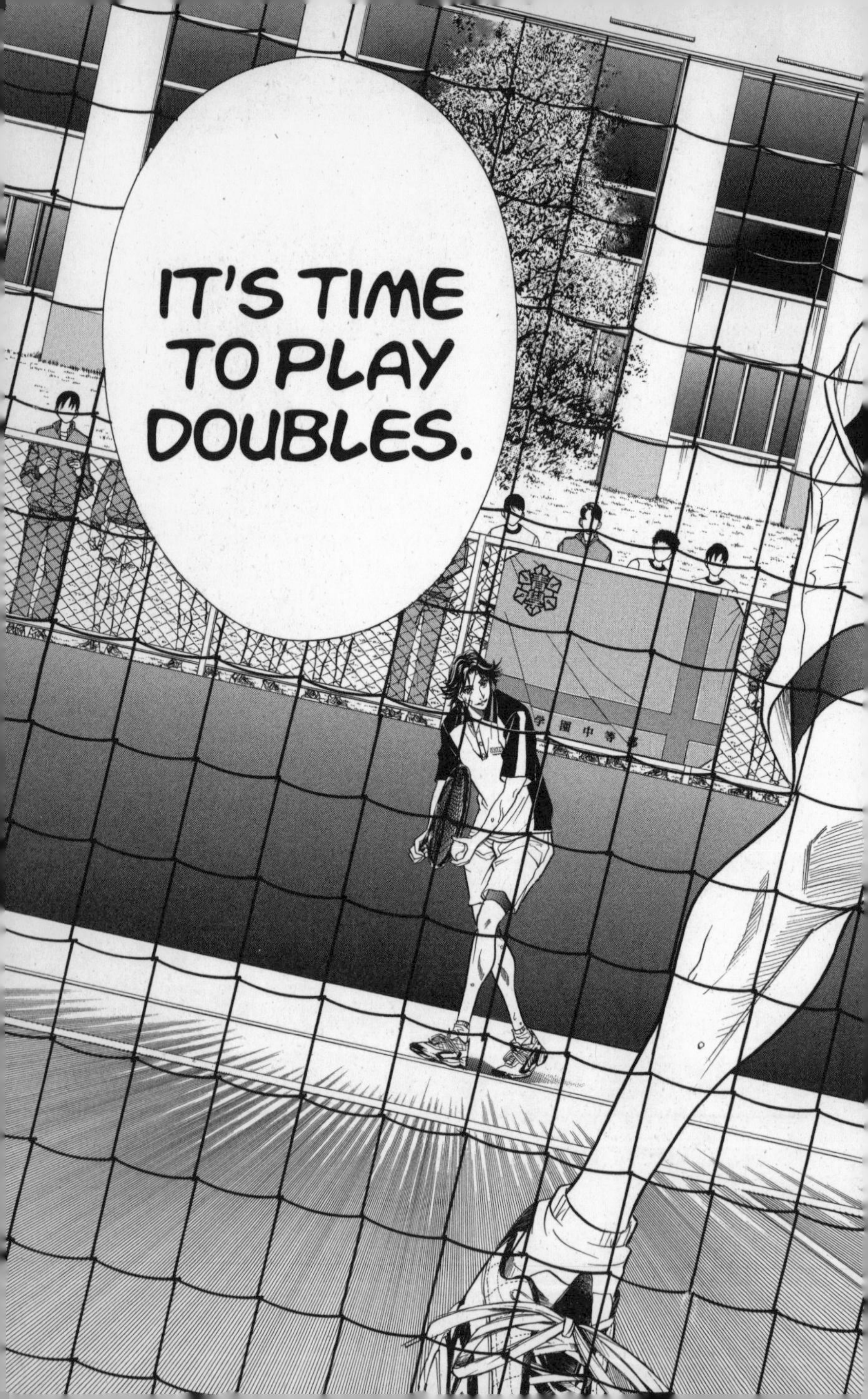
IT'S TIME TO PLAY DOUBLES.

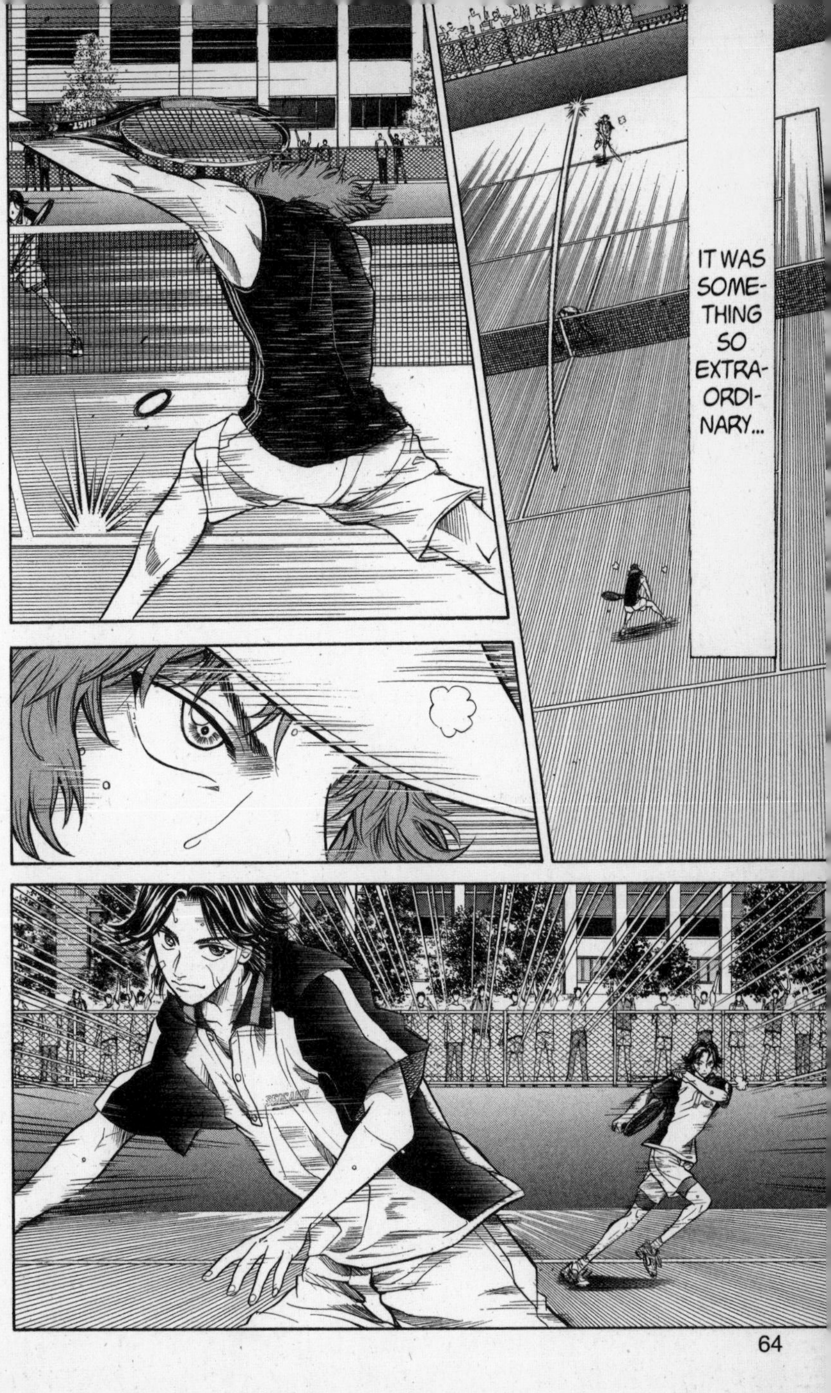
IT WAS SOME-THING SO EXTRA-ORDI-NARY...

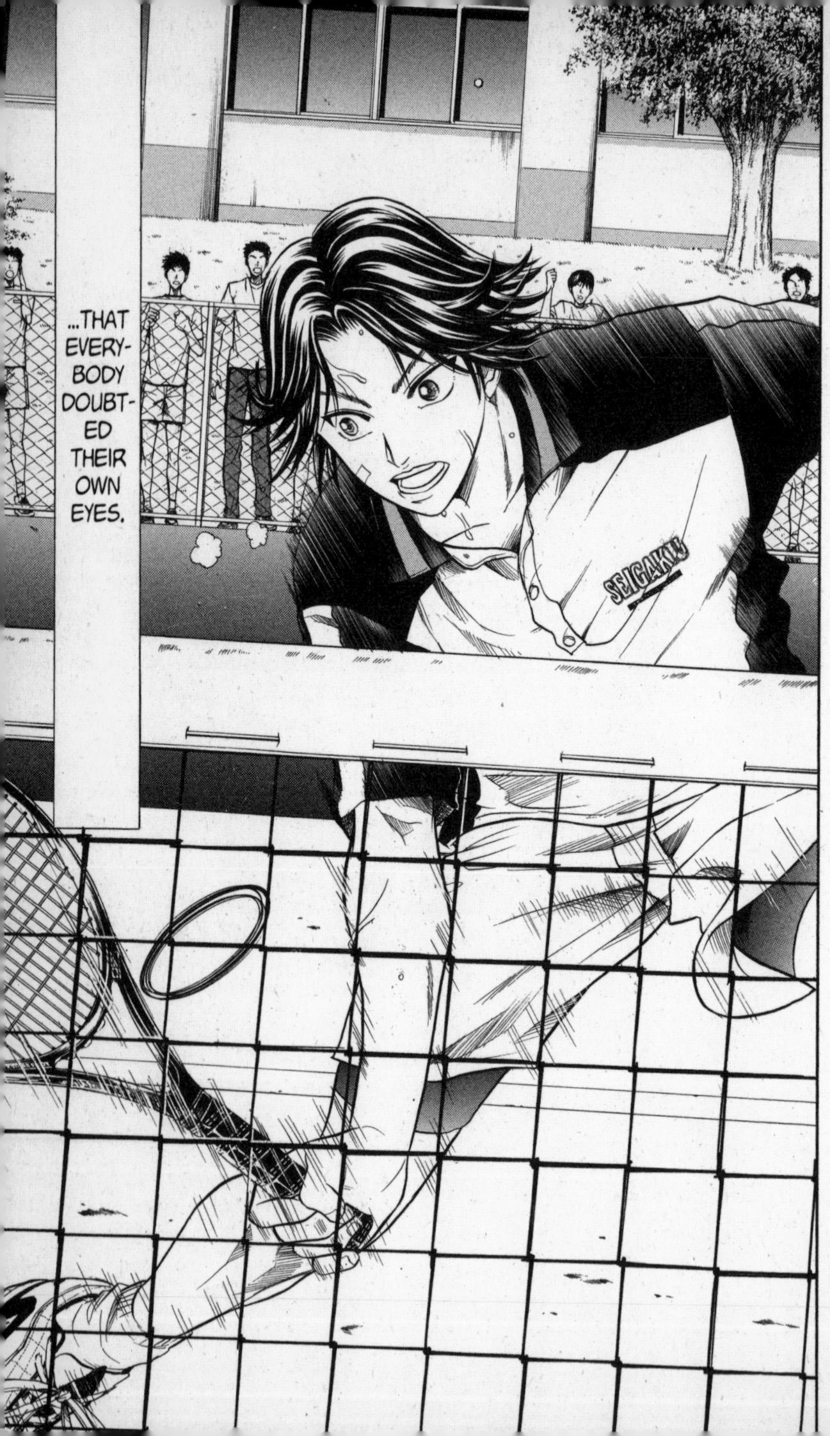
...THAT EVERY-BODY DOUBT-ED THEIR OWN EYES.
SEIGAKU

テニスの王子様

THE PRINCE OF TENNIS

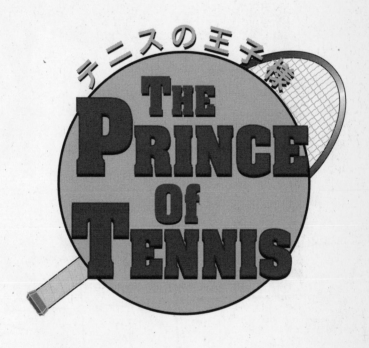

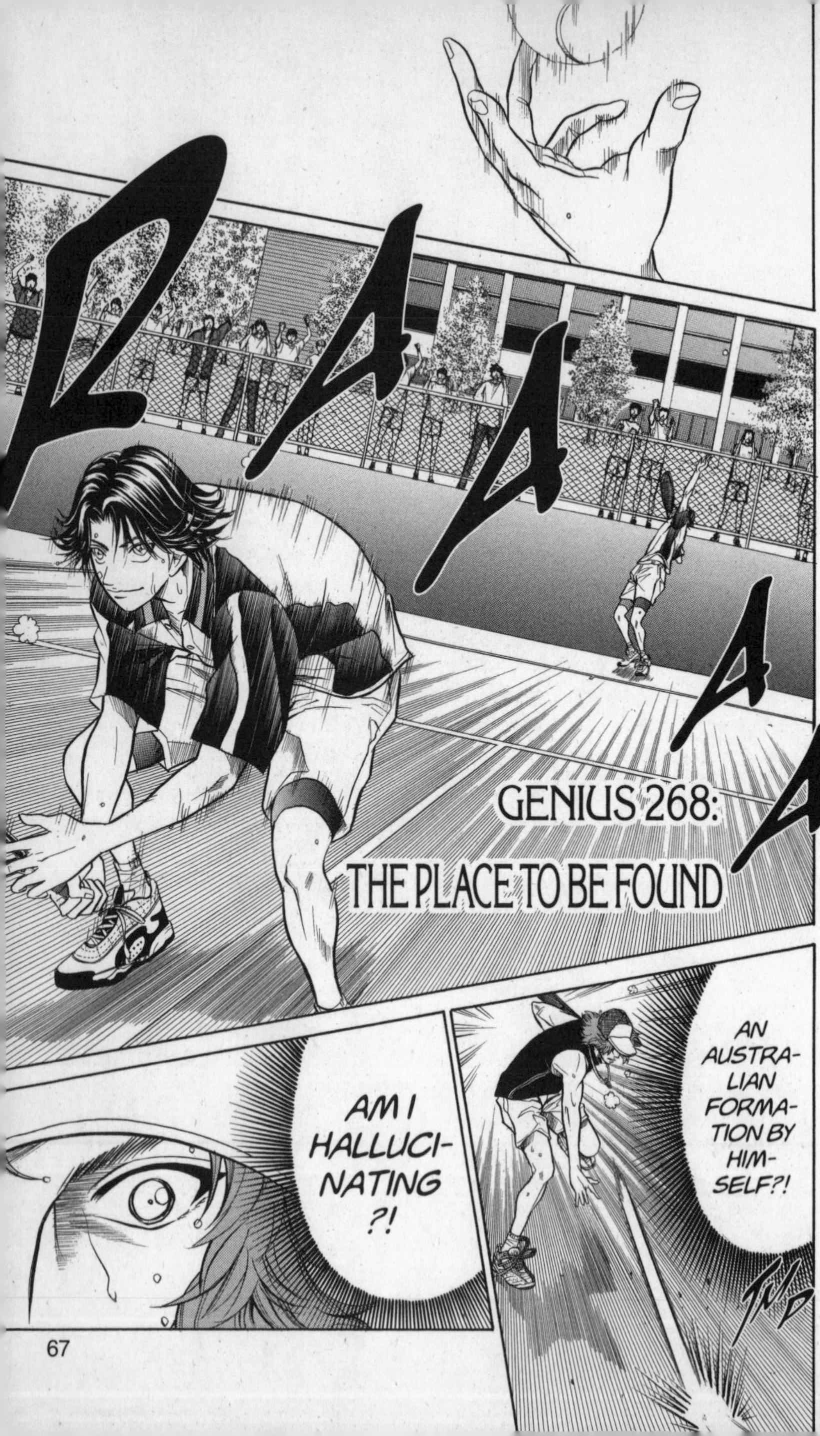
DAAAAA
GENIUS 268:
THE PLACE TO BE FOUND
AN AUSTRALIAN FORMATION BY HIMSELF?!
AM I HALLUCINATING?!

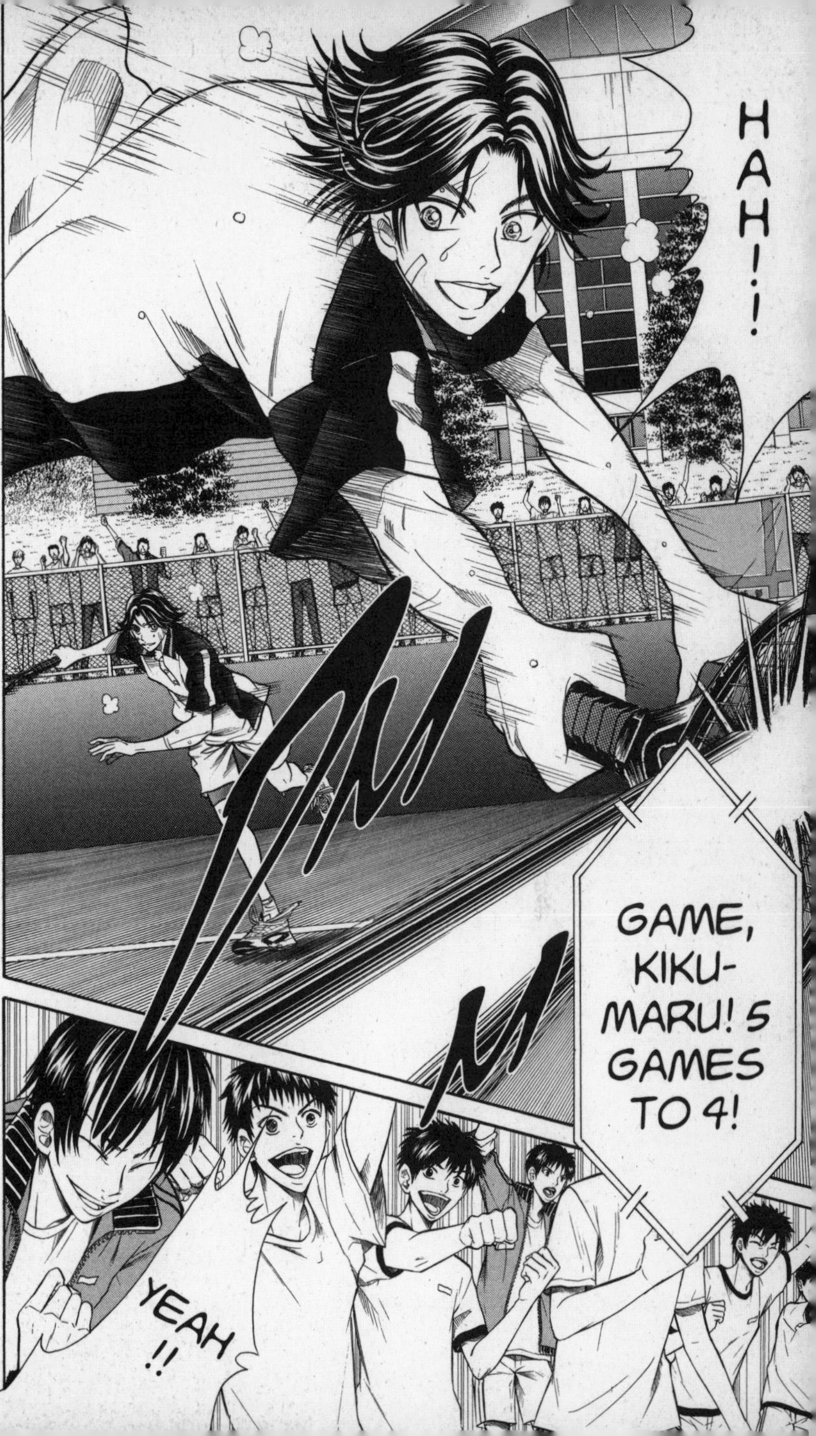
HAH!!
GAME, KIKU-MARU! 5 GAMES TO 4!
YEAH !!

GENIUS 268: THE PLACE TO BE FOUND

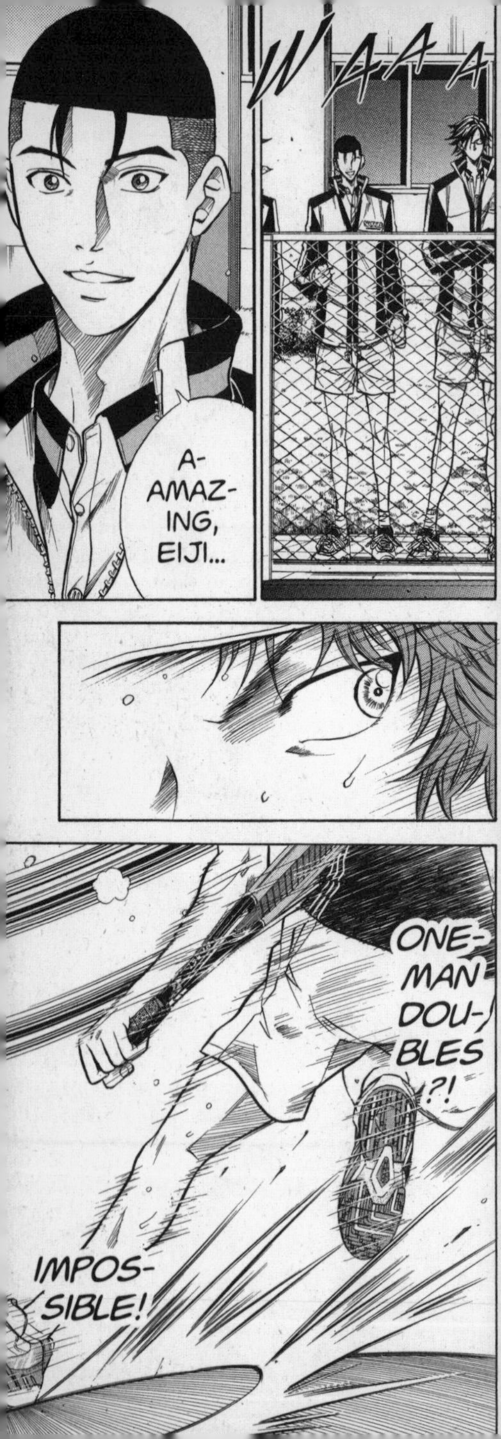
WAAA
A-AMAZING, EIJI...
ONE-MAN DOUBLES?!
IMPOSSIBLE!

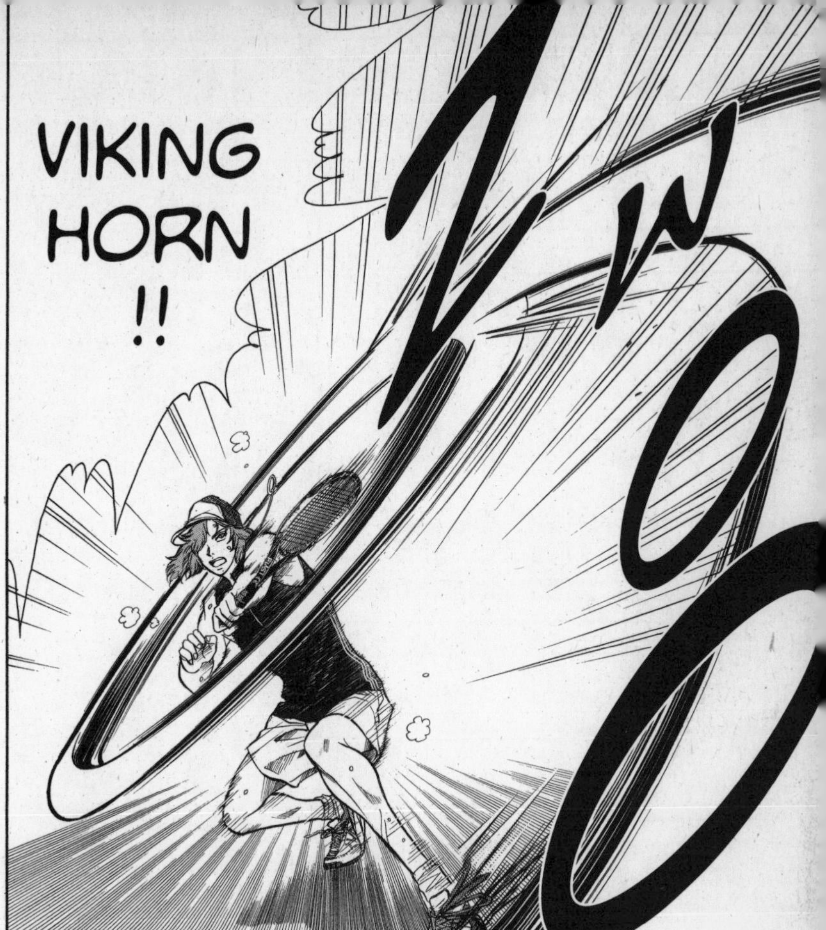
VIKING HORN !!
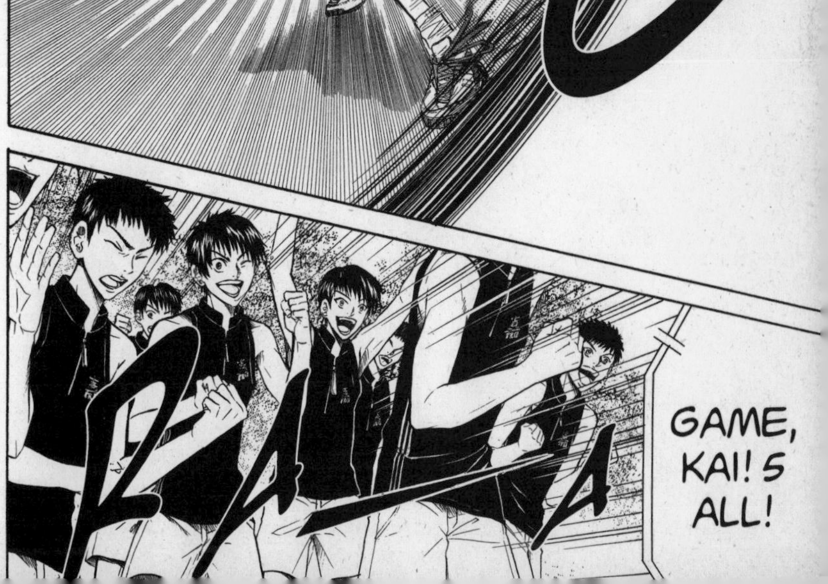
GAME, KAI! 5 ALL!

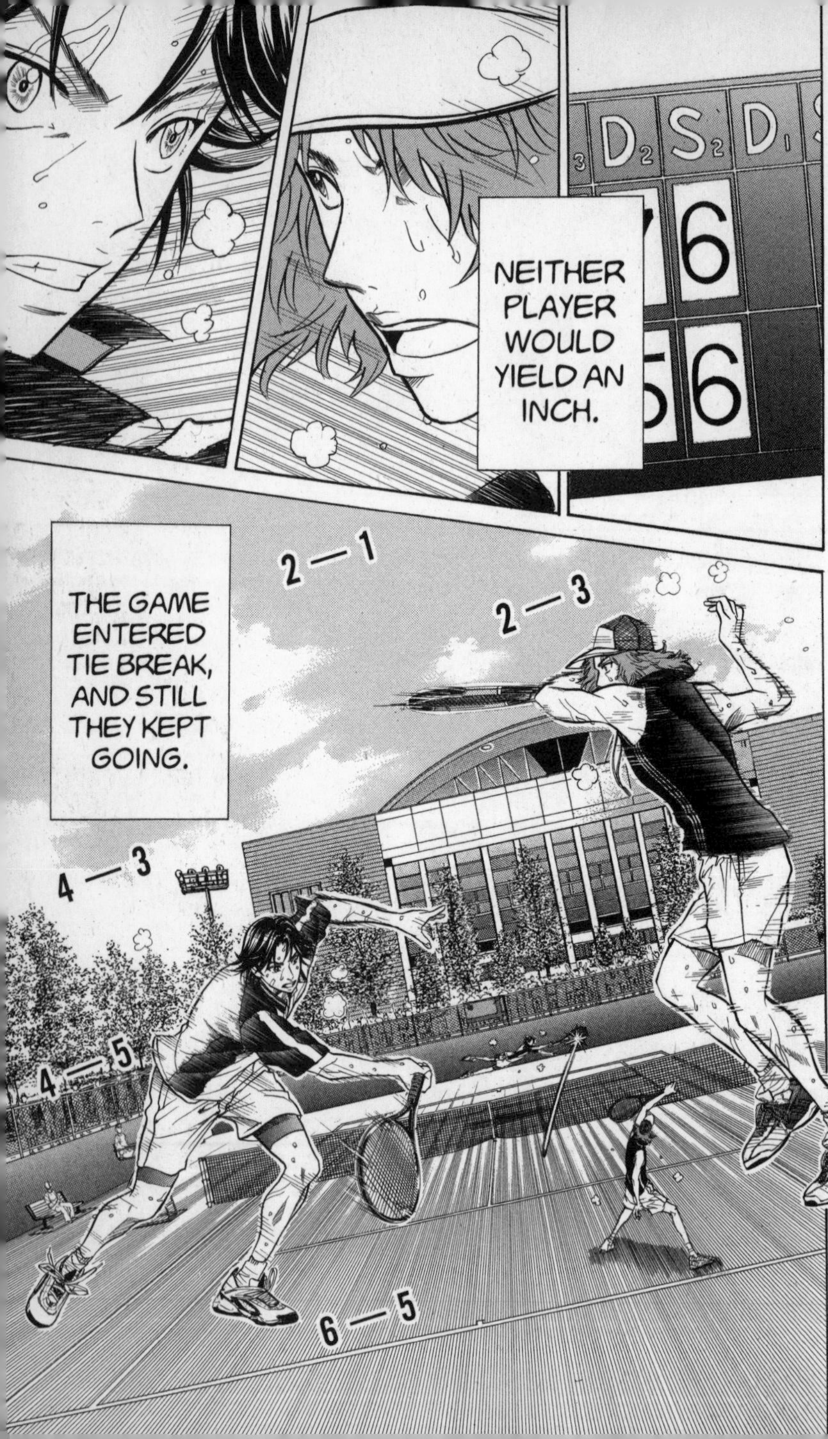
NEITHER PLAYER WOULD YIELD AN INCH.
THE GAME ENTERED TIE BREAK, AND STILL THEY KEPT GOING.
2—1
2—3
4—3
4—5
6—5

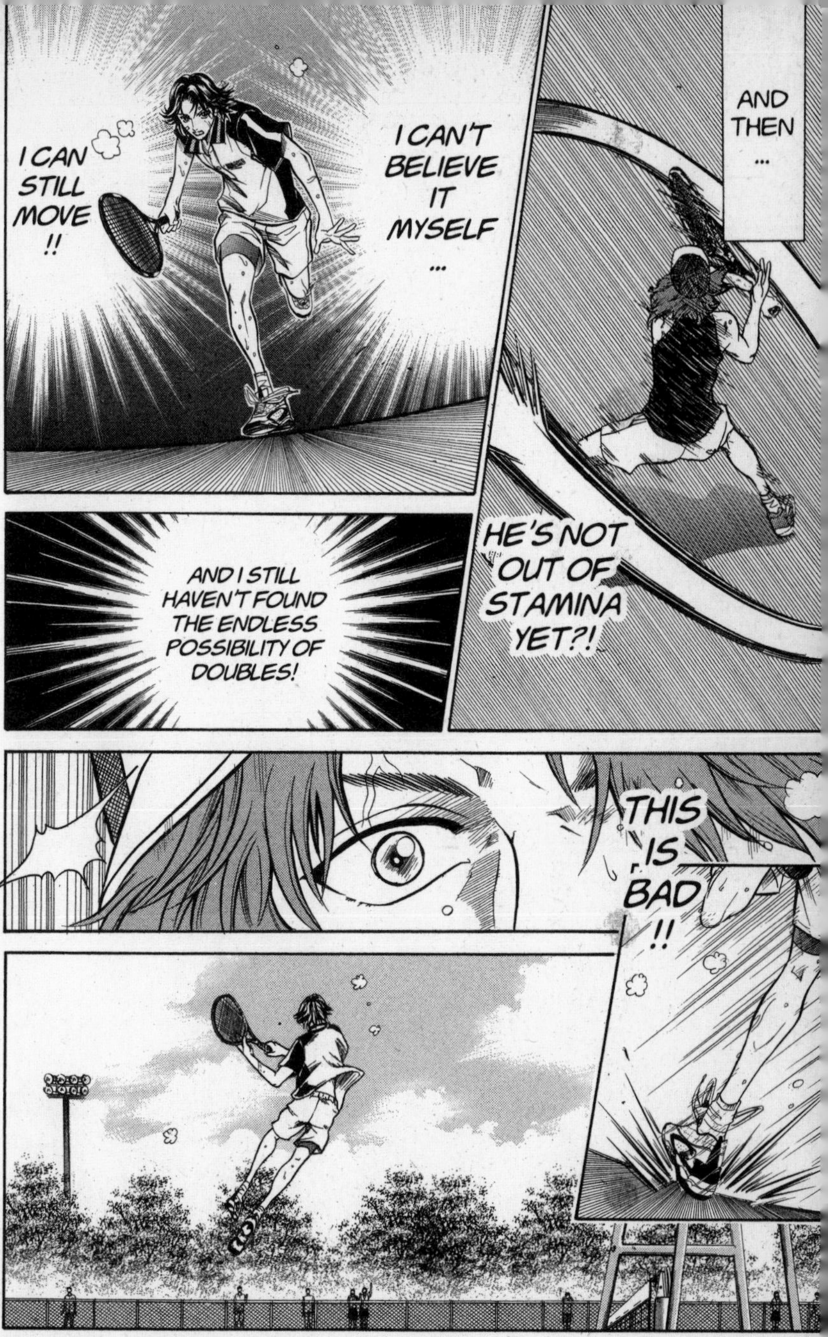
AND THEN ...
HE'S NOT OUT OF STAMINA YET?!
I CAN'T BELIEVE IT MYSELF ...
I CAN STILL MOVE !!
AND I STILL HAVEN'T FOUND THE ENDLESS POSSIBILITY OF DOUBLES!
THIS IS BAD !!

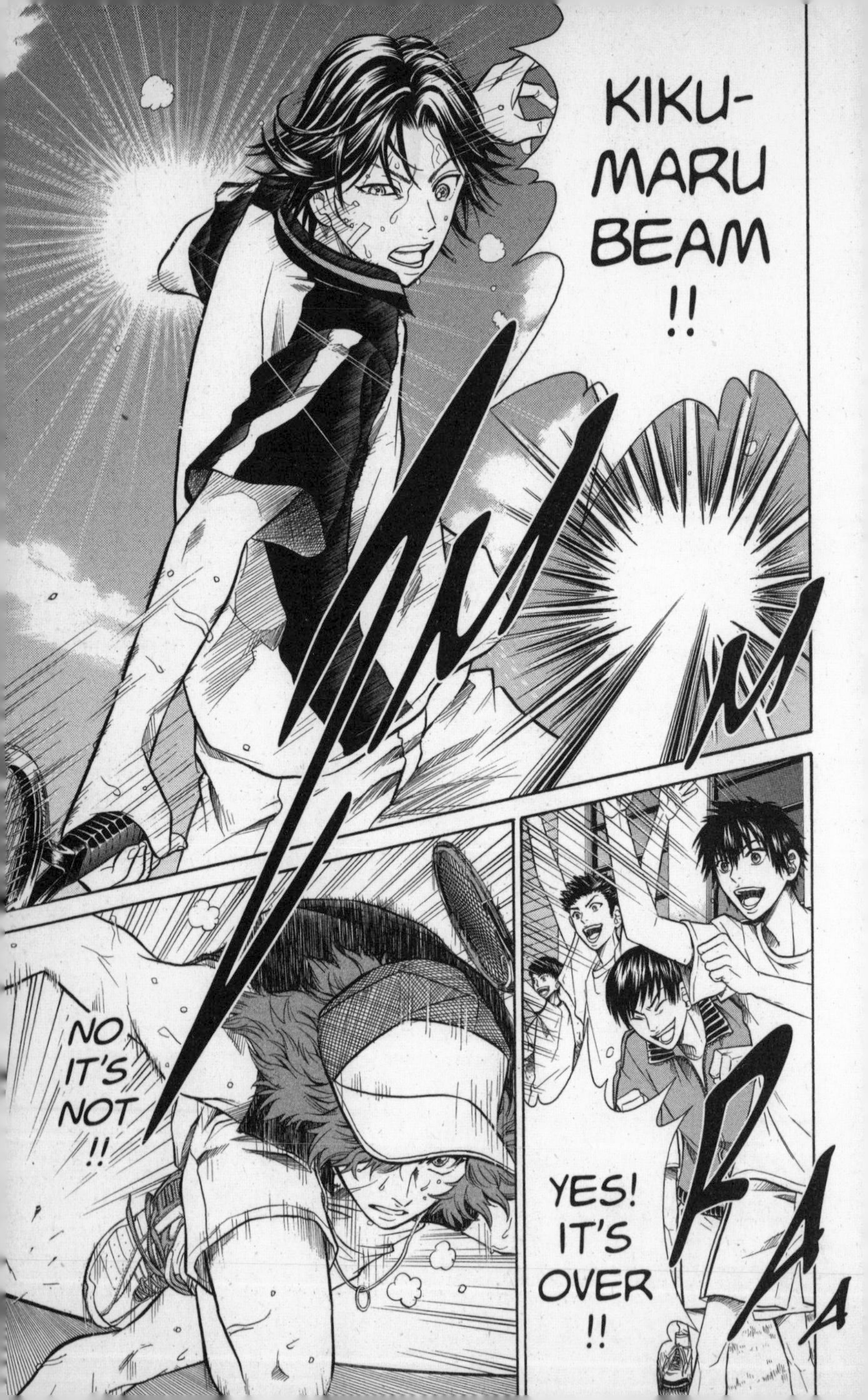
KIKU-MARU BEAM !!
YES! IT'S OVER !!
NO IT'S NOT !!

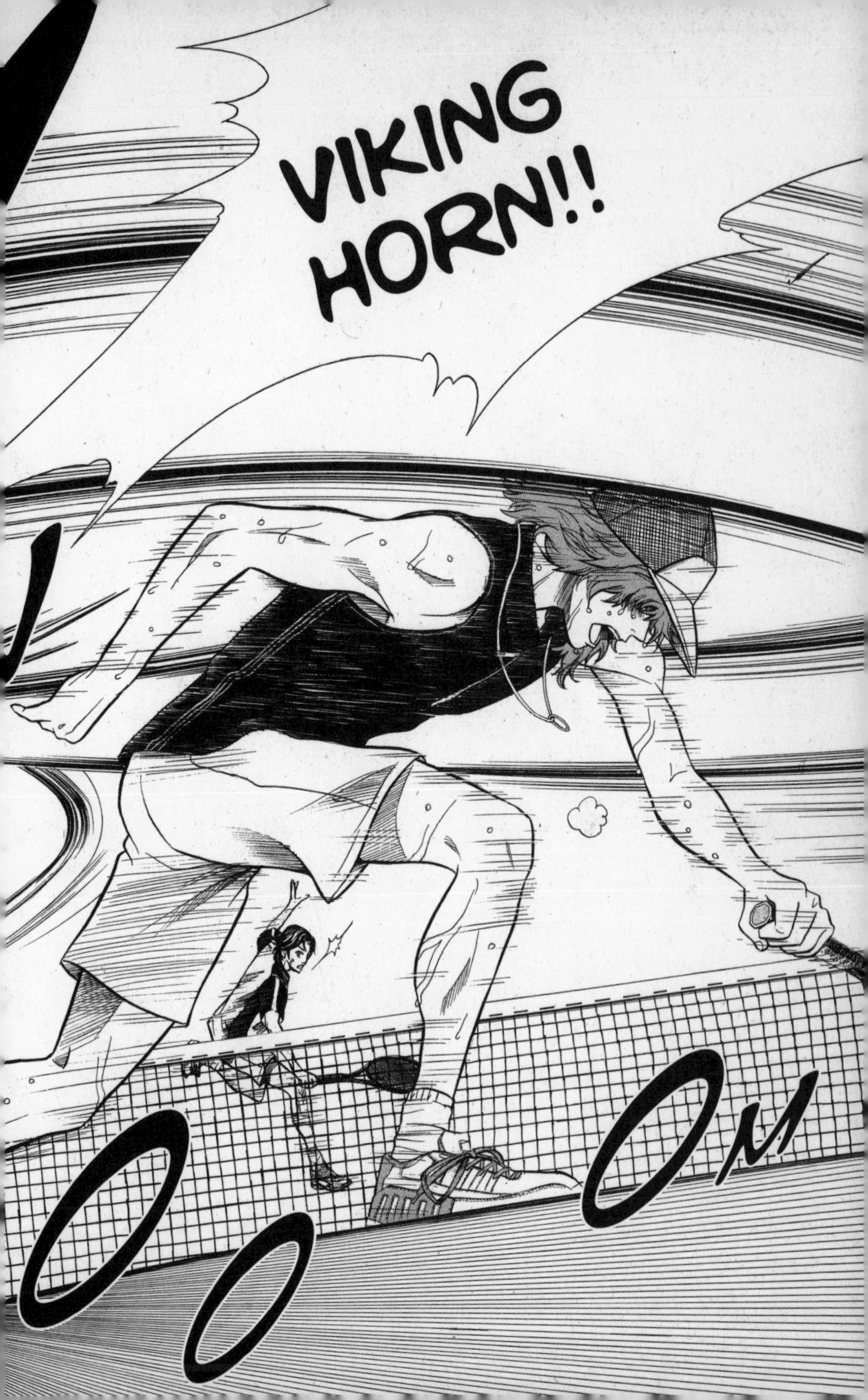
VIKING HORN!!
OOOOM

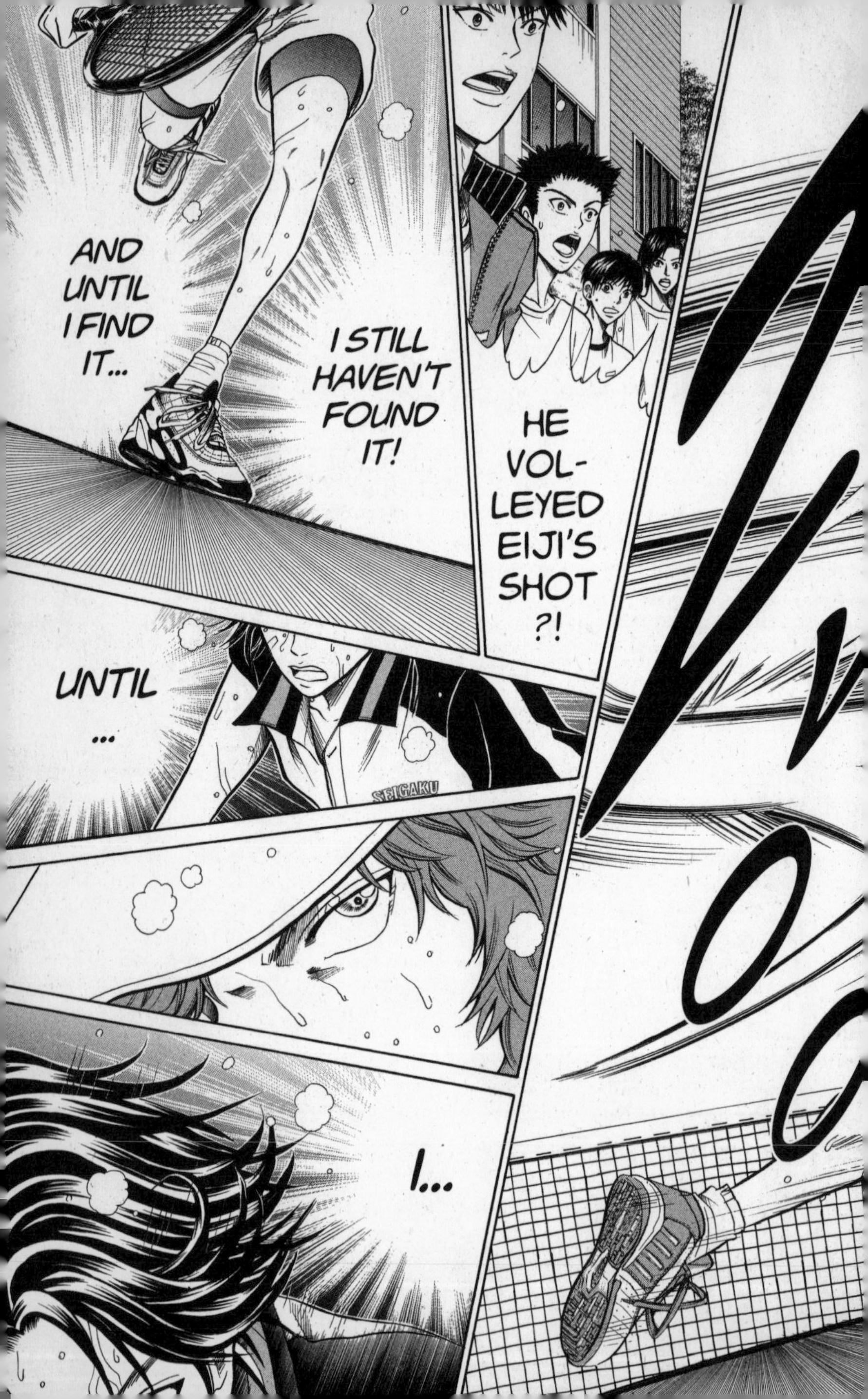
HE VOL-LEYED EIJI'S SHOT ?!
I STILL HAVEN'T FOUND IT!
AND UNTIL I FIND IT...
UNTIL ...
SEIGAKU
I...

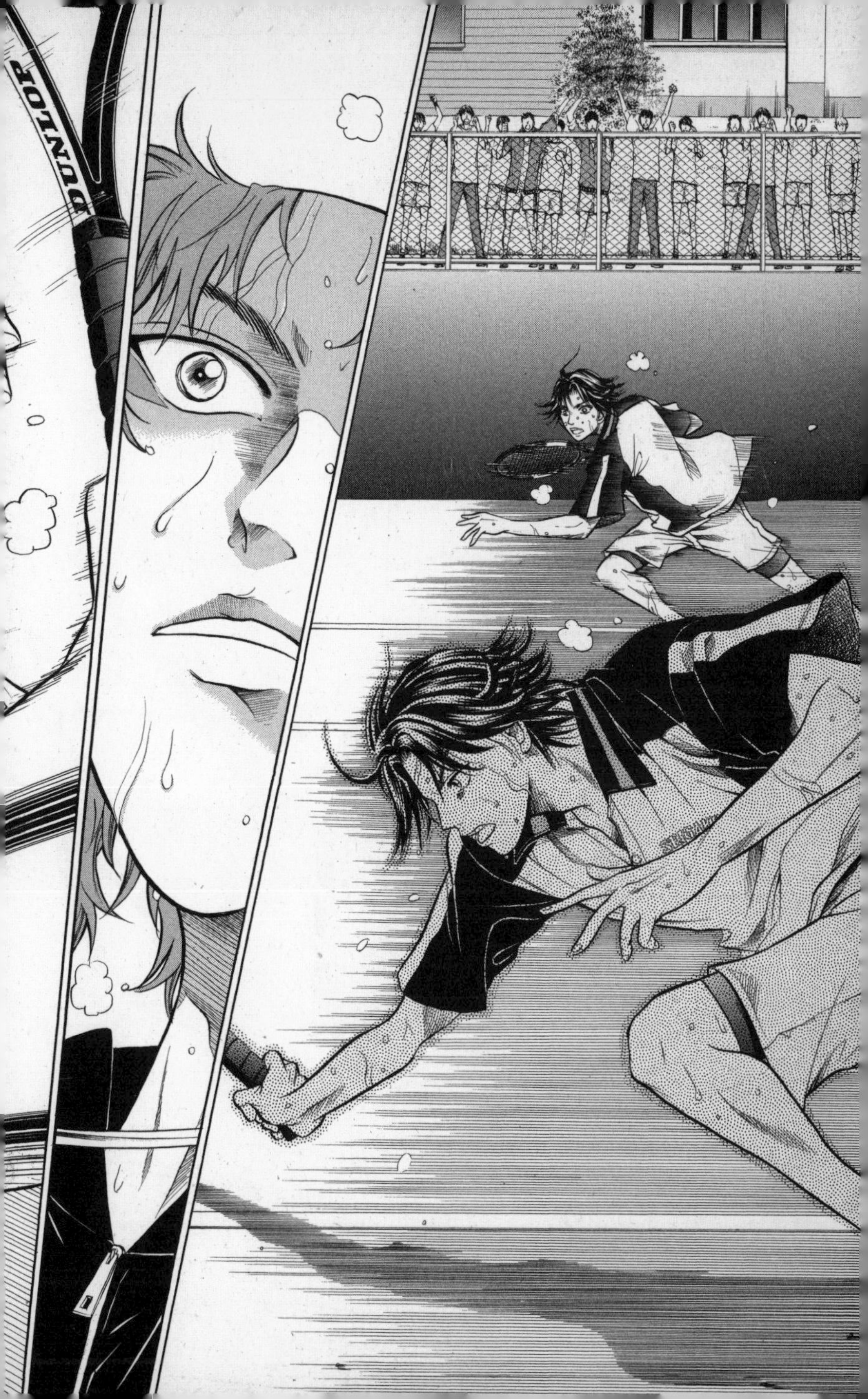
DUNLOP

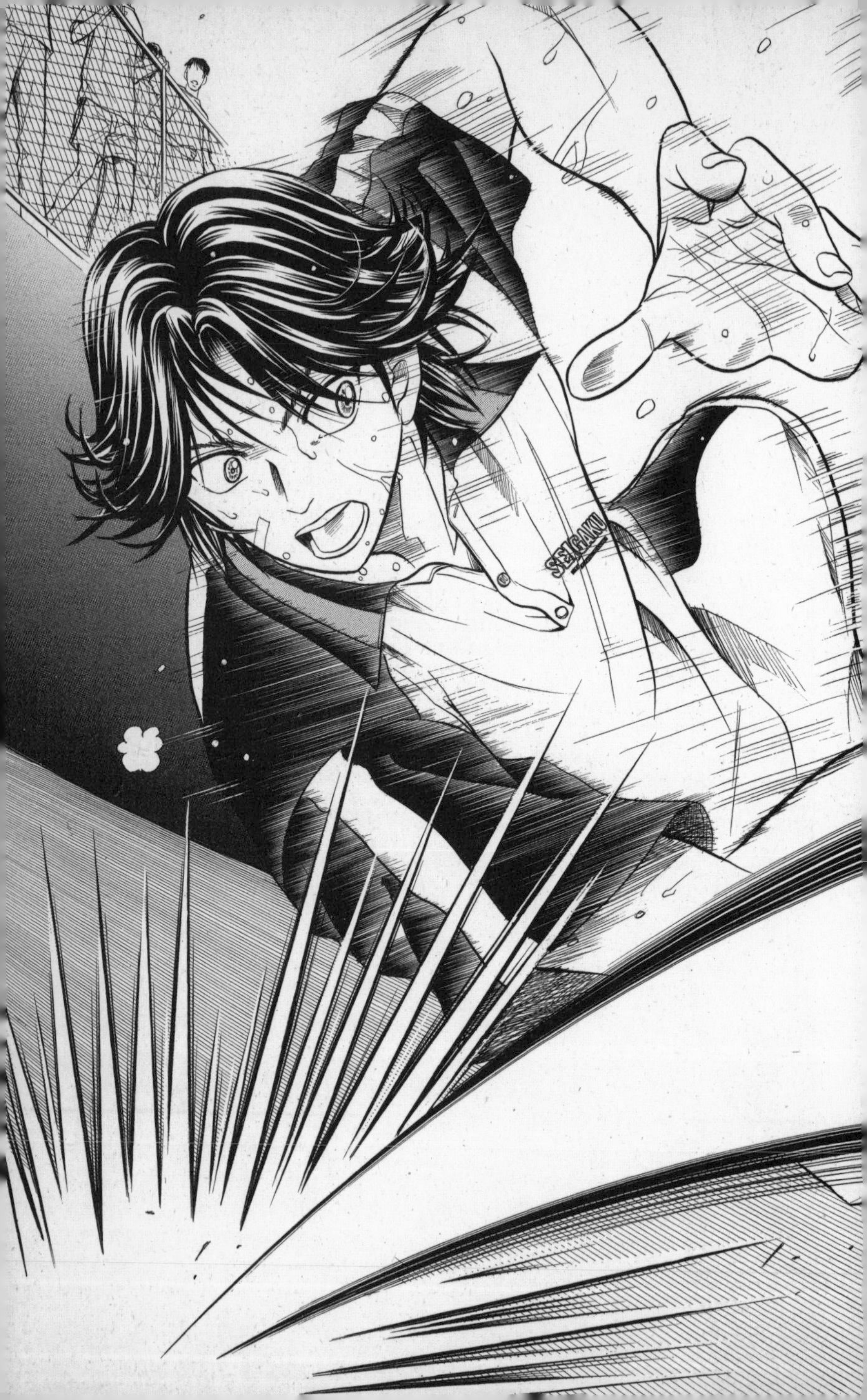
SEIGAKU

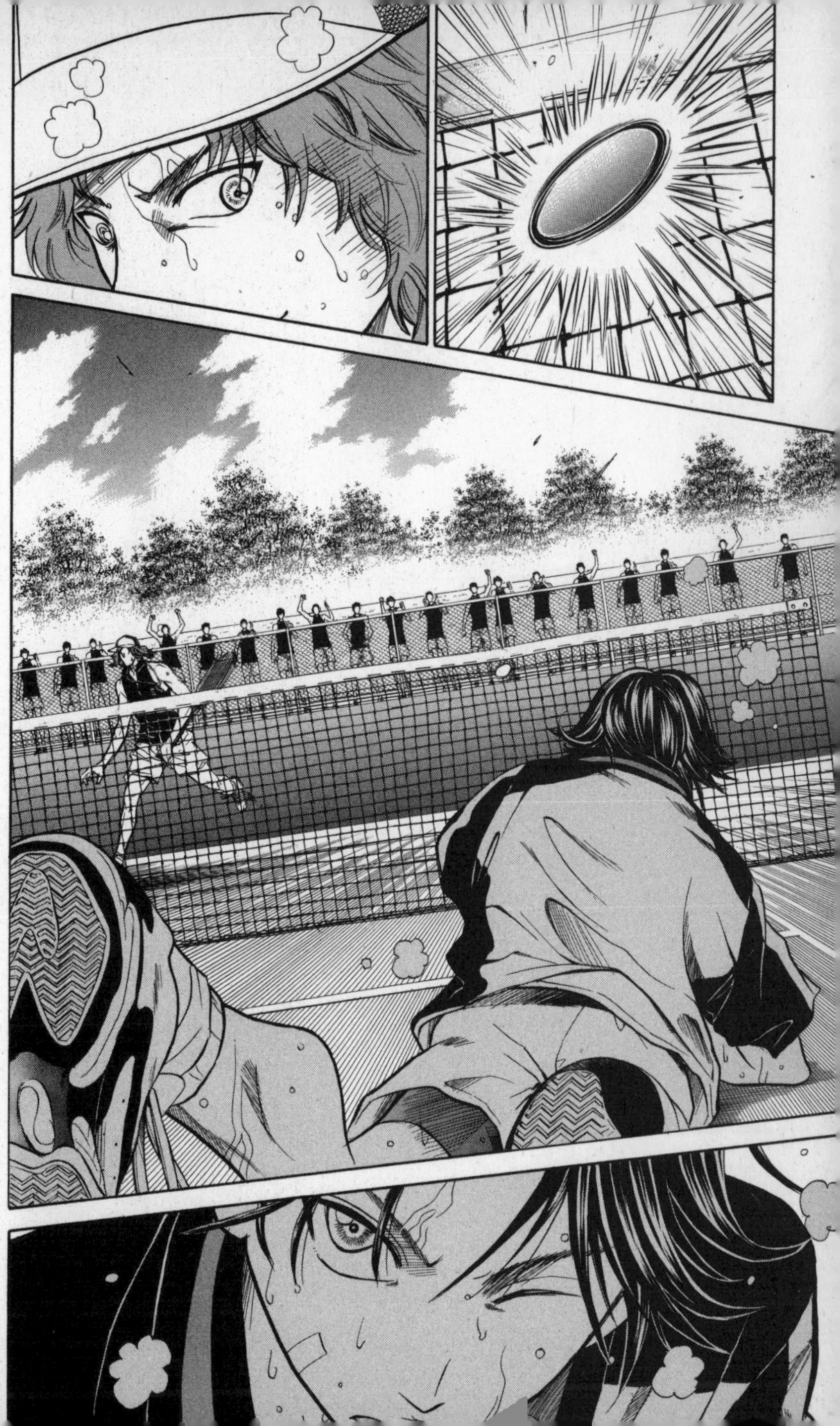

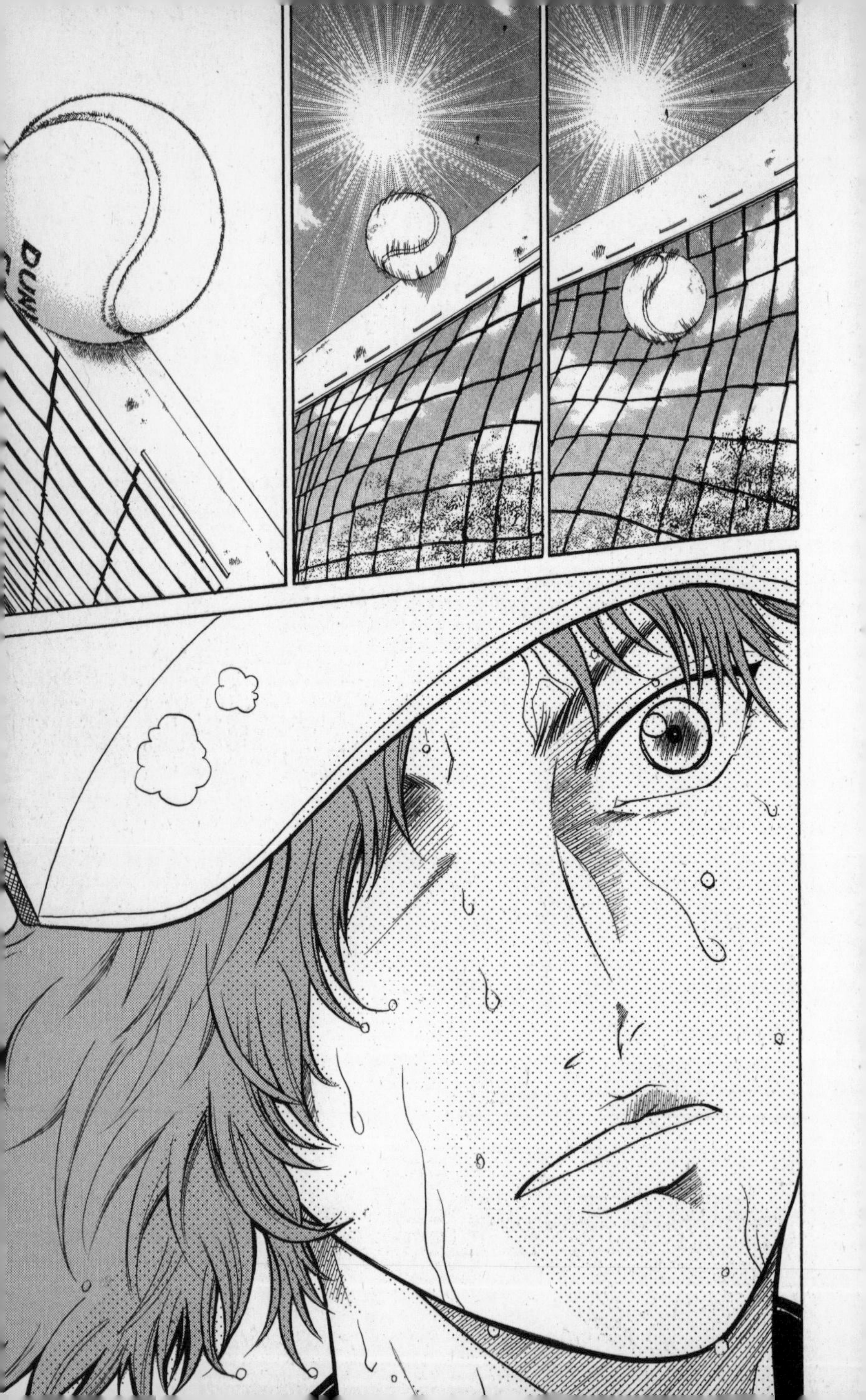

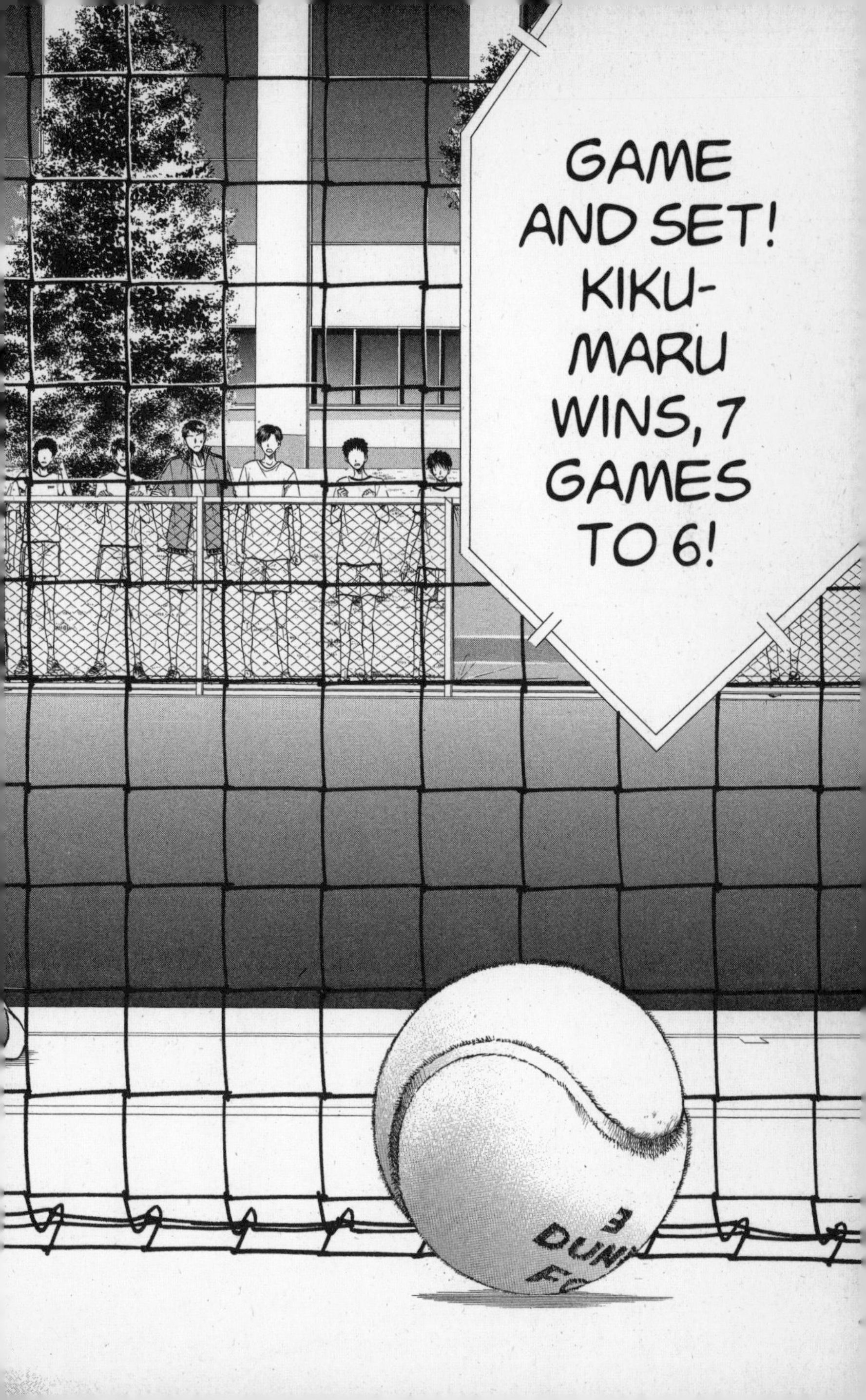
GAME AND SET! KIKU-MARU WINS, 7 GAMES TO 6!

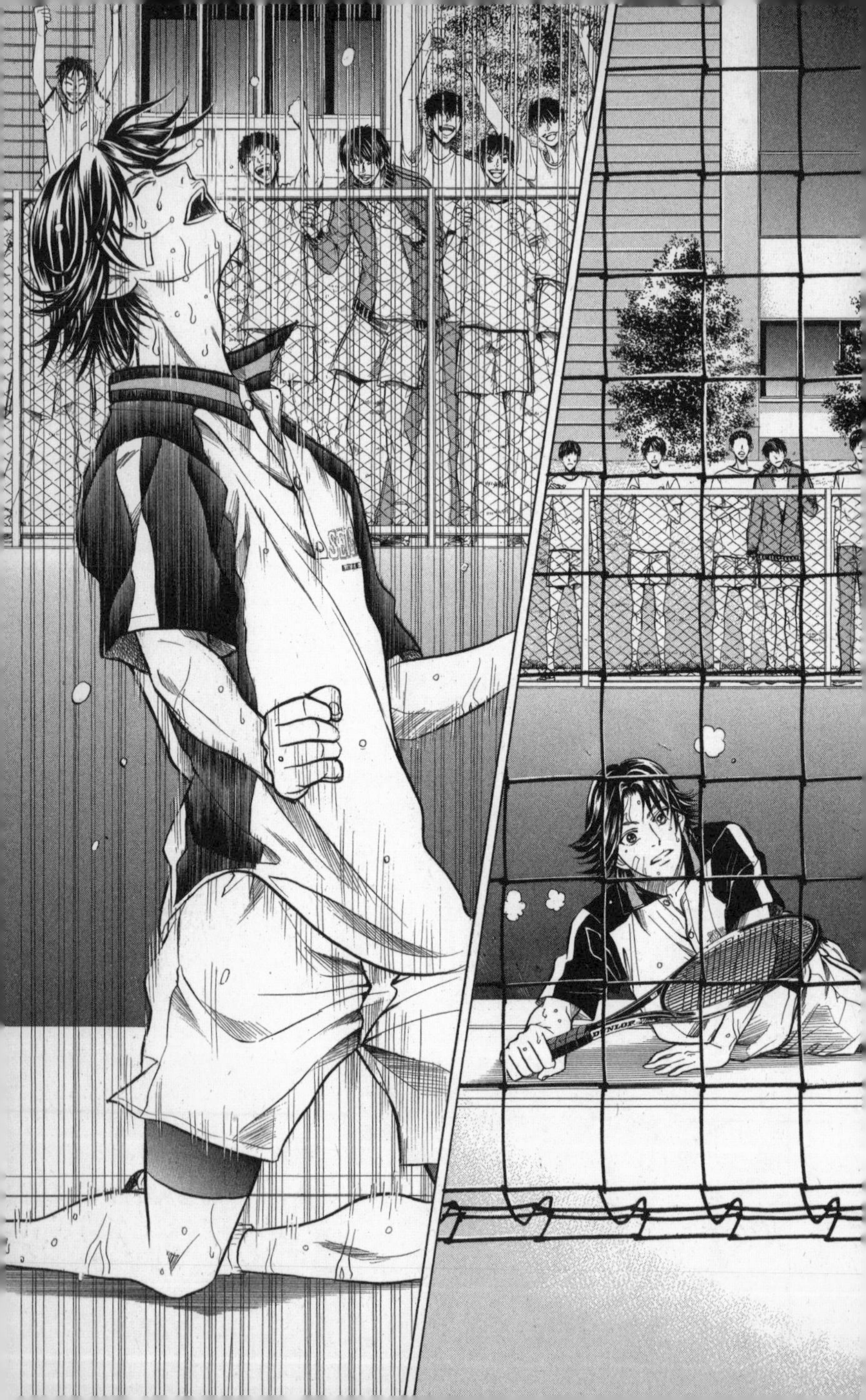
DUNLOP

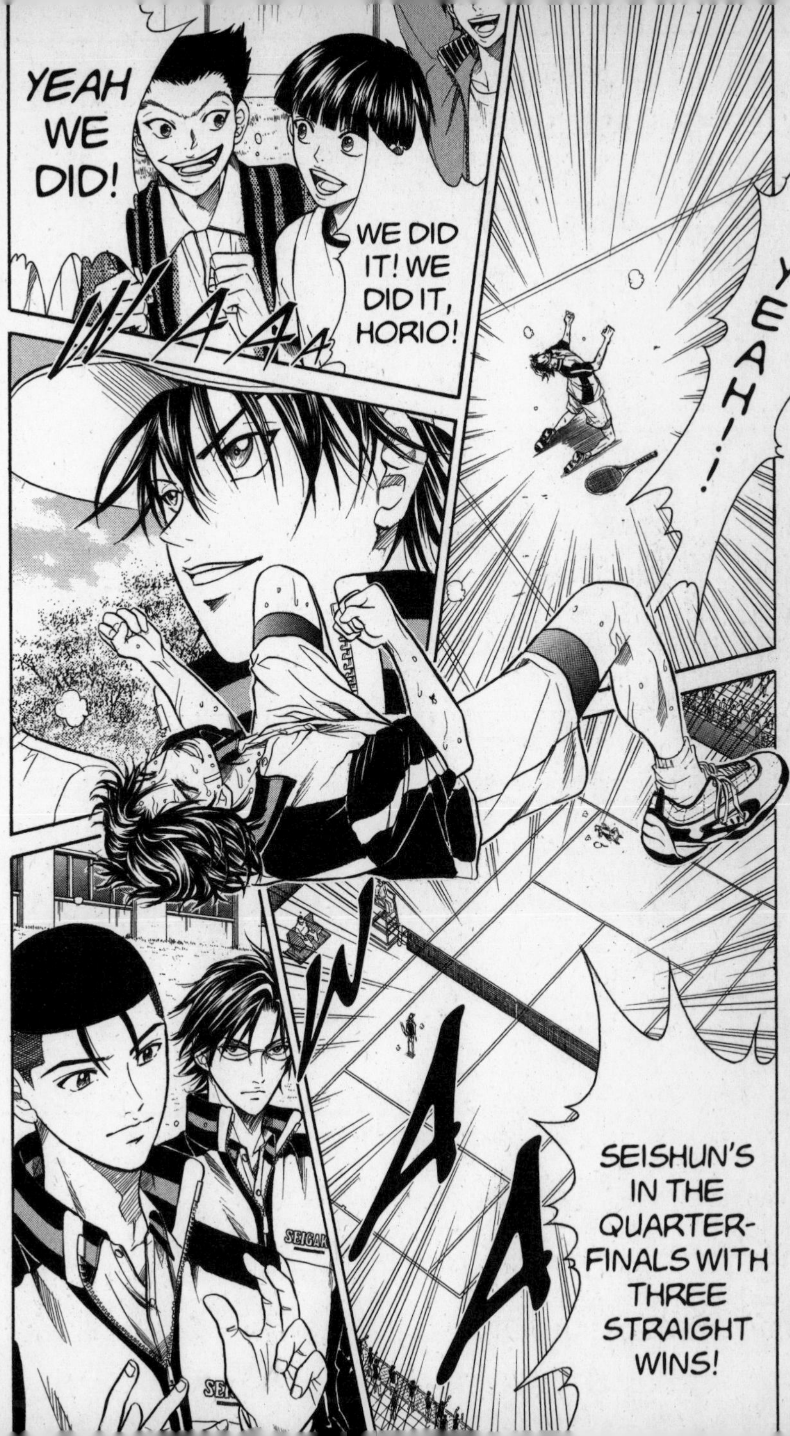
YEAH!!!
WE DID IT! WE DID IT, HORIO!
YEAH WE DID!
WAAAA
WAAA
SEISHUN'S IN THE QUARTER-FINALS WITH THREE STRAIGHT WINS!

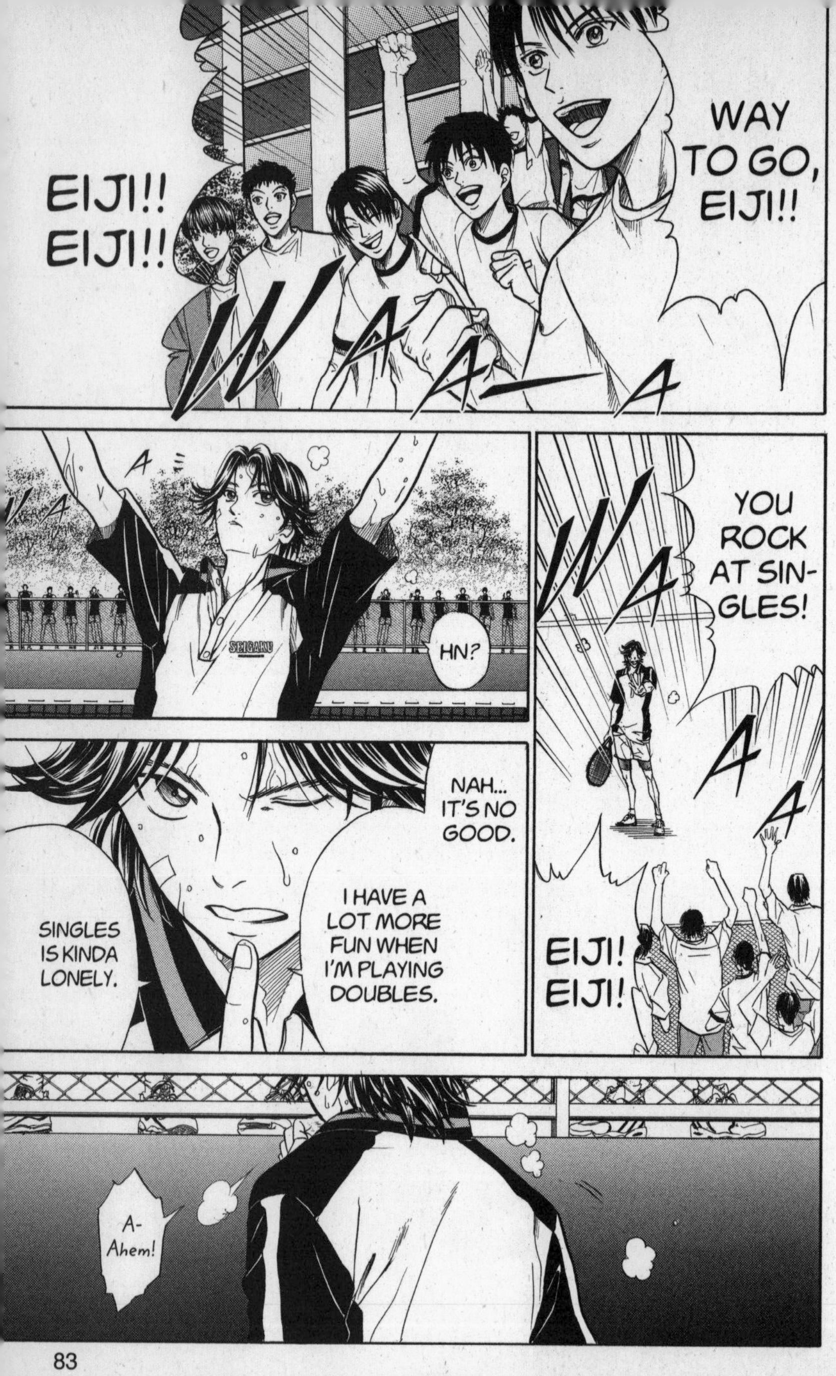
WAY TO GO, EIJI!!
EIJI!! EIJI!!
WA A— A
YOU ROCK AT SINGLES!
WA
A
A
EIJI! EIJI!
WA A A
HN?
NAH... IT'S NO GOOD.
I HAVE A LOT MORE FUN WHEN I'M PLAYING DOUBLES.
SINGLES IS KINDA LONELY.
A- Ahem!

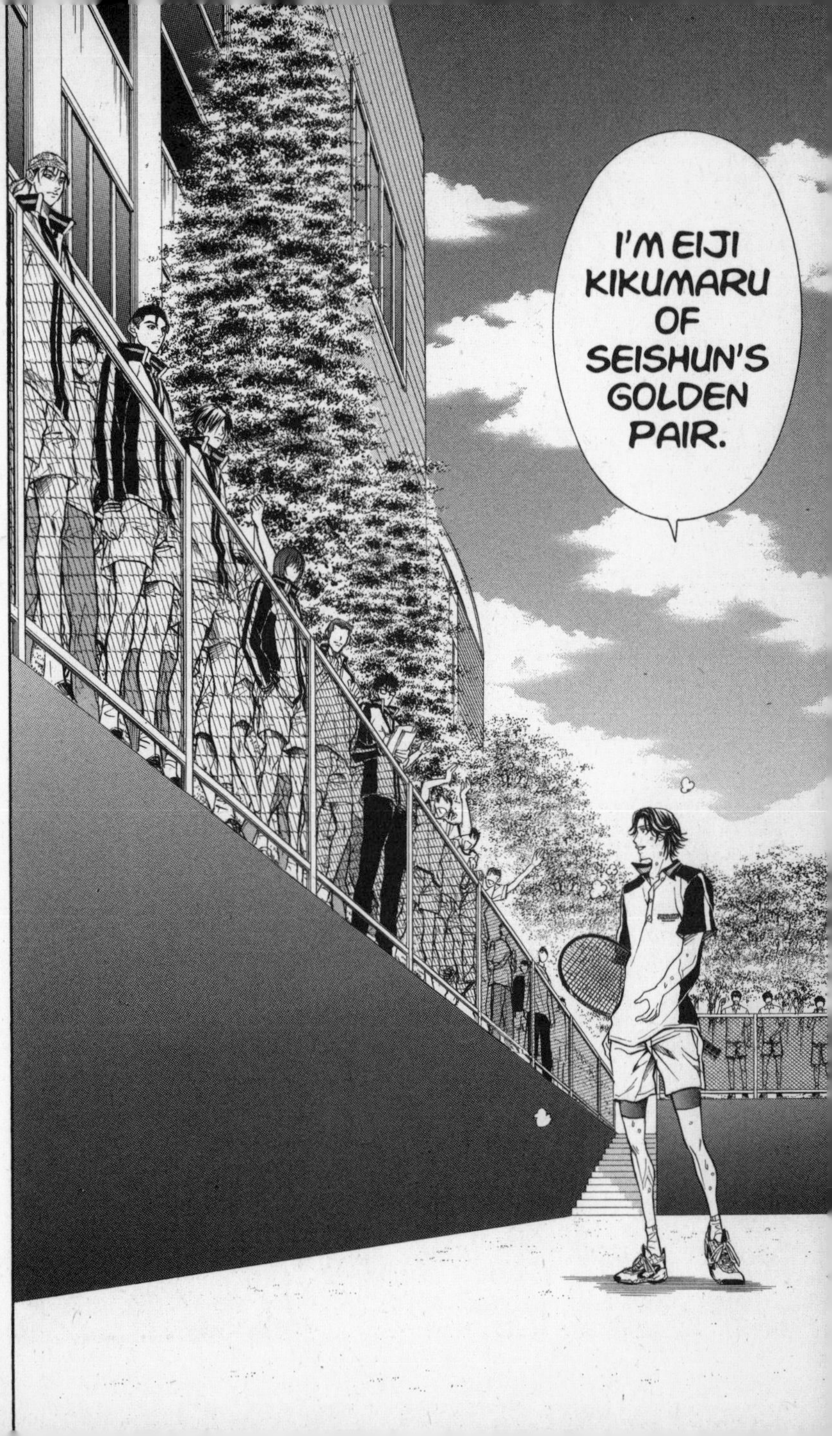
I'M EIJI KIKUMARU OF SEISHUN'S GOLDEN PAIR.

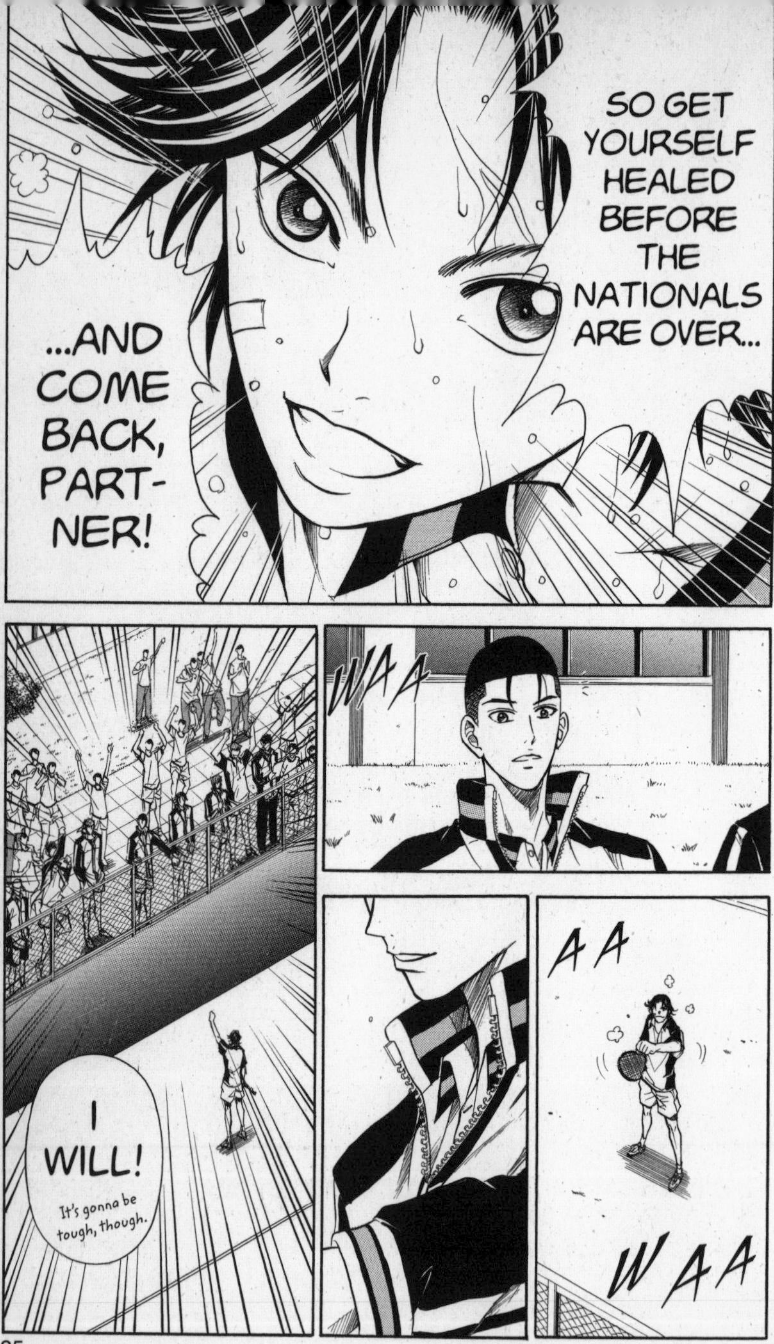
SO GET YOURSELF HEALED BEFORE THE NATIONALS ARE OVER...
...AND COME BACK, PARTNER!
WAA
AA
WAA
I WILL!
It's gonna be tough, though.

テニスの王子様

THE PRINCE OF TENNIS

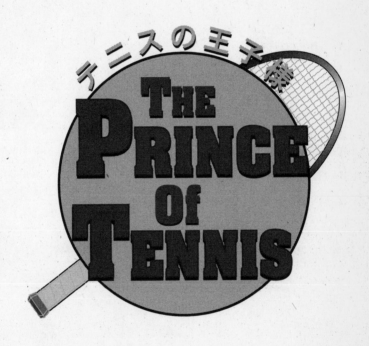

GENIUS 269: A MAN CALLED "KILLER"

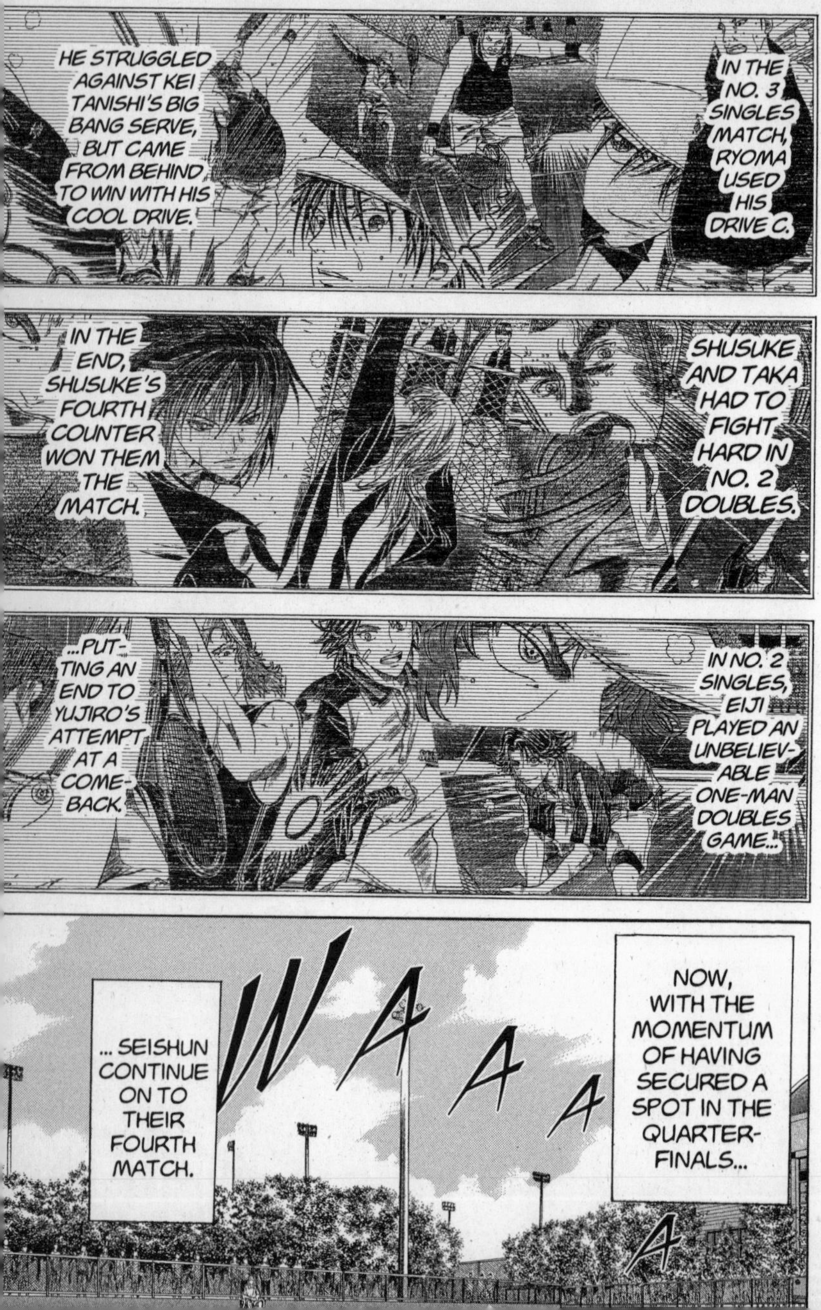
IN THE NO. 3 SINGLES MATCH, RYOMA USED HIS DRIVE C.
HE STRUGGLED AGAINST KEI TANISHI'S BIG BANG SERVE, BUT CAME FROM BEHIND TO WIN WITH HIS COOL DRIVE.
SHUSUKE AND TAKA HAD TO FIGHT HARD IN NO. 2 DOUBLES.
IN THE END, SHUSUKE'S FOURTH COUNTER WON THEM THE MATCH.
IN NO. 2 SINGLES, EIJI PLAYED AN UNBELIEV-ABLE ONE-MAN DOUBLES GAME...
...PUT-TING AN END TO YUJIRO'S ATTEMPT AT A COME-BACK.
NOW, WITH THE MOMENTUM OF HAVING SECURED A SPOT IN THE QUARTER-FINALS...
WAAAA
... SEISHUN CONTINUE ON TO THEIR FOURTH MATCH.

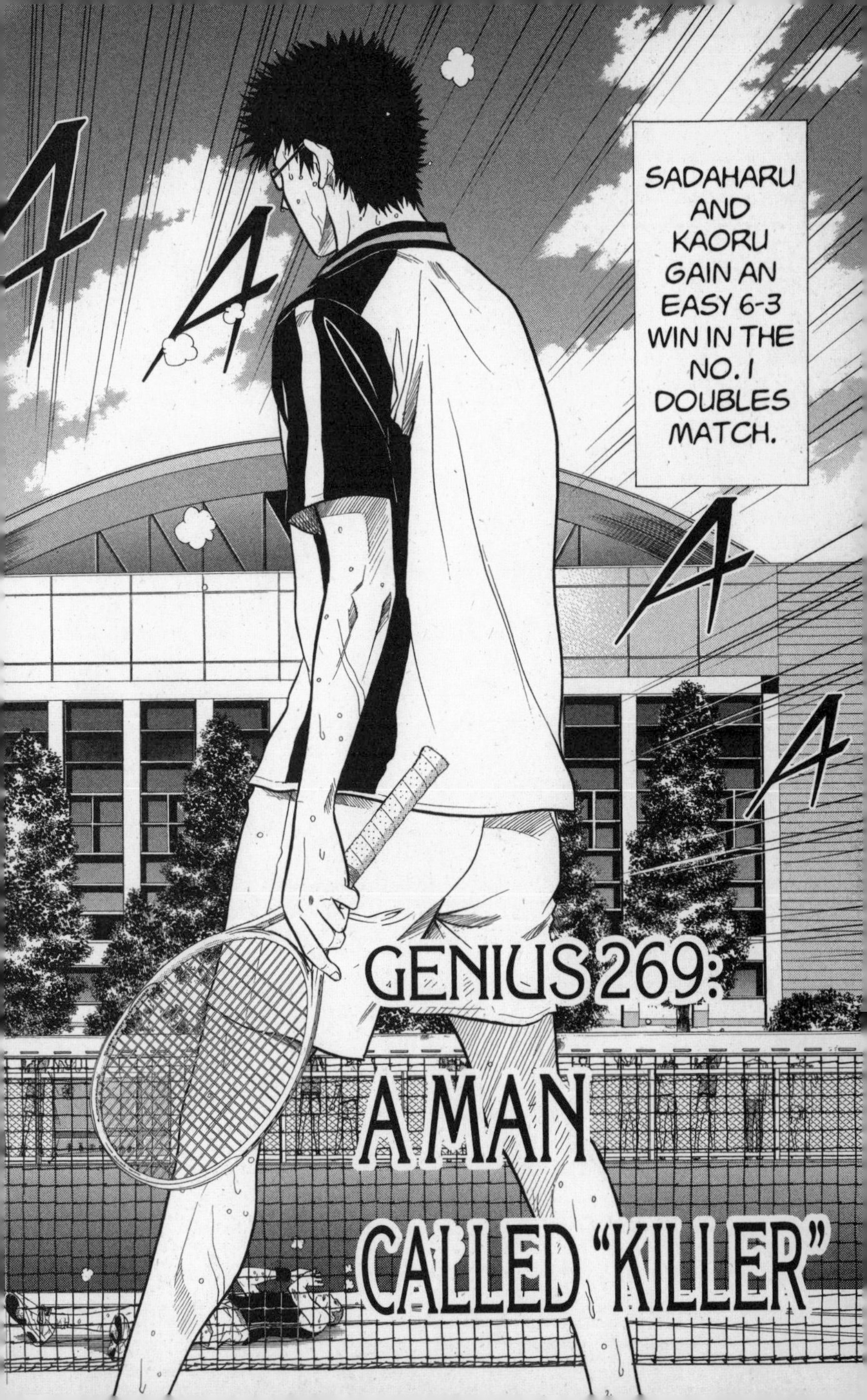
SADAHARU AND KAORU GAIN AN EASY 6-3 WIN IN THE NO. 1 DOUBLES MATCH.
GENIUS 269:
A MAN CALLED "KILLER"

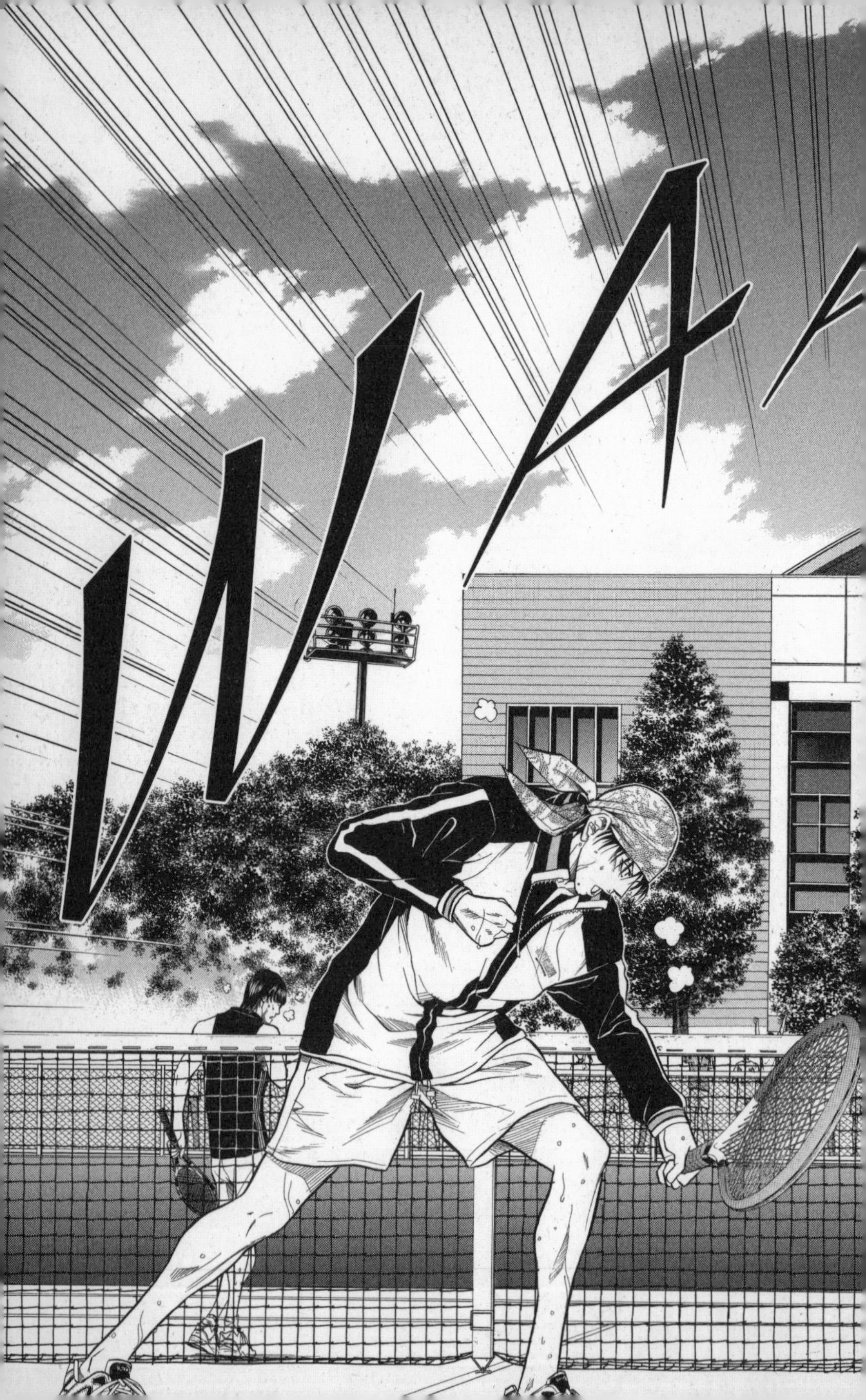
WA

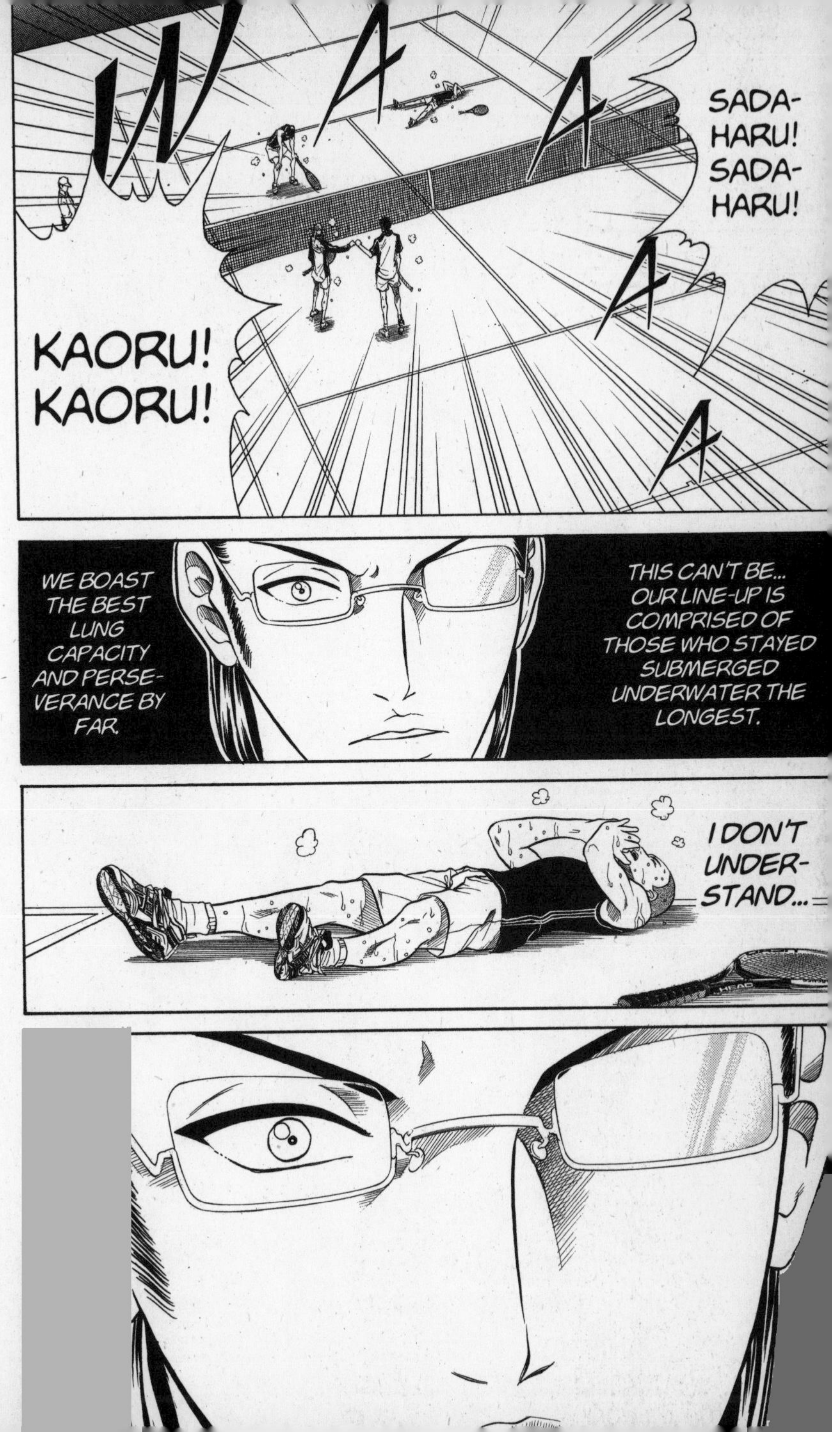
WAAAAA
SADA-HARU! SADA-HARU!
KAORU! KAORU!
THIS CAN'T BE... OUR LINE-UP IS COMPRISED OF THOSE WHO STAYED SUBMERGED UNDERWATER THE LONGEST.
WE BOAST THE BEST LUNG CAPACITY AND PERSE-VERANCE BY FAR.
I DON'T UNDER-STAND...

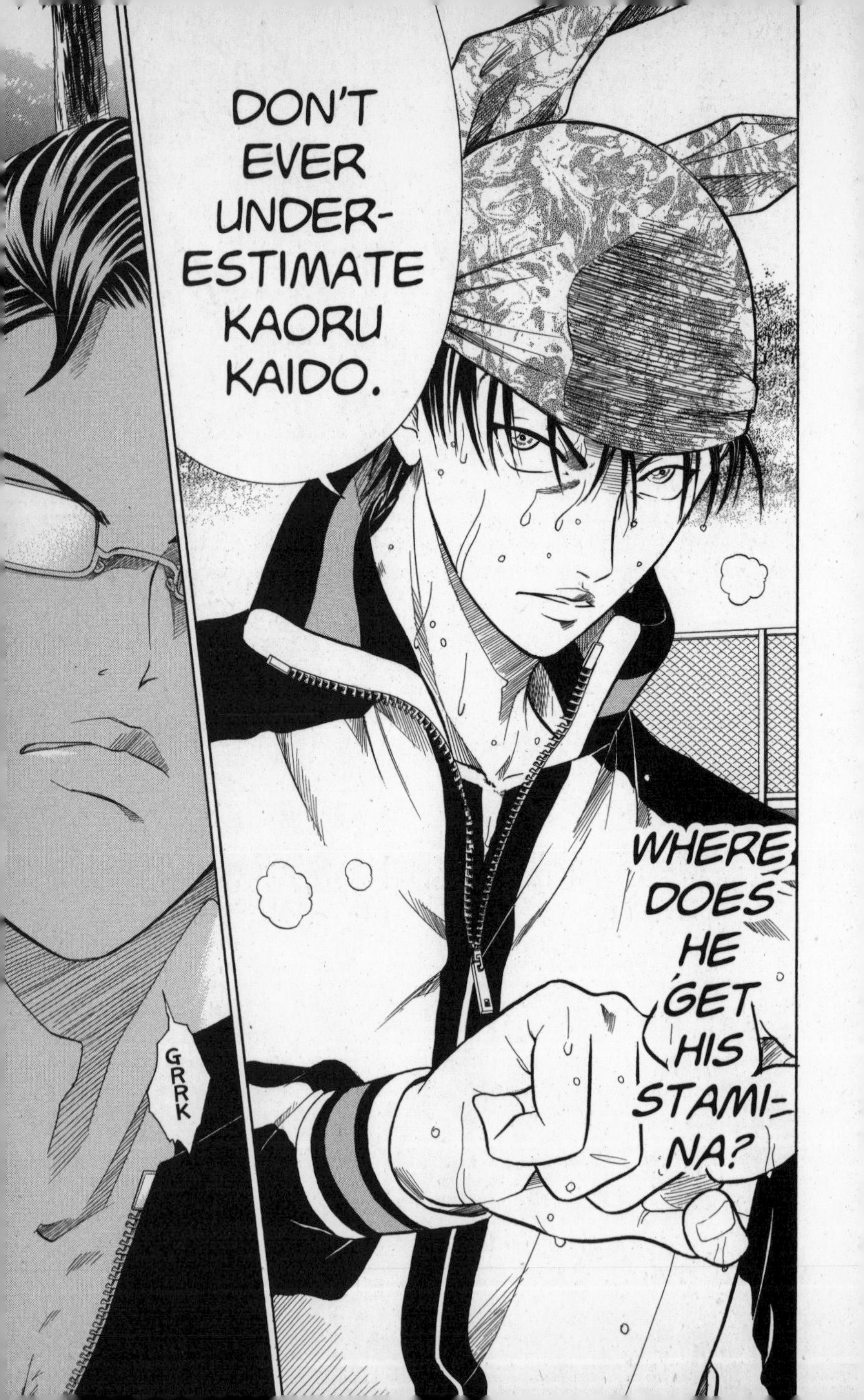
DON'T EVER UNDER-ESTIMATE KAORU KAIDO.
WHERE DOES HE GET HIS STAMI-NA?
GRRK

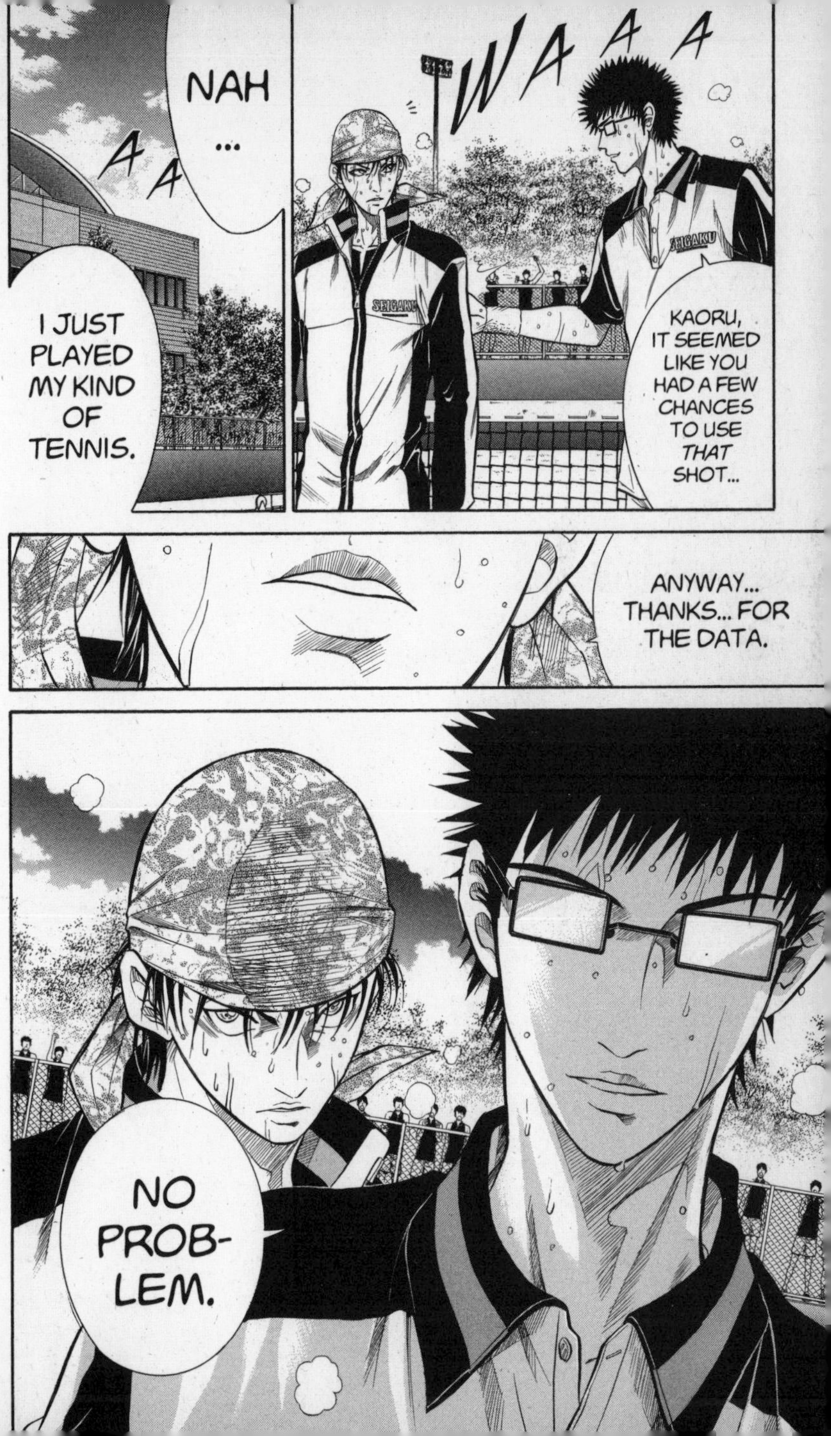
WAAA
KAORU, IT SEEMED LIKE YOU HAD A FEW CHANCES TO USE *THAT* SHOT...
NAH ...
AA
I JUST PLAYED MY KIND OF TENNIS.
ANYWAY... THANKS... FOR THE DATA.
NO PROB-LEM.

READ THIS WAY

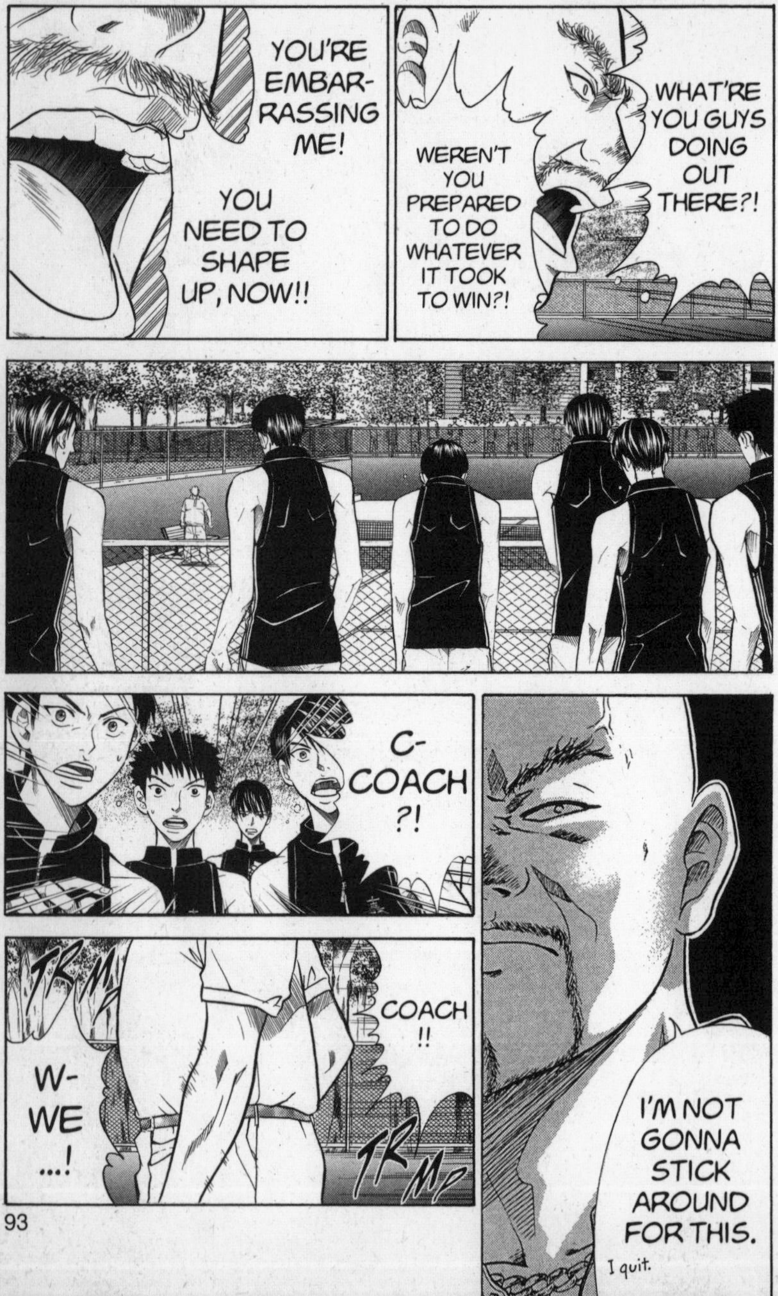
WHAT'RE YOU GUYS DOING OUT THERE?!
WEREN'T YOU PREPARED TO DO WHATEVER IT TOOK TO WIN?!
YOU'RE EMBARRASSING ME!
YOU NEED TO SHAPE UP, NOW!!
I'M NOT GONNA STICK AROUND FOR THIS.
I quit.
C-COACH?!
TRMP
COACH!!
W-WE...!
TRMP

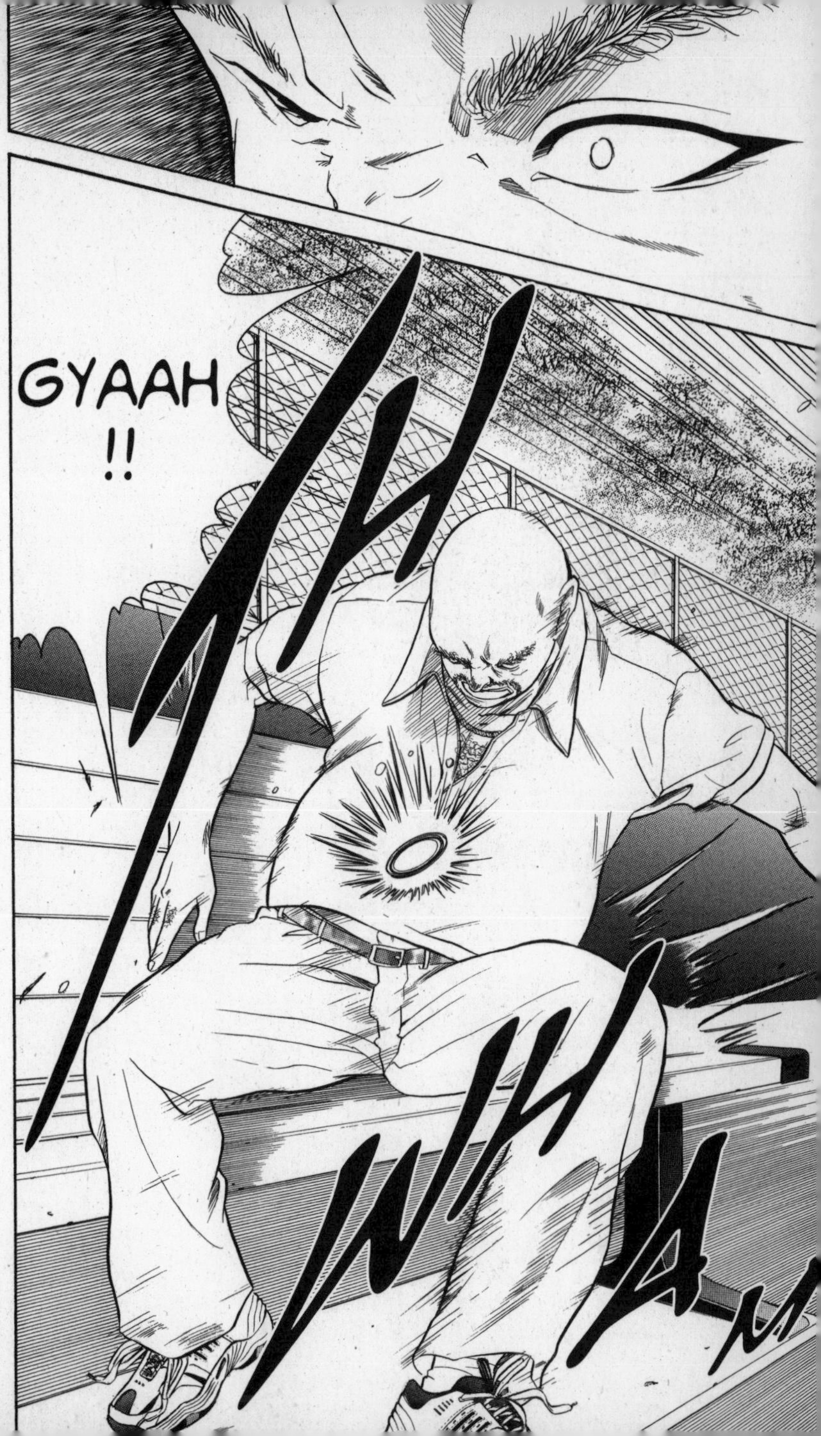
GYAAH
!!

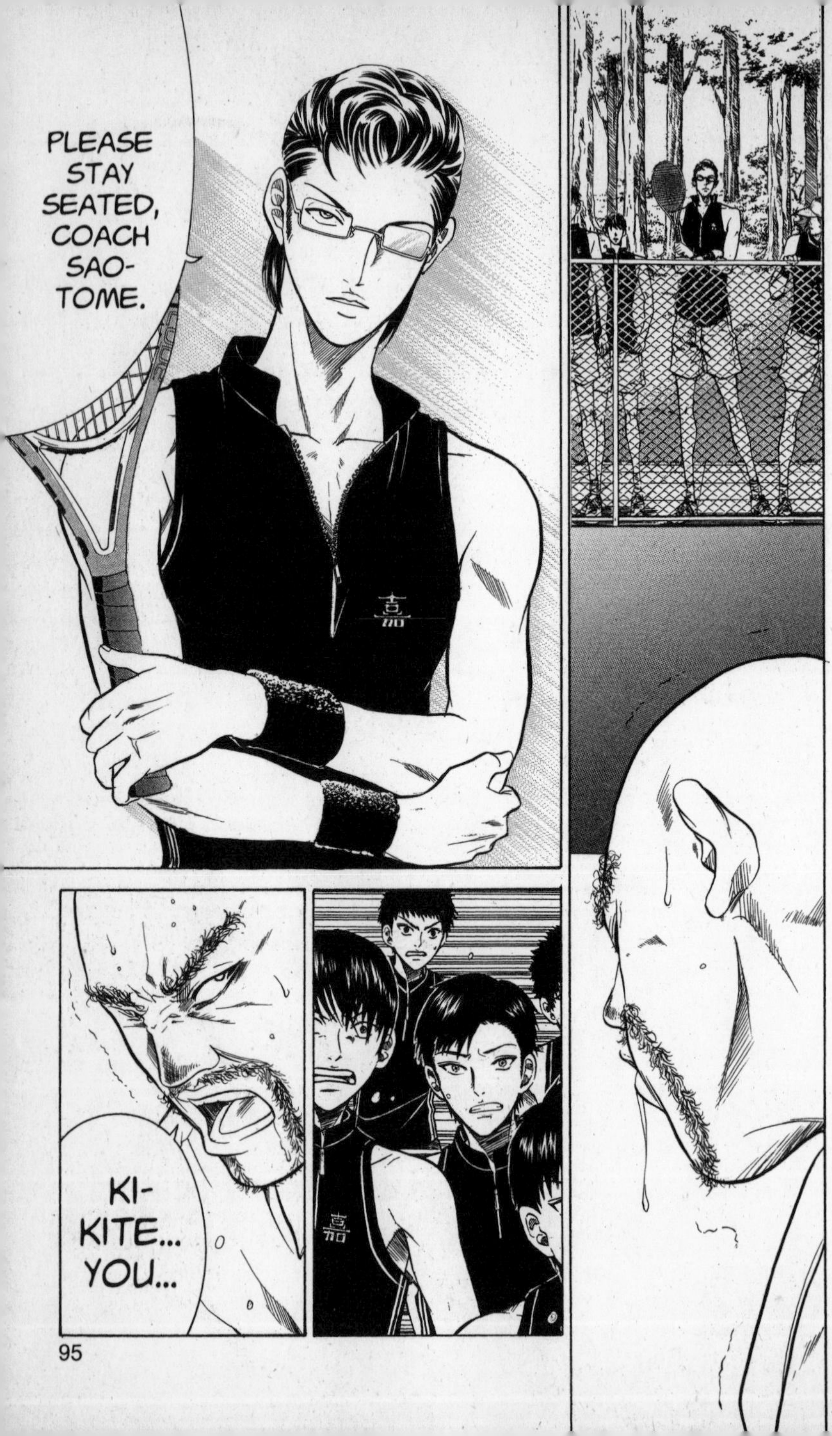
PLEASE STAY SEATED, COACH SAO-TOME.
KI-KITE... YOU...

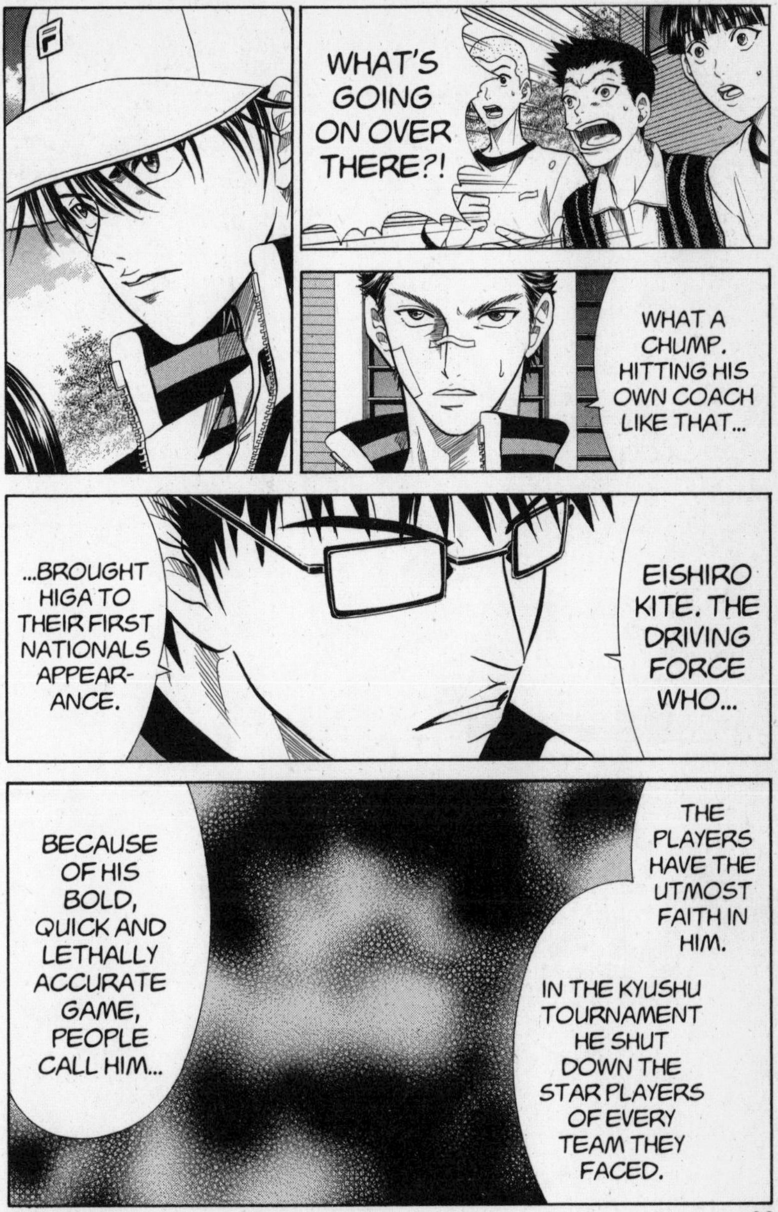
WHAT'S GOING ON OVER THERE?!
WHAT A CHUMP. HITTING HIS OWN COACH LIKE THAT...
EISHIRO KITE. THE DRIVING FORCE WHO...
...BROUGHT HIGA TO THEIR FIRST NATIONALS APPEARANCE.
THE PLAYERS HAVE THE UTMOST FAITH IN HIM.
IN THE KYUSHU TOURNAMENT HE SHUT DOWN THE STAR PLAYERS OF EVERY TEAM THEY FACED.
BECAUSE OF HIS BOLD, QUICK AND LETHALLY ACCURATE GAME, PEOPLE CALL HIM...

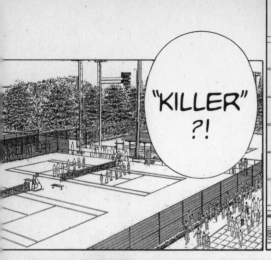

"KILLER"?!

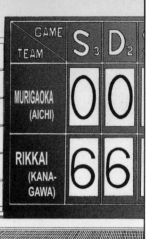

GAME TEAM	S₃	D₂
MURIGAOKA (AICHI)	0	0
RIKKAI (KANA-GAWA)	6	6

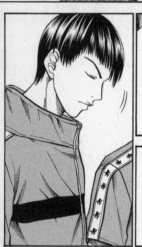

...THE CAPTAIN OF THE OKINAWA TEAM HAS.

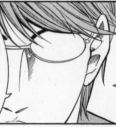

WHAT AN AWFULLY DISTURBING NICKNAME...

IS HE REALLY A TENNIS PLAYER?

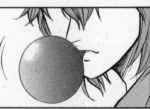

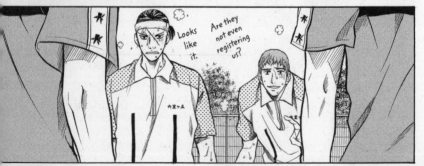

Looks like it.

Are they not even registering us?

97

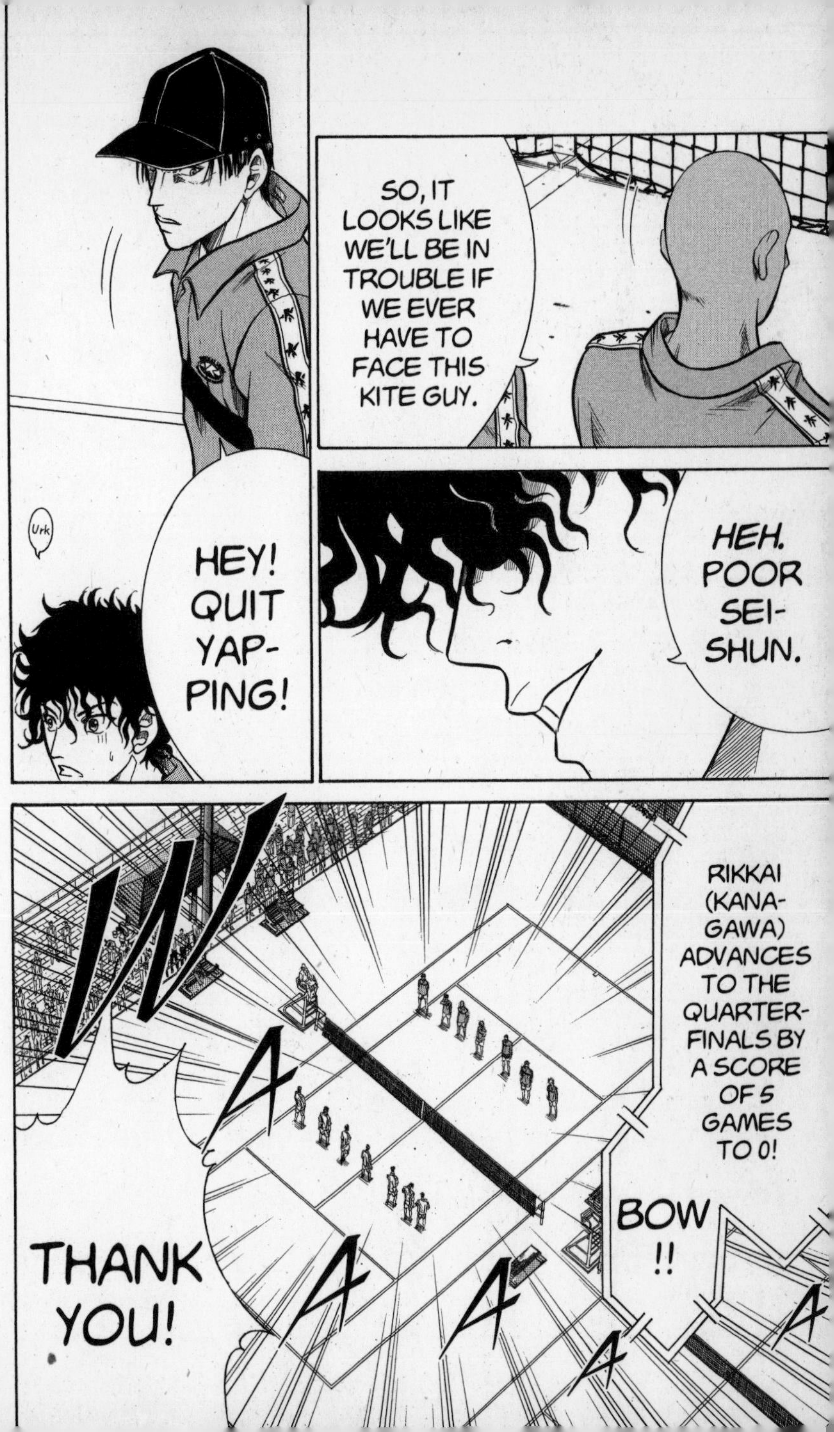
SO, IT LOOKS LIKE WE'LL BE IN TROUBLE IF WE EVER HAVE TO FACE THIS KITE GUY.
HEH. POOR SEI-SHUN.
HEY! QUIT YAP-PING!
Urk
RIKKAI (KANA-GAWA) ADVANCES TO THE QUARTER-FINALS BY A SCORE OF 5 GAMES TO 0!
BOW !!
THANK YOU!
WAAAAA

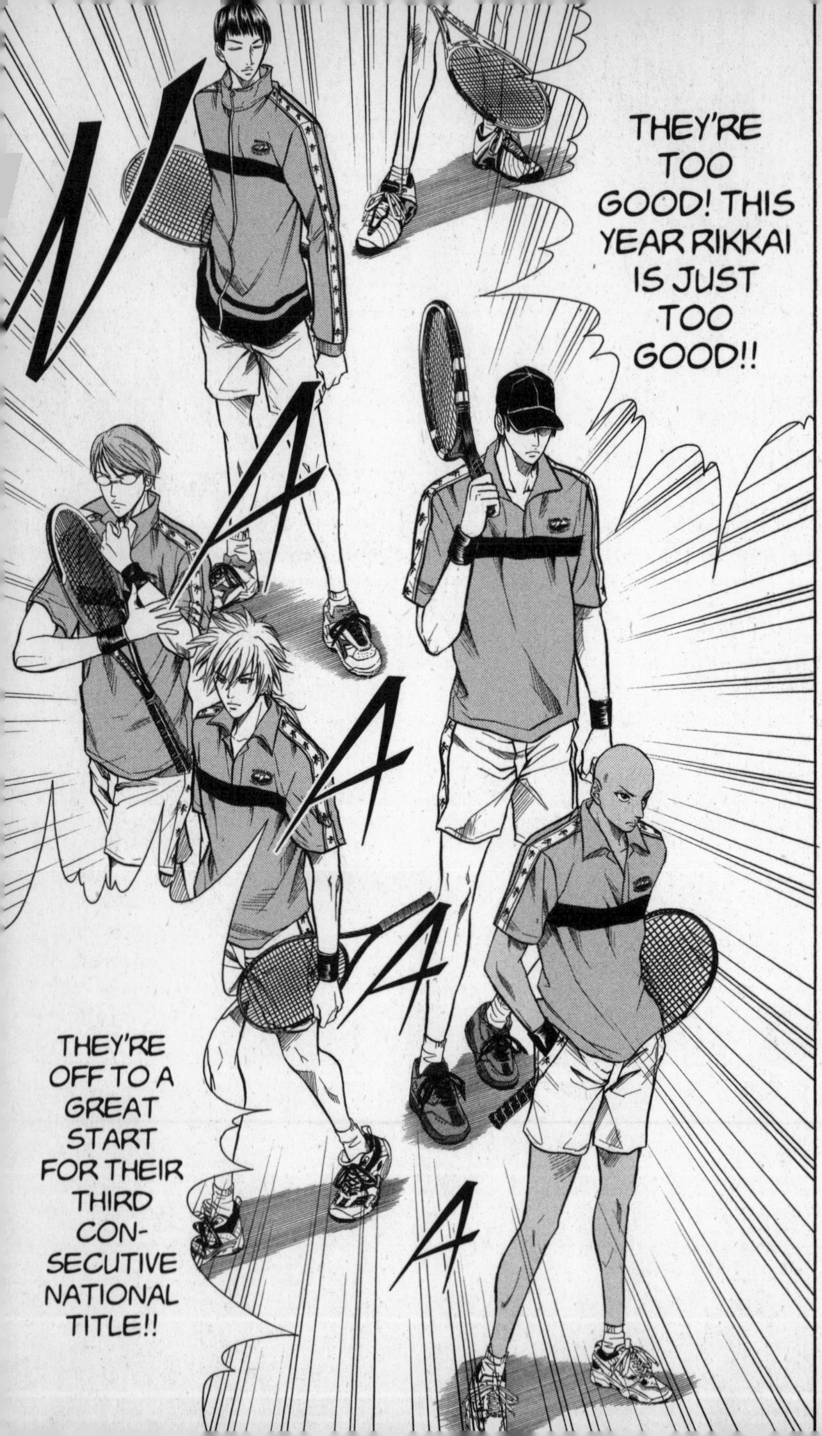
THEY'RE TOO GOOD! THIS YEAR RIKKAI IS JUST TOO GOOD!!
THEY'RE OFF TO A GREAT START FOR THEIR THIRD CON-SECUTIVE NATIONAL TITLE!!

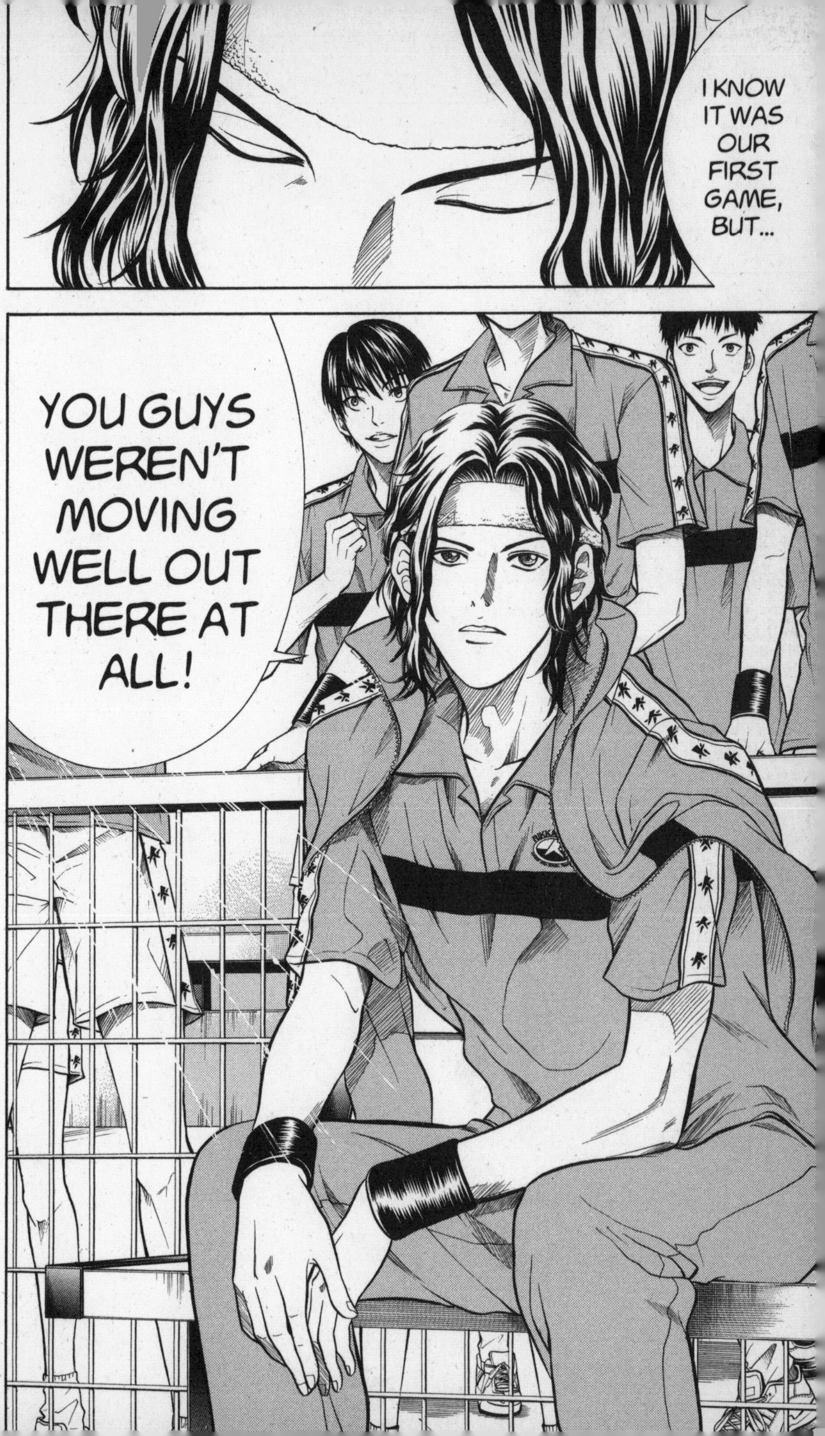
I KNOW IT WAS OUR FIRST GAME, BUT...
YOU GUYS WEREN'T MOVING WELL OUT THERE AT ALL!

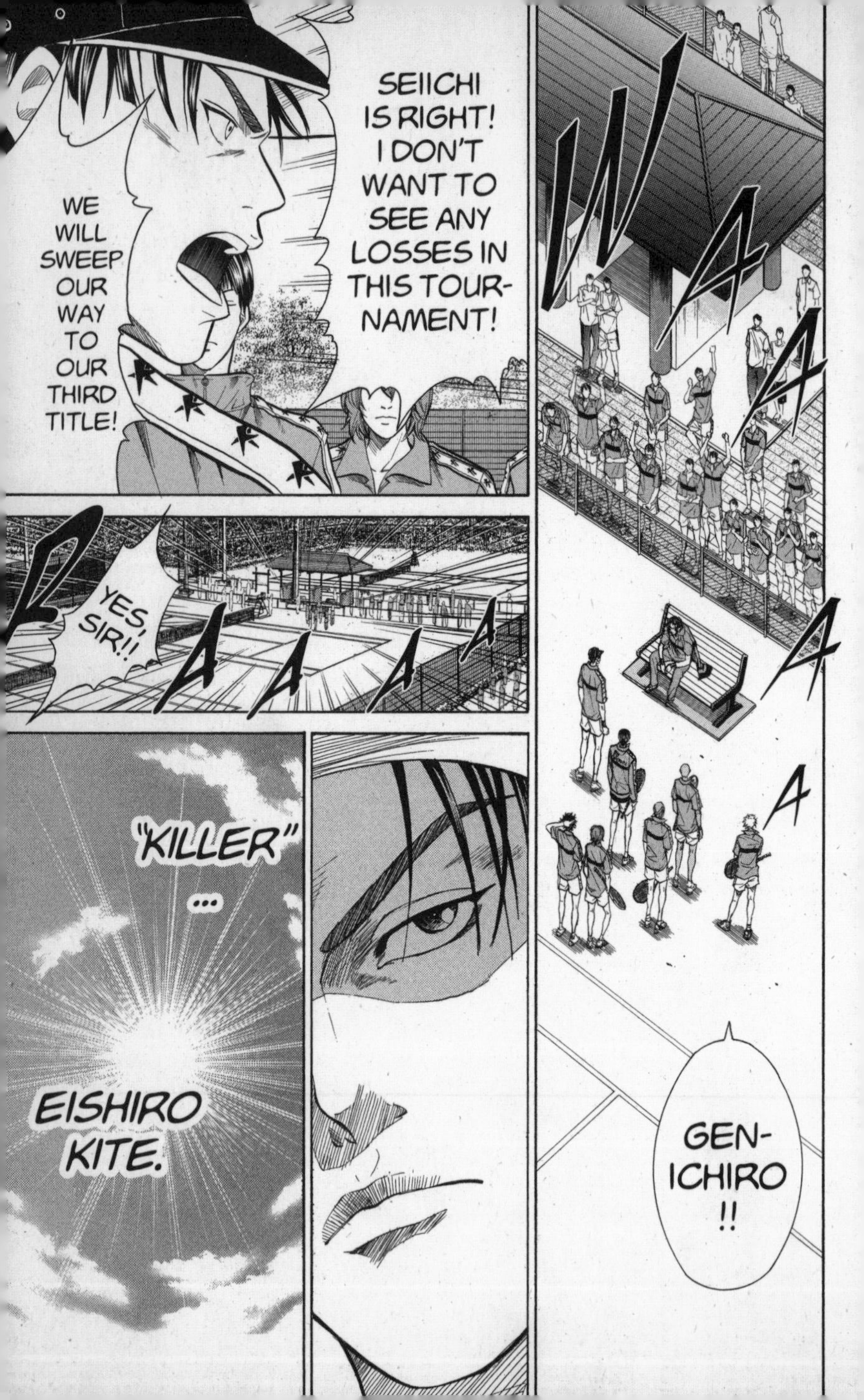
WAAAAA
GEN-ICHIRO!!
SEIICHI IS RIGHT! I DON'T WANT TO SEE ANY LOSSES IN THIS TOURNAMENT!
WE WILL SWEEP OUR WAY TO OUR THIRD TITLE!
YES, SIR!!
BAAAA
"KILLER" ...
EISHIRO KITE.

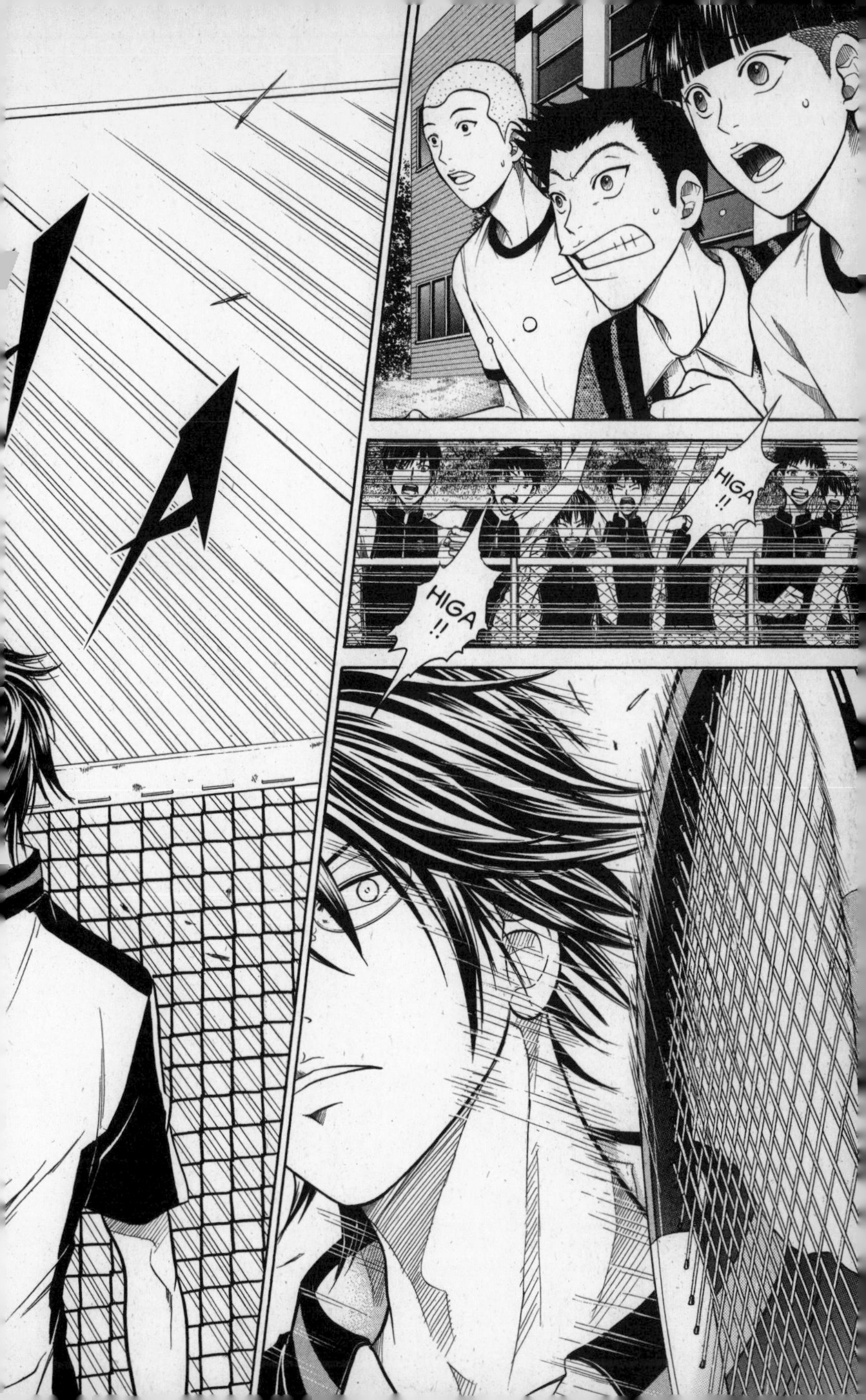
HIGA!!
HIGA!!

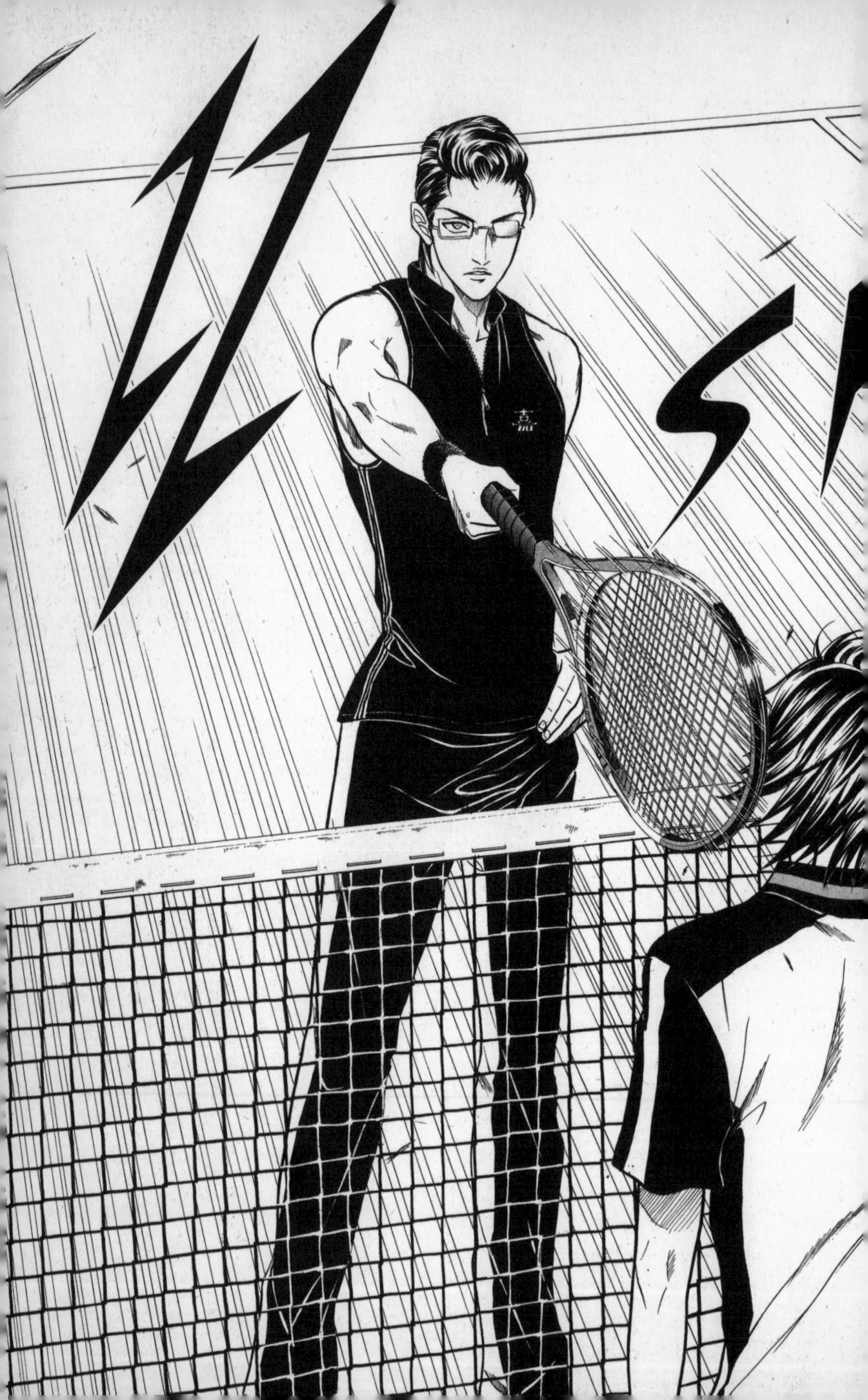

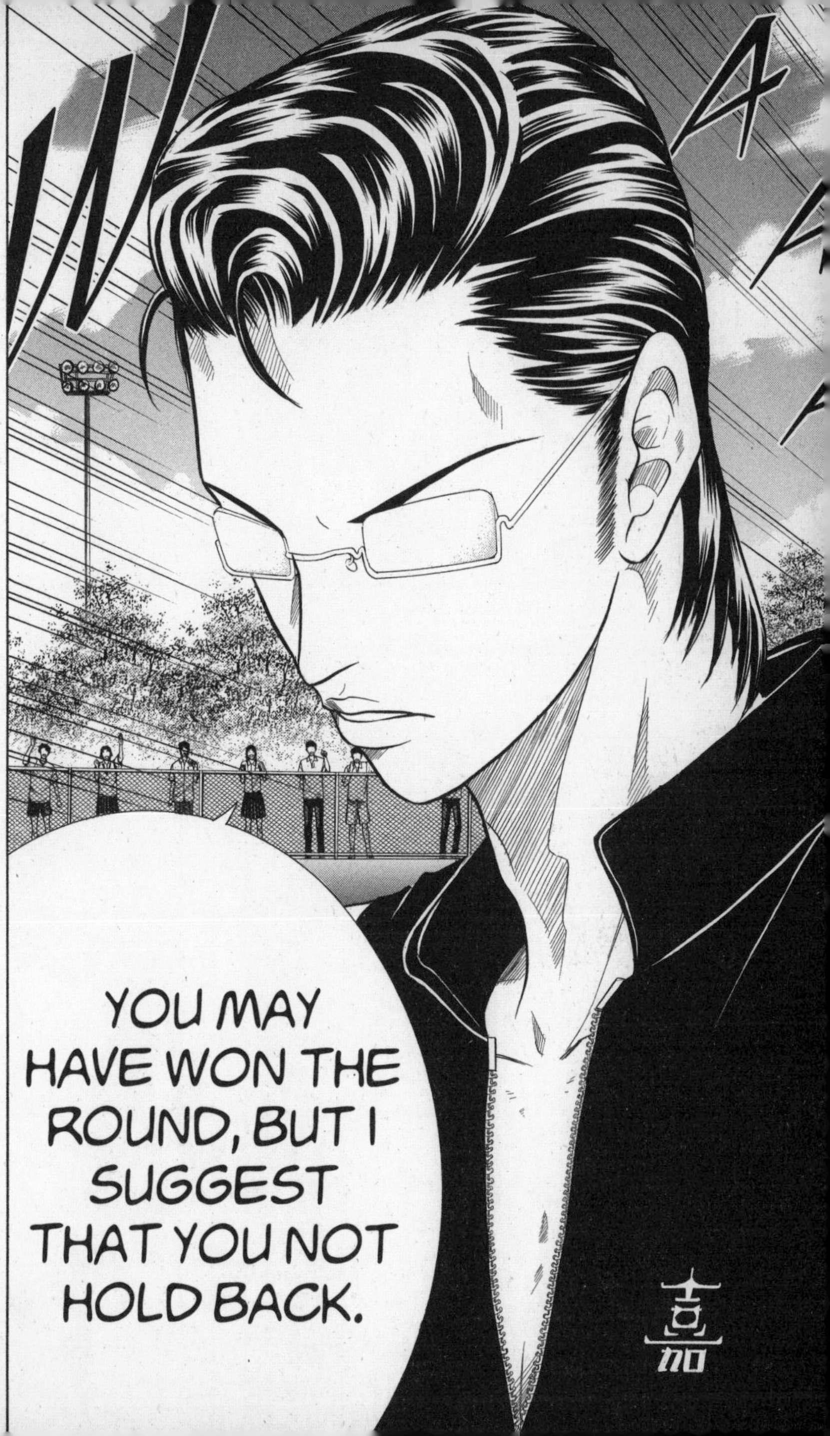
YOU MAY HAVE WON THE ROUND, BUT I SUGGEST THAT YOU NOT HOLD BACK.

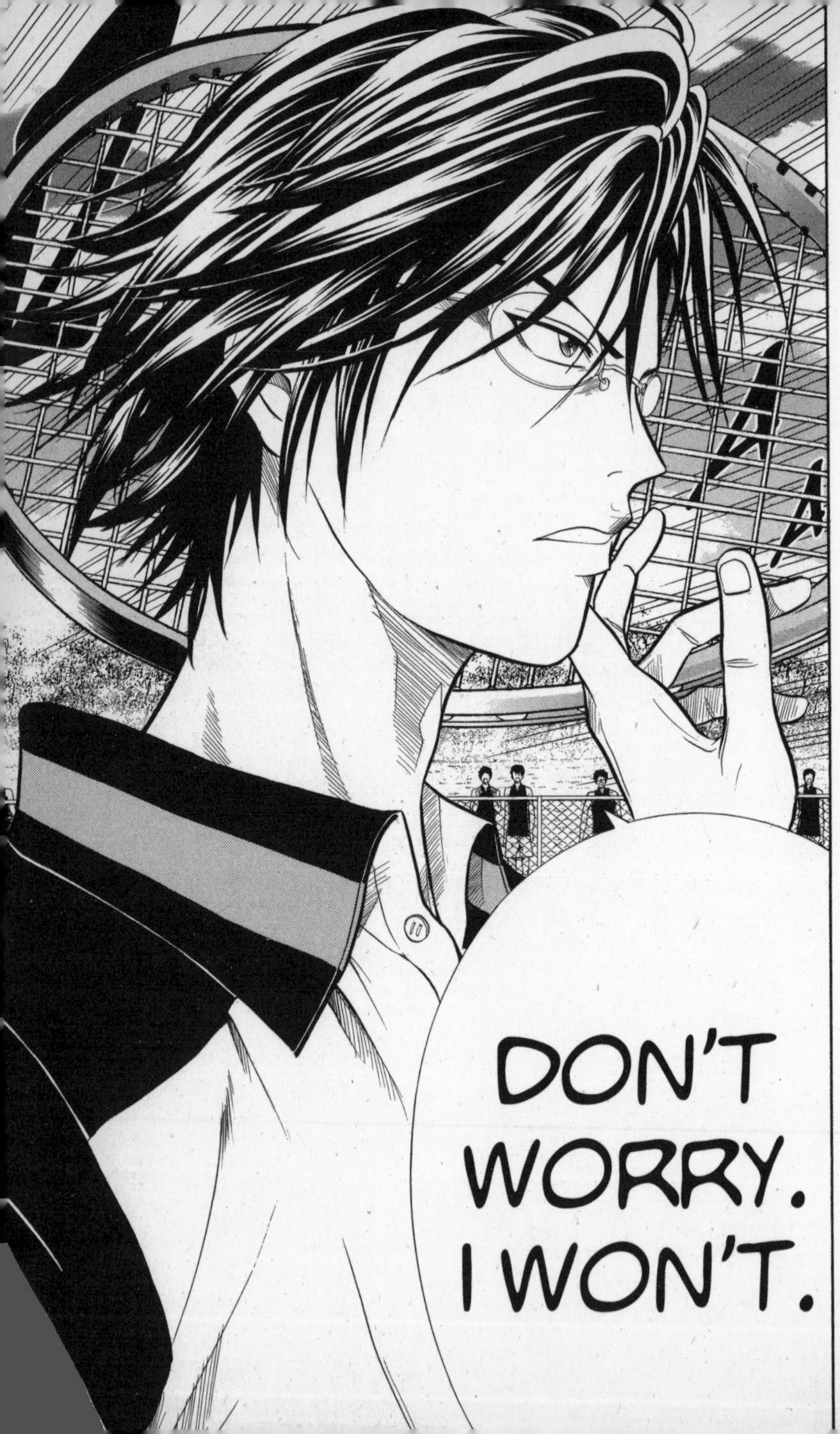
DON'T WORRY. I WON'T.

テニスの王子様

THE PRINCE OF TENNIS

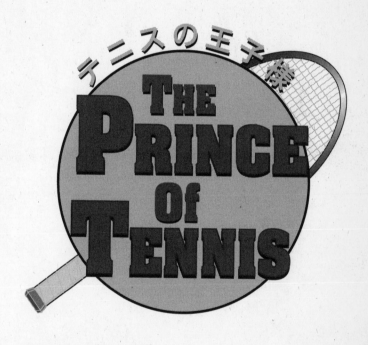

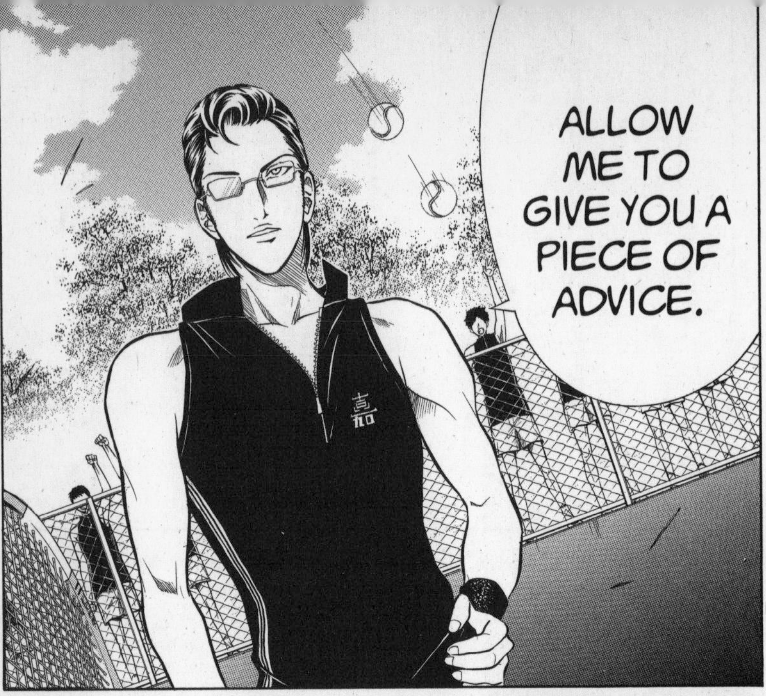
ALLOW ME TO GIVE YOU A PIECE OF ADVICE.

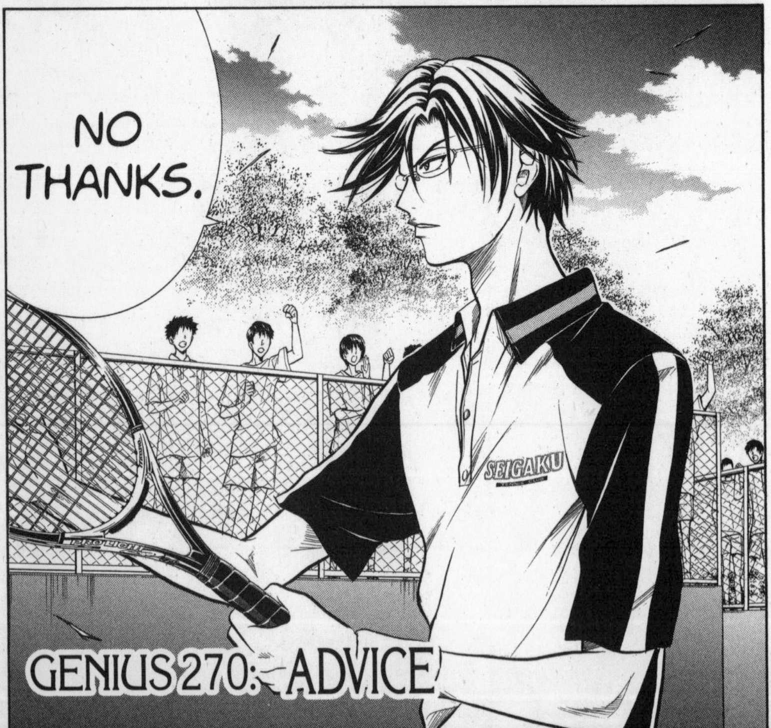
NO THANKS.
SEIGAKU
GENIUS 270: ADVICE

GENIUS 270: ADVICE

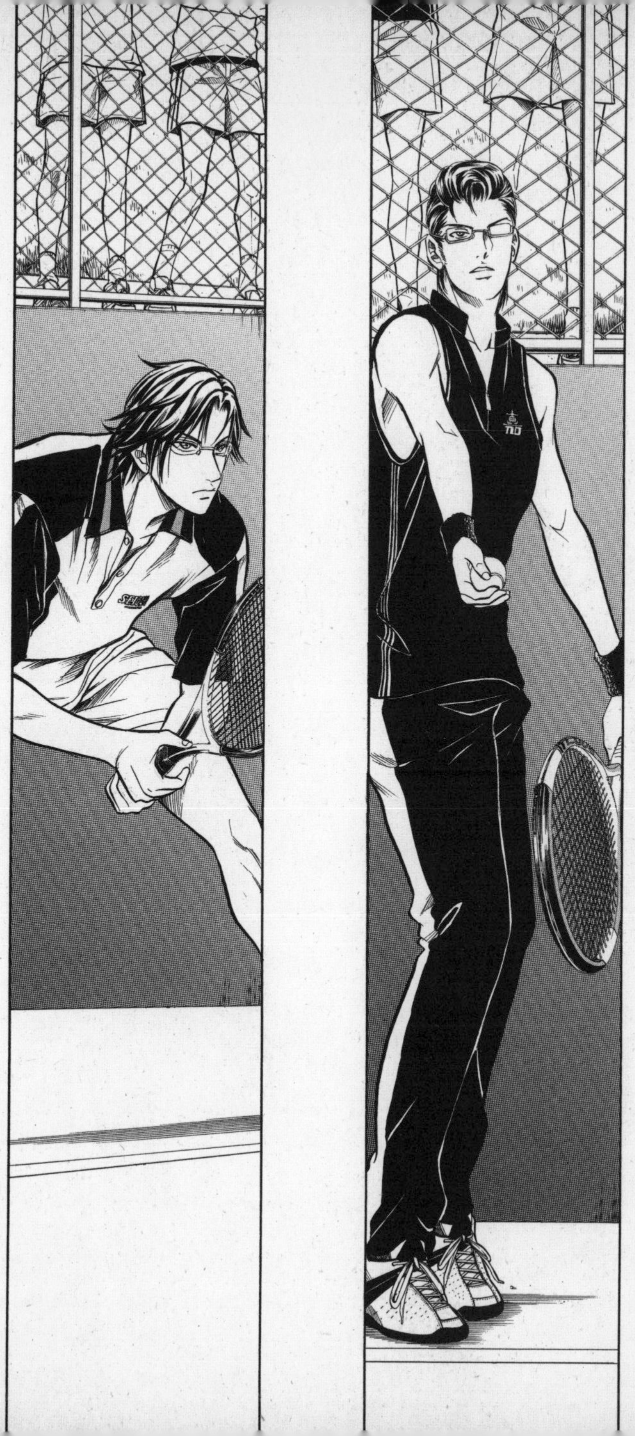

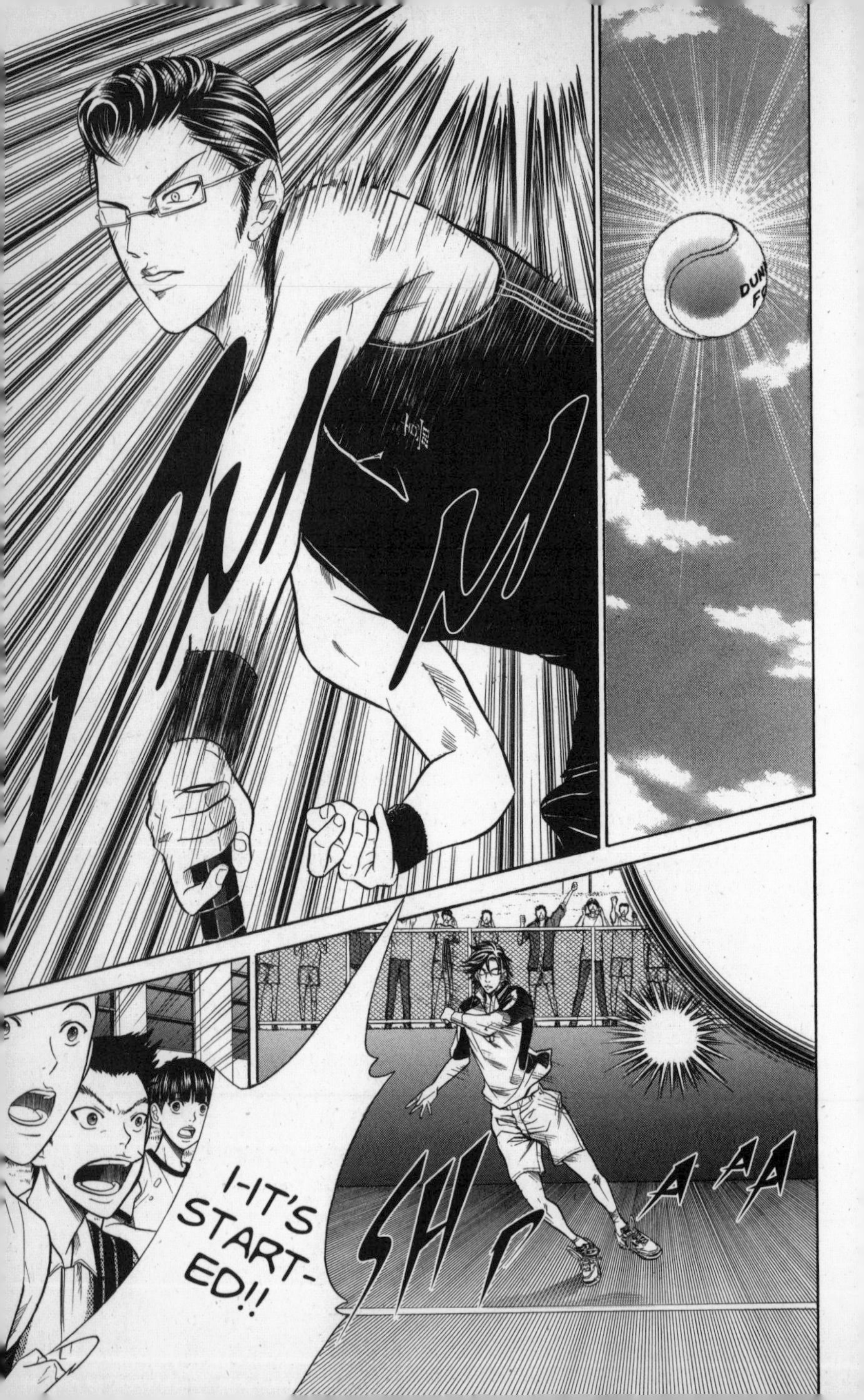
DUNL FO
I-IT'S START-ED!!
SH
A AA

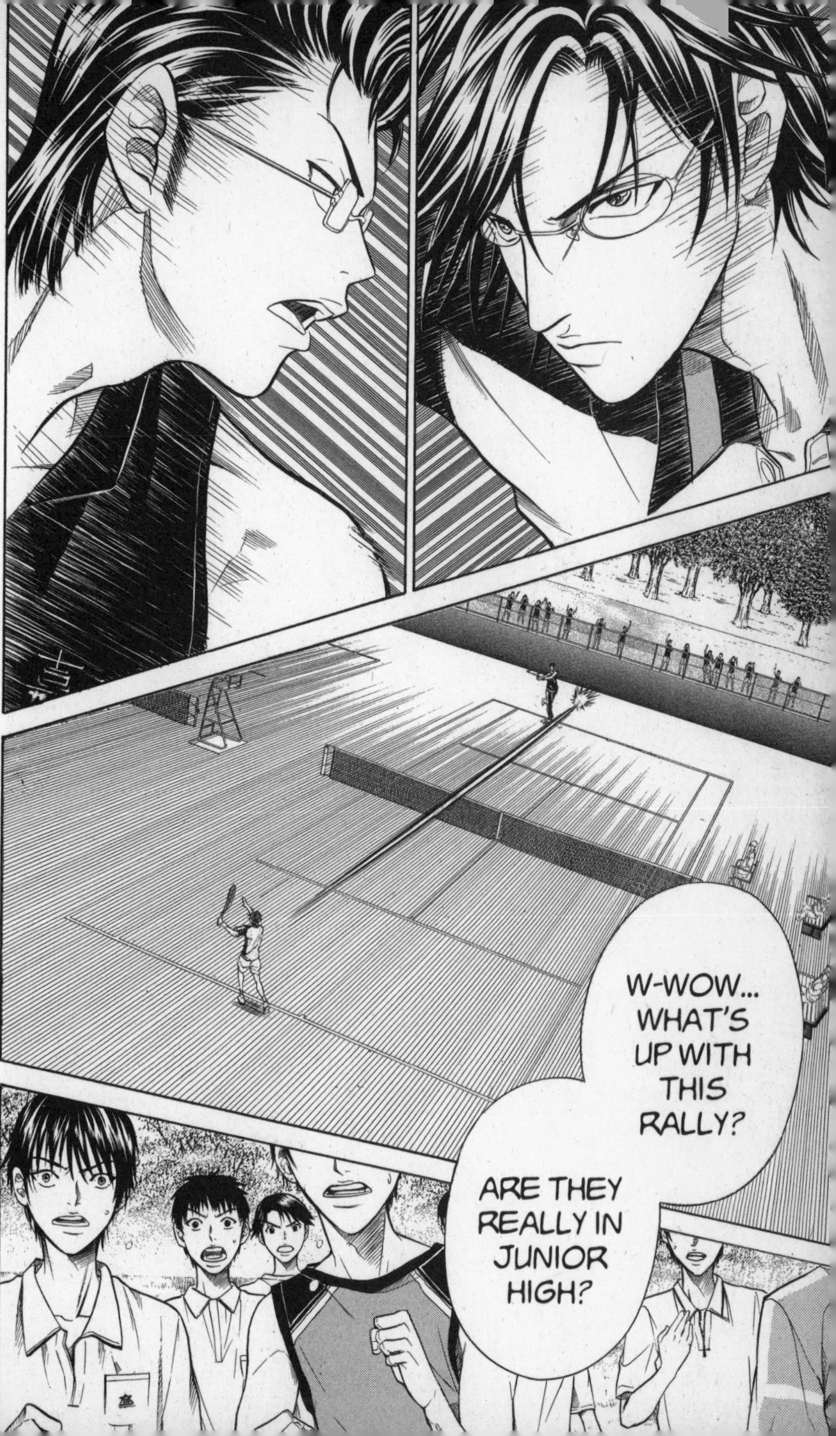
W-WOW... WHAT'S UP WITH THIS RALLY?
ARE THEY REALLY IN JUNIOR HIGH?

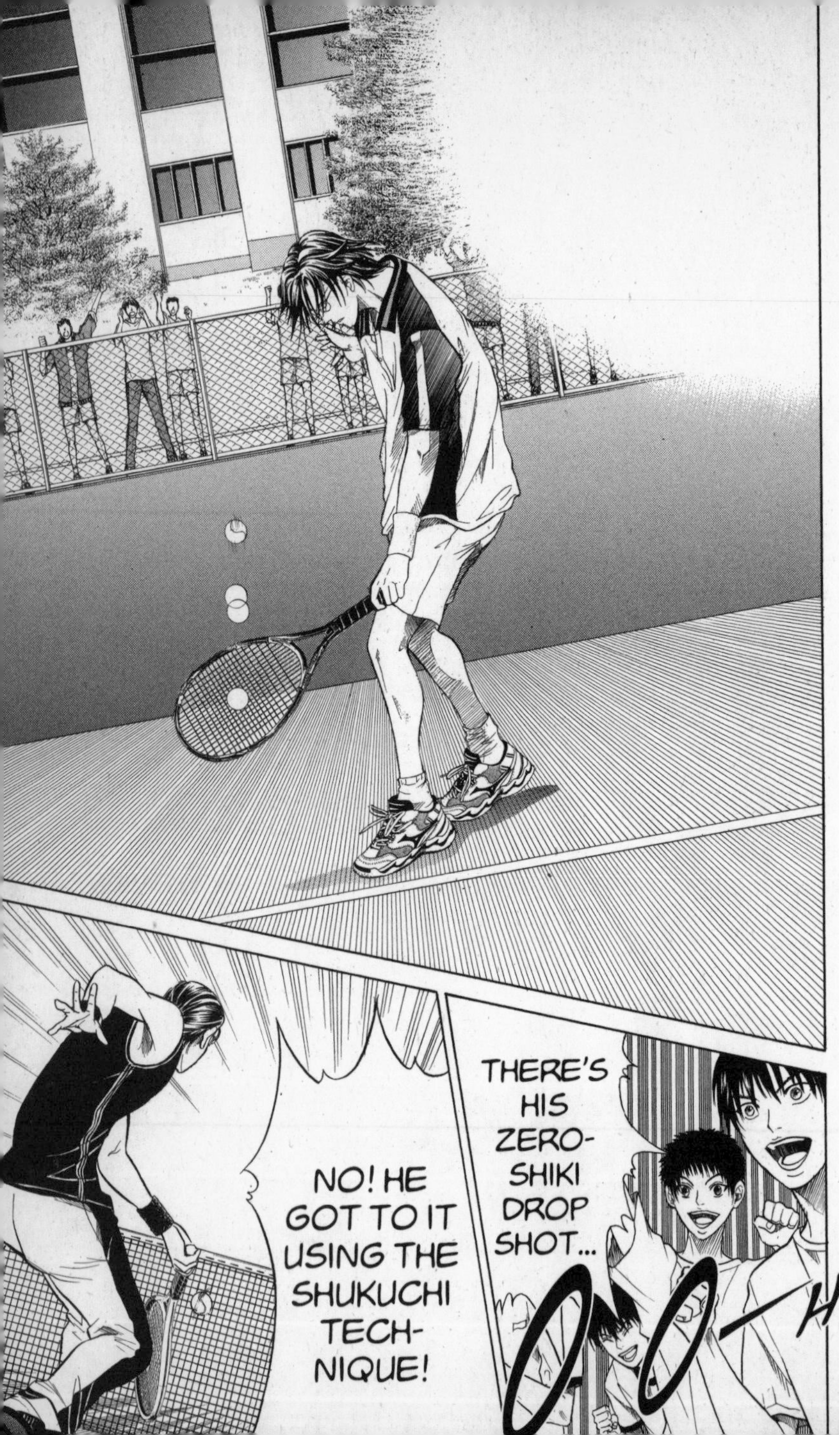
THERE'S HIS ZERO-SHIKI DROP SHOT...
OO—H
NO! HE GOT TO IT USING THE SHUKUCHI TECH-NIQUE!

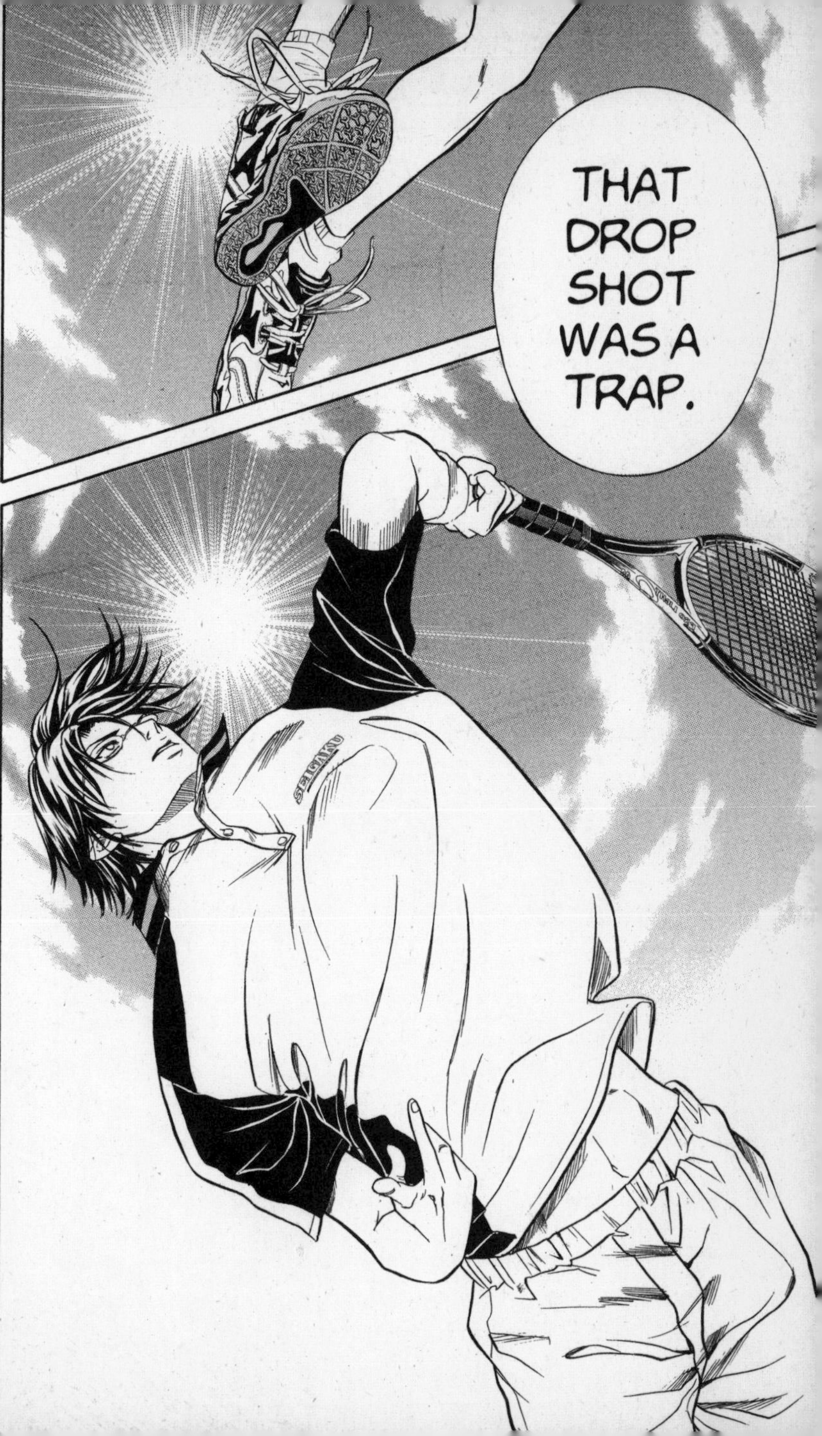
THAT DROP SHOT WAS A TRAP.

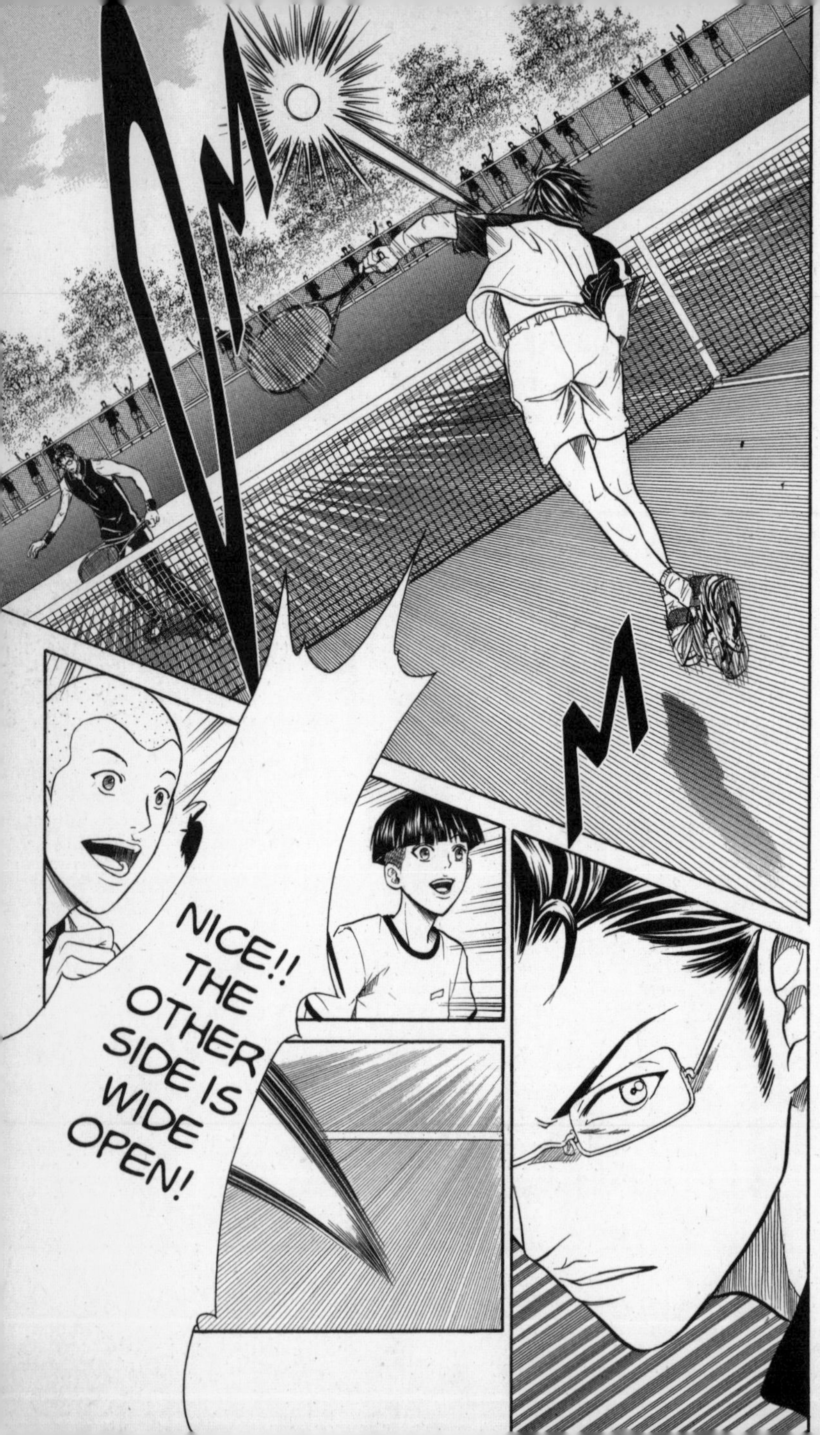
NICE!! THE OTHER SIDE IS WIDE OPEN!

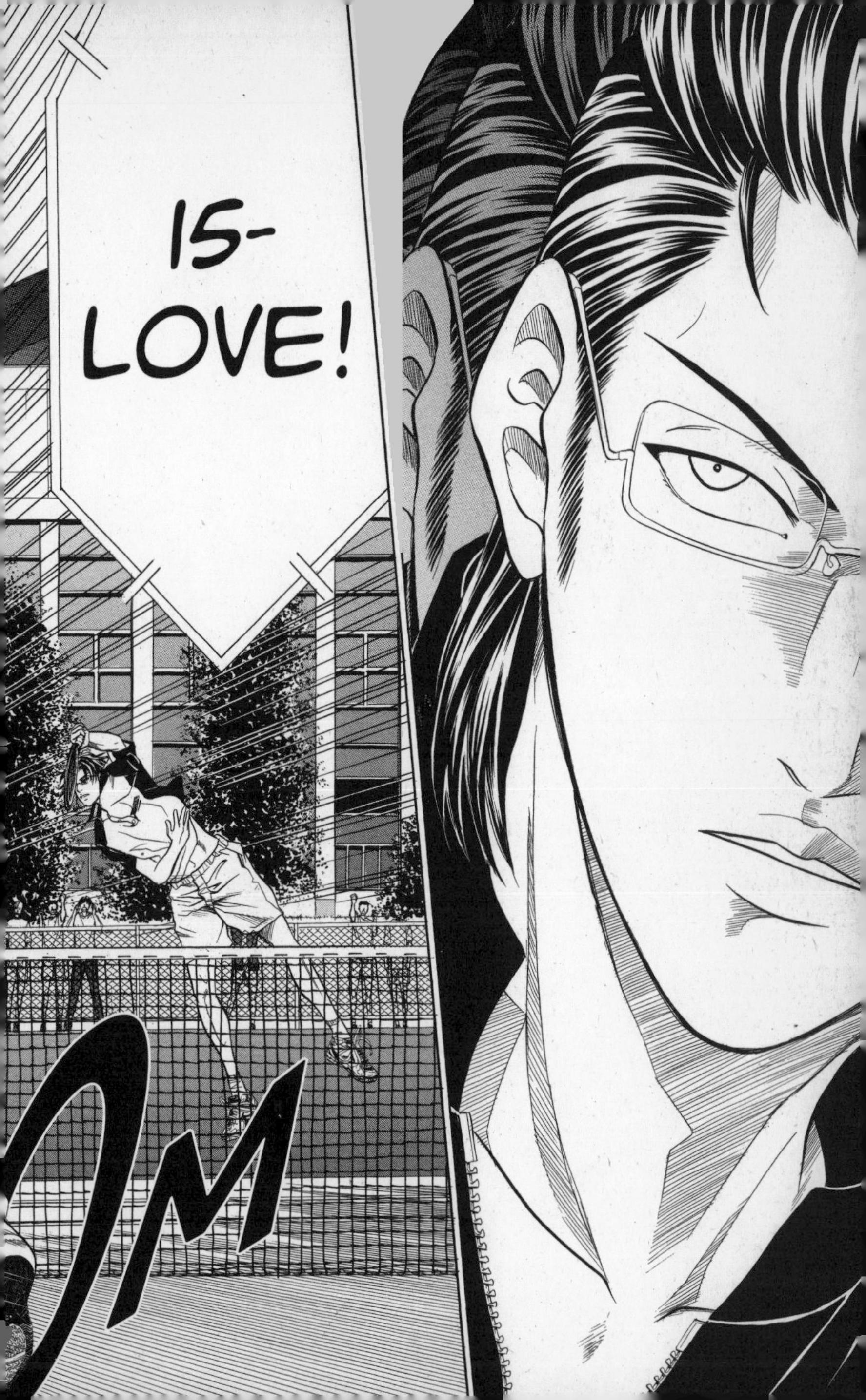
15-
LOVE!

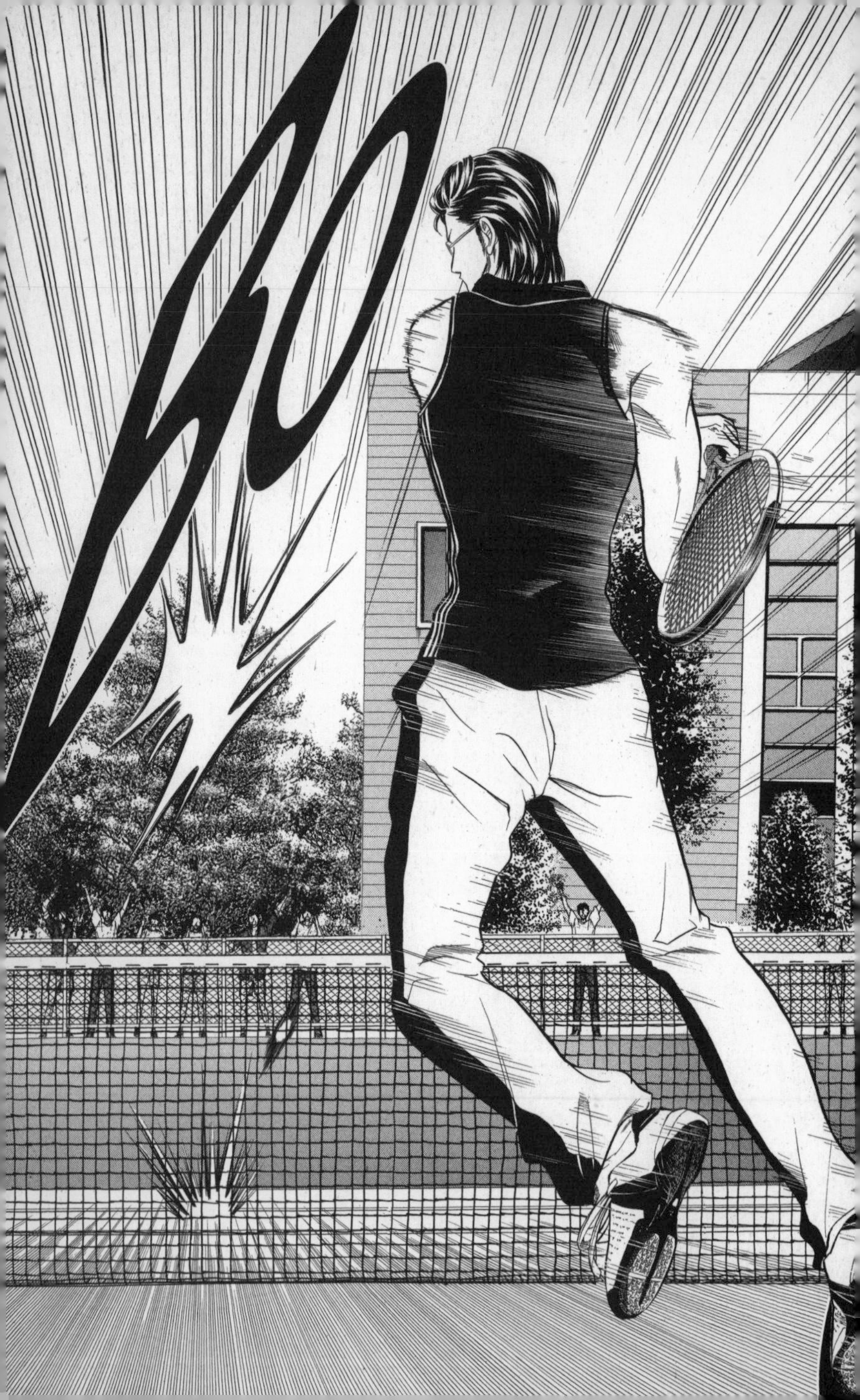

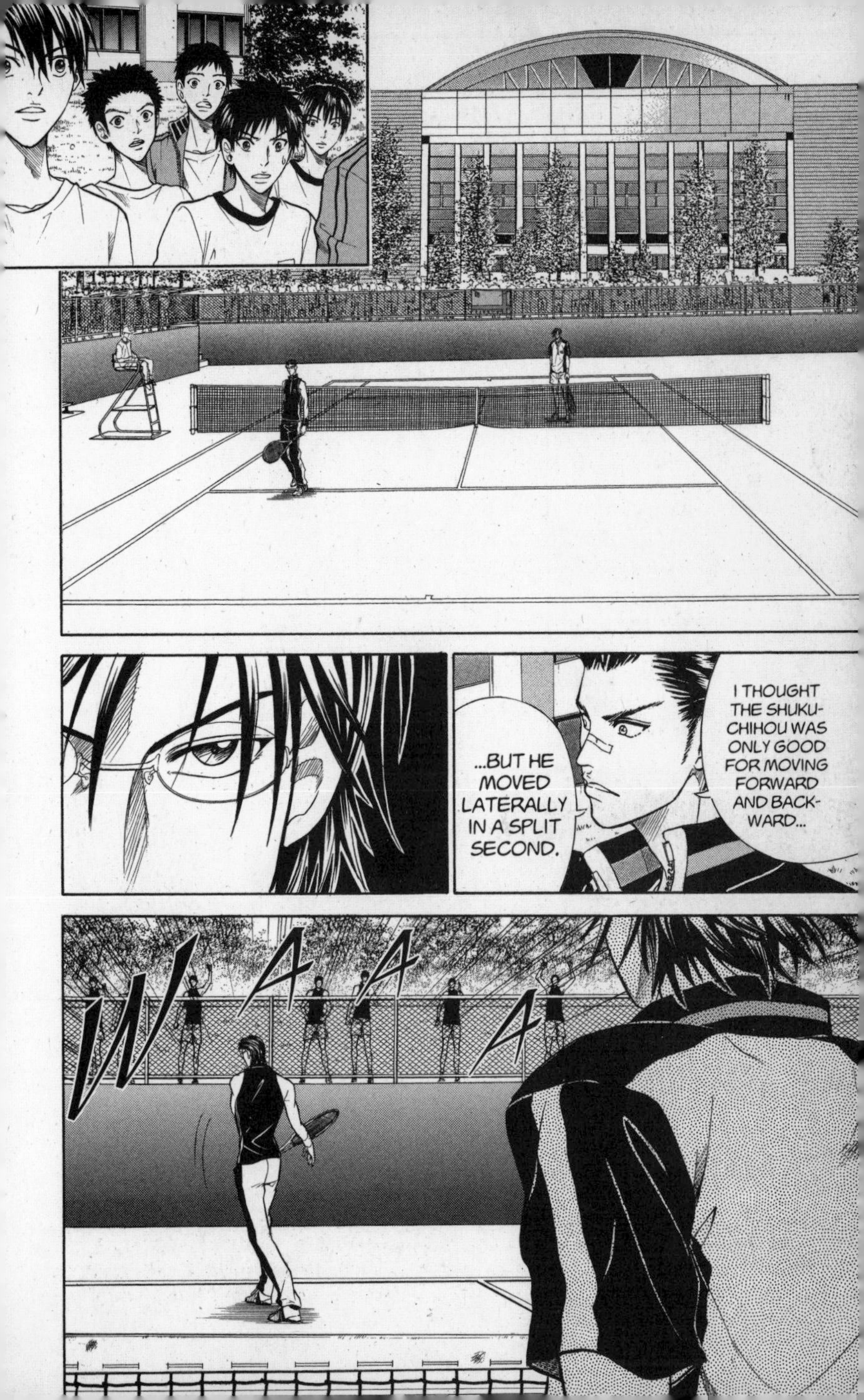
I THOUGHT THE SHUKU-CHIHOU WAS ONLY GOOD FOR MOVING FORWARD AND BACK-WARD...
...BUT HE MOVED LATERALLY IN A SPLIT SECOND.
WAAA

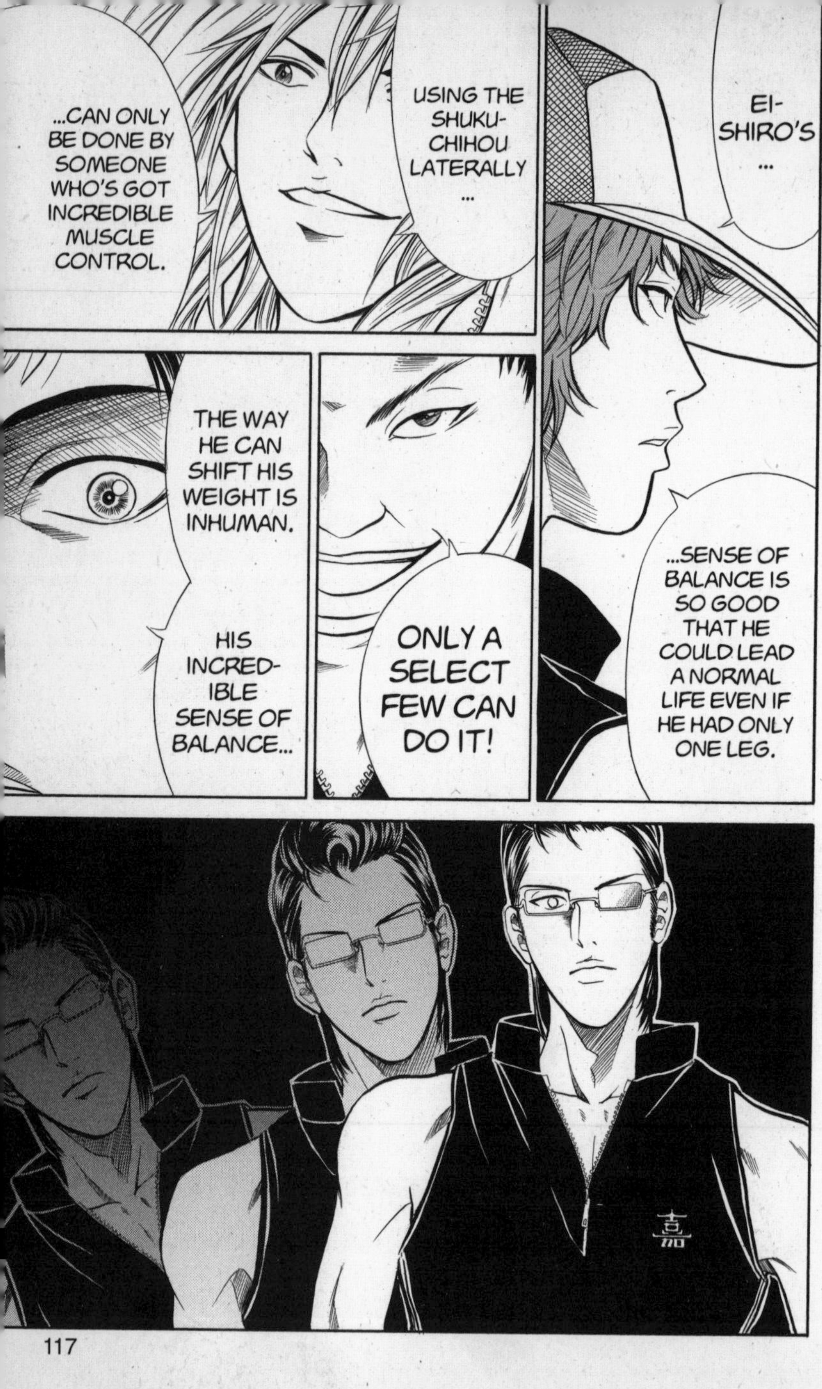
EI-SHIRO'S ...
...SENSE OF BALANCE IS SO GOOD THAT HE COULD LEAD A NORMAL LIFE EVEN IF HE HAD ONLY ONE LEG.
USING THE SHUKU-CHIHOU LATERALLY ...
...CAN ONLY BE DONE BY SOMEONE WHO'S GOT INCREDIBLE MUSCLE CONTROL.
ONLY A SELECT FEW CAN DO IT!
THE WAY HE CAN SHIFT HIS WEIGHT IS INHUMAN.
HIS INCRED-IBLE SENSE OF BALANCE...

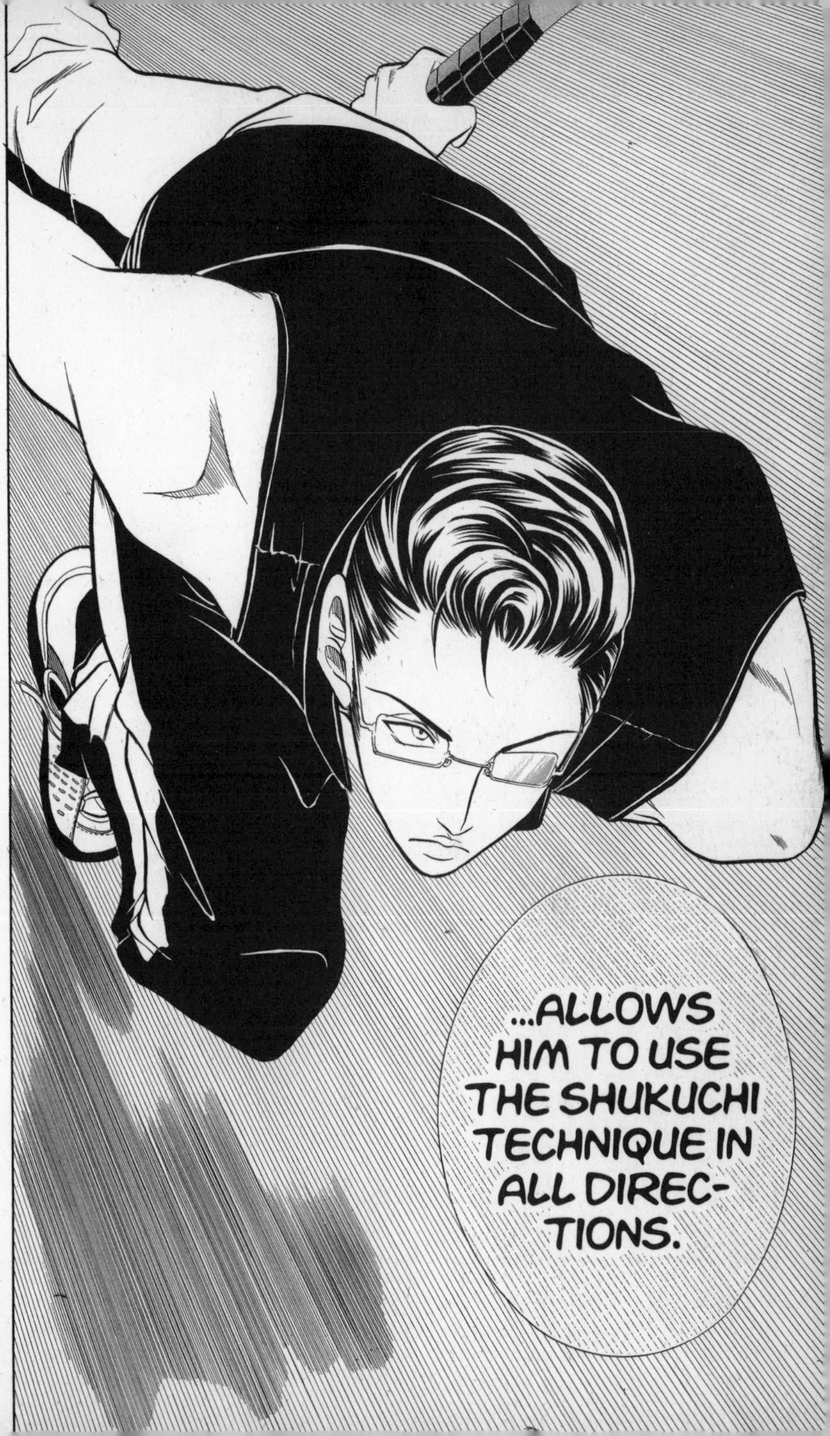
...ALLOWS HIM TO USE THE SHUKUCHI TECHNIQUE IN ALL DIREC- TIONS.

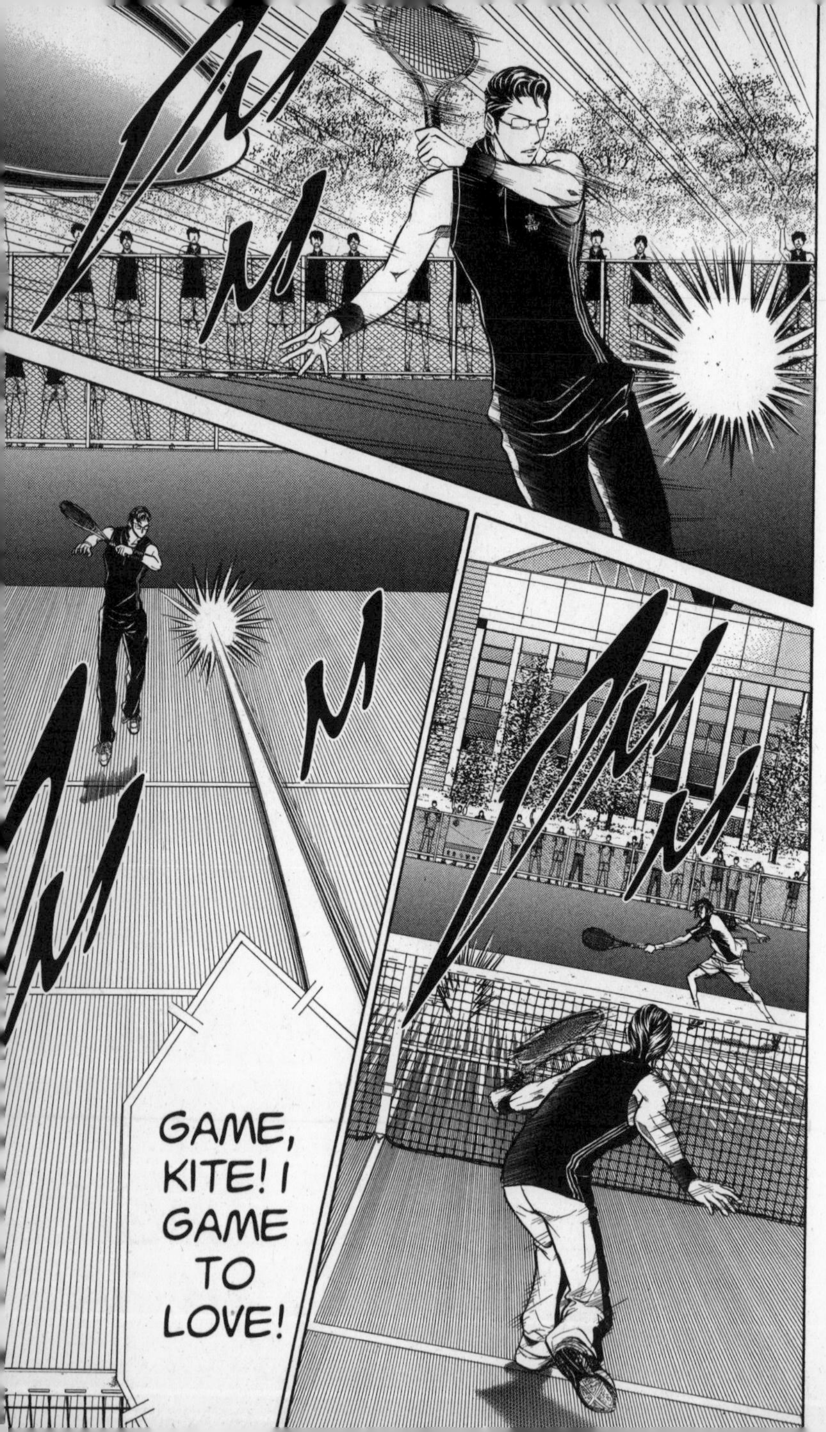
GAME, KITE! 1 GAME TO LOVE!

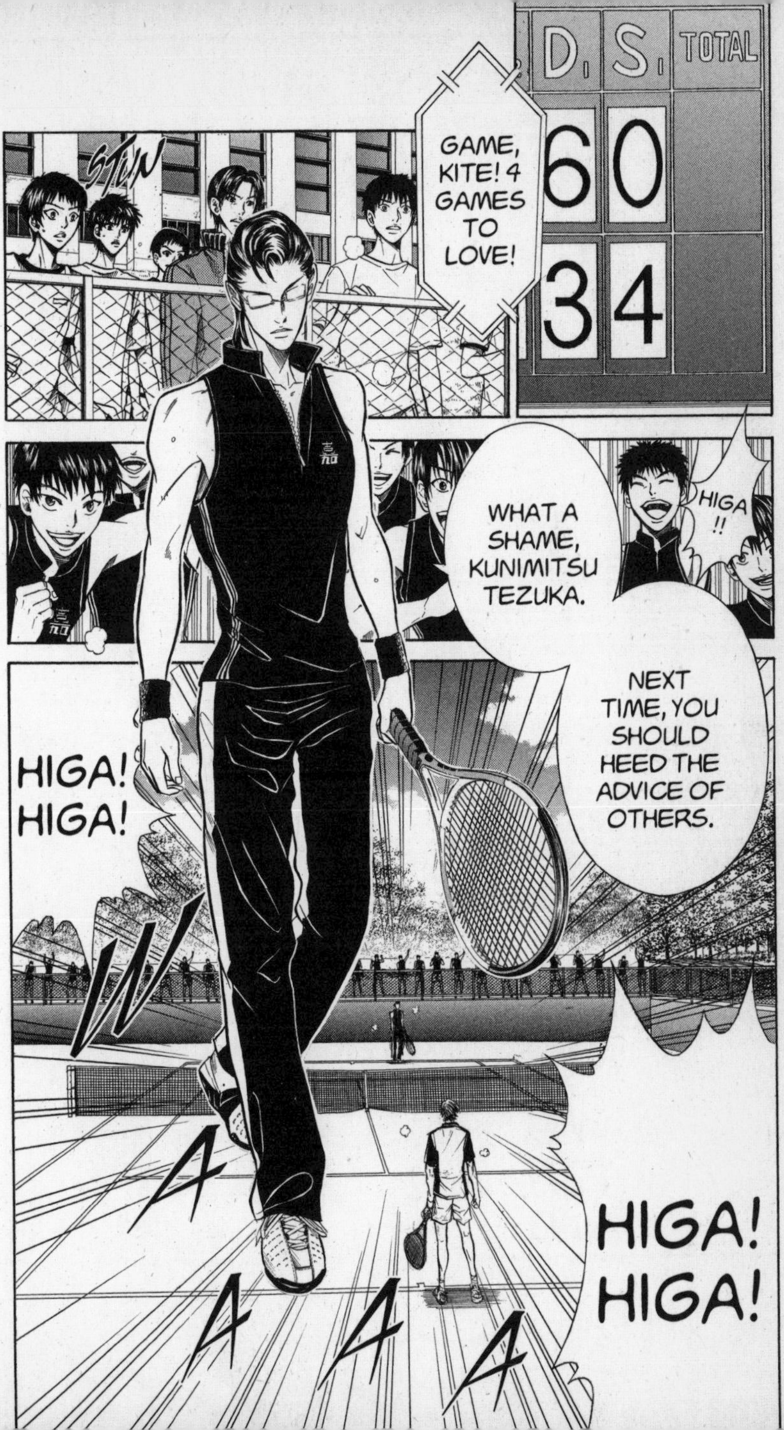
D. S. TOTAL
6 0
3 4
GAME, KITE! 4 GAMES TO LOVE!
STUN
HIGA !!
WHAT A SHAME, KUNIMITSU TEZUKA.
NEXT TIME, YOU SHOULD HEED THE ADVICE OF OTHERS.
HIGA! HIGA!
HIGA! HIGA!
WAAAA

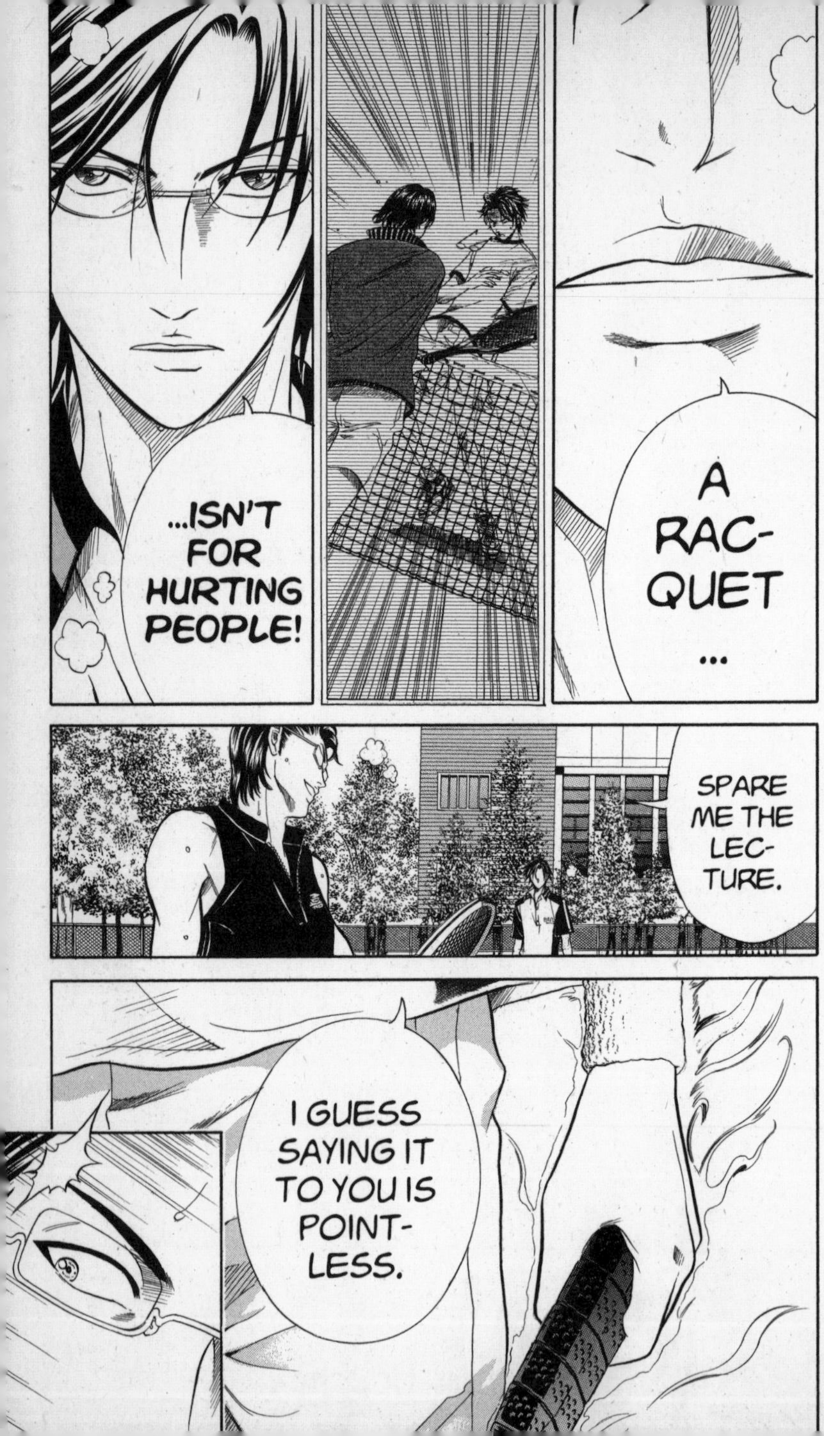
A RAC-QUET ...
...ISN'T FOR HURTING PEOPLE!
SPARE ME THE LEC-TURE.
I GUESS SAYING IT TO YOU IS POINT-LESS.

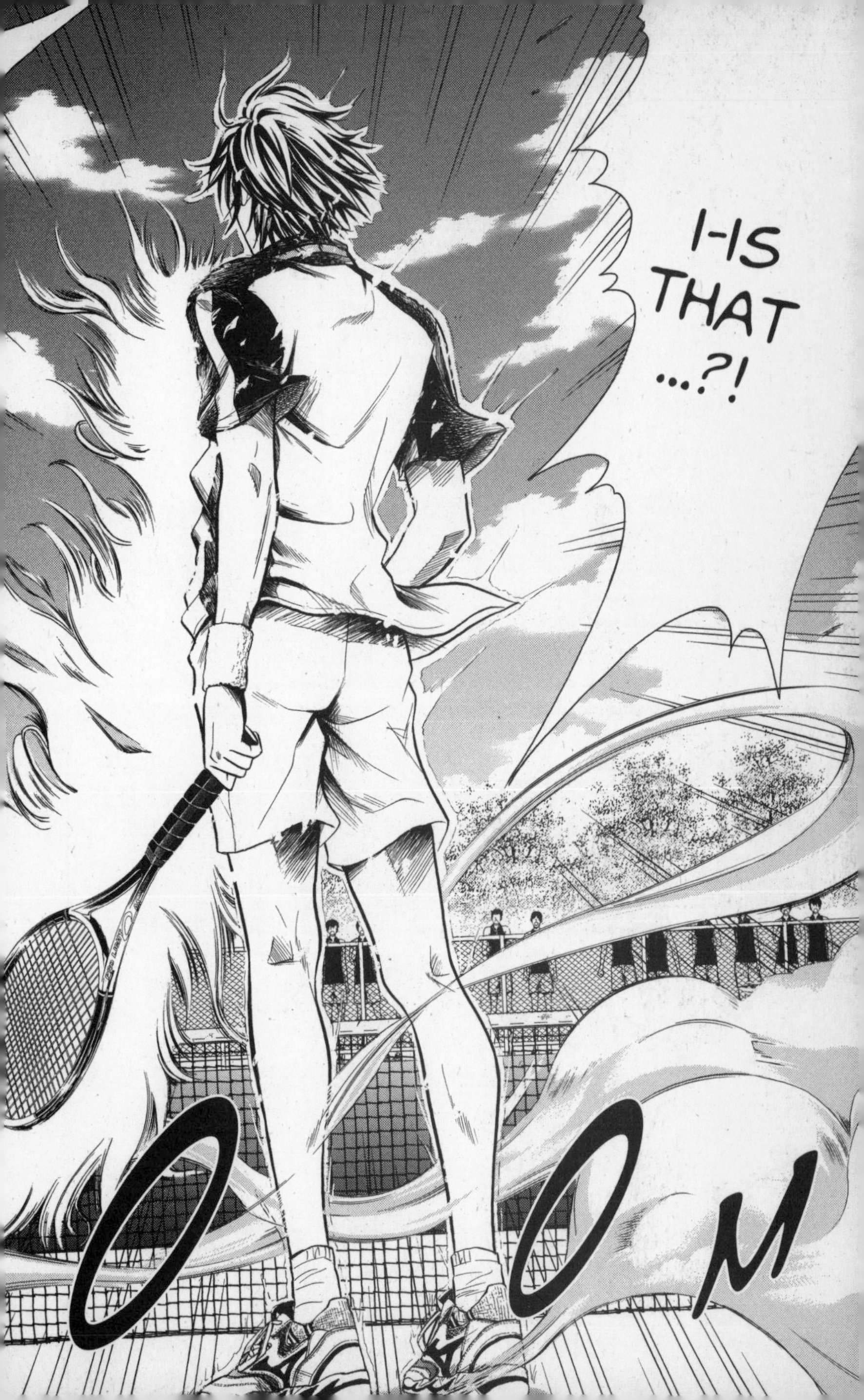
I-IS THAT ...?!
OOM

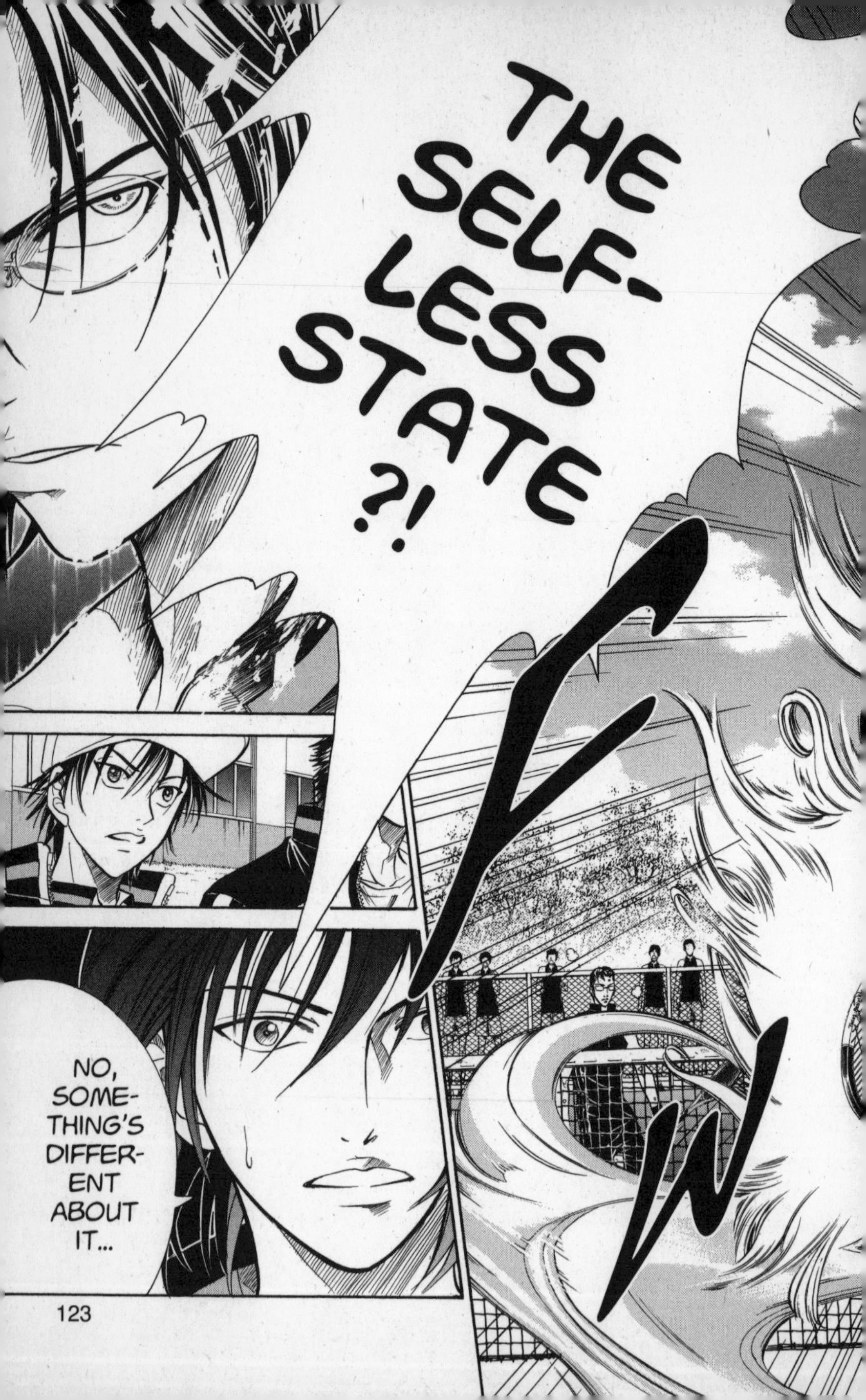
THE SELF-LESS STATE?!
NO, SOME-THING'S DIFFER-ENT ABOUT IT...

テニスの王子様

THE PRINCE OF TENNIS

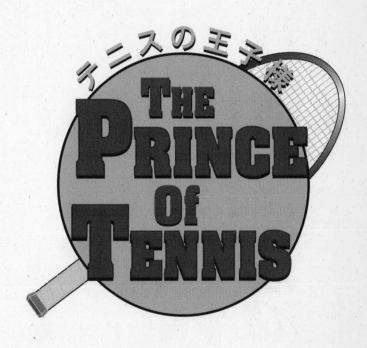

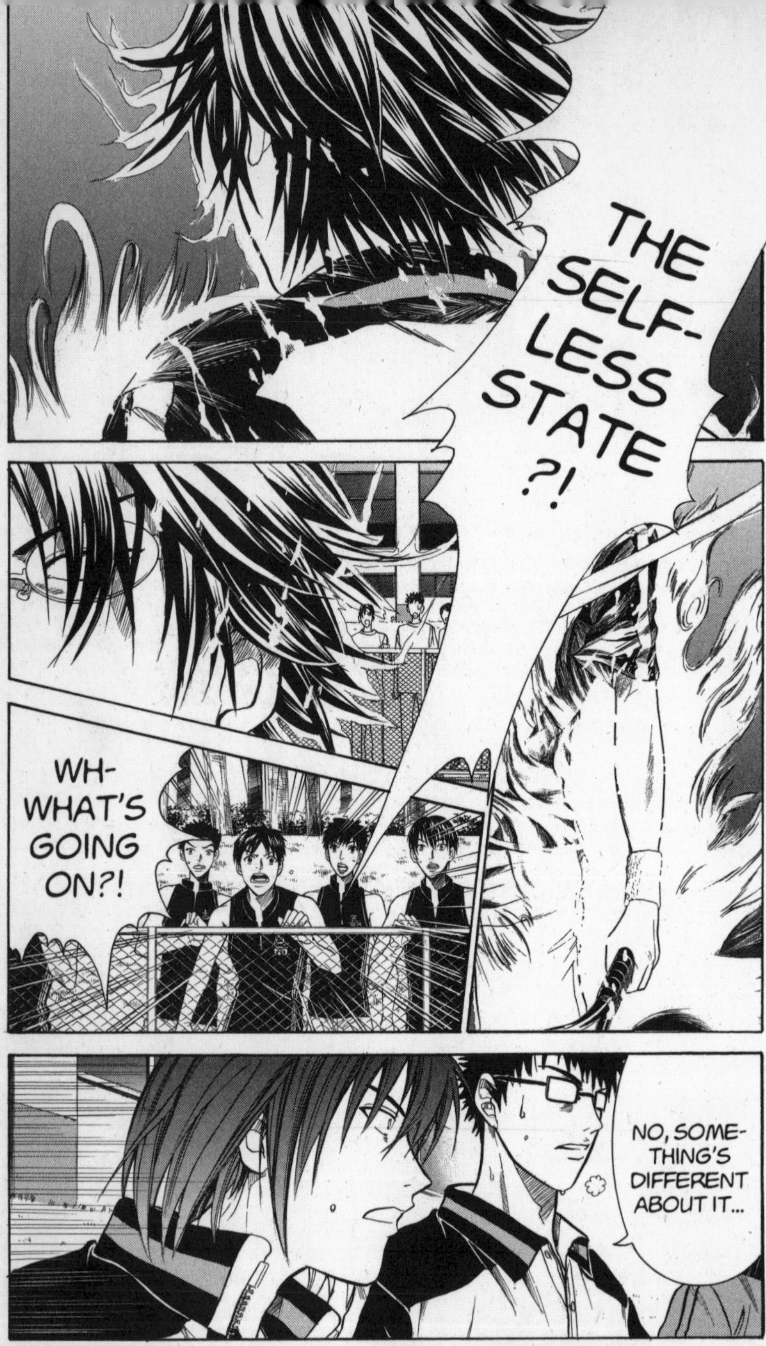
THE SELF-LESS STATE ?!
WH-WHAT'S GOING ON?!
NO, SOME-THING'S DIFFERENT ABOUT IT...

GENIUS 271: TOTAL COMEBACK

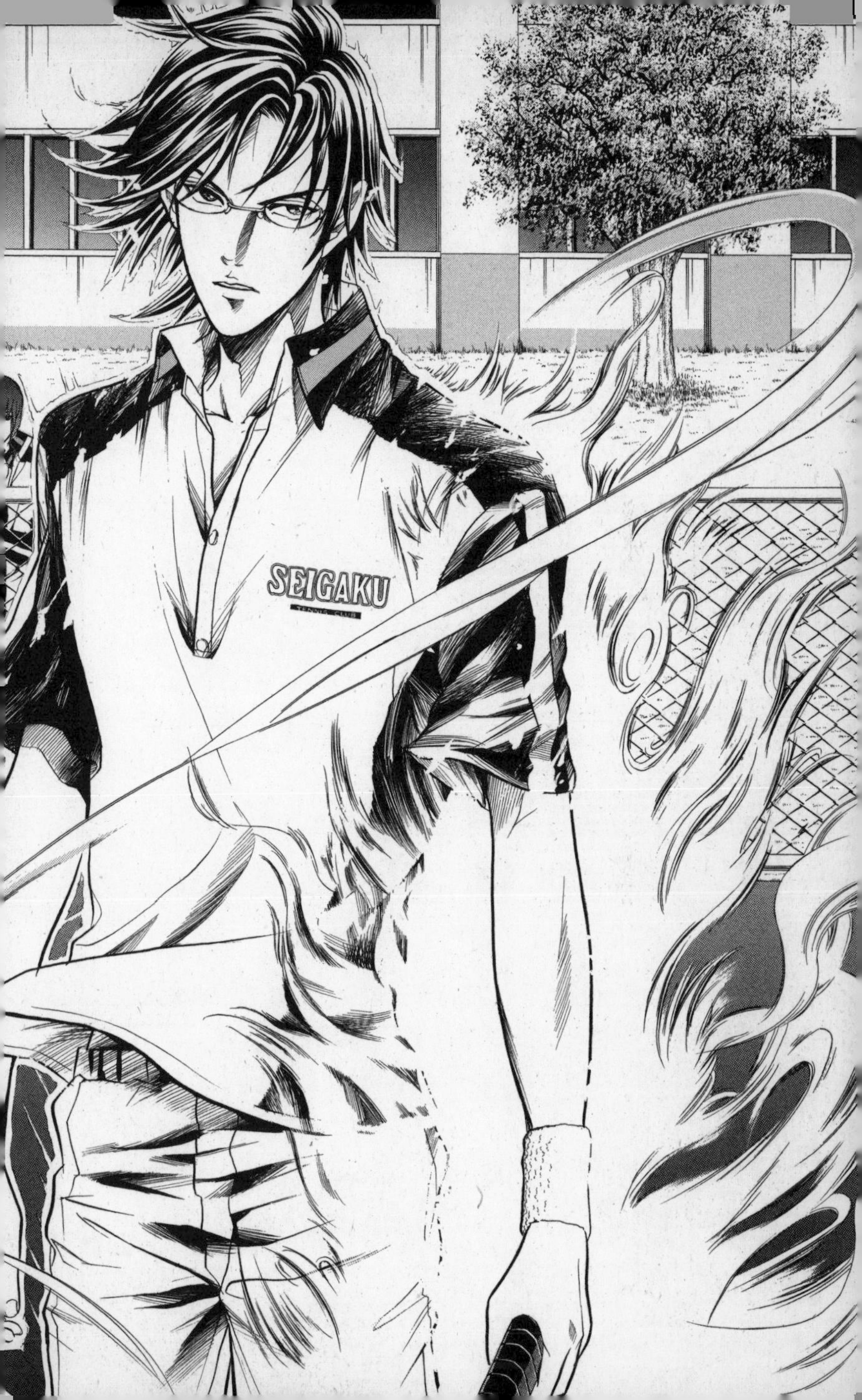
SEIGAKU

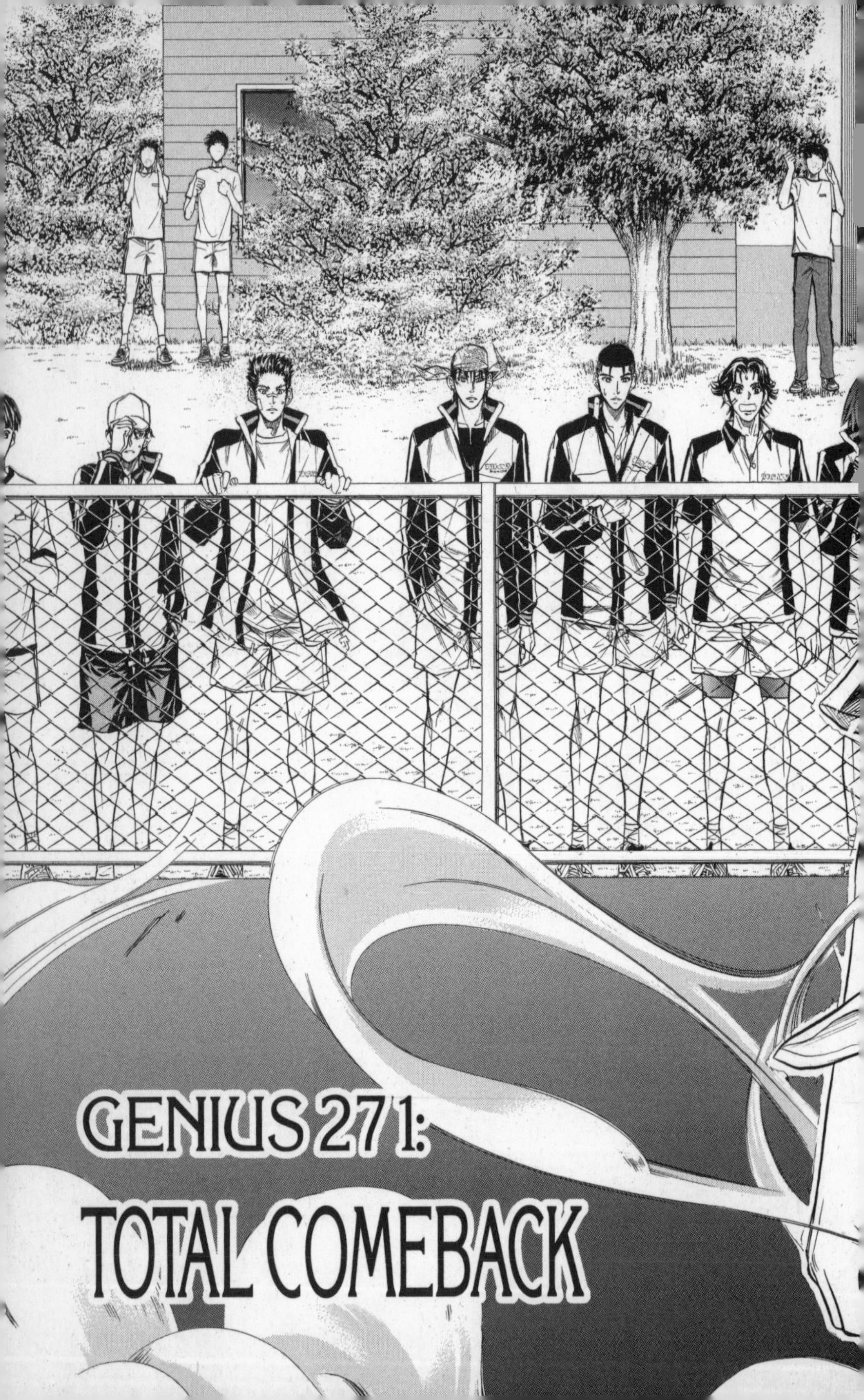
GENIUS 271:
TOTAL COMEBACK

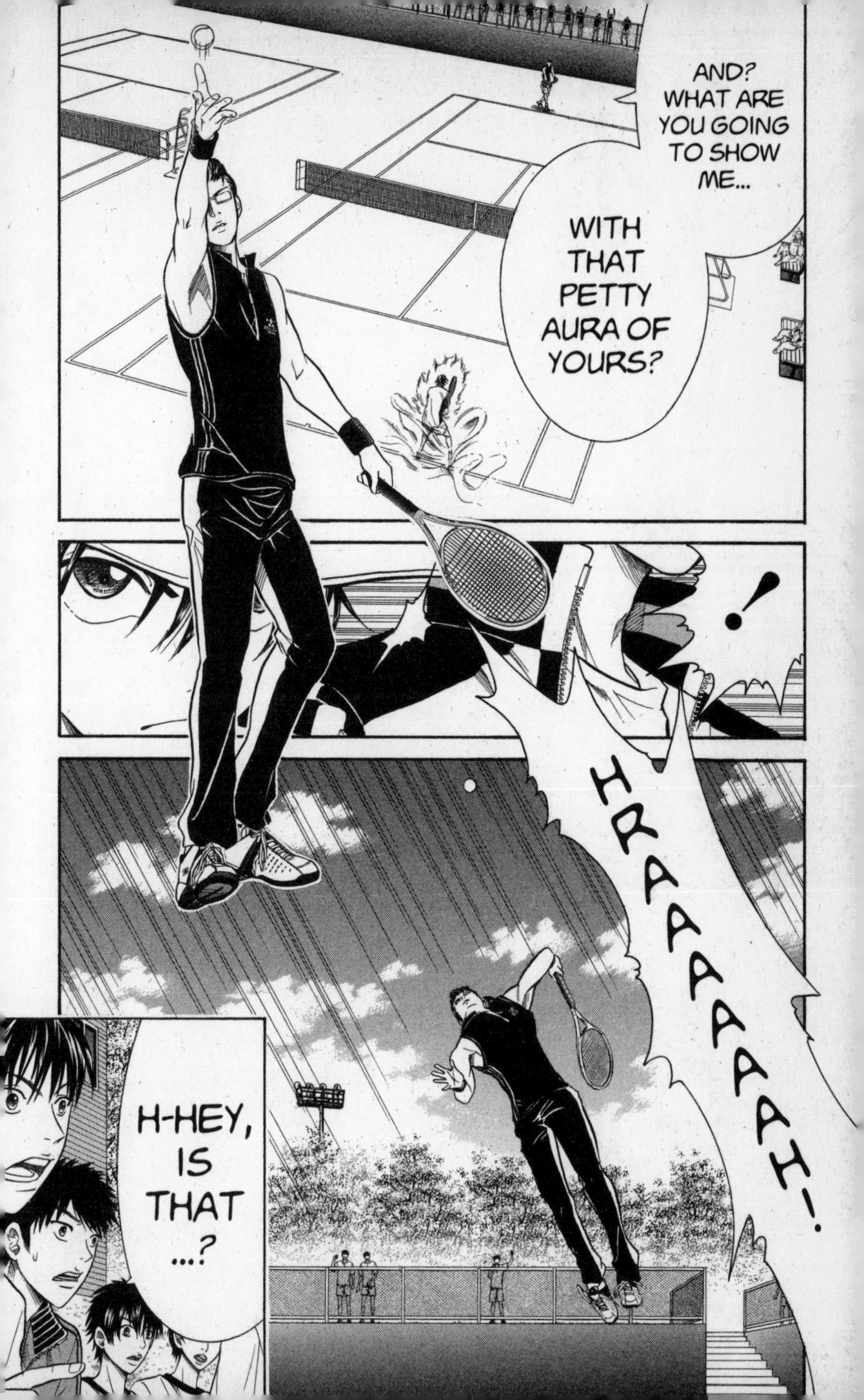
AND? WHAT ARE YOU GOING TO SHOW ME...
WITH THAT PETTY AURA OF YOURS?
!
HRAAAAAAH!
H-HEY, IS THAT ...?

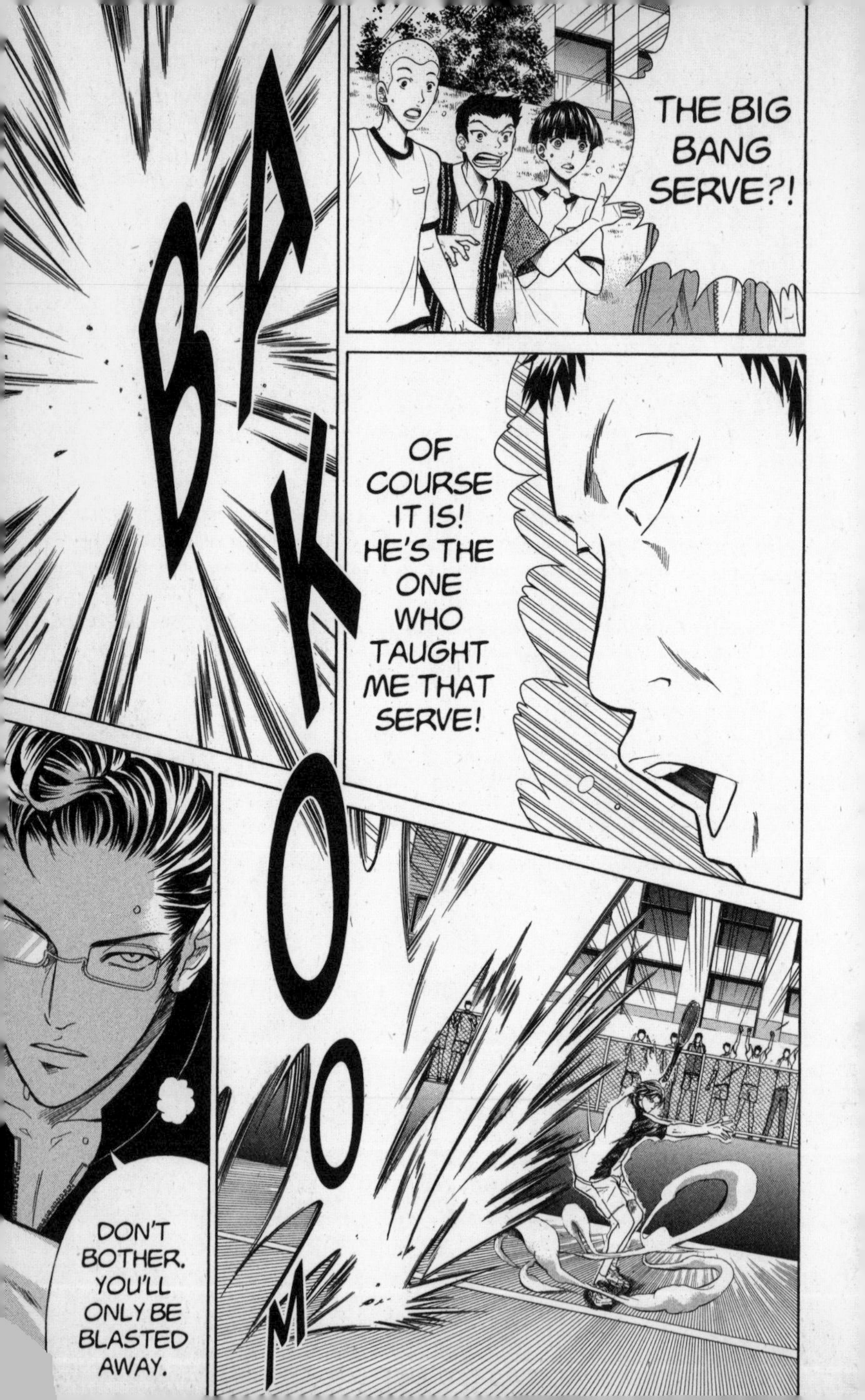
THE BIG BANG SERVE?!
OF COURSE IT IS! HE'S THE ONE WHO TAUGHT ME THAT SERVE!
BAKOOOM
DON'T BOTHER. YOU'LL ONLY BE BLASTED AWAY.

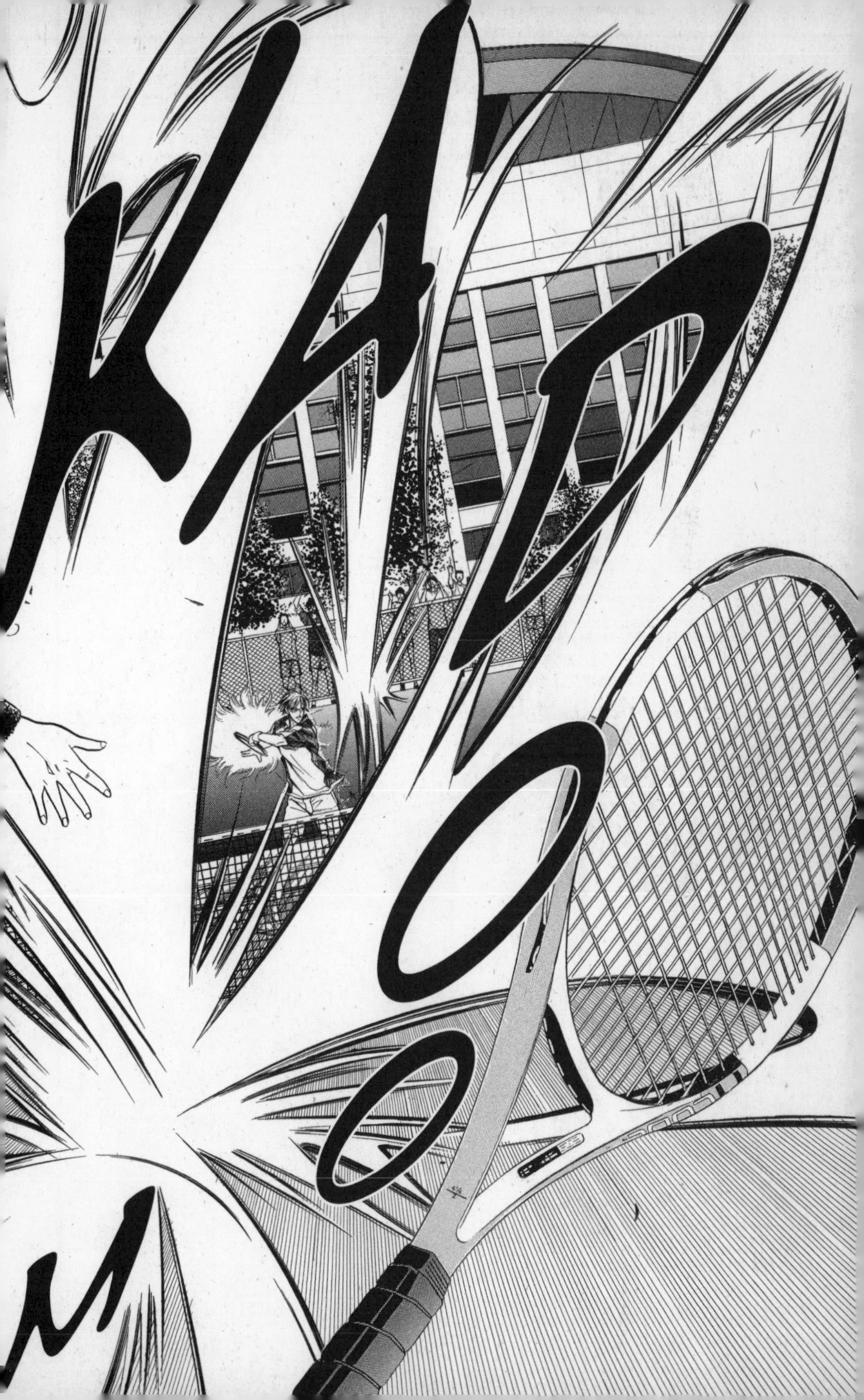
KAPOOM

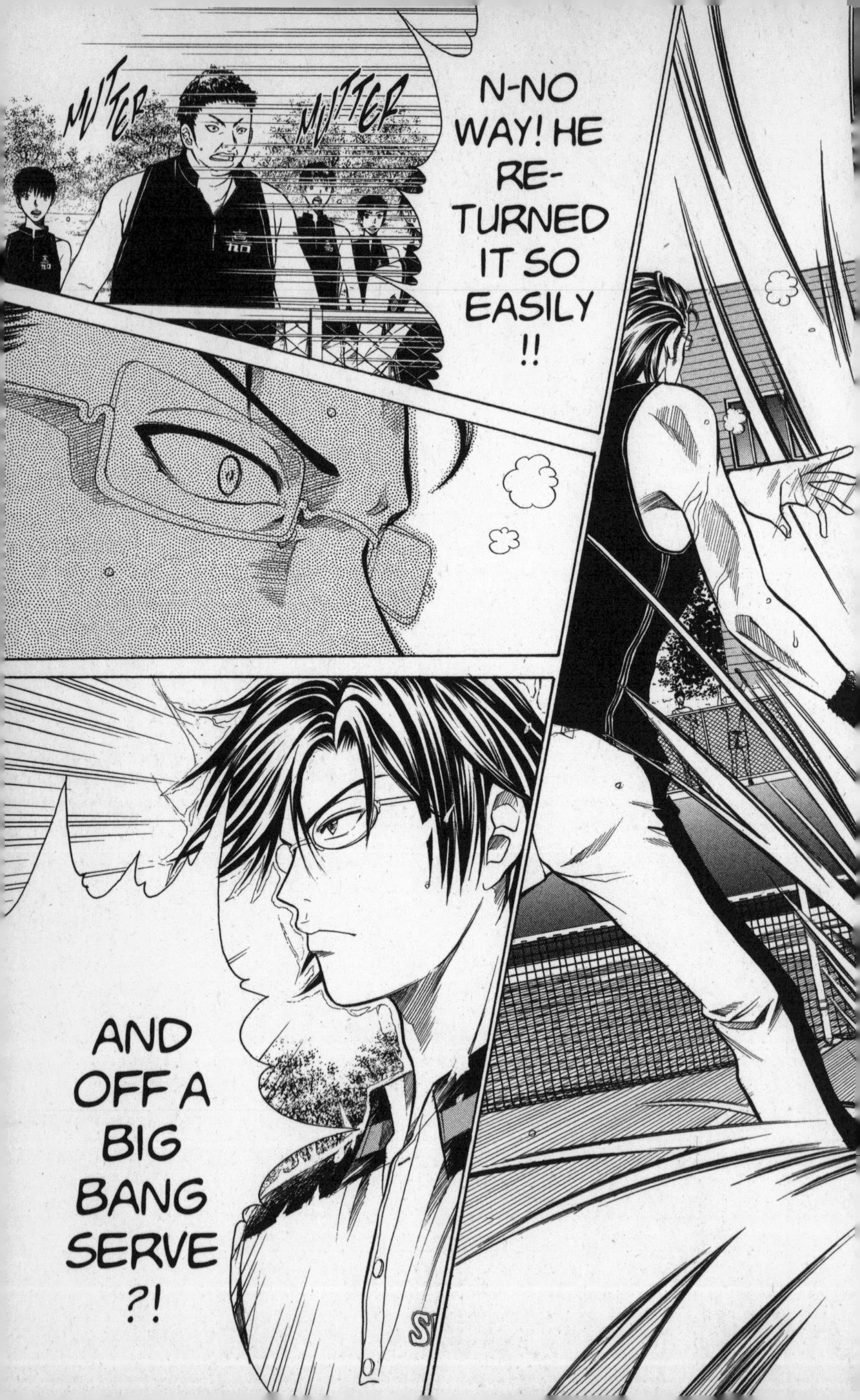
MUTTER
MUTTER
N-NO WAY! HE RE-TURNED IT SO EASILY!!
AND OFF A BIG BANG SERVE?!

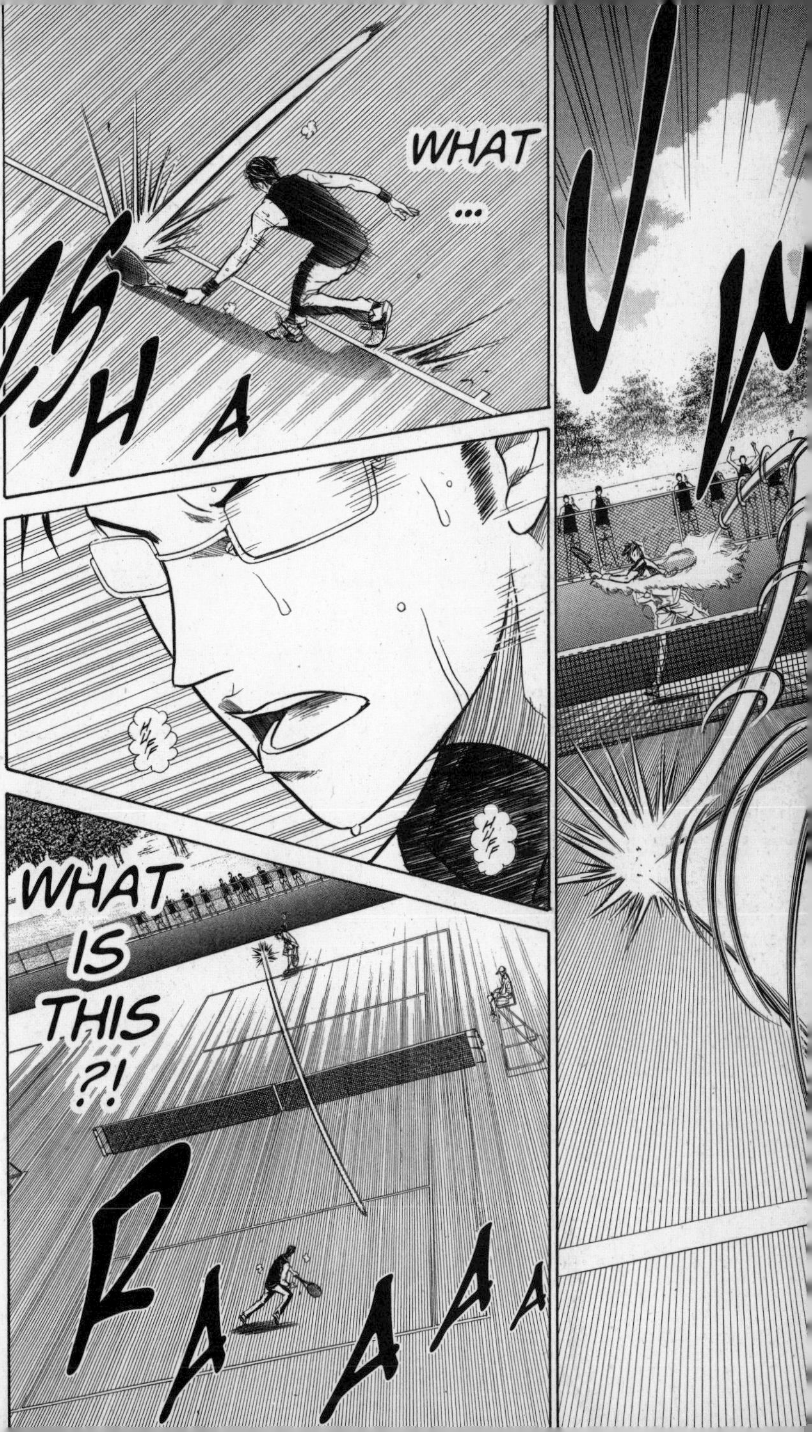
WHAT ...
WHAT IS THIS ?!

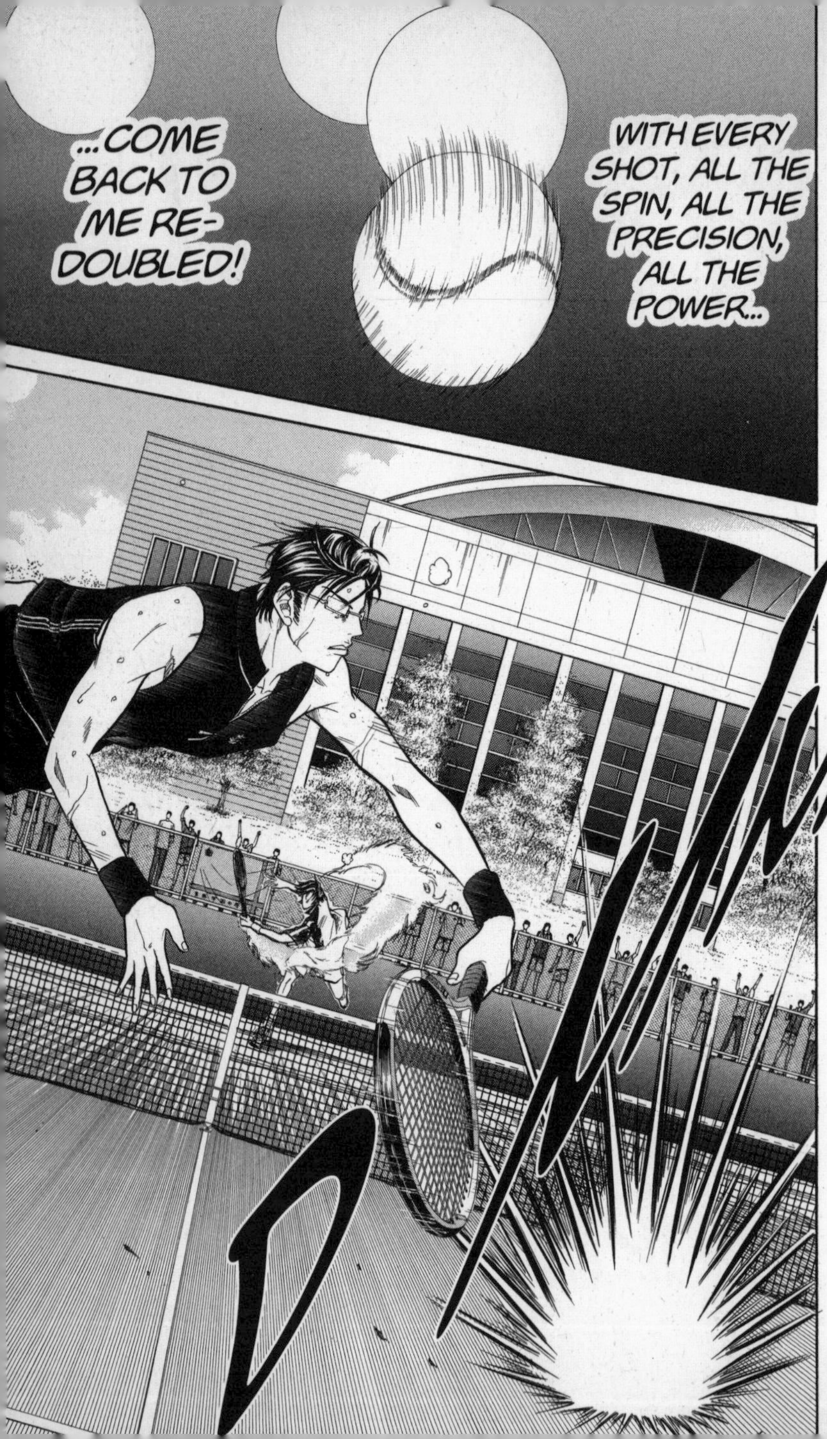
WITH EVERY SHOT, ALL THE SPIN, ALL THE PRECISION, ALL THE POWER...
...COME BACK TO ME RE-DOUBLED!

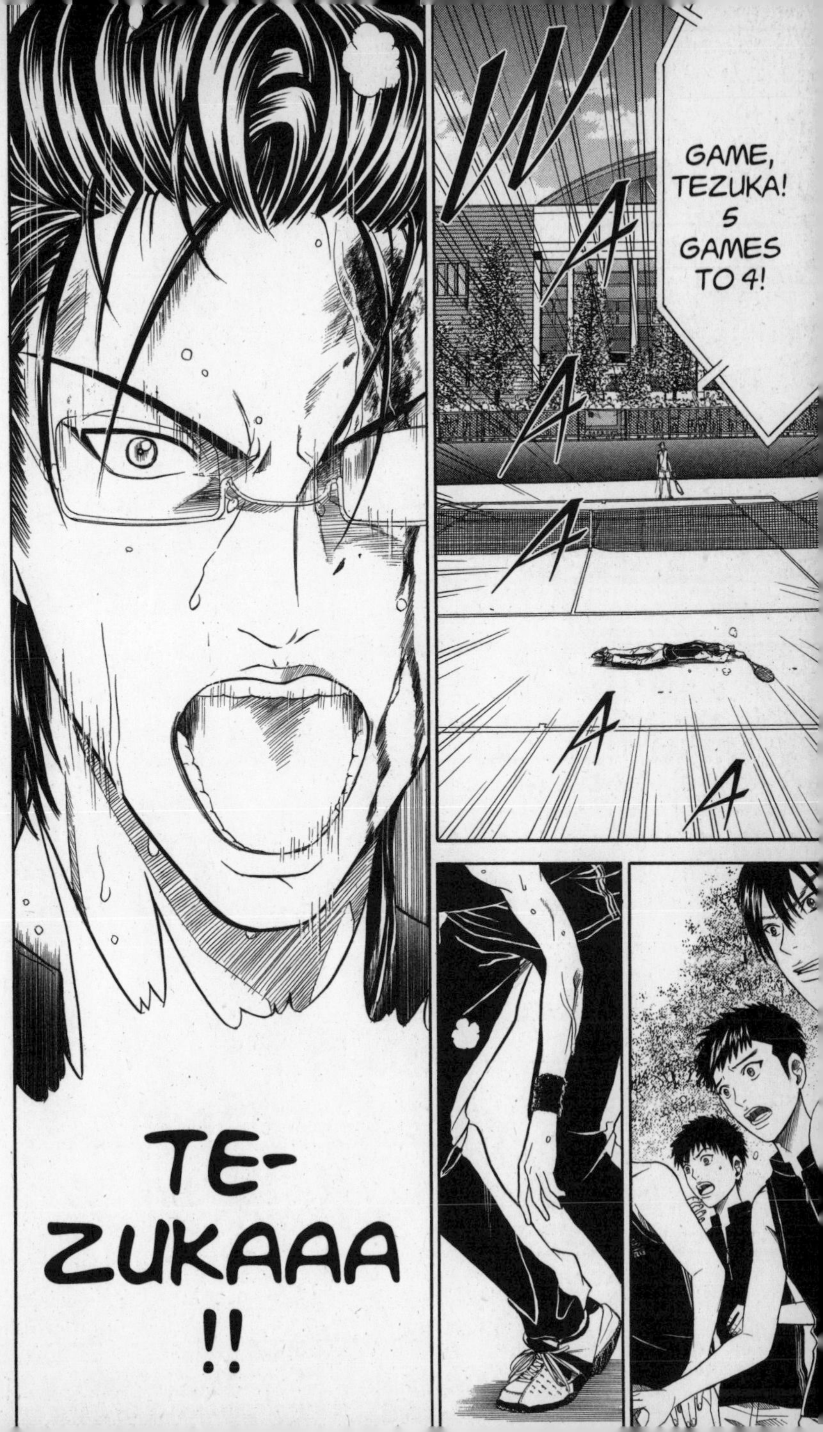
GAME, TEZUKA! 5 GAMES TO 4!
WAAAAAA
TE-ZUKAAAA!!

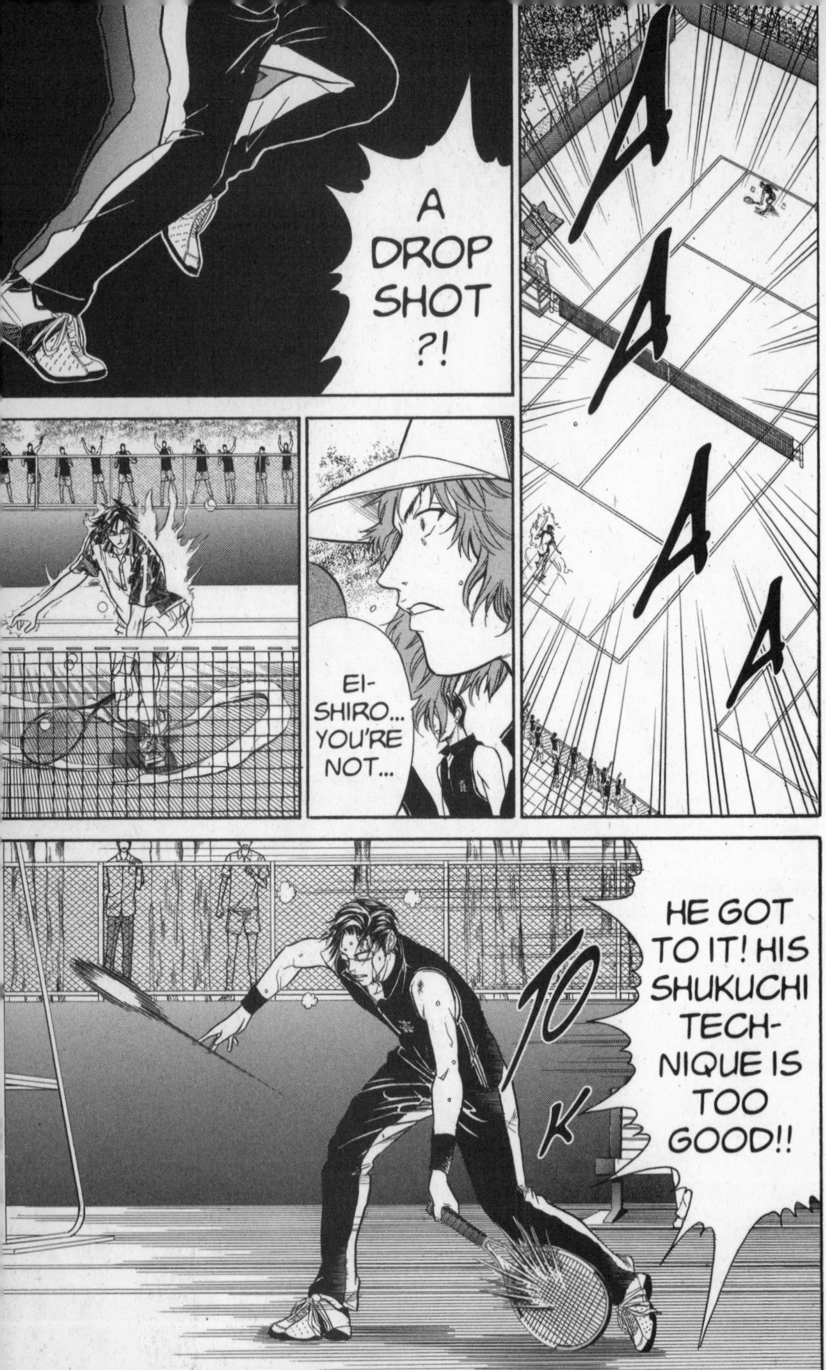
AAAA
A DROP SHOT?!
EI-SHIRO... YOU'RE NOT...
TOK
HE GOT TO IT! HIS SHUKUCHI TECH-NIQUE IS TOO GOOD!!

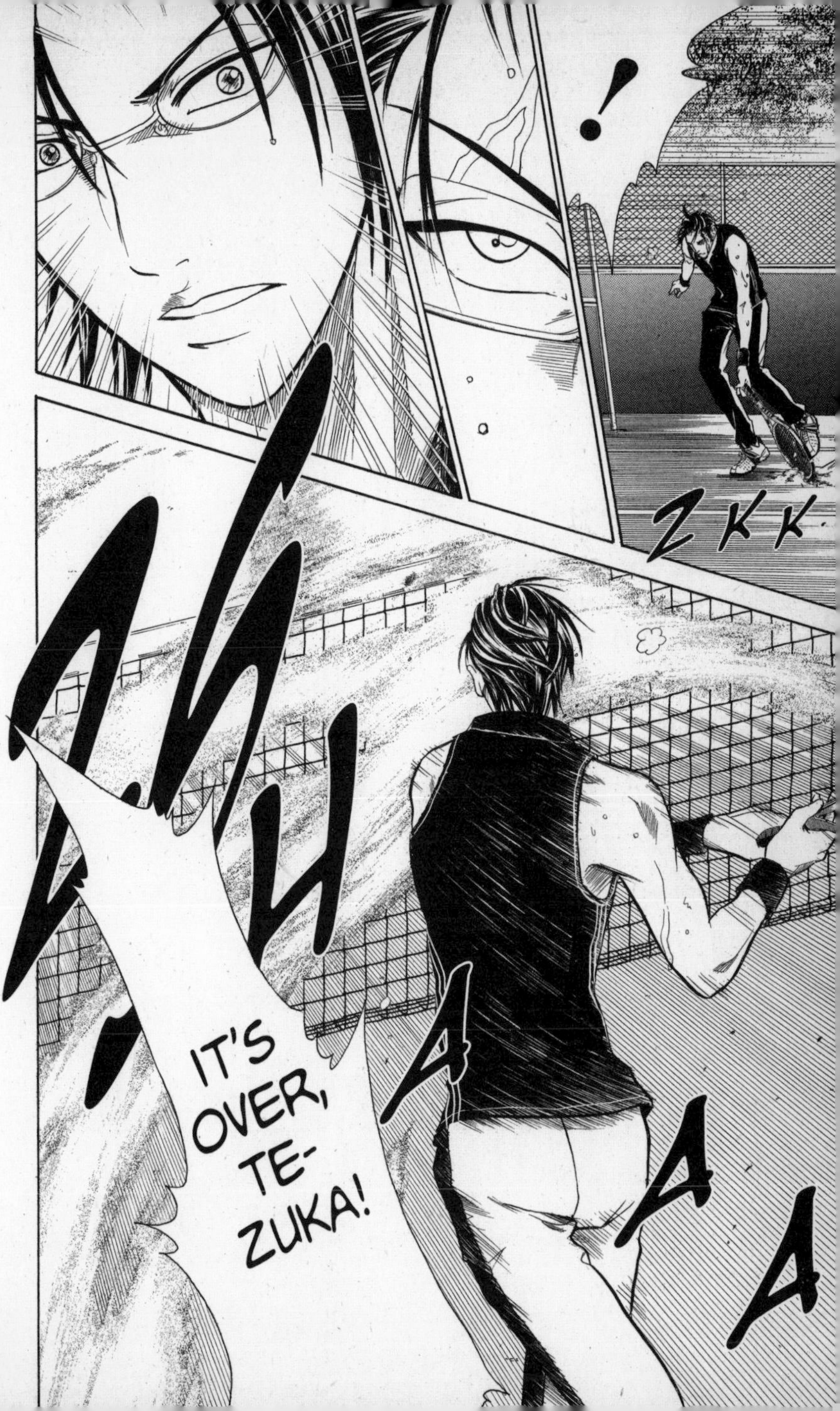
!
ZKK
IT'S OVER, TE-ZUKA!
AAAA

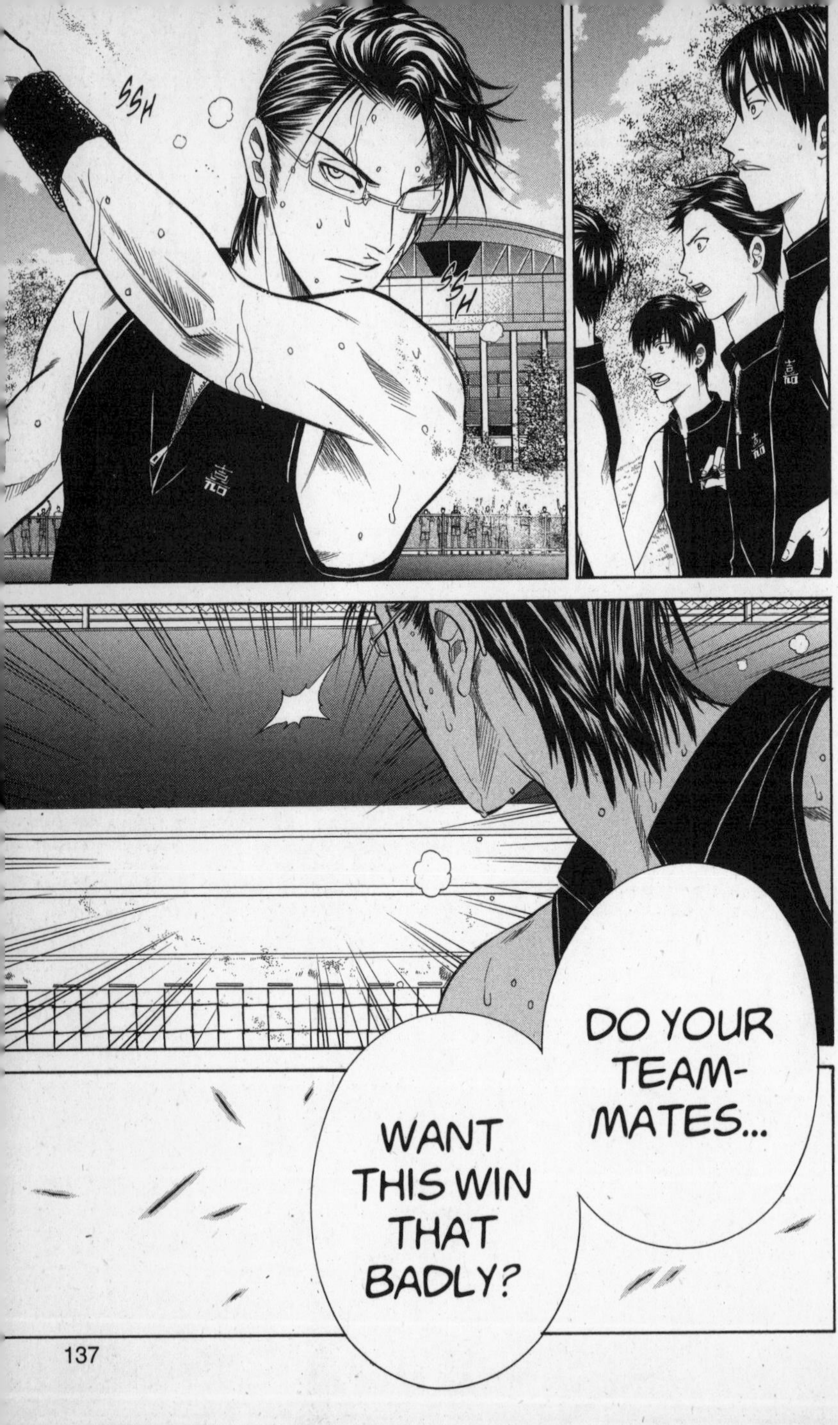
SSH
SSH
DO YOUR TEAM-MATES...
WANT THIS WIN THAT BADLY?

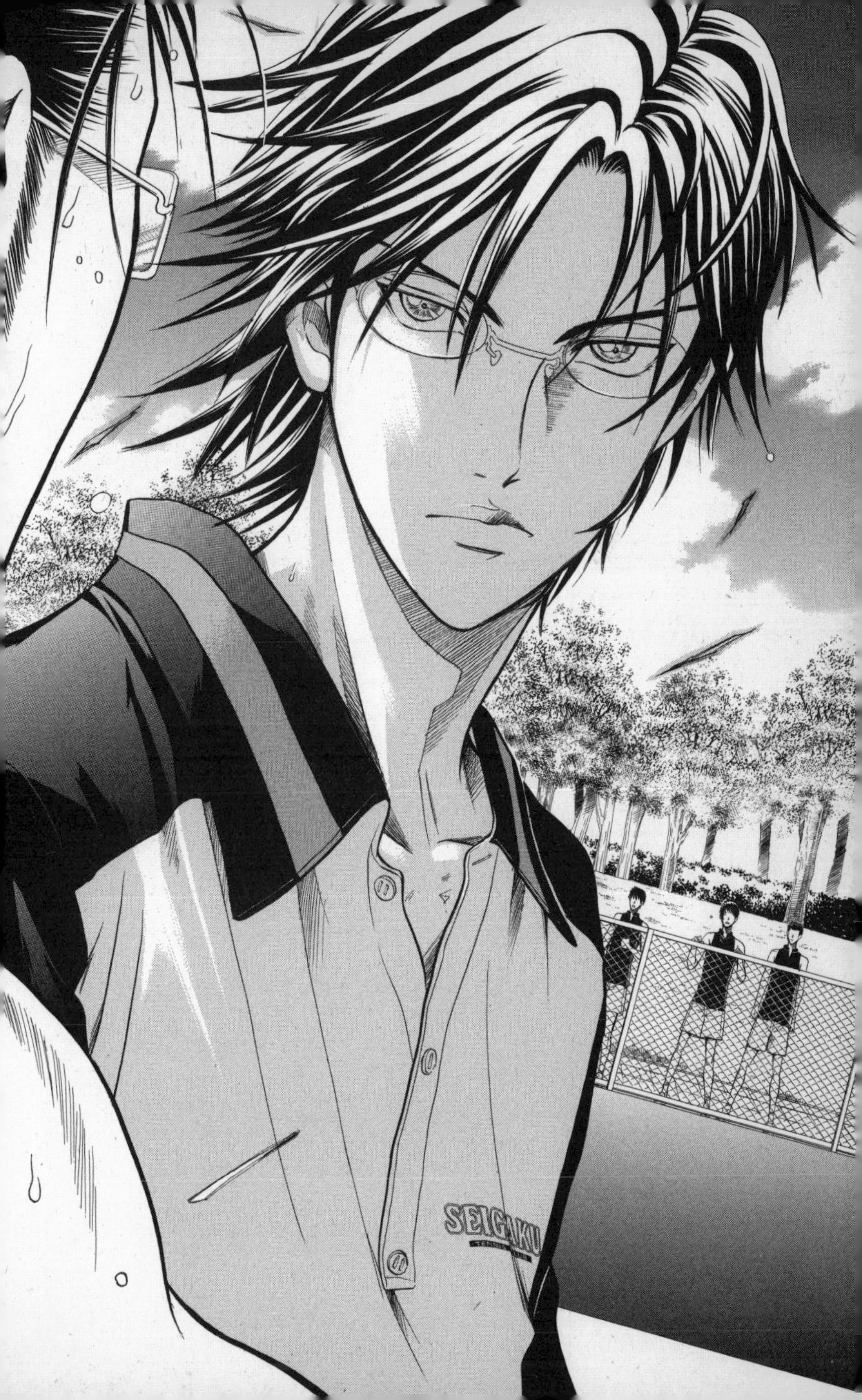
SEIGAKU

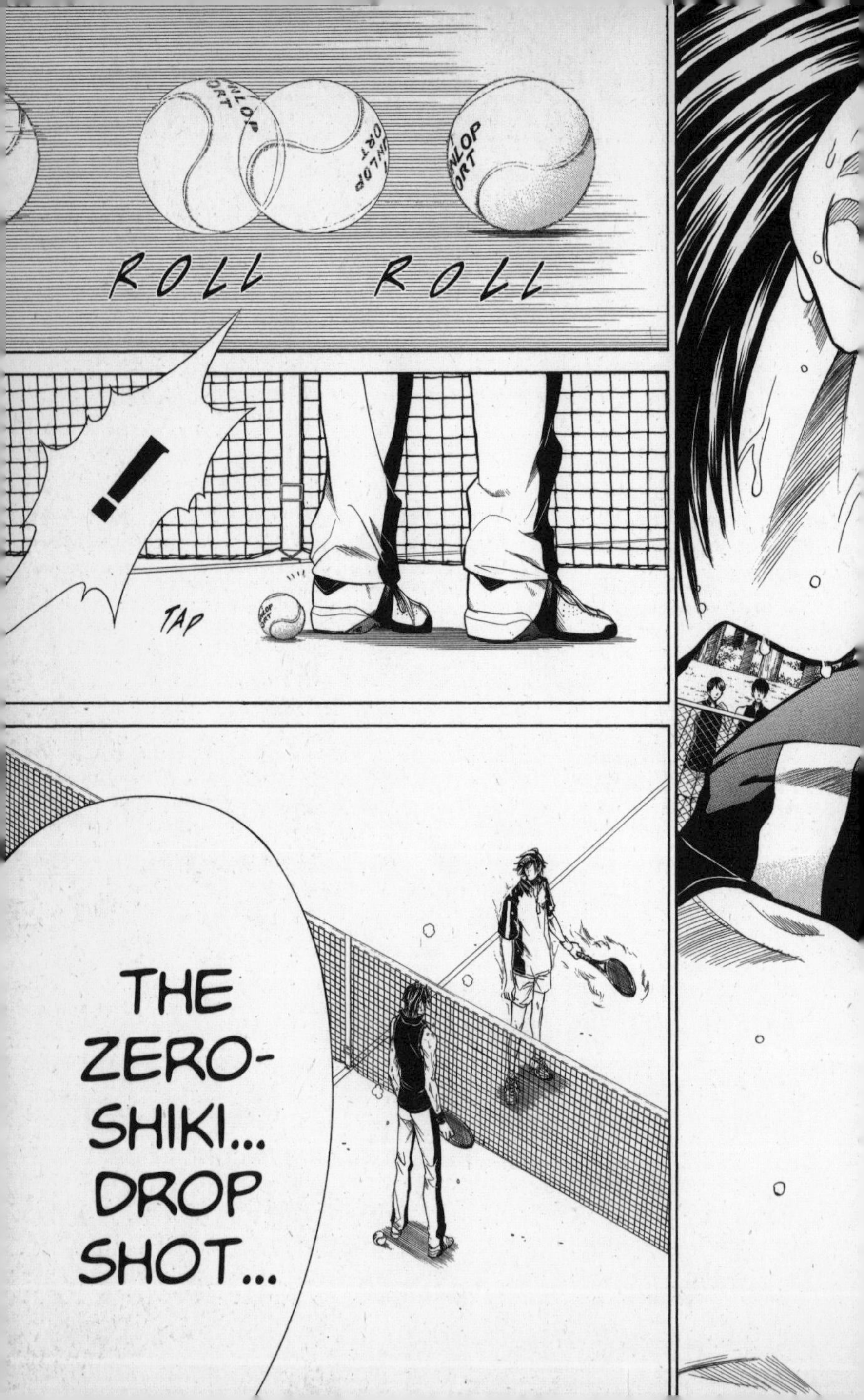
ROLL ROLL
!
TAP
THE ZERO-SHIKI... DROP SHOT...

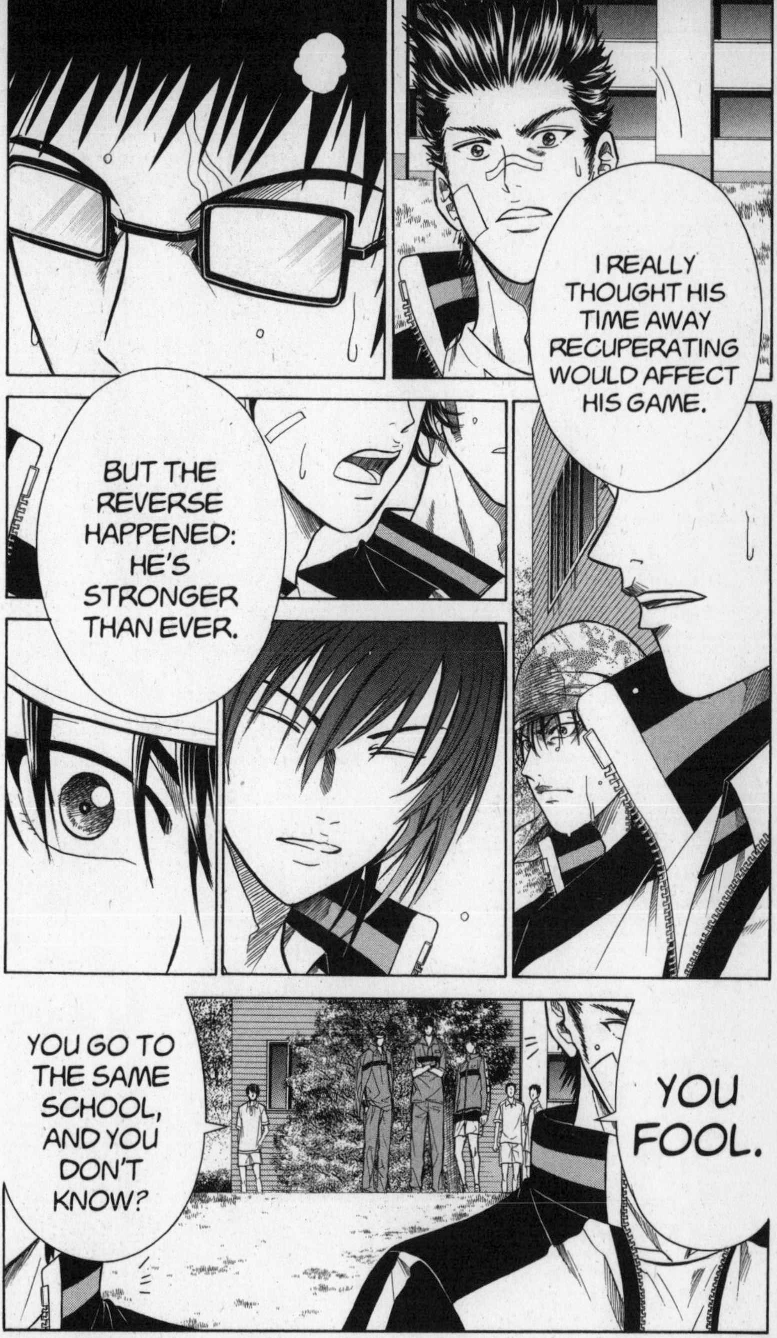
I REALLY THOUGHT HIS TIME AWAY RECUPERATING WOULD AFFECT HIS GAME.
BUT THE REVERSE HAPPENED: HE'S STRONGER THAN EVER.
YOU FOOL.
YOU GO TO THE SAME SCHOOL, AND YOU DON'T KNOW?

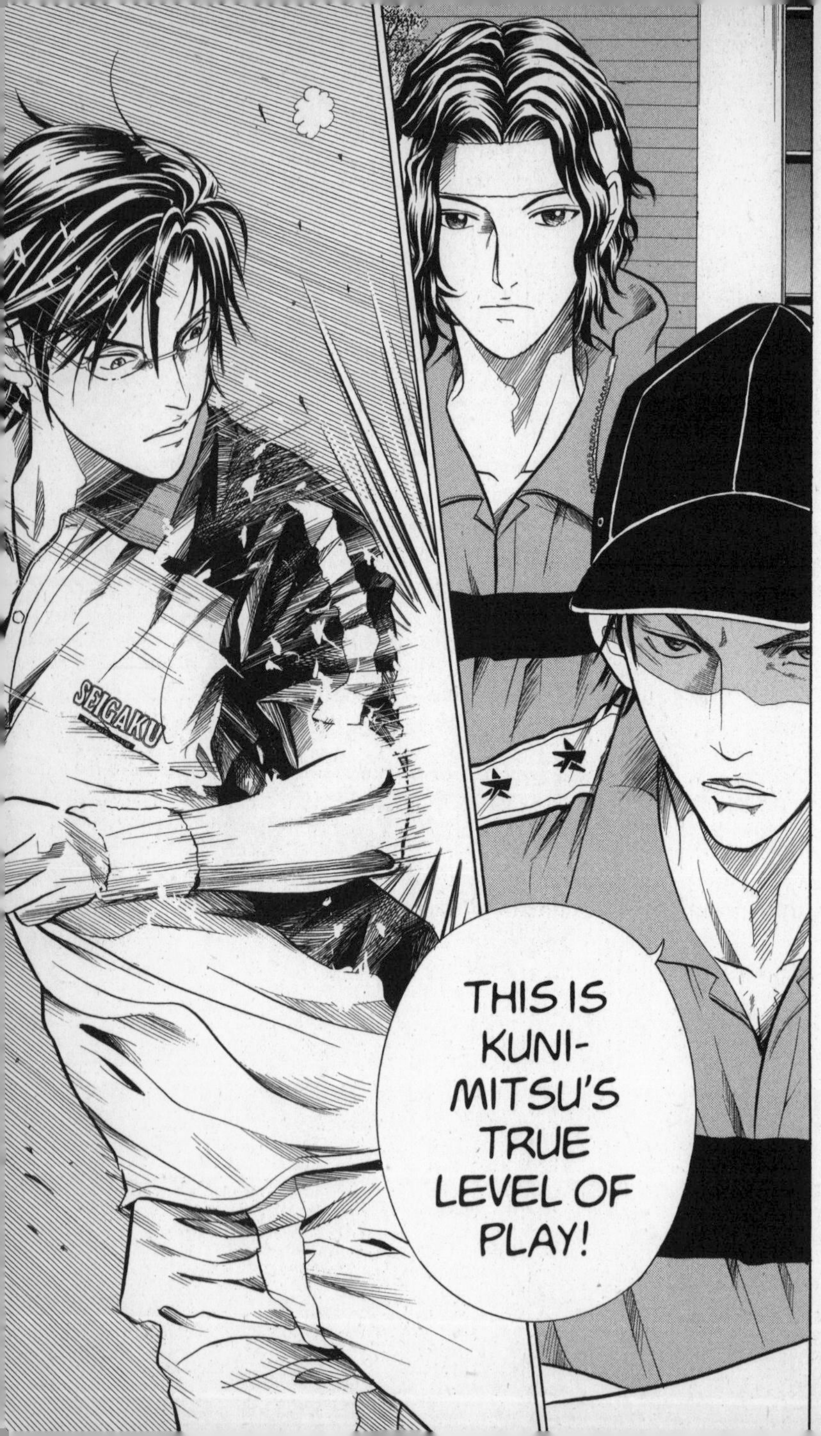
SEIGAKU
THIS IS KUNI-MITSU'S TRUE LEVEL OF PLAY!

テニスの王子様
THE PRINCE OF TENNIS

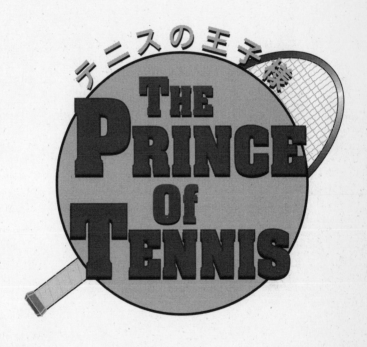

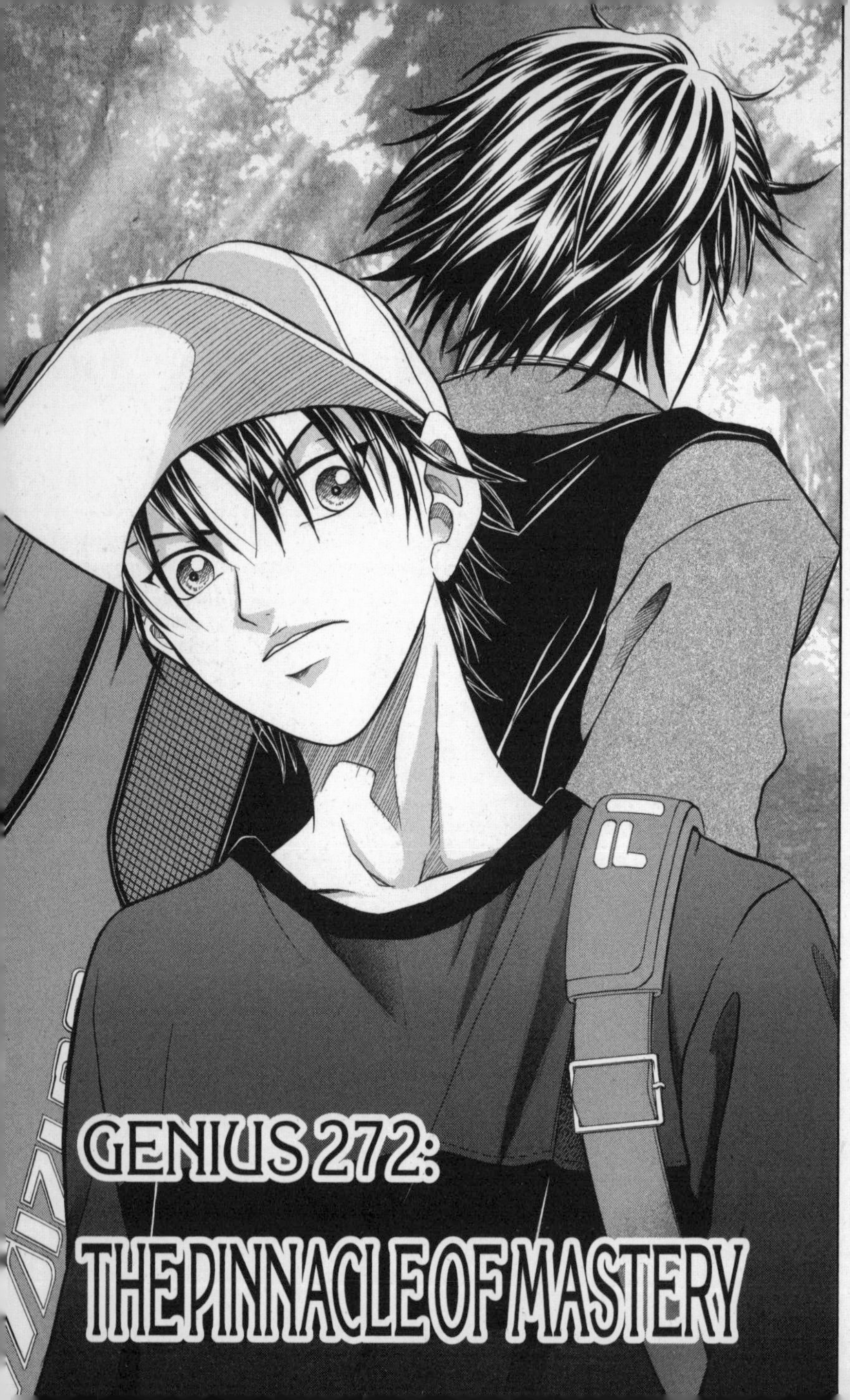
GENIUS 272:
THE PINNACLE OF MASTERY

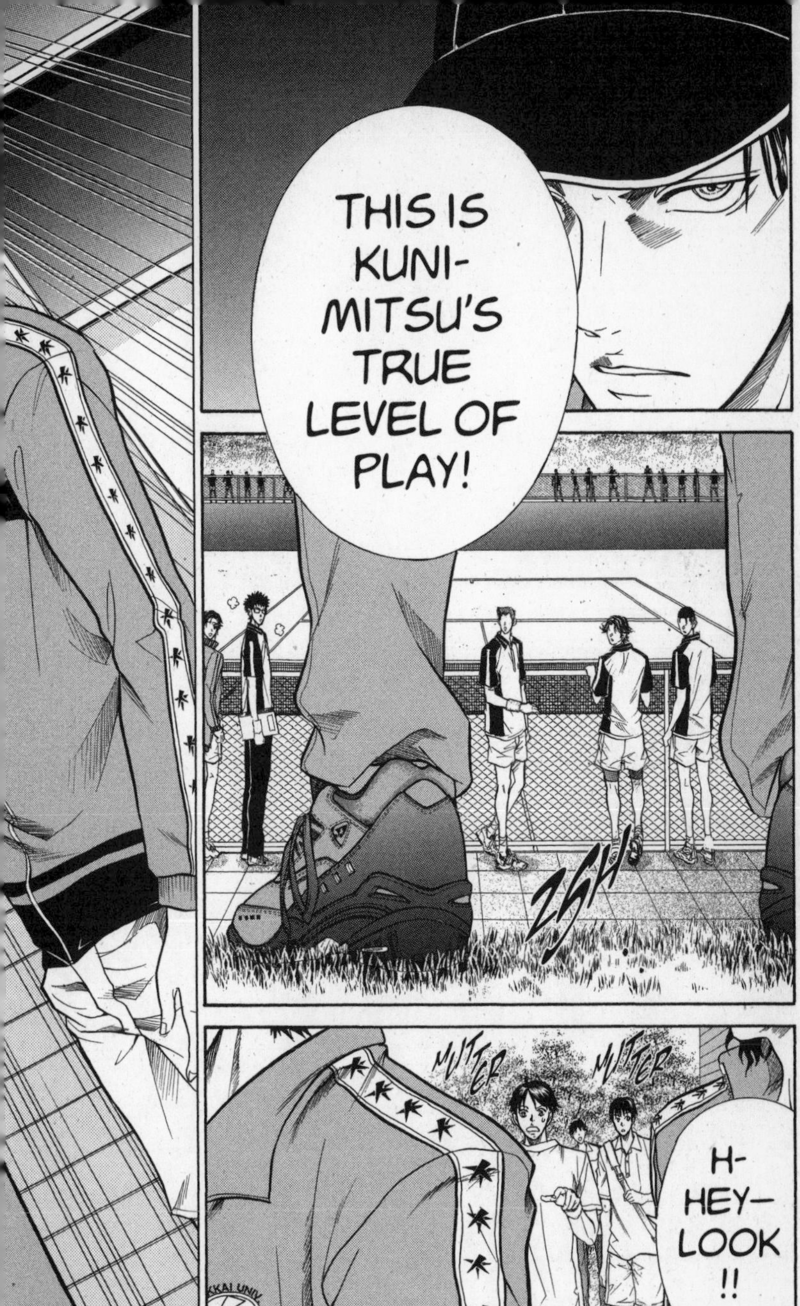
THIS IS KUNI-MITSU'S TRUE LEVEL OF PLAY!
ZSH
MUTTER MUTTER
H-HEY-LOOK!!

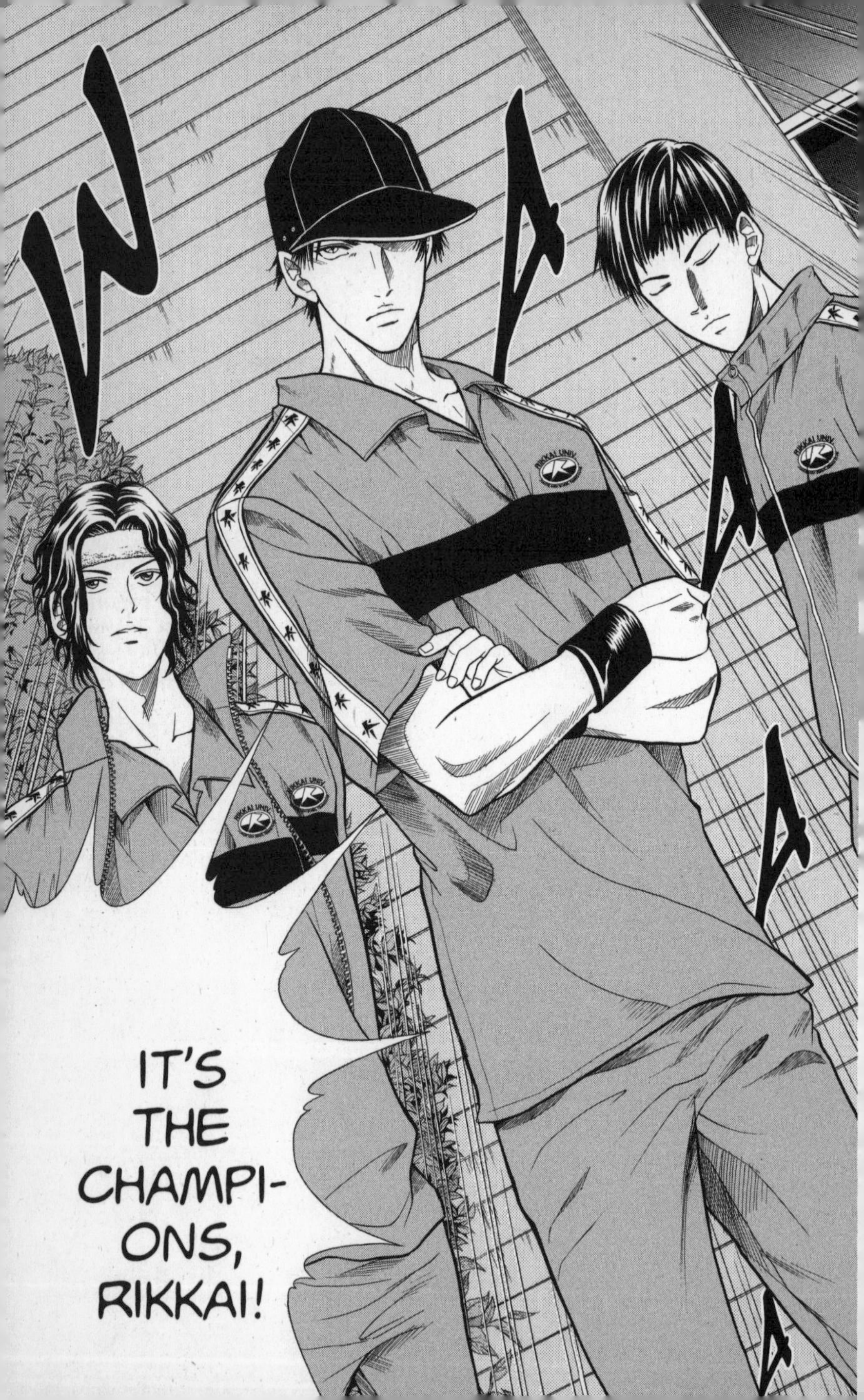
IT'S THE CHAMPI-ONS, RIKKAI!

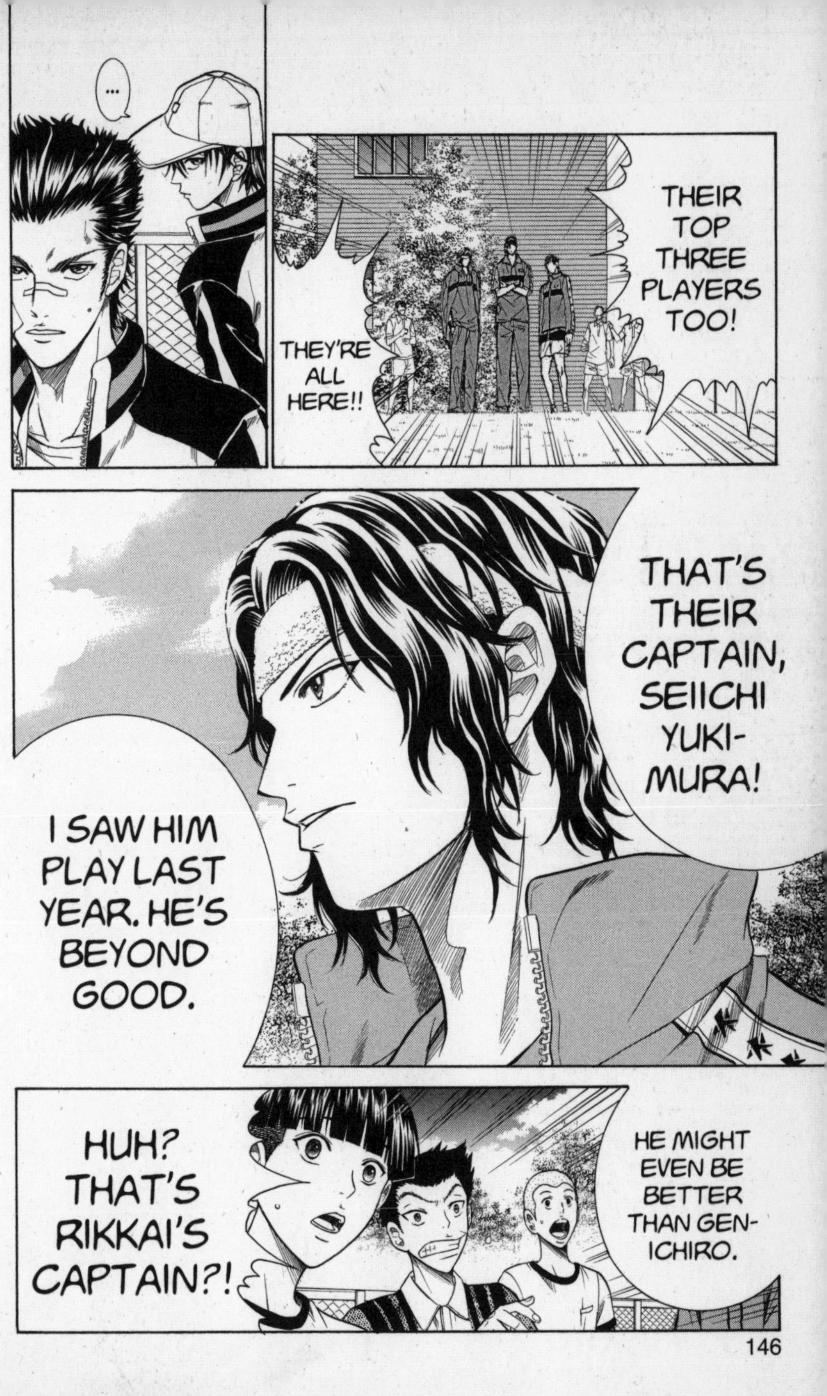
THEY'RE ALL HERE!!
THEIR TOP THREE PLAYERS TOO!
...
THAT'S THEIR CAPTAIN, SEIICHI YUKI-MURA!
I SAW HIM PLAY LAST YEAR. HE'S BEYOND GOOD.
HUH? THAT'S RIKKAI'S CAPTAIN?!
HE MIGHT EVEN BE BETTER THAN GEN-ICHIRO.

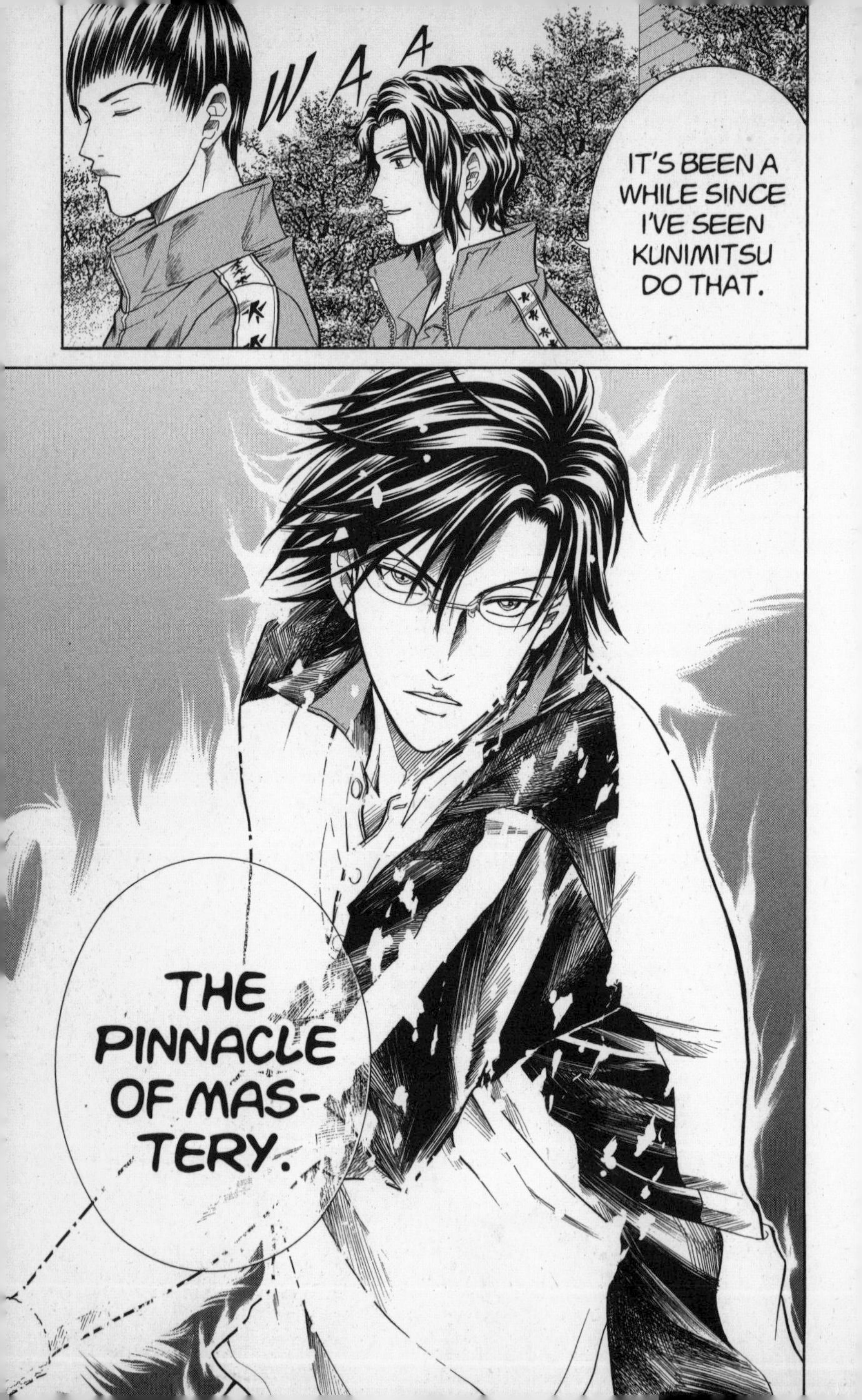
WAA
IT'S BEEN A WHILE SINCE I'VE SEEN KUNIMITSU DO THAT.
THE PINNACLE OF MAS- TERY.

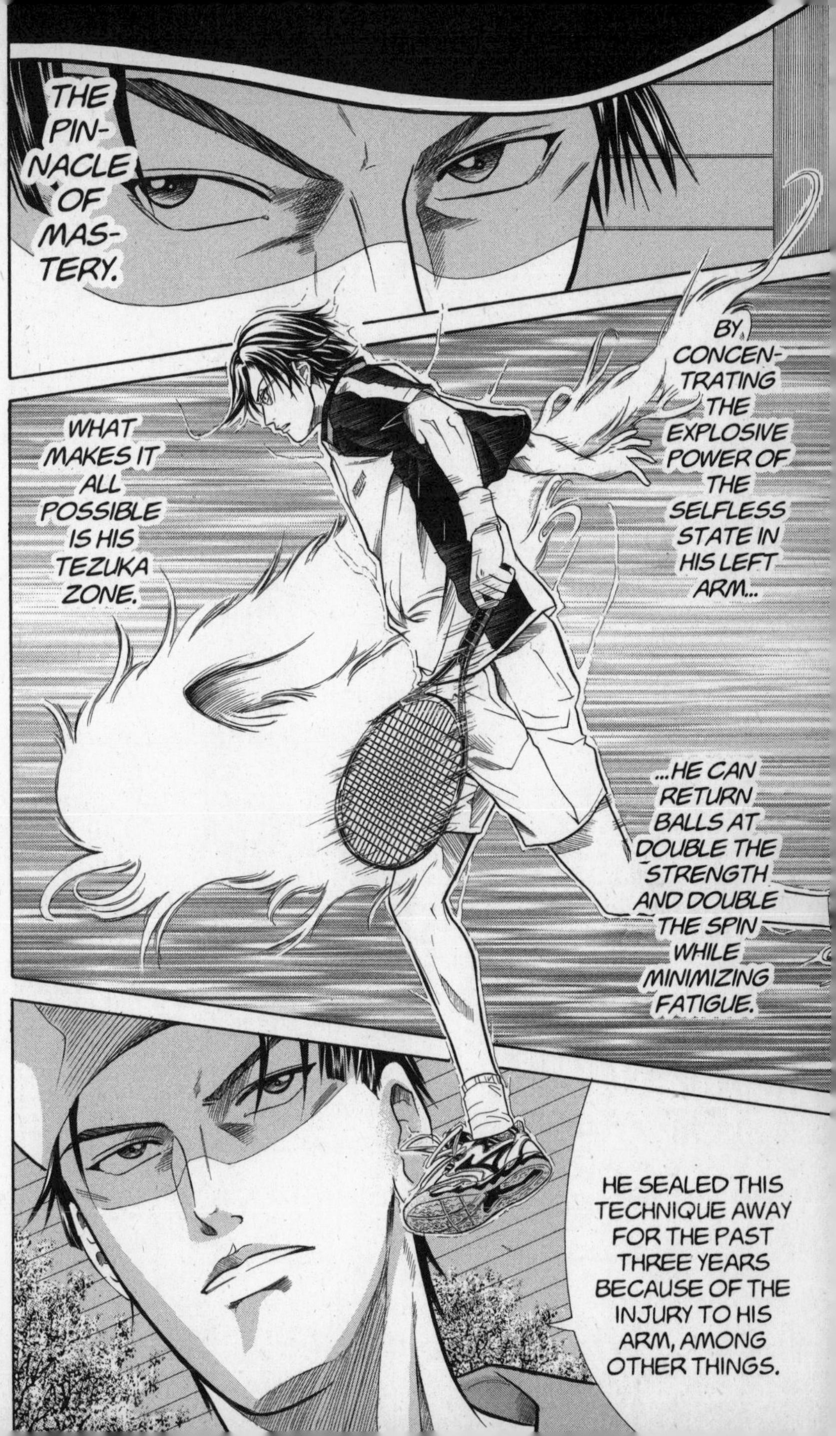
THE PIN-NACLE OF MAS-TERY.
BY CONCEN-TRATING THE EXPLOSIVE POWER OF THE SELFLESS STATE IN HIS LEFT ARM...
...HE CAN RETURN BALLS AT DOUBLE THE STRENGTH AND DOUBLE THE SPIN WHILE MINIMIZING FATIGUE.
WHAT MAKES IT ALL POSSIBLE IS HIS TEZUKA ZONE.
HE SEALED THIS TECHNIQUE AWAY FOR THE PAST THREE YEARS BECAUSE OF THE INJURY TO HIS ARM, AMONG OTHER THINGS.

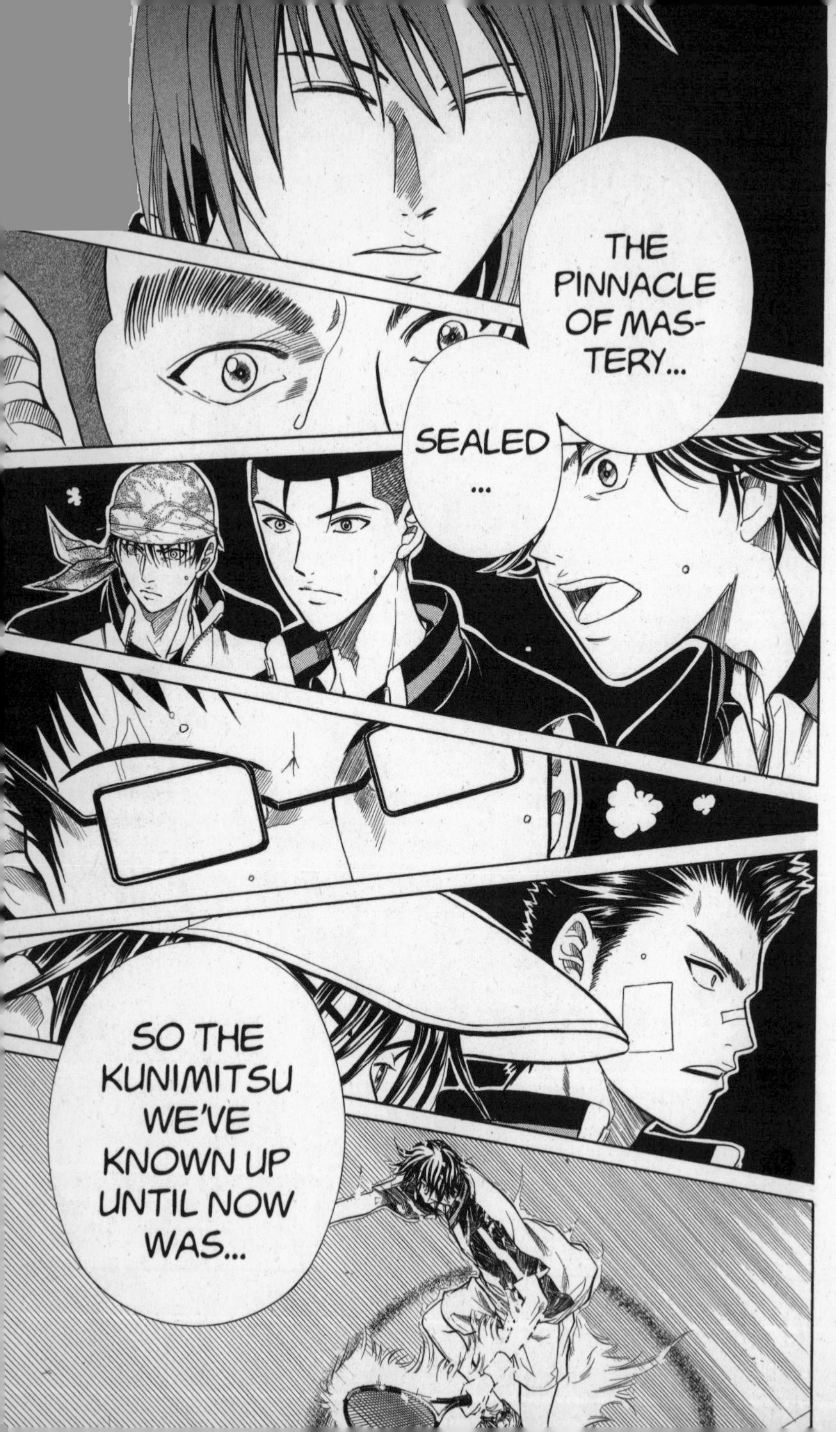
THE PINNACLE OF MAS-TERY...
SEALED ...
SO THE KUNIMITSU WE'VE KNOWN UP UNTIL NOW WAS...

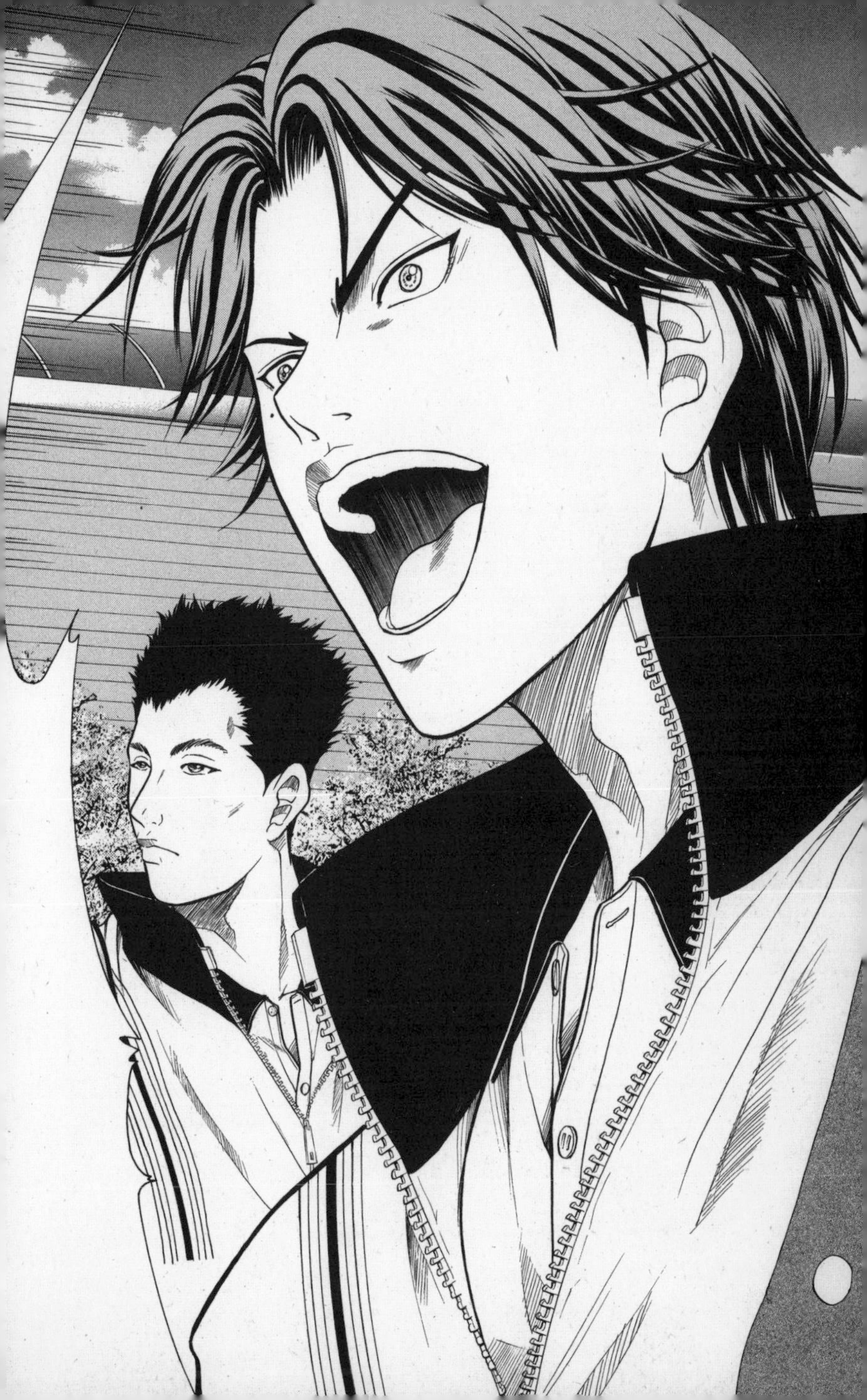

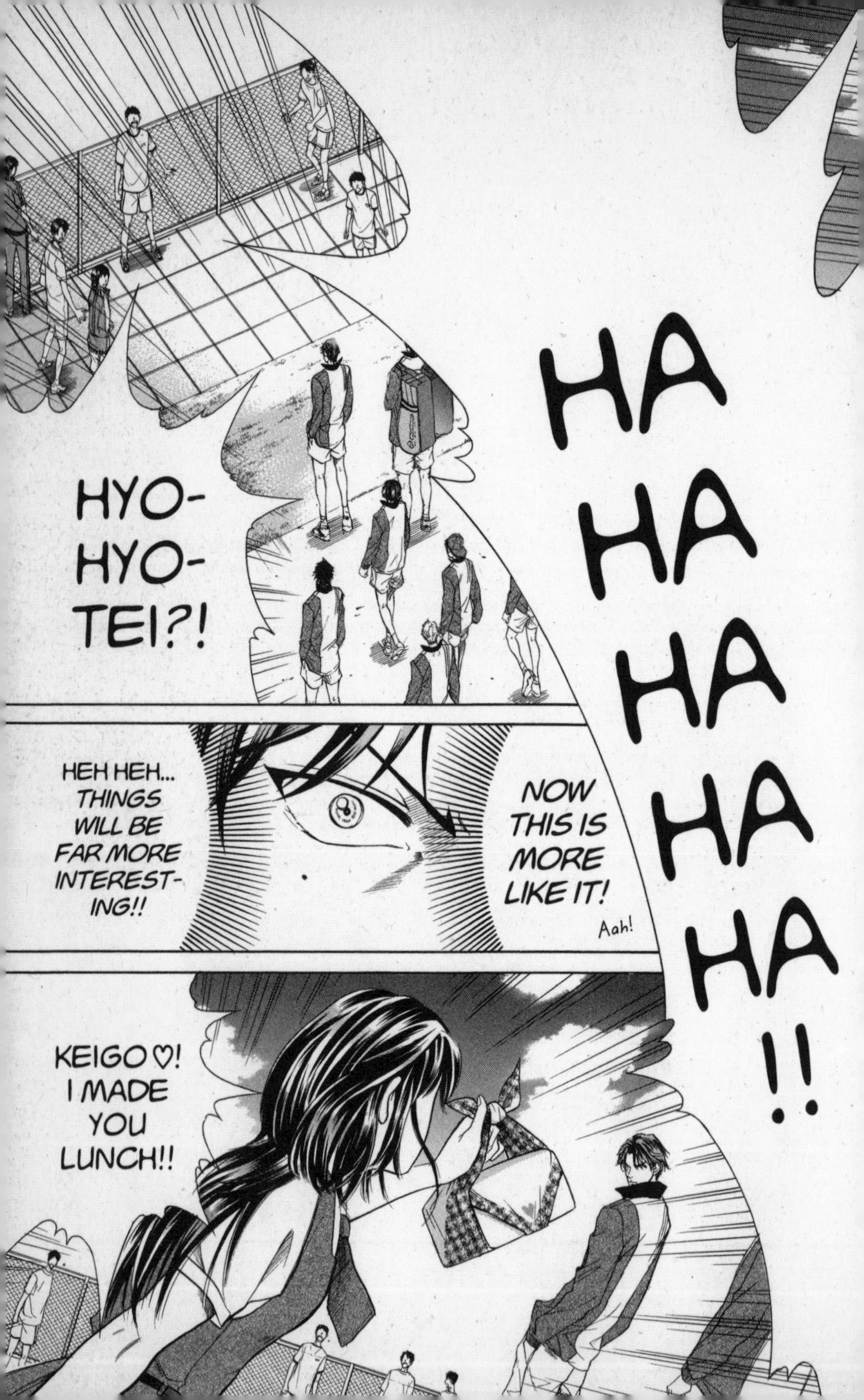
HA HA HA HA HA!!
HYO-HYO-TEI?!
NOW THIS IS MORE LIKE IT!
Aah!
HEH HEH... THINGS WILL BE FAR MORE INTEREST-ING!!
KEIGO♡! I MADE YOU LUNCH!!

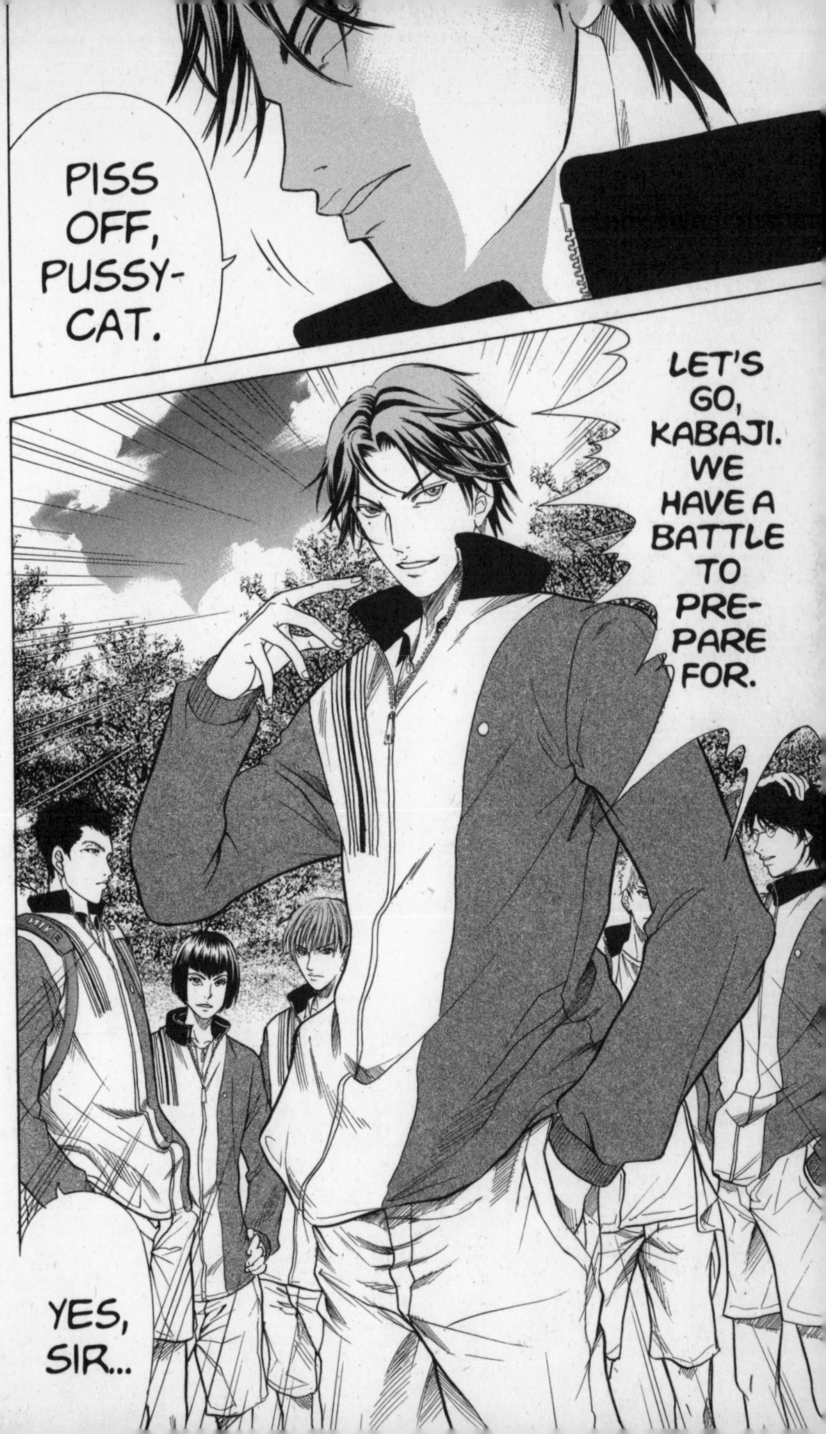
PISS OFF, PUSSY-CAT.
LET'S GO, KABAJI. WE HAVE A BATTLE TO PRE-PARE FOR.
YES, SIR...

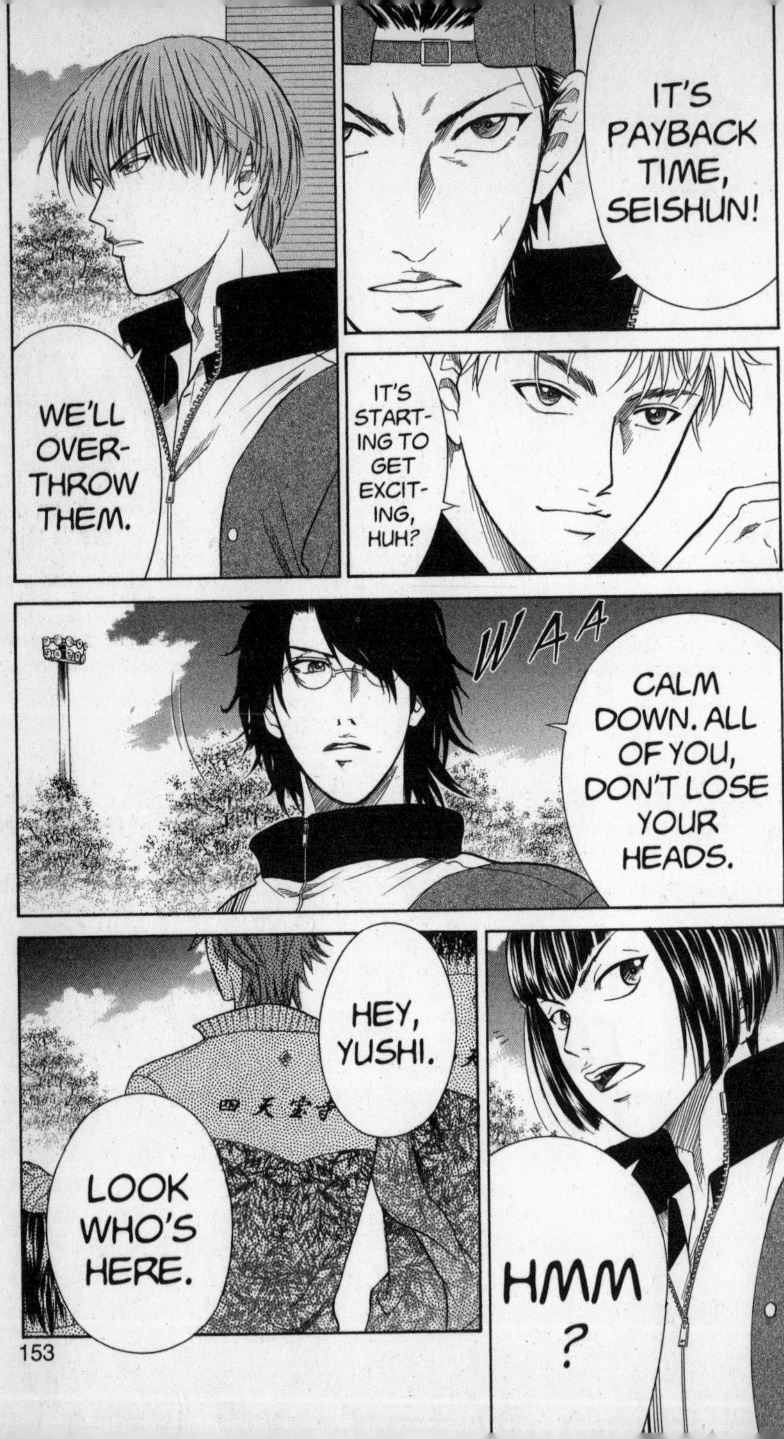
IT'S PAYBACK TIME, SEISHUN!
IT'S STARTING TO GET EXCITING, HUH?
WE'LL OVERTHROW THEM.
WAA
CALM DOWN. ALL OF YOU, DON'T LOSE YOUR HEADS.
HMM ?
HEY, YUSHI.
LOOK WHO'S HERE.

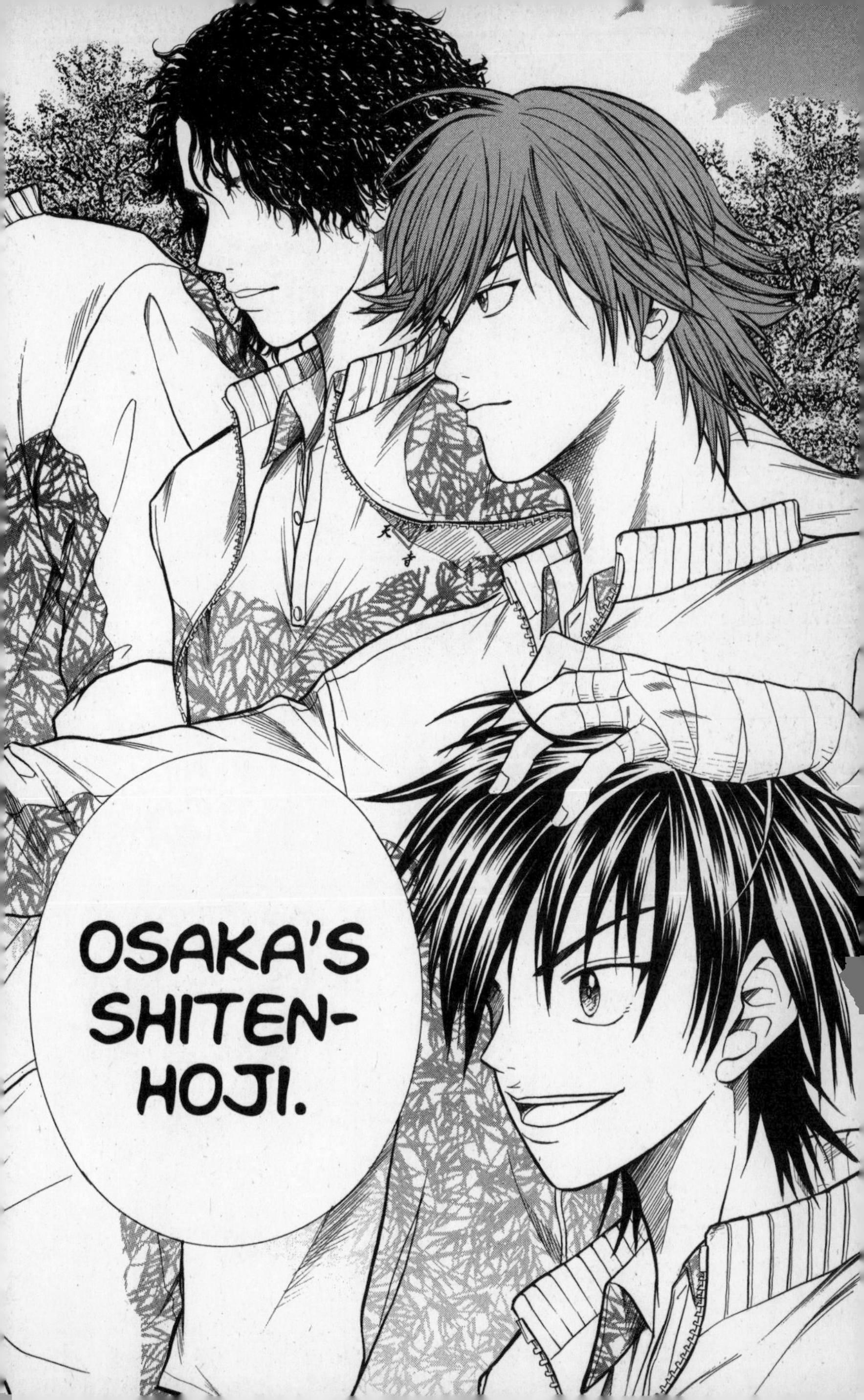
OSAKA'S SHITEN-HOJI.

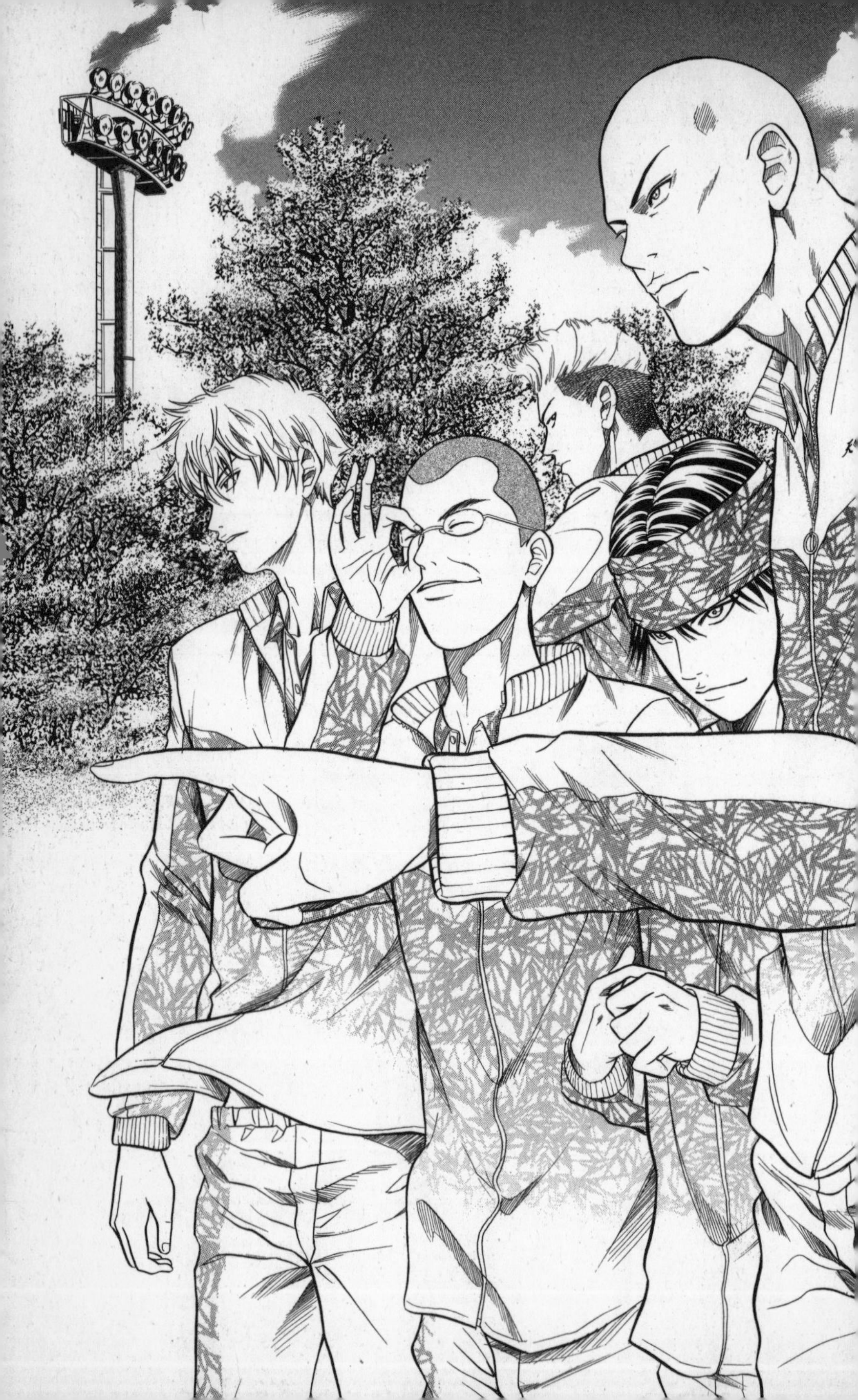

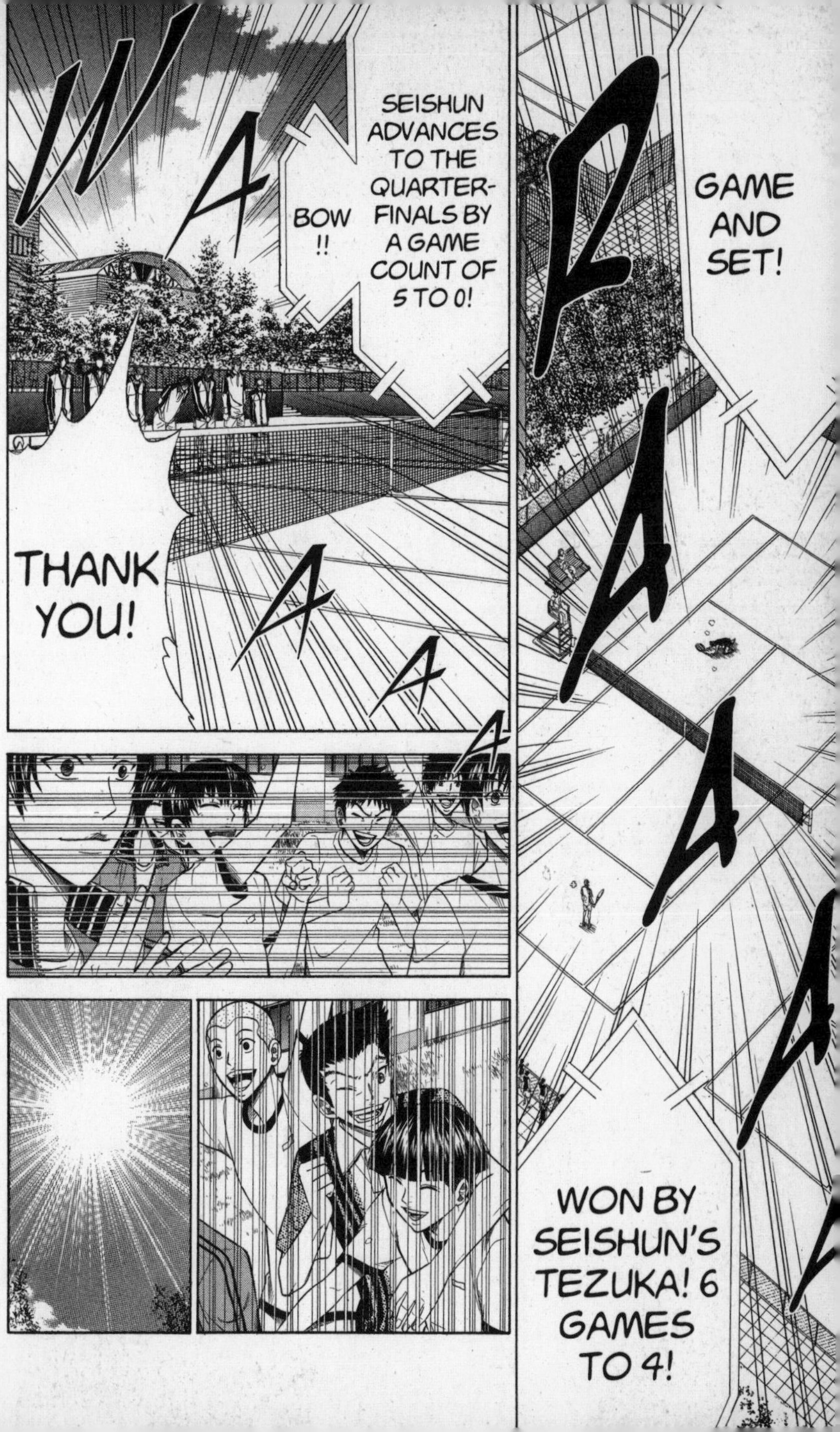
GAME AND SET!
WAAAAAA
WON BY SEISHUN'S TEZUKA! 6 GAMES TO 4!
SEISHUN ADVANCES TO THE QUARTER-FINALS BY A GAME COUNT OF 5 TO 0!
BOW !!
WAAAA
THANK YOU!

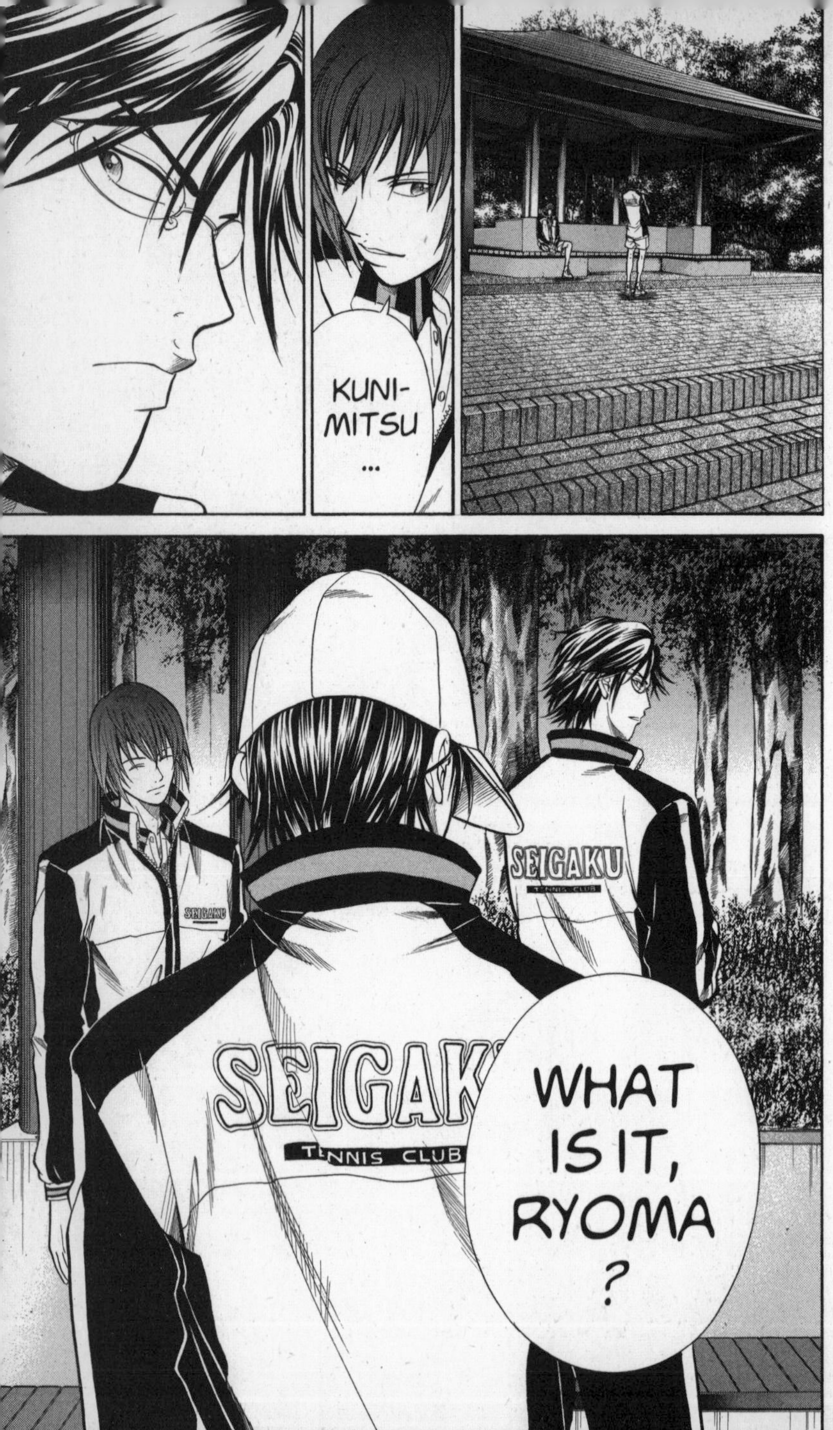
KUNI-
MITSU
...
SEIGAKU
TENNIS CLUB
SEIGAKU
SEIGAKU
TENNIS CLUB
WHAT IS IT, RYOMA ?

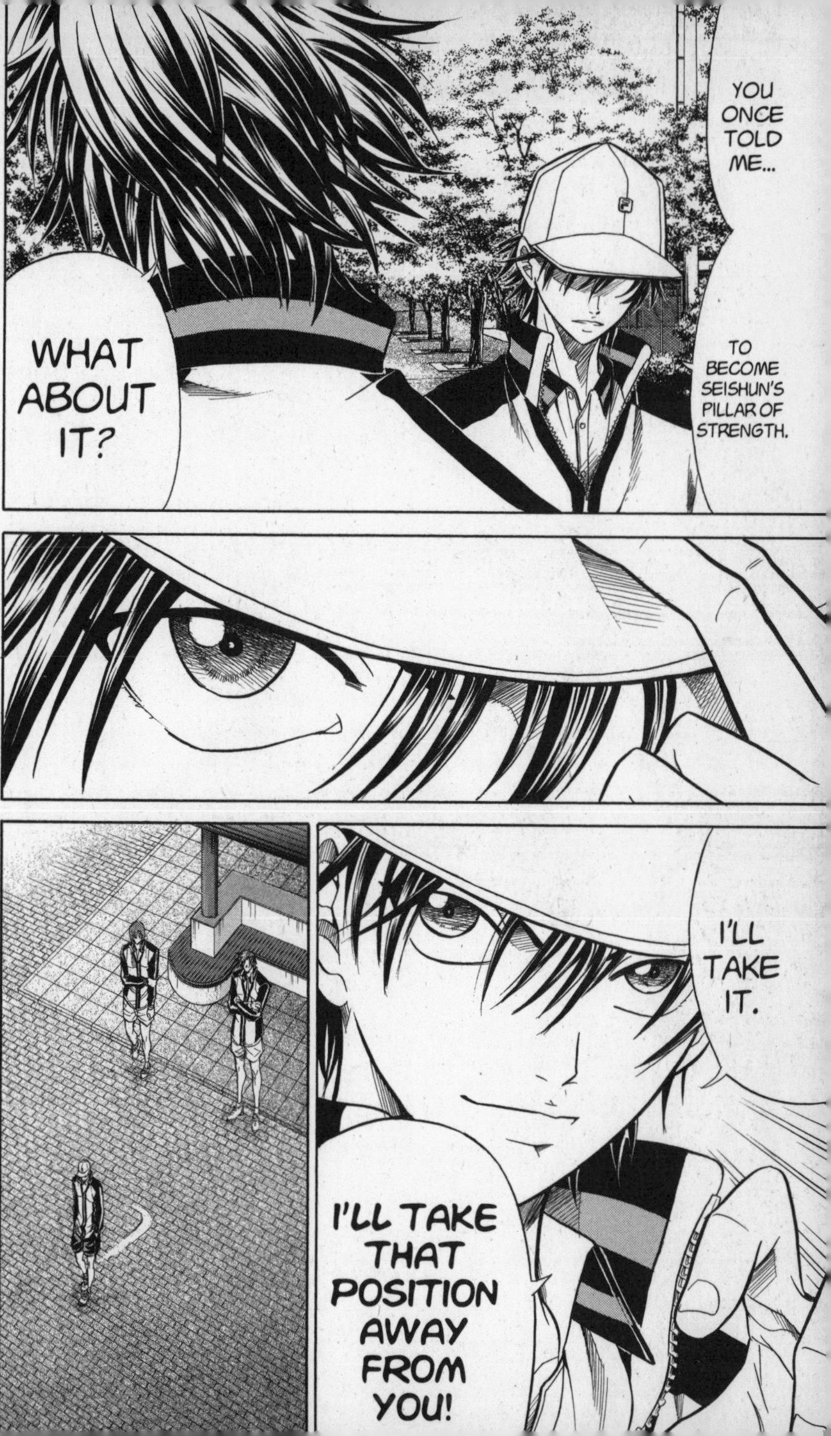
YOU ONCE TOLD ME...
TO BECOME SEISHUN'S PILLAR OF STRENGTH.
WHAT ABOUT IT?
I'LL TAKE IT.
I'LL TAKE THAT POSITION AWAY FROM YOU!

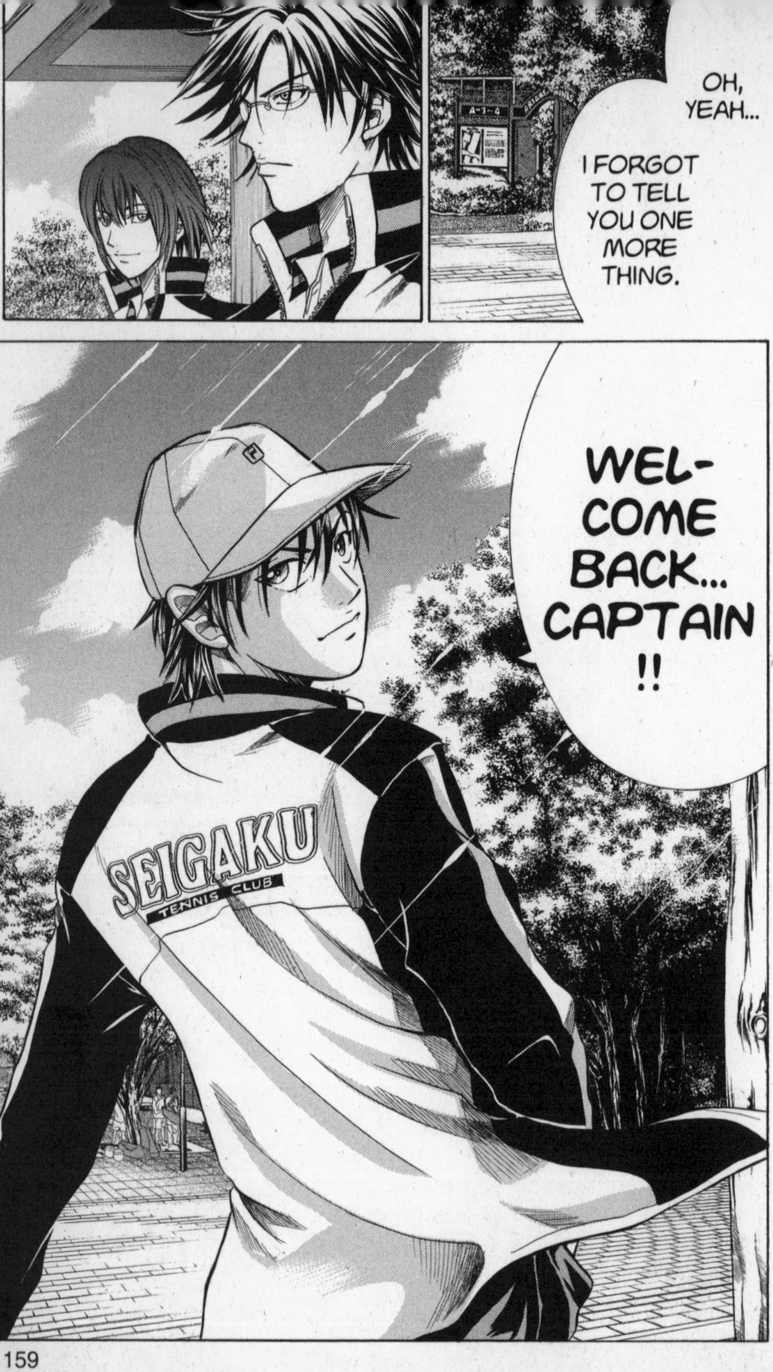
OH, YEAH...
I FORGOT TO TELL YOU ONE MORE THING.
WEL-COME BACK... CAPTAIN!!
SEIGAKU
TENNIS CLUB

テニスの王子様

THE PRINCE OF TENNIS

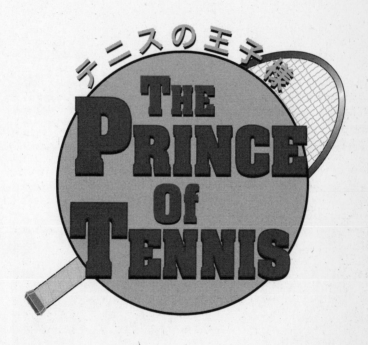

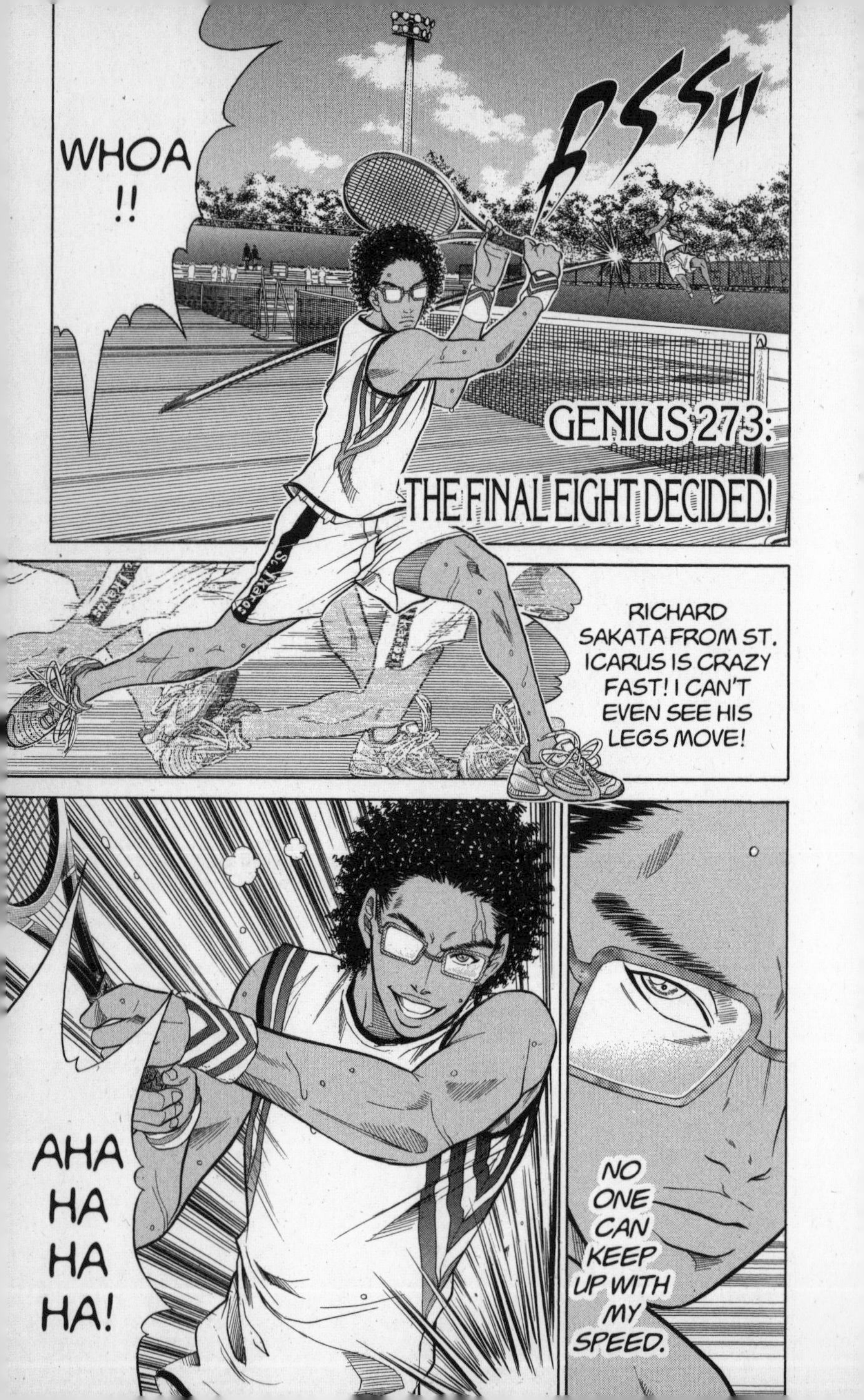
BSSH
WHOA !!
GENIUS 273: THE FINAL EIGHT DECIDED!
St. Ikarus
RICHARD SAKATA FROM ST. ICARUS IS CRAZY FAST! I CAN'T EVEN SEE HIS LEGS MOVE!
NO ONE CAN KEEP UP WITH MY SPEED.
AHA HA HA HA HA!

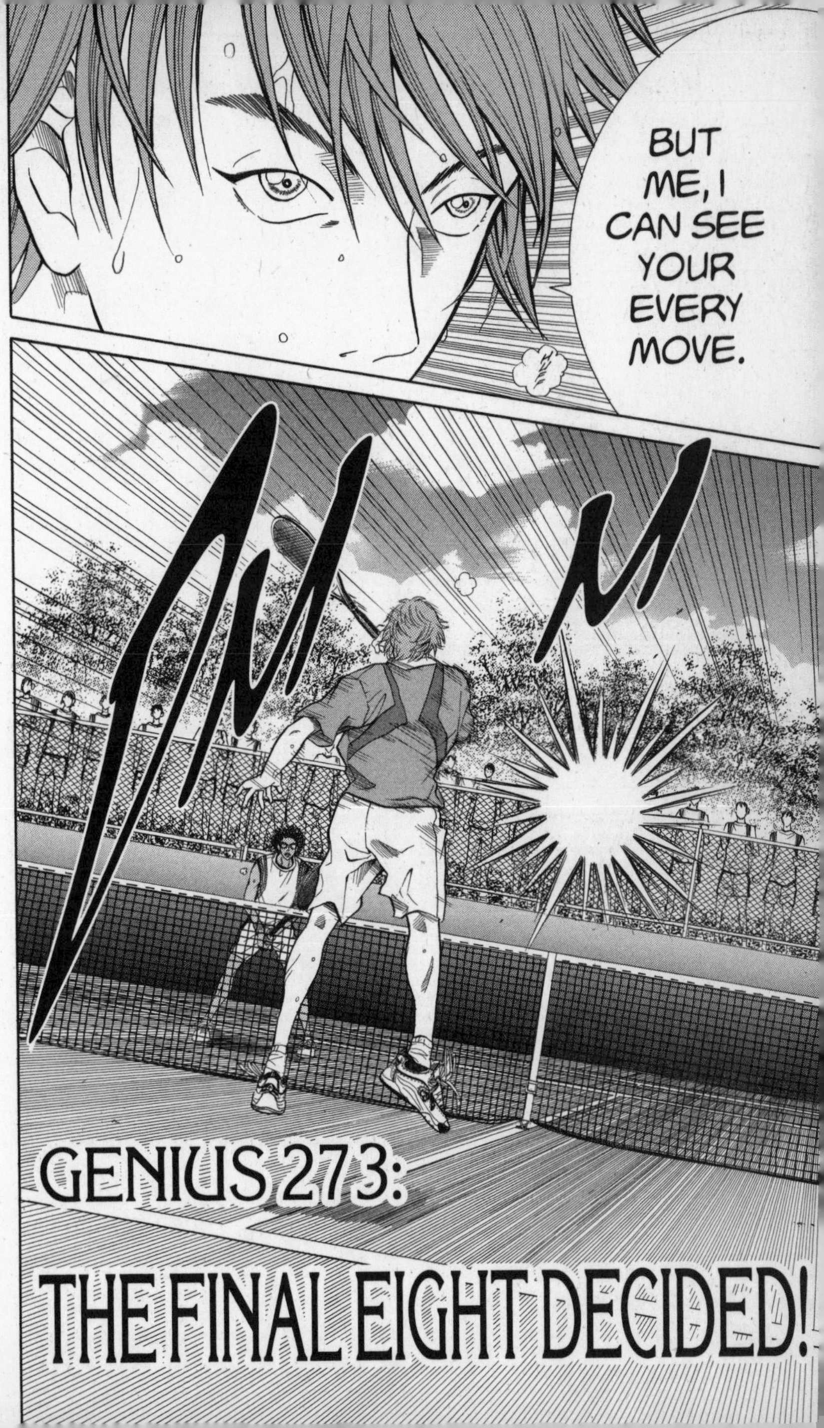
BUT ME, I CAN SEE YOUR EVERY MOVE.
GENIUS 273:
THE FINAL EIGHT DECIDED!

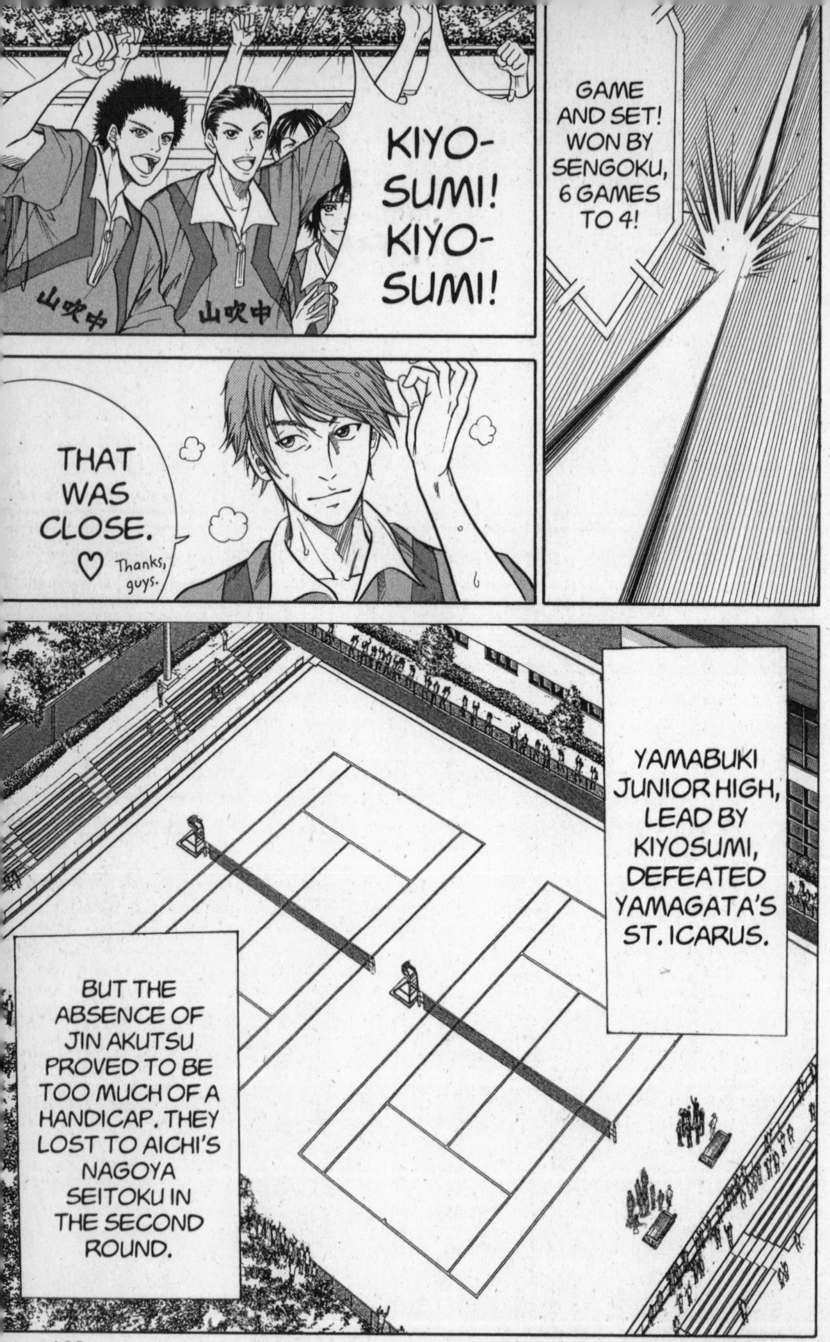
GAME AND SET! WON BY SENGOKU, 6 GAMES TO 4!
KIYO-SUMI! KIYO-SUMI!
山吹中
山吹中
THAT WAS CLOSE. ♡
Thanks, guys.
YAMABUKI JUNIOR HIGH, LEAD BY KIYOSUMI, DEFEATED YAMAGATA'S ST. ICARUS.
BUT THE ABSENCE OF JIN AKUTSU PROVED TO BE TOO MUCH OF A HANDICAP. THEY LOST TO AICHI'S NAGOYA SEITOKU IN THE SECOND ROUND.

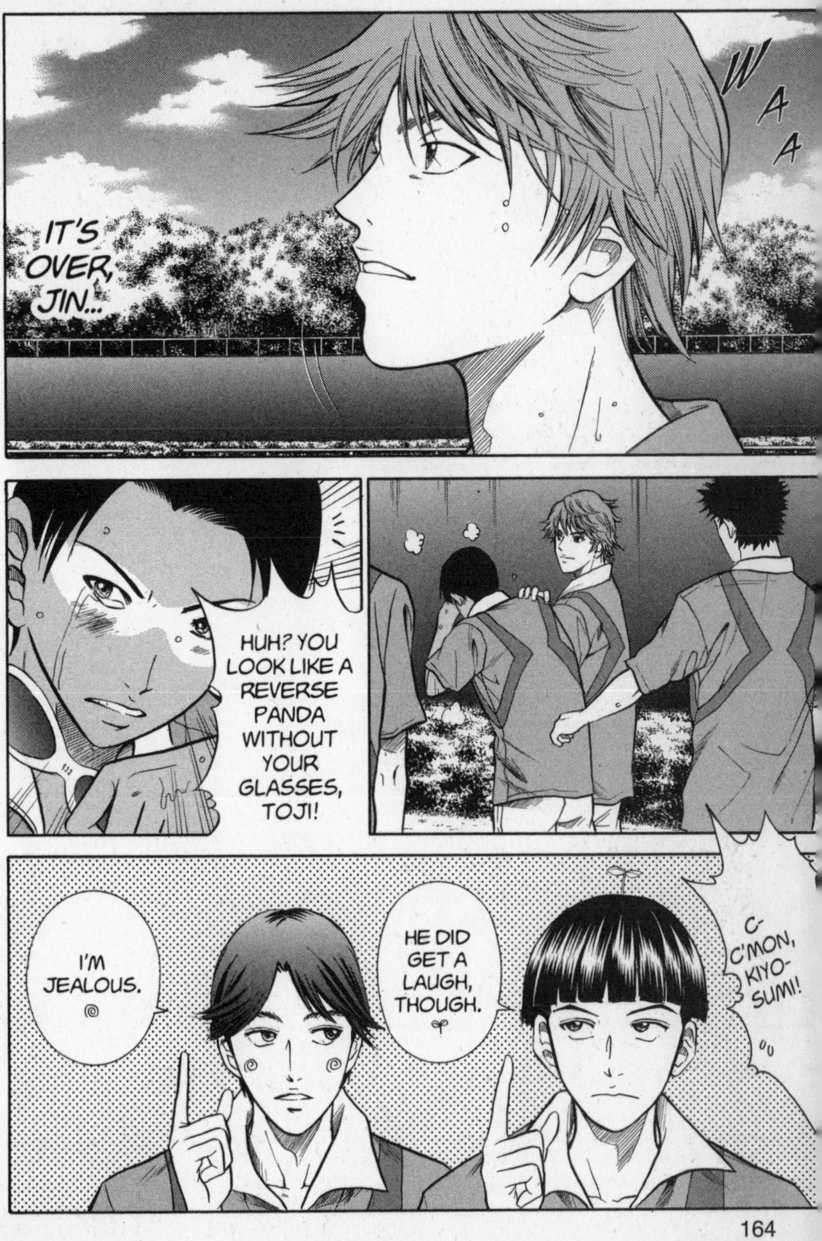
WAAA
IT'S OVER, JIN...
HUH? YOU LOOK LIKE A REVERSE PANDA WITHOUT YOUR GLASSES, TOJI!
C-C'MON, KIYOSUMI!
HE DID GET A LAUGH, THOUGH.
I'M JEALOUS.

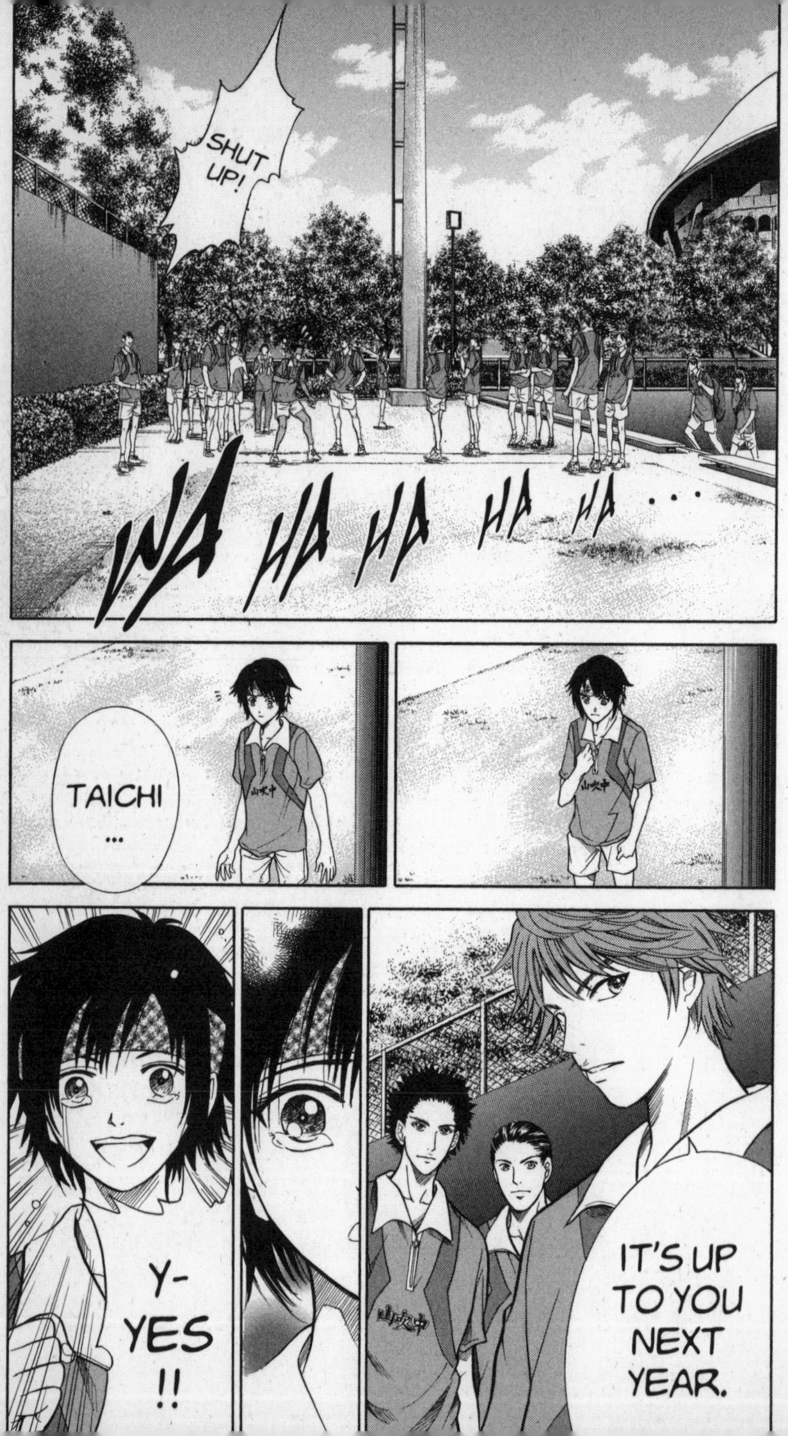
SHUT UP!
WA HA HA HA HA...
TAICHI ...
IT'S UP TO YOU NEXT YEAR.
Y-YES!!

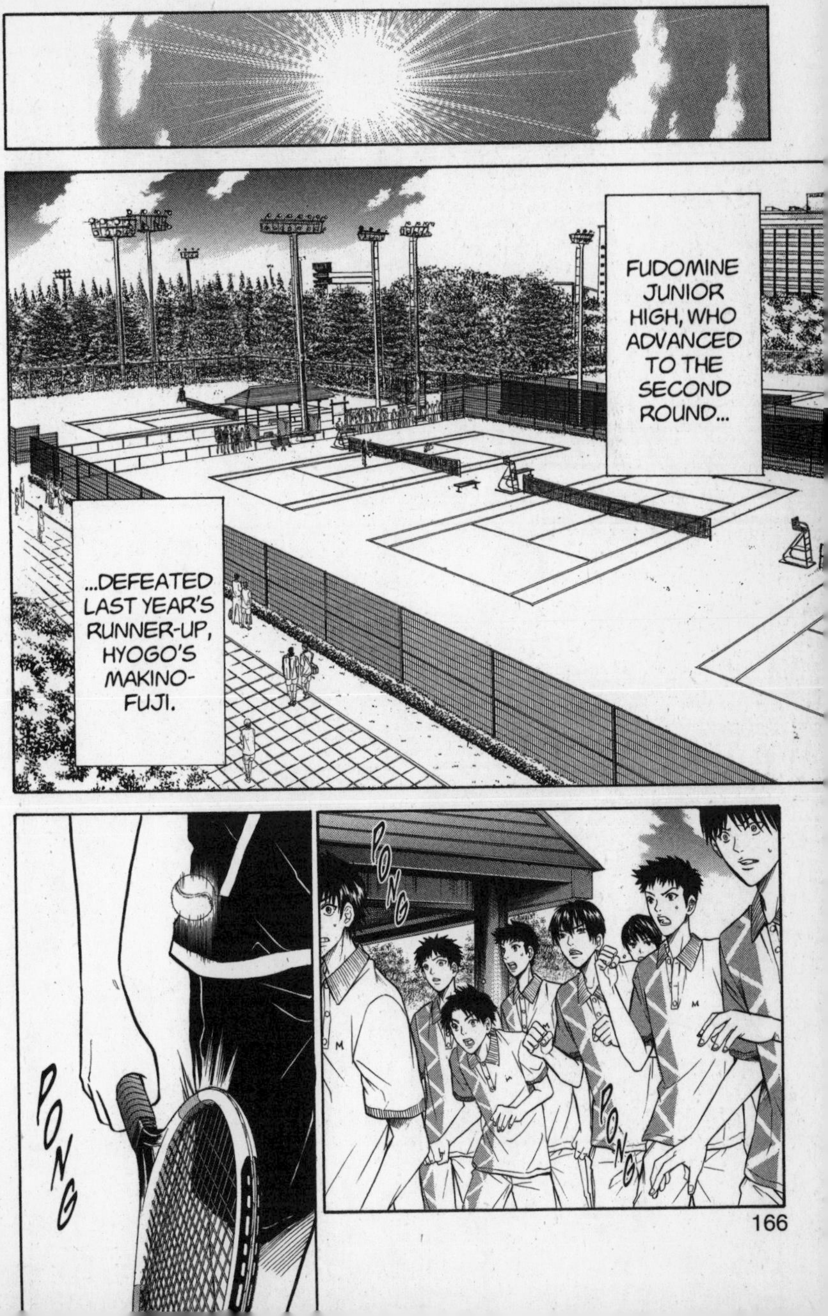
FUDOMINE JUNIOR HIGH, WHO ADVANCED TO THE SECOND ROUND...
...DEFEATED LAST YEAR'S RUNNER-UP, HYOGO'S MAKINO-FUJI.
PONG
PONG
PONG

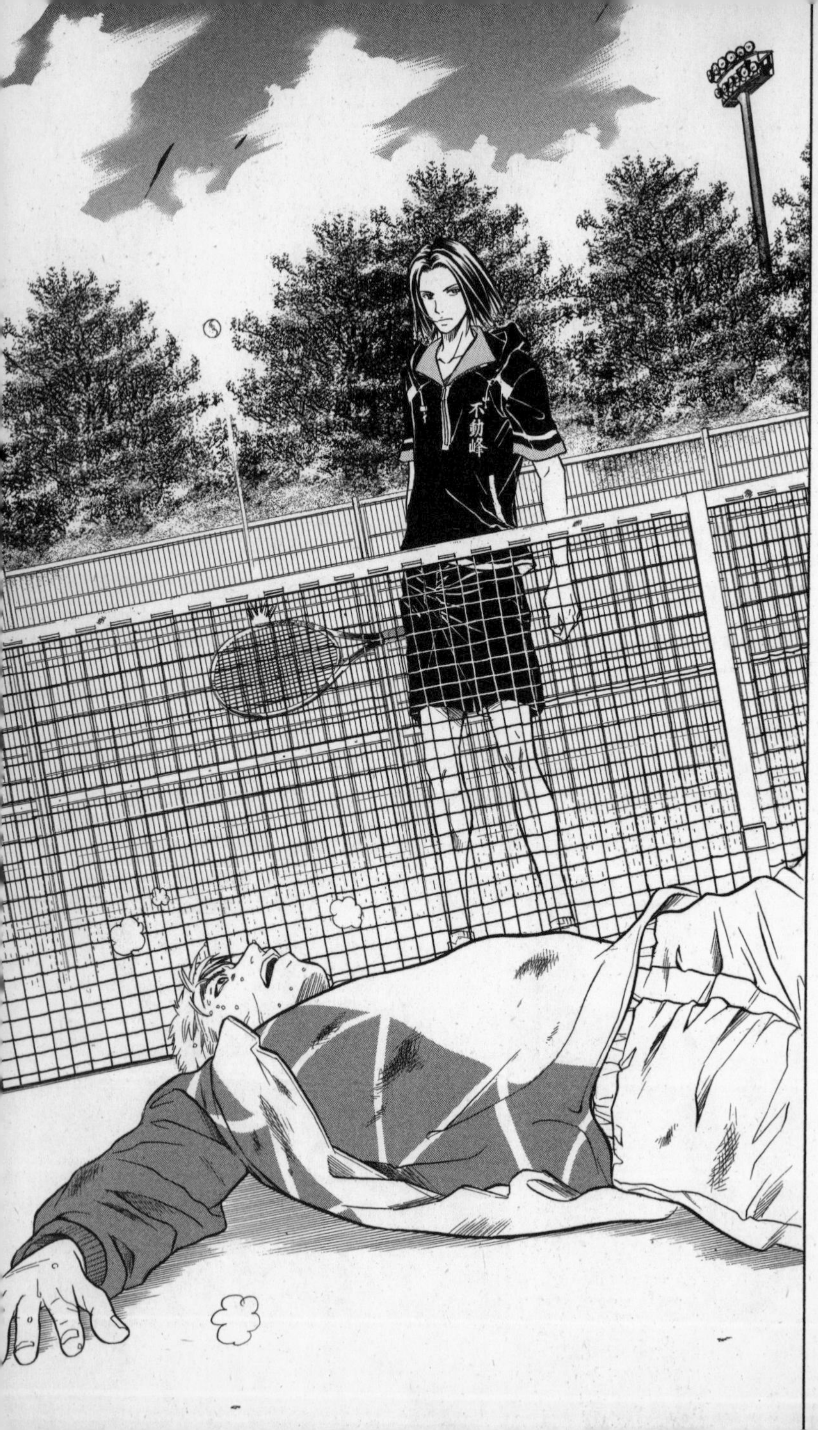
不動峰

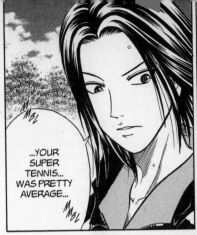

...YOUR SUPER TENNIS... WAS PRETTY AVERAGE...

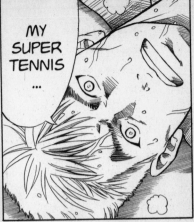

MY SUPER TENNIS...

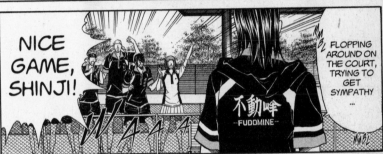

NICE GAME, SHINJI!

FLOPPING AROUND ON THE COURT, TRYING TO GET SYMPATHY...

WAAAA

不動峰 -FUDOMINE-

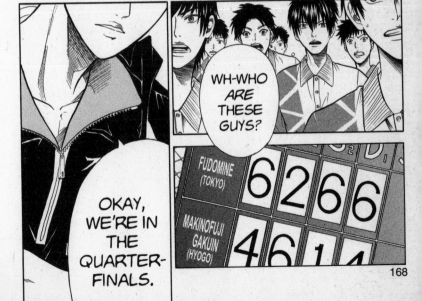

OKAY, WE'RE IN THE QUARTER-FINALS.

WH-WHO ARE THESE GUYS?

FUDOMINE (TOKYO)	6	2	6	6
MAKINOFUJI GAKUIN (HYOGO)	4	6	1	4

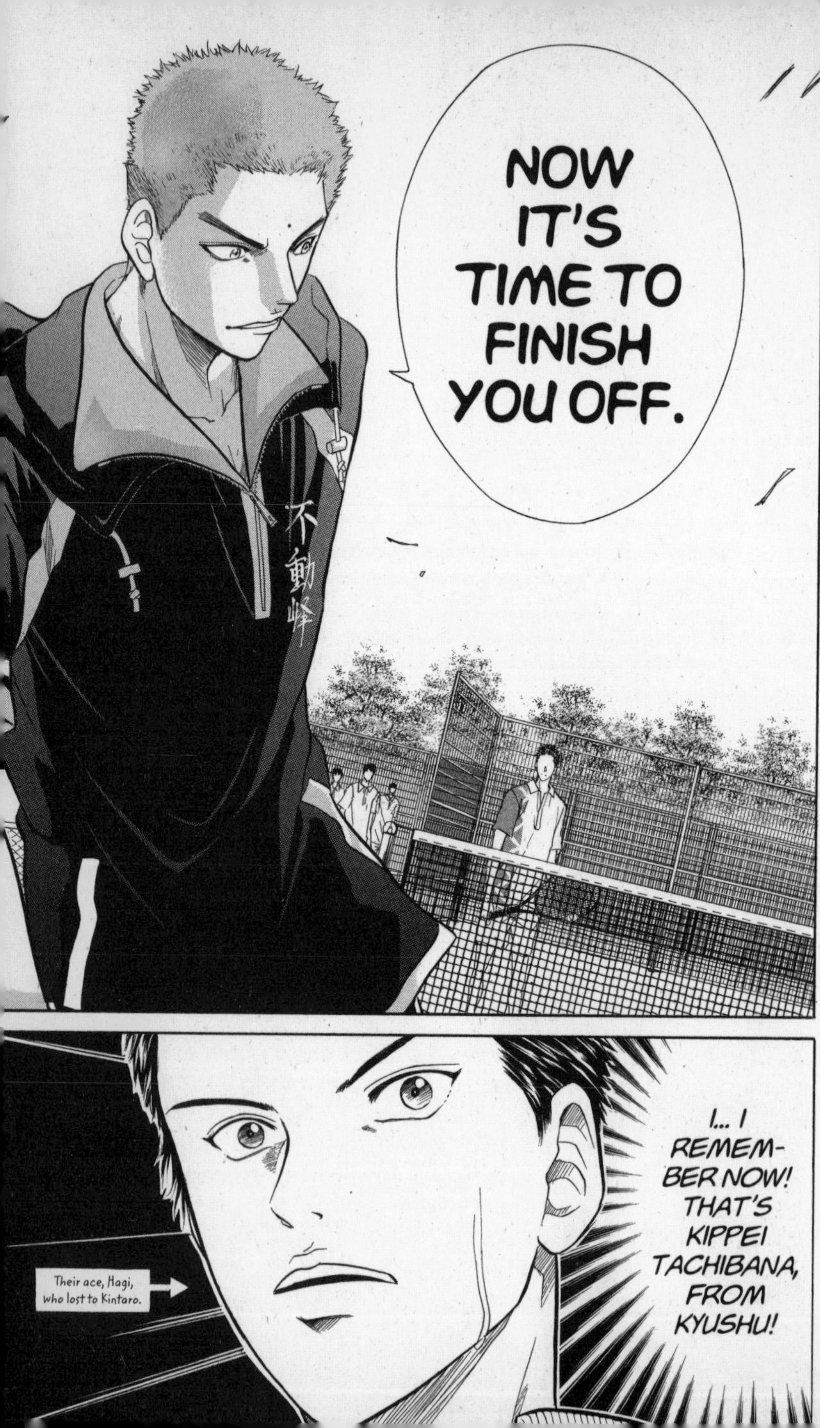
NOW IT'S TIME TO FINISH YOU OFF.
I... I REMEMBER NOW! THAT'S KIPPEI TACHIBANA, FROM KYUSHU!
Their ace, Hagi, who lost to Kintaro.

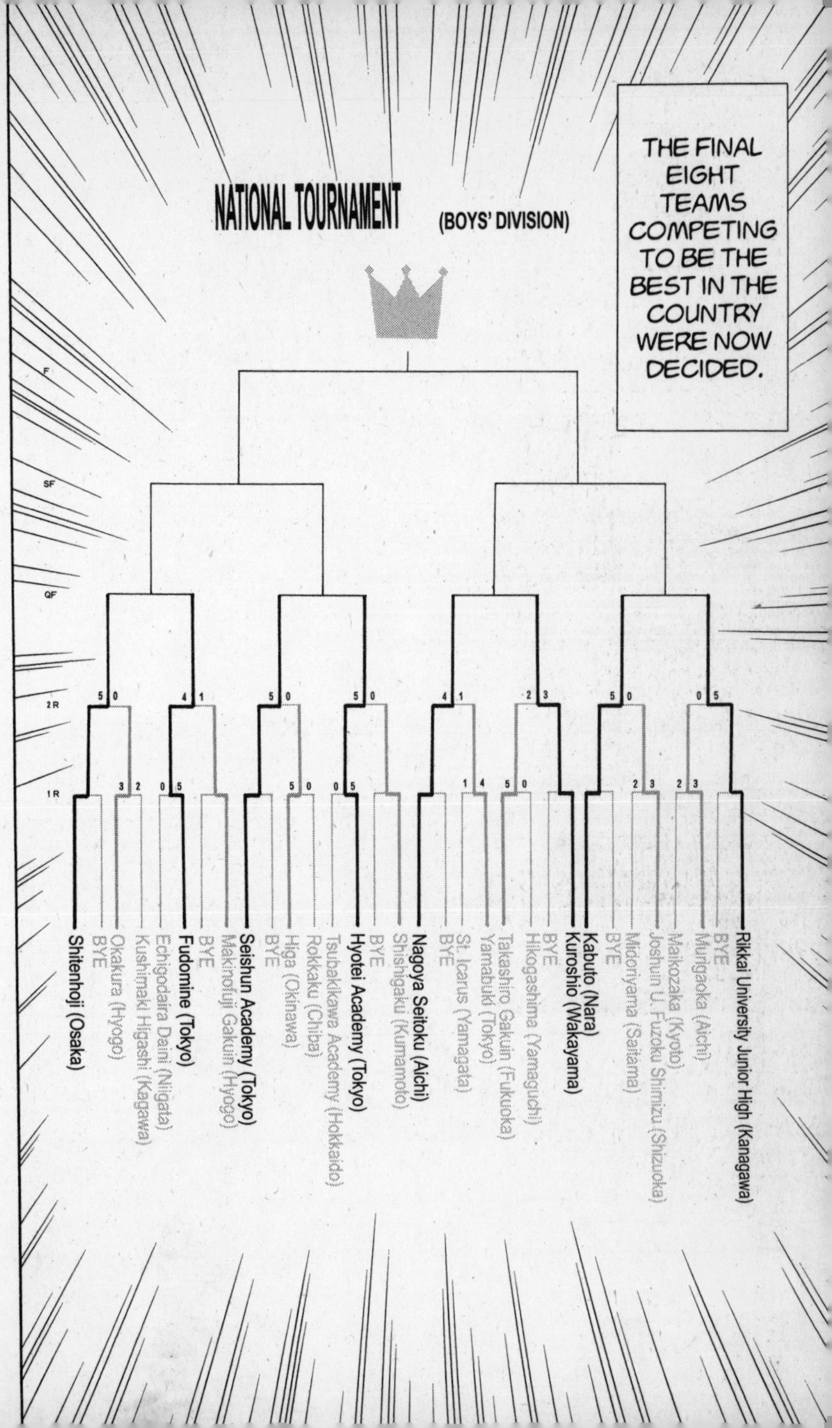
THE FINAL EIGHT TEAMS COMPETING TO BE THE BEST IN THE COUNTRY WERE NOW DECIDED.
NATIONAL TOURNAMENT
(BOYS' DIVISION)
F
SF
QF
2 R
1 R
Shitenhoji (Osaka)
BYE
Okakura (Hyogo)
Kushimaki Higashi (Kagawa)
Echigodaira Daini (Niigata)
Fudomine (Tokyo)
BYE
Makinofuji Gakuin (Hyogo)
Seishun Academy (Tokyo)
BYE
Higa (Okinawa)
Rokkaku (Chiba)
Tsubakikawa Academy (Hokkaido)
Hyotei Academy (Tokyo)
BYE
Shishigaku (Kumamoto)
Nagoya Seitoku (Aichi)
BYE
St. Icarus (Yamagata)
Yamabuki (Tokyo)
Takashiro Gakuin (Fukuoka)
Hikogashima (Yamaguchi)
BYE
Kuroshio (Wakayama)
Kabuto (Nara)
BYE
Midoriyama (Saitama)
Joshuin U. Fuzoku Shimizu (Shizuoka)
Maikozaka (Kyoto)
Murigaoka (Aichi)
BYE
Rikkai University Junior High (Kanagawa)

READ THIS WAY

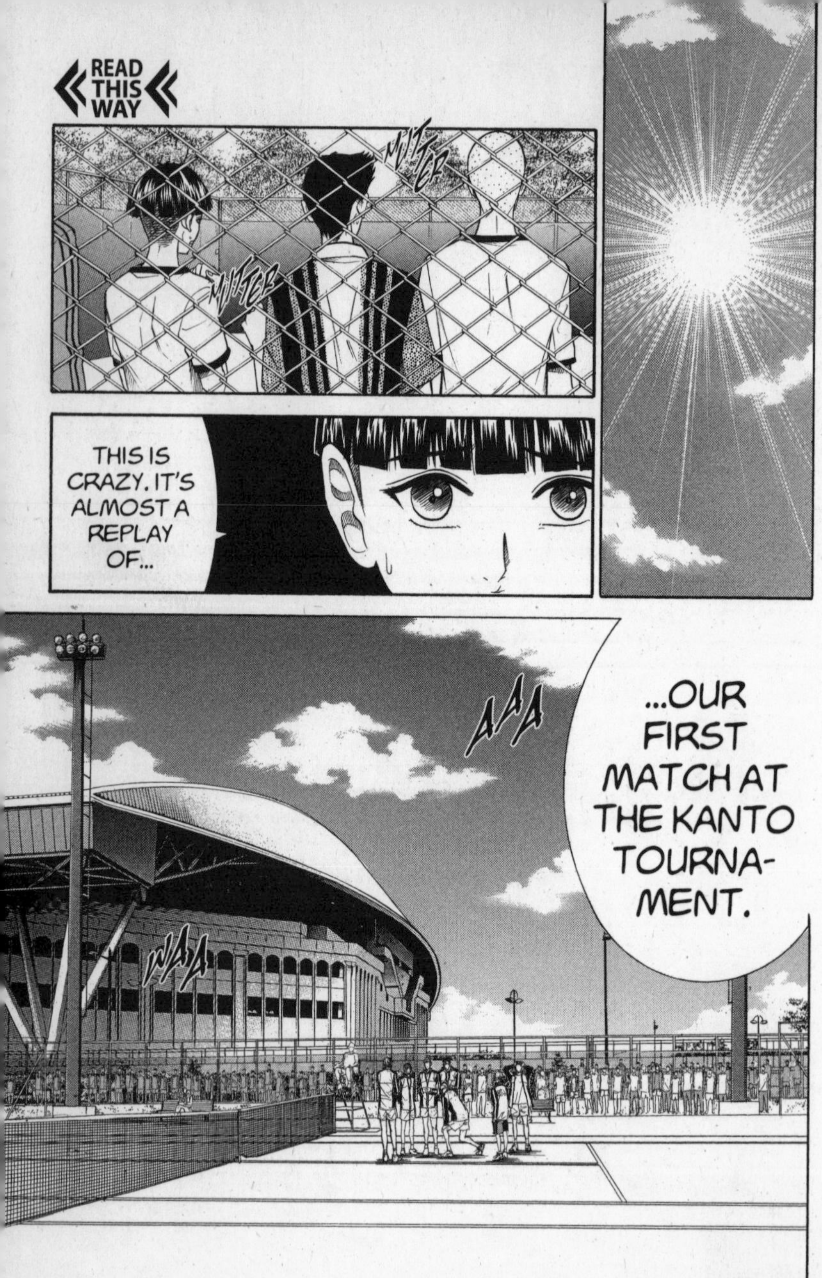
MUTTER
MUTTER
THIS IS CRAZY. IT'S ALMOST A REPLAY OF...
AAA
...OUR FIRST MATCH AT THE KANTO TOURNA-MENT.
WAA

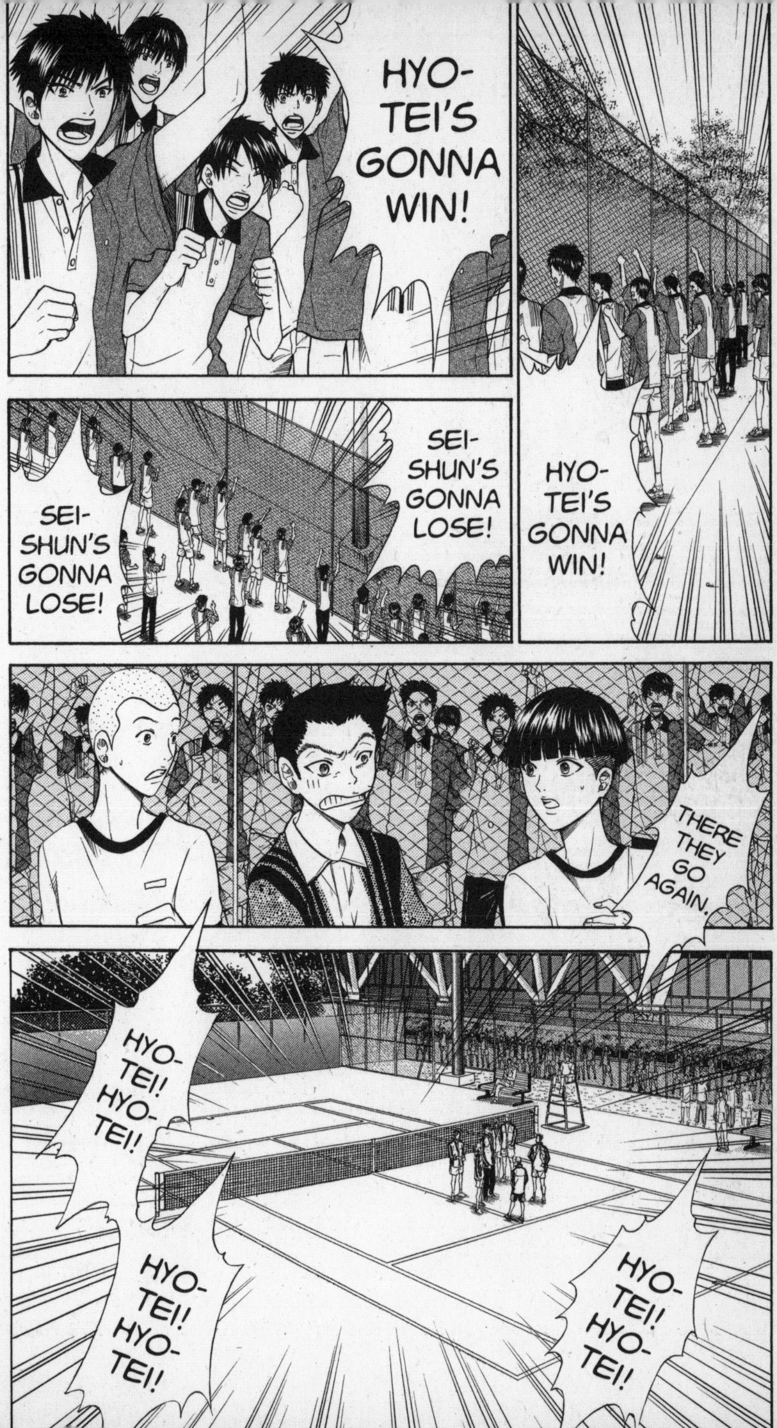
HYO-TEI'S GONNA WIN!
HYO-TEI'S GONNA WIN!
SEI-SHUN'S GONNA LOSE!
SEI-SHUN'S GONNA LOSE!
THERE THEY GO AGAIN.
HYO-TEI! HYO-TEI!
HYO-TEI! HYO-TEI!
HYO-TEI! HYO-TEI!

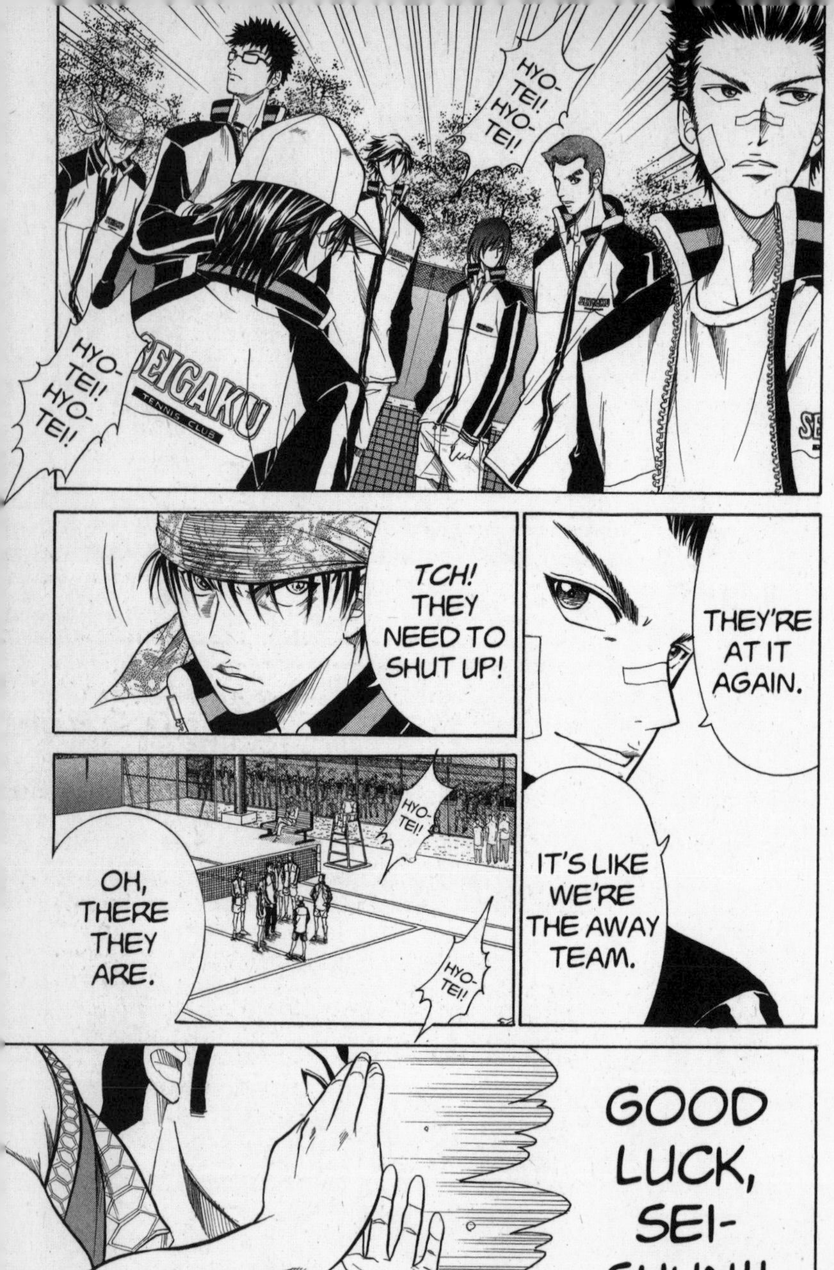
HYO-TEI!! HYO-TEI!!
HYO-TEI!! HYO-TEI!!
THEY'RE AT IT AGAIN.
IT'S LIKE WE'RE THE AWAY TEAM.
TCH! THEY NEED TO SHUT UP!
HYO-TEI!
HYO-TEI!!
OH, THERE THEY ARE.
GOOD LUCK, SEI-SHUN!!

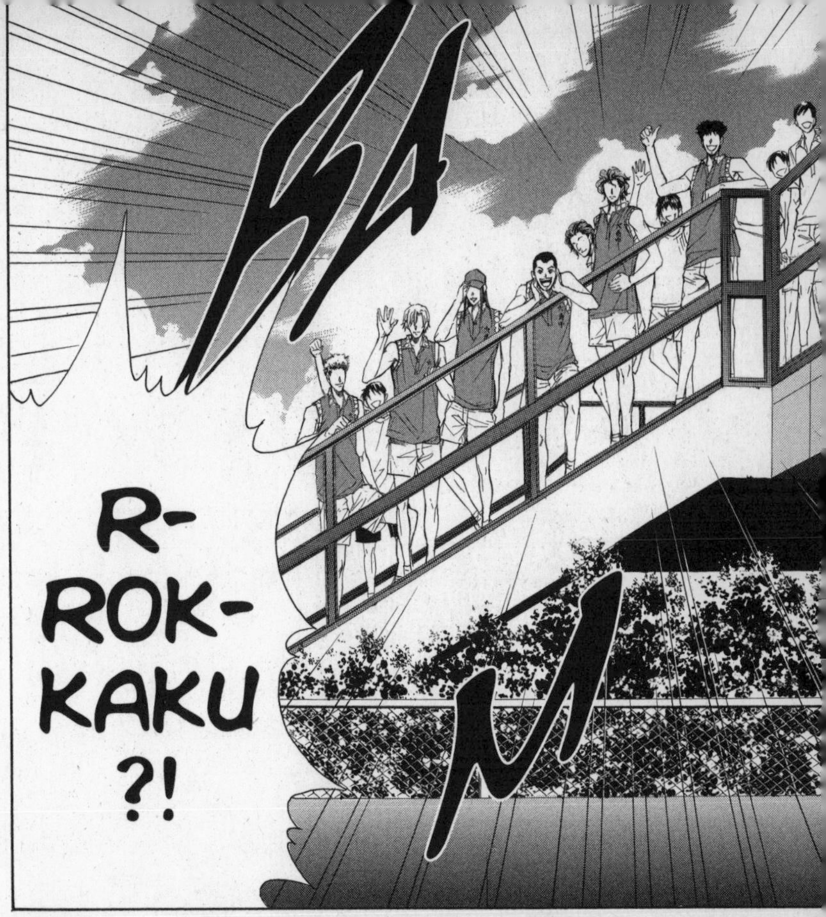
R-ROK-KAKU?!

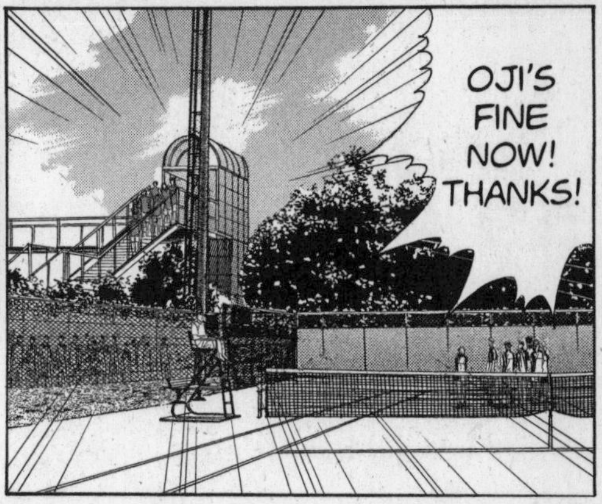
OJI'S FINE NOW! THANKS!

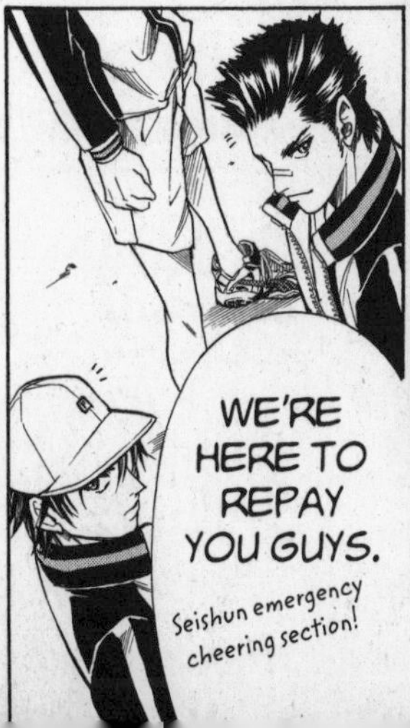
WE'RE HERE TO REPAY YOU GUYS.
Seishun emergency cheering section!

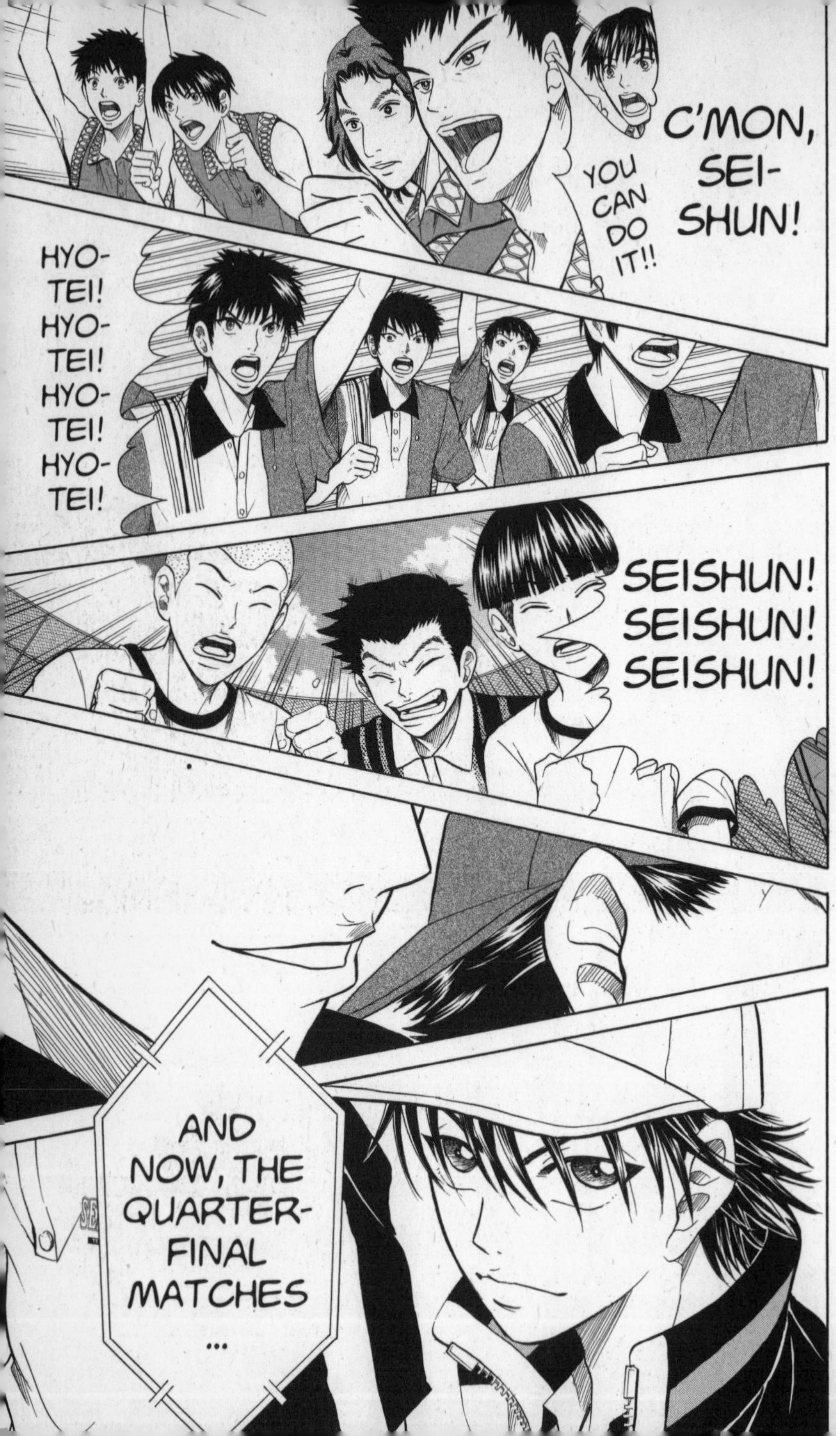
C'MON, SEI-SHUN!
YOU CAN DO IT!!
HYO-TEI! HYO-TEI! HYO-TEI! HYO-TEI!
SEISHUN! SEISHUN! SEISHUN!
AND NOW, THE QUARTER-FINAL MATCHES ...

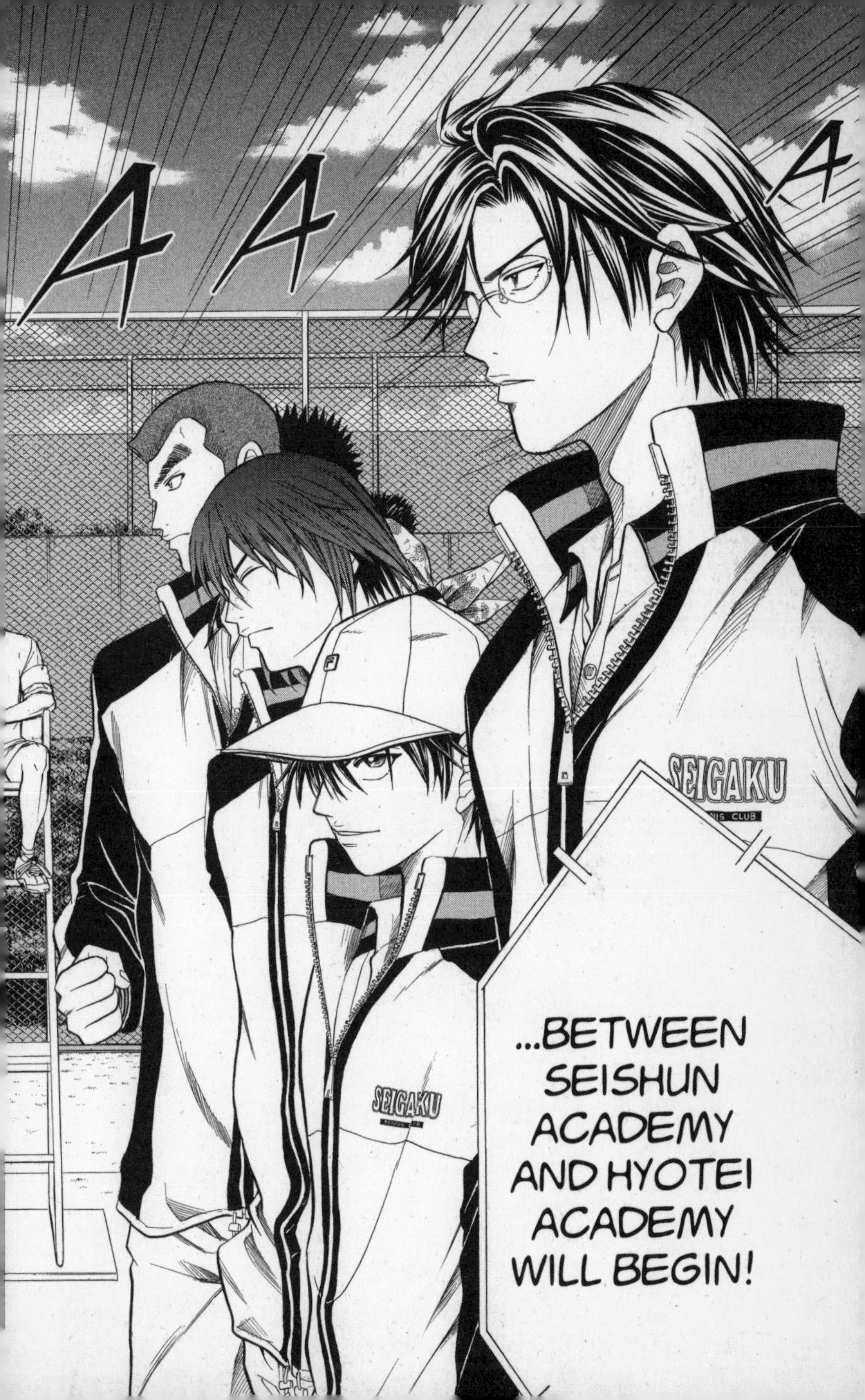
AAAA
...BETWEEN SEISHUN ACADEMY AND HYOTEI ACADEMY WILL BEGIN!
SEIGAKU
SEIGAKU

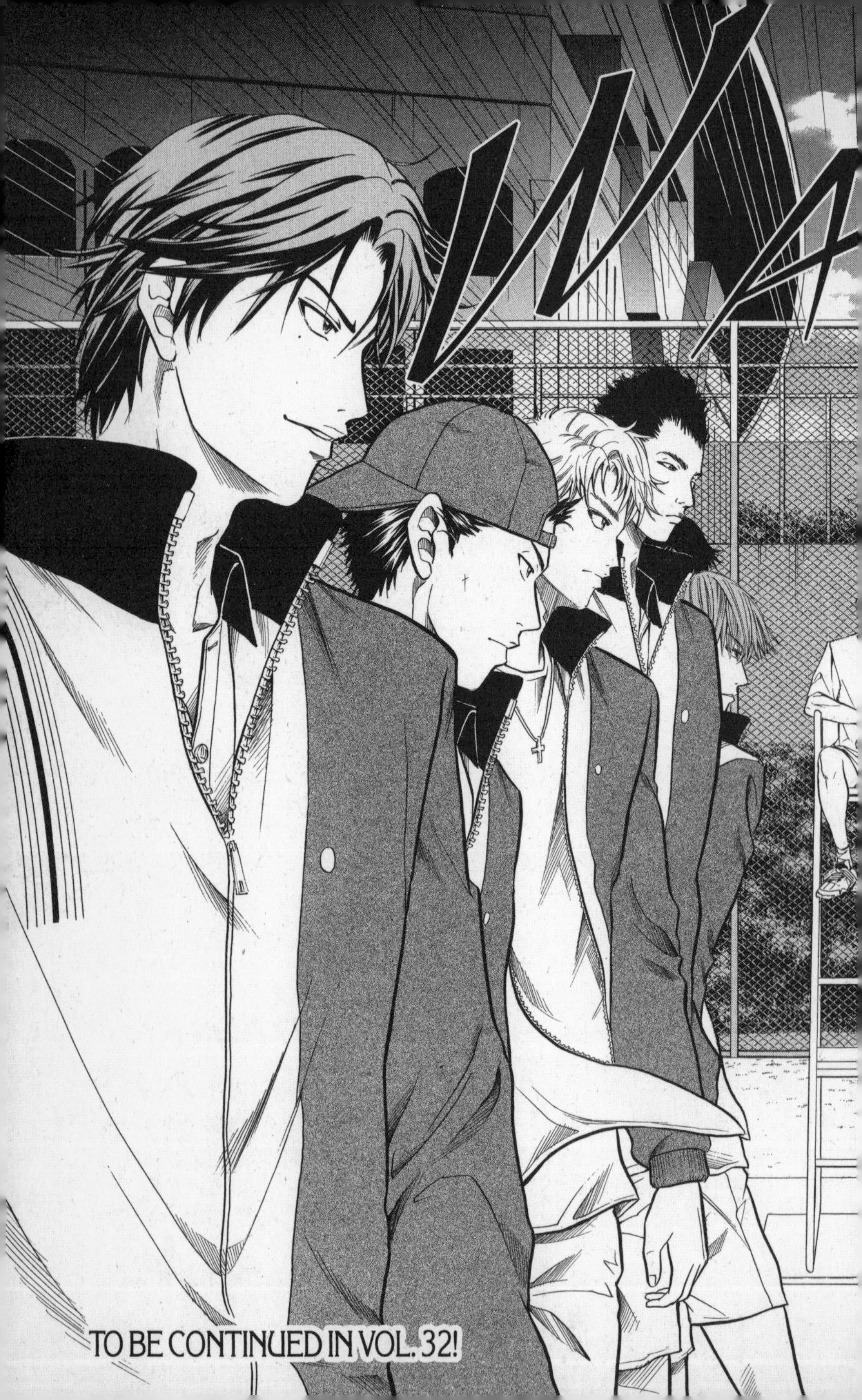
TO BE CONTINUED IN VOL. 32!

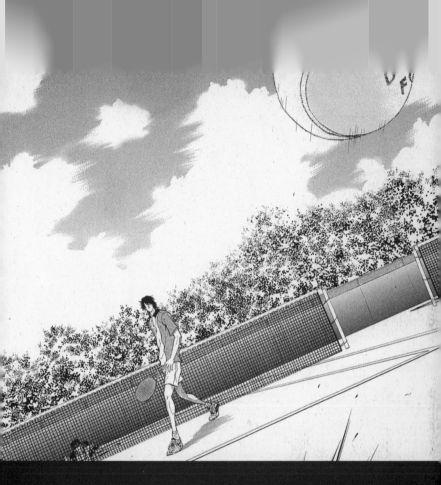

Two of a Cunning Kind

The National Tournament moves into the quarterfinal stage, and the Seishun players find themselves pitted against their old rivals, Hyotei. Kicking things off is the No. 3 Singles match between Momoshiro and Hyotei's resident "genius," Yushi Oshitari. Will all of Momo's strength and cunning be enough to defeat the "Player of a Thousand Techniques"?

Available July 2009!

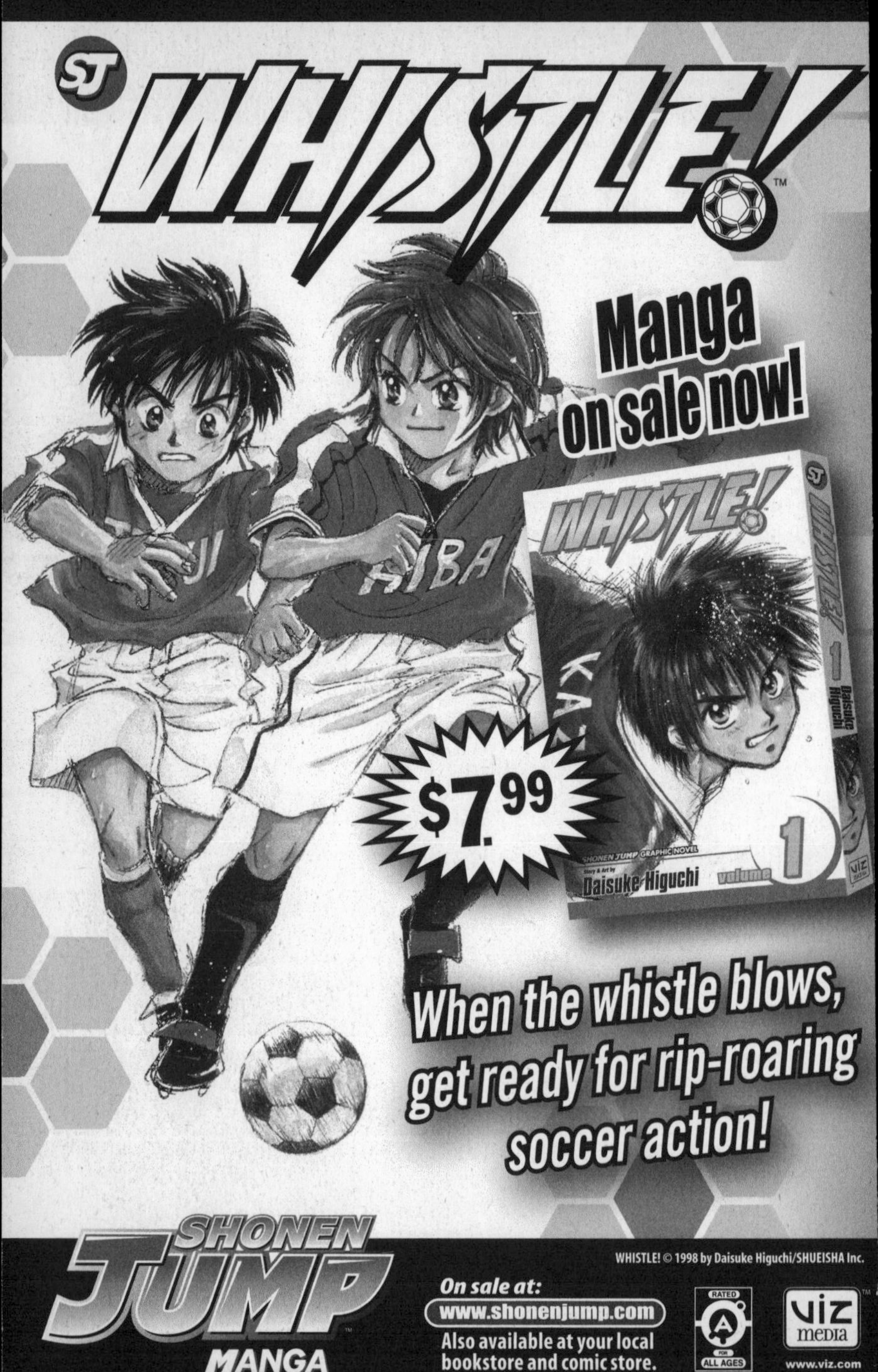
SJ
WHISTLE!™
Manga on sale now!
WHISTLE!
SJ WHISTLE! 1 Daisuke Higuchi
SHONEN JUMP GRAPHIC NOVEL
Story & Art by Daisuke Higuchi
volume 1
$7.99
When the whistle blows, get ready for rip-roaring soccer action!
SHONEN JUMP MANGA
WHISTLE! © 1998 by Daisuke Higuchi/SHUEISHA Inc.
On sale at:
www.shonenjump.com
Also available at your local bookstore and comic store.
RATED A FOR ALL AGES
VIZ media
www.viz.com

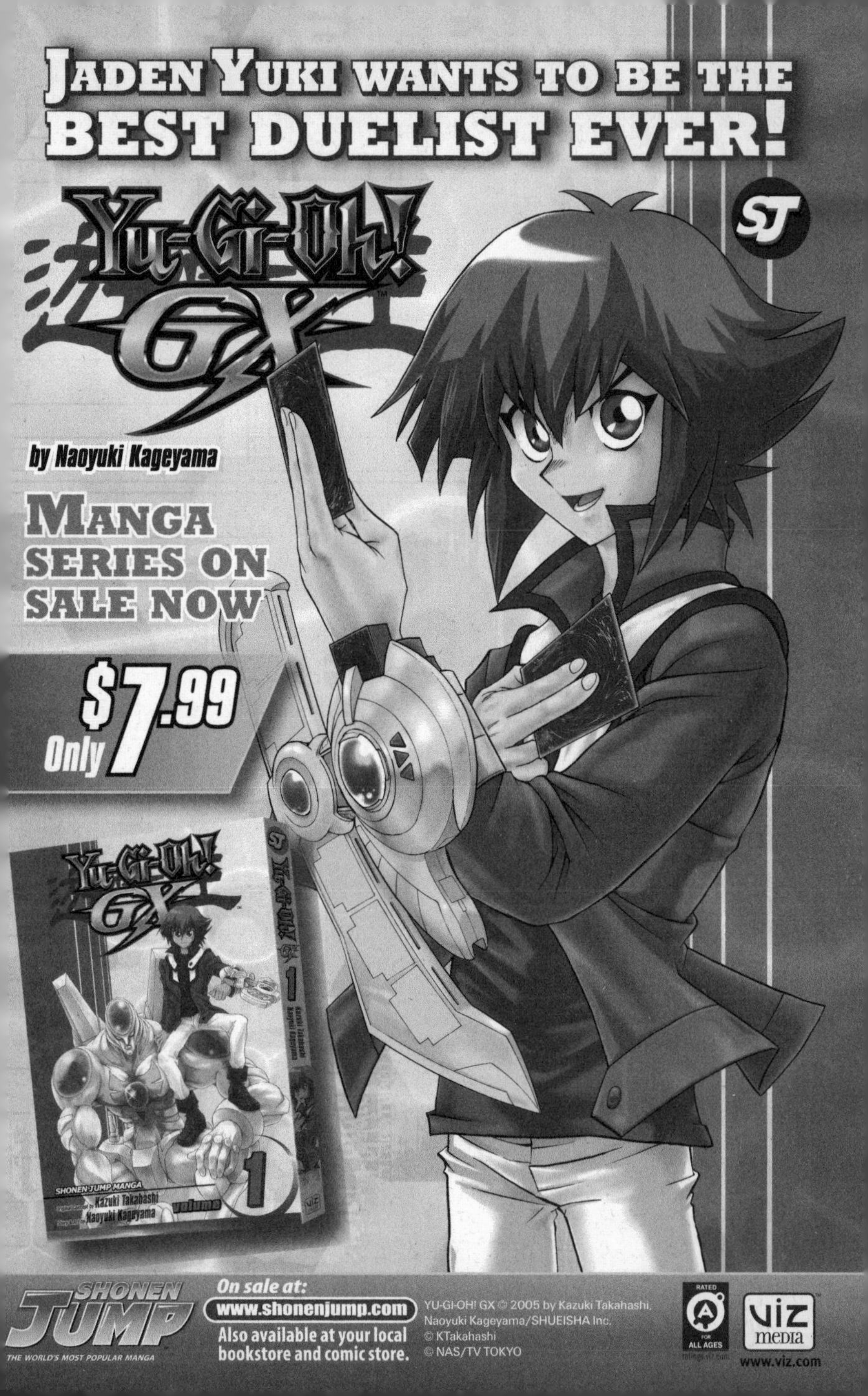
JADEN YUKI WANTS TO BE THE BEST DUELIST EVER!
Yu-Gi-Oh! GX™
SJ
by Naoyuki Kageyama
MANGA SERIES ON SALE NOW
Only $7.99
Yu-Gi-Oh! GX
SHONEN JUMP MANGA
Kazuki Takahashi
Naoyuki Kageyama
volume 1
SHONEN JUMP
THE WORLD'S MOST POPULAR MANGA
On sale at:
www.shonenjump.com
Also available at your local bookstore and comic store.
YU-GI-OH! GX © 2005 by Kazuki Takahashi, Naoyuki Kageyama/SHUEISHA Inc.
© KTakahashi
© NAS/TV TOKYO
RATED A FOR ALL AGES
VIZ media
www.viz.com

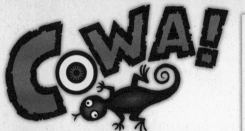
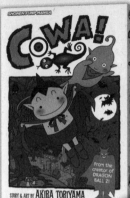
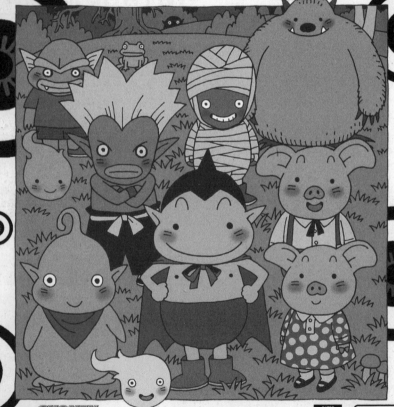

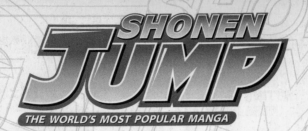
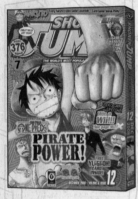
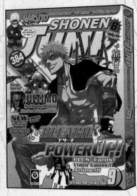
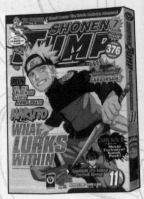

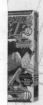